DEVELOPMENT AND UNDERDEVELOPMENT

Series editors: Ray Bromley and Gavin Kitching

Latin American Theories of Development and Underdevelopment

In the same series

Already published:

Development and Underdevelopment in Historical Perspective:
Populism, nationalism and industrialization
Gavin Kitching

Development Projects as Policy Experiments:
An adaptive approach to development administration
Dennis A. Rondinelli

Development and the Environmental Crisis:
Red or green alternatives?
Michael Redclift

Regions in Question:
Space, development theory and regional policy
Charles Gore

The Fragmented World:
Competing perspectives on trade, money and crisis
Chris Edwards

Transnational Corporations and Uneven Development:
The internationalization of capital and the third world
Rhys Jenkins

Socialism and Underdevelopment
Ken Post and Phil Wright

LATIN AMERICAN THEORIES OF DEVELOPMENT AND UNDERDEVELOPMENT

Cristóbal Kay

Routledge
London and New York

First published 1989 by Routledge
11 New Fetter Lane, London EC4P 4EE
29 West 35th Street, New York, NY 10001

© 1989 Cristóbal Kay

Typeset by LaserScript Limited, Mitcham, Surrey
Printed and bound in Great Britain by
Biddles Ltd, Guildford and King's Lynn

British Library Cataloguing in Publication Data
Kay, Cristóbal, 1944–
    Latin American theories of development and underdevelopment.
    (Development and underdevelopment)
    1. Economic development
    I. Title II. Series
    330.9

    ISBN 0-415-01422-0

Library of Congress Cataloging in Publication Data
Kay, Cristóbal.
    Latin American theories of development and underdevelopment /
    Cristóbal Kay.
    p.   cm. — (Development and underdevelopment)
    Bibliography: p.
    ISBN 0-415-01422-0. — ISBN 0-415-01423-9 (pbk.)
    1. Economic development—Research—Latin America.   I. Title.
    II. Series.
    HD77.5.L29K39   1989
    338.9—dc19   88-30330
                                                       CIP

Contents

Preface

My aim in writing this book is to acquaint a wider audience with the various currents of thought within the Latin American development school. While the ideas of a few prominent Latin American social scientists have travelled beyond Latin America, little or nothing is known about many others who have made key contributions to the thinking on underdevelopment and development. Thus, in this book I present the ideas of many of these thinkers and I often let them speak in their own voices. To what extent I have succeeded in presenting a sufficiently original, distinctive, and coherent body of thought which can be labelled 'Latin American theories of development Studies and underdevelopment' is for the reader to judge.

The writing of this book on the history of a particular set of ideas often led me to reminisce about my own personal history. I met many of the authors discussed here during my days as a student at the University of Chile in the early and mid–1960s and later as a Fellow of the Centre of Socio–Economic Studies at the same university. I came across their ideas by listening to their lectures, seminars, and conference papers in Chile and other parts of the world. I hope this personal acquaintance with some authors has added to my comprehension of their writings and that it has not impaired my understanding of the ideas of others whom I have not had the privilege of meeting or observing at such close range. The social sciences were particularly creative in Chile during the 1960s and early 1970s benefiting greatly from the contribution of Latin American intellectuals exiled at the time in Chile. I was also fortunate to be a postgraduate student in the Institute of Development Studies at the University of Sussex in the late 1960s. I shared in the excitement of its first steps, particularly because it was one of the few institutions in the developed world which was receptive to the ideas of the Latin American development school.

I wish to thank the University of Glasgow for providing me with a home since late 1973, and particularly to the Centre for Development Studies for giving material support in the writing of this book. I am grateful to Ray Bromley and Gavin Kitching, the editors of this Series on Development and Underdevelopment, for giving me the opportunity to write this book. Special thanks go to Ray for supporting this venture during its long gestation period and, above all, for his detailed and very helpful comments. My greatest debt is to Diana Kay who commented on and skilfully edited the entire text, not only transforming my poor English but above all contributing to the development of my ideas and teaching me how to convey these more clearly.

Finally, all quotations which have been taken from foreign language publications have been translated into English by me and all the added emphases in these quotations are those of the authors, unless specified otherwise. The usual disclaimers apply.

CRISTÓBAL KAY
Glasgow, June 1988

1

The challenge from the periphery

Nobody is in possession of the revealed truth today, neither in the North nor in the South. We all catch glimpses of the truth, we have carried out analyses, some of which are promising, but we cannot accept what the North thinks as the revealed truth. I have every respect for the ideas of the North, but they must not necessarily be taken at their face value. It is essential that some day all of us, those of the North and those of the South together, set ourselves to explore the nature of our problems, discarding dogmas and preconceived ideas, until we reach a measure of common ground. (From a speech delivered by Raúl Prebisch (1986a: 16) shortly before his death in 1986.)

DEVELOPMENT THEORY: CRISIS AND RENEWAL?

In recent years development economists have engaged in a process of critical introspectionr egarding the state of their discipline.[1] This can be interpreted as reflecting either a state of crisis or a sign of growing maturity. In this process key questions about the discipline have been raised such as what has been achieved, what are the failings, and what is the way forward?

Great prominence has been given to some of these reflections. Nobel prize–winner, Sir Arthur Lewis, delivered his presidential address to the ninety–sixth meeting of the American Economic Association in 1983 on the state of development theory. This was subsequently published as a leading article in the Association's journal, which is not noted for giving special attention to development economics (Lewis, 1984). Another leading economics journal, *The Economic Journal* of the Royal Economic Society, likewise highlighted the plight of development studies by publishing Amartya Sen's (1983) reflections on the issue which he presented in his presidential address to the Development Studies Association's annual conference in 1982.

Some participants in the debate on the state of development economics propose that the best way forward is for the discipline to become interdisciplinary: development economics should evolve or merge into development studies (Seers, 1979a: 712–13; Livingstone, 1981: 11–14). Dudley Seers, one of the pioneers of development economics, further proposed that another source of revitalization for the discipline could be provided by the development theories which have emerged from the Third World (ibid.: 714). Already in the early 1960s he argued that 'the writings of the Latin American school of structuralism' could provide the basis for the reconstruction of *economics*, which he considered to be in crisis, as it did not answer to the needs of the Third World countries (Seers, 1967: 26–7). As yet these theories have not been fully considered and incorporated into the mainstream of development economics, and even less so by the economics profession. I share Seers's assessment and aim through this book to make some of these Third World theories more accessible and widely recognized.

The dominant paradigms in the early post–war period

This book aims to contribute to the discussion on the state of development theory by presenting the key ideas of what I call the Latin American school of development. There are two main strands in this school: structuralism and dependency. [2] Structuralism developed as a critique of neoclassical analysis, while dependency analysis engaged in a critique of modernization theory. Neoclassical and modernization theories were proposed by economists and sociologists from the centre, and especially the Anglo–Saxon world. The Marxist strand within dependency analysis is critical of orthodox Marxism as well as of structuralism. Thus, there is a critique of theories emanating from the centre as well as an ongoing debate between Latin American social scientists themselves.

The Latin American school of development was born in the late 1940s at a time when the neoclassical and Keynesian theories were dominant in economics and modernization theory in sociology. These ideas had shaped the minds of many social scientists in the Third World. 'In a sense, their theoretical equipment was twice removed from reality – it reflected the doctrines developed for *other* countries in response to *earlier* events.' (Seers, 1980: 6.) In a seminal essay

Seers, who just before writing this essay had worked for some years in the United Nations Economic Commission for Latin America (ECLA), the hotbed of structuralism, argued that orthodox economics was built in and for developed industrial economies and therefore really deals with what is 'a highly special case' (Seers, 1967: 5). What is particularly important to consider is that:

> The chief theoretical schools of Europe and North America promoted their own recipes for accelerating growth as universally valid. At one extreme, the Chicago school ... argued for opening the doors to foreign trade and investment, and avoiding planning and controls. IMF economists, from the same stable, saw inflation and payments problems – already widespread, especially in Latin America – as due to lack of monetary discipline. If this were put right, the basis would be established for a fast growth of output and employment.
>
> (Seers, 1980: 6)

Furthermore, development economics only began to emerge as a discipline in the 1950s, so it could not offer much guidance to the Latin American school, and the structuralists in particular, in their quest to formulate alternative development policies for the region.

Given their overwhelming influence, it required independent minds to point out that these Northern paradigms corresponded to the needs and characteristics of mature capitalism and were therefore of limited value in addressing the development problems of the Third World. Indeed, few underdeveloped countries satisfied the assumptions underlying neoclassical and Keynesian economics (Sunkel, 1977: 7). The assumptions of these theories were particularly restrictive and even irrelevant given the major differences which existed between the developed and the less developed world. In many Third World countries, for example, money was not a universal means of exchange and financial institutions hardly existed, a large proportion of the rural population were subsistence peasant farmers, infrastructure (such as roads, communications, and energy) was limited, education and literacy poor, and so on. This meant that capital and labour markets as well as the price mechanism worked very differently in these countries compared with their equivalents in the industrial nations.

Development specialists in Latin America and elsewhere questioned the utility of these dominant paradigms for explaining the causes and the persistence of underdevelopment and for proposing policies to overcome that state of affairs. It was felt that the policies recommended by neoclassical and perhaps even by Keynesian economics would, at best, delay development and, at worst, continually reproduce the underdevelopment of the Third World.

> It became clear that there was no real reason why theories and approaches based on the idealisation and simplification of the history of Western industrial capitalist countries should apply to societies with completely different structural characteristics and historical experience – not to mention their particular type of insertion in the international system in a radically changed contemporary world. Dissatisfaction with this type of development thinking was, then, a powerful factor in favour of evolving an alternative.
>
> (Oteiza, 1978: 15)

A key contribution of the Latin American school was the emphasis on the specificity of the peripheral countries and the insistance that new theories were required to explain their different structures, dynamics, and realities. Although some neoclassical and Keynesian economists might have noticed the differences between what today is called the North and the South, a commonly held attitude was that: 'If theory did not correspond to reality, so much the worse for reality: it would have to be changed so that it would correspond to the assumptions of neoclassical and macrodynamic [Keynesian] theory.' (Sunkel, 1977: 8.) Neoclassical economics was particularly influential in Latin America because it provided a powerful rationale for the continuance of the existing international division of labour which favoured the interests of the primary exporting sector and of foreign capital. However, emergent industrial and popular interests began to challenge this old coalition of forces and these changing class forces found expression at the level of ideas. Thus:

> Two main lines of thinking and policy emerged. On one hand were the conservatives – intellectual representatives of the old order – who maintained that the traditional specialisation in primary exports constituted the best engine of growth, provided that the industrial countries also achieved full employment and growth. The benefits of specialisation and comparative advantage would then be spread from the export sector to the rest of society and development would eventually be achieved.
>
> (ibid.)

Structuralists questioned in particular neoclassical trade theory and

Samuelson's (1948; 1949) factor price equalization theory. Paul Samuelson (well-known US economist and Nobel prize-winner):

> proved that, on certain assumptions conventionally accepted in the theory of international trade, free trade would equalize wages throughout the world, so that a United States worker and an Indian worker would be paid the same, and trade could therefore perform precisely the same function as free international movement of factors.
>
> (Streeten, 1979: 23–4)

Similarly, but in a less ironic manner, Love (1980: 63) writes:

> the economics profession had just been treated to a formal demonstration by Paul Samuelson in 1948–49 that, under certain conventional (but unrealistic) assumptions, trade could serve as a complete substitute for the movement of factors of production from one country to another, indicating that international trade could potentially equalize incomes among nations. Thus the less rigorous (but much more realistic) arguments of Prebisch and Singer burst upon the scene just after Samuelson had raised neoclassical trade theory to new heights of elegance, and against this theory the new ideas would have to struggle.

Jacob Viner (1953), an influential neoclassical economist, shared Samuelson's belief that free international trade would gradually reduce, if not close, the income gap between the rich and poor countries. Viner also firmly held the view that free market conditions would spontaneously bring into action forces which would industrialize and develop the 'backward' countries (Ady, 1967: 112). He was against state–promoted industrialization as it distorts the free operation of the market and also because he questioned Prebisch's belief in the inherent superiority of industry over agriculture.

The policy implications of these theories were that free international trade and free internal market forces were the best way to promote the development of the Third World. 'Prebisch and Singer, however, developed a thesis with very different policy implications, based on an apparent tendency for the terms of trade of primary producers to deteriorate, which led to an emphasis on industrialisation and justified tariff protection.' (Seers, 1980: 6.) This will be analysed in Chapter 2 where I will examine the structuralist theories which were critical of the doctrines of free trade and international specialization, attributed underdevelopment to the lack of industrial development, and 'provided the rationalisation for protection, for investment in infrastructure and manufacturing and for planning' (Sunkel, 1977: 8).[3]

Another common characteristic of economists of those times (whether Marxists or members of the Chicago school) was a basic optimism. Inequalities within and between countries could and would in one way or another be reduced eventually, bringing an homogenised, modernised world within the reach of the next generation.

(Seers, 1980: 7)

A common central question concerned the way in which traditional societies could best achieve the economic prosperity, social welfare systems, and parliamentary democracy of the modern societies. The prevailing thinking held that 'backward' countries should follow the example of the advanced countries which was idealized and presented as resulting from free-market policies and the Protestant work ethic. These factors would lead to growth which would automatically take care, sooner or later, of poverty, unemployment, and income inequality, inasmuch as these were of concern to the neoclassicals.

'Development' was essentially an economic problem. Economic growth was considered a suitable yardstick for it (indeed almost a synonym). In the end, growth would mean reduced inequality, unemployment and poverty (viz the Kuznets 'U-curve'). Such progress would be all the easier because the necessary technologies were already available.

(ibid.: 5)

With respect to sociological modernization theories, the key point to stress here is that they were impregnated with a profound dualism and ethnocentricity. According to J. Taylor (1979: 33),

the functionalist theory of change, together with the Parsonian concepts of structure and functional prerequisites constituted the foundation of what came to be known as the 'modernisation theory' of the 'Sociology of Development' as it emerged during the post-war period.

Bert Hoselitz (1960) introduced the modern-traditional dichotomy to the analysis of social change and economic development using Talcott Parsons's (1948: 1951) set of pattern-variables.

Whilst one side of the pattern variable choices was held to characterise traditional societies, the other side characterised modern societies. Hoselitz constructed two ideal–types of society, the one combining universalism, functional specificity, achievement–orientation, and collectivity–orientation (the modern type); and the other, combining particularism, diffuseness, ascription and self–orientation (the traditional type). Modernisation (to be achieved through a process of increasing differentiation) then became the problem of ensuring a transition from dominance by the traditional to the modern type of orientation of action.

(J. Taylor, 1979: 34)

In other words the general features of developed societies 'are abstracted as an ideal type and then contrasted with the equally ideal typical features of a poor economy and society. In this mode, development is viewed as the transformation of one type into the other.' (Nash, 1963: 5.)

The modernization paradigm of the sociology of development argued that Third World countries should follow a path similar to that of the advanced capitalist countries. It also viewed the economic, social, and cultural penetration by the modern West into the traditional South as furthering modernization.

The West (taken here as the Atlantic community of developed nations and their overseas outliers) diffuses knowledge, skills, organization, values, technology and capital to a poor nation, until over time, its society, culture and personnel become variants of that which made the Atlantic community economically successful.

(ibid.: 5)

The traditional–modern dichotomy was transformed into a theory of stages of economic growth by Walt W. Rostow (1960), who subtitled his then extremely popular (but now much discredited) book 'A Non–Communist Manifesto'. He distinguished five stages in the evolution of societies and argued that all societies started from the traditional stage and that the best way for achieving and speeding–up the transition to the more advanced stages was to follow a similar path of change to that pursued by the developed capitalist countries. [4]

This is the background against which the Latin American development school had to assert itself. Undoubtedly it was an uphill struggle both against the dominant paradigms of the centre and against the dominant class interests in the periphery. Even in the late 1970s Seers was of the opinion that the ideas of the structuralists were not taken very seriously by the profession (Seers, 1979a: 718). The

Argentinian economist Raúl Prebisch also recalled 'a sense of arrogance toward these poor underdeveloped economists of the periphery' (Prebisch, cited in Love, 1980: 63), especially in the early period and by neoclassical economists from the centre. Whilst the contribution which the Latin American school has made to the analysis of underdevelopment and development is increasingly recognized, its significance is still undervalued (Toye, 1987: 106–8).

The impact of the Latin American school

There have been few (if any) systematic and comprehensive attempts to present and evaluate the body of writing which constitutes the Latin American development school. [5] This is partly explained by the variety of the contributions themselves, which cross many disciplinary boundaries and encompass many different ideological positions and levels of analysis. Additionally many contributions were not initially presented in a systematic and comprehensive manner as they did not set out to construct an all–inclusive theory but to criticize particular aspects of orthodox theories originating from the centre or to analyse particular problems in a novel manner. Some of these ideas need to be developed further still in order to achieve full theoretical status. Whilst developing a common approach to the problem of underdevelopment and development of the world economy, the particular issues addressed vary over time. It is only with hindsight that these underlying common methodological and analytical elements can be fully appreciated and the full significance of the early writings reinterpreted by situating them within a wider context: the Latin American development school.

Social scientists from the centre have tended to focus on particular aspects of these theories, partly because these became available in a piecemeal manner but also because they failed to grasp the distinctiveness and significance of the wider theoretical framework which was emerging. This applies in particular to the writings of the structuralist development thinkers. Thus, Prebisch's thesis on the deterioration of the terms of trade between centre and periphery was first picked up in the Anglo–Saxon world during the mid–1950s, but many neoclassical critiques overlooked the genuineness of the problem raised by Prebisch and the underlying significance of his vision. The same is true, though to a lesser extent, of the structuralist discussion on inflation which sparked off the structuralist–monetarist controversy during the late 1950s and early 1960s.

The prolific Brazilian economist Celso Furtado, by contrast, fully appreciated the importance of Prebisch's early work, and in his assessment,

> Possibly no concept has had so much significance for the advance of studies on development as Raúl Prebisch's concept of the centre–periphery structure. Though Prebisch's main concern was the international propagation of the business cycle – the diversity of behaviour of economies which export primary products by comparison with economies which export industrial products – the concept was based on an overall view of the capitalist system, and opened the way to a perception of its structural diversity, a knowledge of which is essential in order to understand the special character of underdevelopment. The elaboration of this concept by Prebisch himself, and by the group of social scientists which met at ECLA ...– a group known as the Latin American structuralist school – gave rise to a trend of thought which has had considerable influence.
>
> (Furtado, 1980: 211–12)

The idea of structural heterogeneity in the capitalist system arising from asymmetries in the distribution of benefits from trade and foreign investment ran contrary to the neoclassical position, which argued that international trade and foreign investment not only provided an engine of growth but was also a factor in reducing inequalities in living standards between countries. 'Another idea of considerable importance, brought to the fore by the Latin American school in the early 1950s, was that of the harmful effects of the type of technology incorporated in equipment imported by late developing countries.' (ibid.: 212.) Thus, they also perceived much earlier than many other economists the problems associated with imported modern technology whose benefits at that time went widely unquestioned. [6]

Within the Latin American school, dependency theory has undoubtedly had the most widespread appeal and impact on development studies both in the periphery and in the centre. However, dependency 'consumers' in the centre have tended to focus on the more accessible and familiar aspects of dependency theory, such as the writings of André Gunder Frank (see F. Cardoso, 1977a). This is partly because Frank writes in English whilst many of the Latin American dependency authors have yet to be translated from Spanish or Portuguese. [7] This book aims to correct this one–sided reception of dependency theory in the developed countries by giving prominence to a wider range of dependency–analysis authors. In this way it is hoped that some misrepresentations and misplaced critiques can be rectified. Some work has already been undertaken in this direction, notably by Philip O'Brien (1975; 1984), Gabriel Palma (1978), and Colin Henfrey (1981).

With respect to the structuralist school of thought, this is far less well–known in the developed countries than dependency theory. This is a regrettable omission, not only because structuralism was the first original body of development theory to emanate from the Third World but also because, arguably, a full understanding of dependency theory can only be gained through consideration of the ground first charted by Latin American structuralism. [8] Only then can the crucial and pervasive influence of structuralism on dependency analysis be assessed – an influence even ignored by some dependency writers themselves. Thus, a further aim of this book is to explore the interconnections between the structuralist and dependency schools of thought.

Those few authors of the centre who have taken issue with these theories have generally referred to one aspect alone and thereby missed the added comprehension which an overview provides. In addition, disciplinary boundaries have rarely been crossed. This book aims to provide such an interdisciplinary overview and thereby hopes to make a contribution to development studies. It is almost inevitable that an exercise of this nature will fail to please the experts in each of the separate disciplines but then the interdisciplinary overview given in this book of the Latin American school might yield new insights into the development problems which might not otherwise come to the fore. Thus, this book inserts itself firmly within the discipline of development *studies* which, in my view, has interdisciplinarity as its core methodological foundation.

This book examines a contribution from the periphery to development studies. It might appear as paradoxical that development studies, which is primarily concerned with the analysis of the development problems of the underdeveloped countries, should for so long be dominated by institutions and writers from the centre. It is less surprising given the greater availability of resources for research in the centre. Most international agencies undertaking studies on the South are located in the North, even attracting many social scientists from the South who fall under their spell. After being initially ignored and often derided, the ideas presented here gained some prominence in the centre during the student movement of the late 1960s, a movement which eagerly embraced some Third World liberation figures such as Ernesto 'Ché' Guevara as its heroes. This new generation of students was not only rebelling against the culture and values of its parents but was above all seeking to reinterpret the world and was thus avidly searching for alternative ideas to those of the established orthodoxies. In this new openness, students espoused these ideas from the Third World which combined their concern for a more humane and just world with their search for a new paradigm.

The neo-conservative challenge

During the early 1970s the 'new neoclassical' or neo-liberal counter-revolutionary attack on the structuralists' advocacy of import-substituting industrialization and of an inward-directed development strategy for the periphery, first formulated in the 1950s, began to emerge and gather force. In arguing for a new international economic order, structuralists came under fierce attack from neoclassical economists in the developed countries. Structuralists became easy targets as the inward-directed development strategy had by then been exhausted. However, as Sunkel comments:

> It is easy now with hindsight to point to the weaknesses and limitations of the new development policies pursued since the 1950s. But at the time when the socio-political and economic interests related to the primary export sectors were still very strong, and when threats to them were automatically labelled a communist plot and harshly suppressed, it is convenient to recall that these programmes of nationalist and social democratic reform were regarded as a revolutionary challenge to the existing internal and international order.
>
> (Sunkel, 1977: 8)

In their eagerness to dismiss this challenge from the periphery, the neoclassical economists failed to notice that structuralists were among the first to recognize the limitations of import-substitution industrialization as it was being implemented in various Latin American countries.

With the harsher world economic climate of the 1980s, the decline of development studies, and the renaissance of neoclassical and neo-conservative thought, the progressive voice from the periphery is in danger of being ignored, if not suppressed, yet again. The theories of neo-conservative or neo-liberal economics not only dominate today's intellectual debate but are followed, or proclaimed to be adhered to, by most governments of the major capitalist countries. Keynesian ideas are discredited and monetarist ideas prevail. Powerful institutions such as the International Monetary Fund (IMF) and the World Bank proclaim the neo–liberal ideas to all four corners of the world (even to some socialist countries such as Yugoslavia and China) and exercise pressure on those governments in the Third World which have been reluctant to follow their uniform and unilateral 'advice' as speedily or as fully as they desired. While some countries have little choice but to swallow these prescriptions, others which have the ability to resist these pressures have nonetheless willingly adopted those policies.

Chile was one of the first Latin American countries to adopt such policies in the mid–1970s, pursuing them in the most extreme form. Under the military regime, Chile became an ideal laboratory where the theories of neo–liberal economists could be tested to the full without regard to democratic 'niceties'. It was a technocrat's dream but a nightmare for the majority of the Chilean population who had to pay a high price for this experiment. Monetarist gurus like Nobel prize–winners Friedrich von Hayek and Milton Friedman, the doyen of the Chicago school, were invited to Chile and showered with honours before the model ran into trouble in the early 1980s. However, it was a group of Chilean economists who preached the neo–conservative gospel and who were put in charge of running the economy (O'Brien, 1981). Many of these economists had pursued postgraduate studies at the University of Chicago, the hotbed of monetarism, and because of their slavish adherence to the ideas emanating from the Chicago school they were dubbed the 'Chicago Boys' (the English expression being used in Latin America itself). This represents a major reversal from the spirit which guided structuralist and dependency thinkers and from the days when their ideas were influential. Although the 'Chicago Boys' have lost their glamour they are still entrenched in dominant positions and can thus continue to marginalize structuralist and dependency ideas.

Latin American social scientists were among the first in the South to create a distinctive school of thought which challenged established orthodoxies from the North. This in no way implies that social scientists from other peripheral regions have not gone on to provide equally important contributions, or that writers from outside Latin America did not have a powerful influence on the authors of the region.[9] The case of Paul Baran serves to illustrate the cross–fertilization of ideas. Baran, an economist of Central European origins, was, along with his intellectual companion Paul Sweezy, a major neo–Marxist figure in the United States after the Second World War. His writings were known to structuralists and he exercised a major influence on dependency thinkers, i.e. *dependentistas.* [10]

I hope that this book will be of interest to all those in the centre and the periphery who are concerned with the development problems of the Third World. This book should also have some relevance for those analysing development problems in the developed countries, especially those facing regional and structural problems. Let the neo–conservative counter–revolution not drown out the contribution from the periphery to development theory and policy! Let there be a renaissance of progressive ideas from the periphery and the centre!

DISTINCTIVENESS OF THE LATIN AMERICAN SCHOOL

When surveying the contribution of Latin American social scientists to development studies one is struck by their widespread commitment to change prevailing social and economic structures to benefit the poorer and disadvantaged groups. Indeed, many intellectuals are, or have been, actively engaged in bringing about political changes. The desperate conditions of large sectors of the population in the Third World call for, and have led to, a more prominent role for their intellectuals than in the developed world. The group of writers whose ideas are presented here are acutely and collectively aware that they carry a special and urgent social responsibility.

Part of this responsibility and commitment involves a conscious and continuous effort to determine the specificities of their region with respect to the First World, i.e. the capitalist developed countries. During the populist and reformist period of the 1960s and early 1970s, which saw the rapid expansion of higher education in many Latin American countries, centres for the study of 'the national reality' (as they were often called) sprung up in most countries. These research institutes were often staffed by economists, sociologists, political scientists, and historians who attempted to gain an interdisciplinary or total view of their societies and its relationship with the rest of the world.

A related feature of Latin American social scientists is their propensity to think in regional terms (A. Rodríguez, 1983). Many writings deal with Latin America as a whole and those studies which focus on a particular country are often inserted into a wider regional framework. Latin America's common luso–hispanic colonial heritage facilitates such a regional perspective. The liberation struggles from colonial and oligarchic rule were often led by figures with a Latin American rather than a national vision, such as Bolívar in the nineteenth century and 'Ché' Guevara in the twentieth.

Nationalism in the countries of the centre is often associated with imperialism and right wing political ideologies and movements. In the context of the Third World, by contrast, nationalism acquires a progressive connotation, being the expression of anti–colonial, anti–imperialist, or even anti–capitalist struggles. Latin American nationalist sentiment is directed particularly against the economic and political dominance of US capital in the internal affairs of the region. This search for authentic national independence also informs Latin American intellectuals' desire to 'decolonize the social sciences' by constructing alternative theories to the dominant orthodoxies from the centre (Stavenhagen, 1971b). They want to see the periphery through their own eyes and develop alternative theories which provide a more truthful interpretation of their reality.

The chapters which follow should be understood within the context outlined above. From the many contributions made by Latin American writers to development studies, I have chosen to focus on structuralism, internal colonialism, marginality, and dependency because they are the most distinctive and original. In particular, structuralism and dependency lie at the core of the Latin American school and have had the widest impact on development studies. More could certainly be said on the contribution by political scientists, in particular Guillermo O'Donnell's (1973; 1978) discussion of the 'bureaucratic–authoritarian state', and by Marxist historians and social scientists on the theory of 'modes of production' in the Third World. [11] The latter theme would merit a book on its own and would have to consider the important contribution of Asian and other scholars (mainly French and British). I say nothing on the innovative theories of the educationalist Paulo Freire (1970; 1972; 1985) on 'conscientization' and the 'pedagogy of the oppressed', nor on the 'theology of liberation' adopted by progressive Catholic priests who take the 'option for the poor' in Latin America. Their theology, which has inspired events in Nicaragua, makes an explicit commitment to social justice by helping to empower the poor and adapting the Catholic message to the socio–economic reality under which the oppressed live in Latin America and the Third World (Gutiérrez, 1973).

REFORM OR REVOLUTION?:
THE HAYA DE LA TORRE – MARIÁTEGUI DEBATE

A central theme underlying the discussions of the Latin American school is the question of reform or revolution. As mentioned earlier a major motivation of many Latin American social scientists in their quest for understanding the world in which they live is their desire for change to overcome poverty and underdevelopment. In aspiring to change their societies, the Latin American writers discussed here are driven to uncover the dynamics or logic of the system and the various mechanisms of domination and exploitation which it engenders. At the risk of oversimplifying, the Latin American authors discussed can be divided into two groups: one group argues that this can be done by reforming the existing capitalist system while the other believes that only its overthrow and replacement by a socialist system can tackle the root of the problem.

There exists, of course, a third group of authors in Latin America who want to change the system in a counter–revolutionary direction. They are not concerned with alleviating poverty or inequity but with furthering or re–establishing the dominance of the big bourgeoisie and injecting a new dynamism into the capitalist economic system. These writers have gained some prominence in the wake of the counter–revolutionary movements of the last two decades or so in Latin America, and the resurgence of neo–conservative thought in recent years, especially in the countries of the centre. However, as mentioned earlier their contribution to the social sciences has been lacking in originality. Their main merit (or demerit) has been to apply neo–liberal ideas from the centre to those Latin American countries where they have been influential in formulating policy. They certainly do not form part of a distinct Latin American school of thought as is the case with the reformist and revolutionary thinkers discussed in this study.

This book examines the Latin American contribution to social sciences, and development studies in particular, since the Second World War. However, many of the contributions have their origins in earlier debates such as that between Victor Raúl Haya de la Torre and José Carlos Mariátegui in the late 1920s and early 1930s. It is difficult to assess the extent of this influence as few of the writers examined in this book directly refer to this debate, but many of the ideas of Haya de la Torre and Mariátegui filtered through to the public domain, forming part of the political programmes of social democratic and revolutionary parties in Latin America and particularly in Peru. [12]

Both Haya and Mariátegui undertook an analysis of the Latin American economy and society and its relationship to imperialism in order to define the character of the revolution. Both derived their political positions and programmes of action from a prior analysis of the economic, social, and political reality and the common colonial heritage of Latin America. Both characterized the mode of production in the countryside as feudal or semi–feudal, condemned the landlord class and imperialism for Perú's and Latin America's underdevelopment, and favoured industrialization. Finally, both agreed that the development process in Latin America differs from the classical European model and that the bourgeoisie in Latin America is unable to perform the progressive role it did in Europe.

Haya de la Torre argued that imperialist penetration initiated a process of capitalist development which coexists with feudal relations from the colonial period. In his view the revolution has to be anti–feudal and anti–imperialist so as to liberate the nation from feudal and foreign domination. It cannot be a socialist revolution as, in his view, it is not possible to skip the historical stages of development, and thus it is necessary first to develop capitalism fully. This revolution was to be led by the middle class or petty bourgeoisie, the proletariat being too small and the peasantry too backward. Haya de la Torre called for the establishment of an anti–imperialist state which, owing to the weakness of the national bourgeoisie and the strength of the feudal class and imperialism, has to be state–capitalist. However, he recognized some progressive aspects of imperialism (modern technology and industrial capital) and thus the struggle is only against the negative aspects of imperialism (pillage and domination). The objective of the revolution is to achieve Latin America's economic independence and development within capitalism (Germaná, 1977: 149).

Mariátegui was the first outstanding Marxist to apply Marxism to the concrete conditions of Latin America leading him to new insights and revisions of some Marxist theses. He thus can be considered a neo–Marxist and some authors regard him as a Latin American Gramsci. According to Vanden, 'Mariátegui...anticipates much of the current neo–Marxist and dependency literature...[and] realizes that the remnants of the feudal *latifundio* system are tied to the international capitalist system.' (Vanden, 1986: 44.) For Mariátegui, feudal and capitalist relations are part of one single economic system and do not constitute two separate economies as in Haya's dualistic conception. Imperialist capital is seen as linked to and profiting from pre–capitalist relations. Mariátegui saw no scope for the development of an autochthonous or independent national capitalism. In his view the development of capitalism would not eliminate pre–capitalist relations and would only intensify the domination of imperialist monopoly capital in Peru. Furthermore, for Mariátegui the socialist revolution cannot wait until capitalism has fully developed in Peru and he held that the indigenous peasant communities (the *ayllu*) could constitute the germ of the socialist transformation in the countryside. He argued that Haya de la Torre undervalued the revolutionary potential of the peasantry. Thus, Mariátegui advocates a socialist revolution which will be brought about by a political alliance between workers, peasants, and 'the conscious elements of the middle class' under the leadership of the proletarian party (Baines, 1972: 150).

Haya de la Torre considered that the national bourgeoisie was oppressed externally by imperialism and internally by feudalism and that the struggle for national liberation should therefore take precedence over the class struggle. Meanwhile, Mariátegui held the opposite view. He argued that the local bourgeoisie was organically linked to imperialism and feudalism and that they jointly oppressed and exploited the urban and rural workers. Thus, the fight for national liberation does not neutralize the class struggle and, on the contrary, is subordinated to the class struggle. The local bourgeoisie is unable to fulfil this task, which can only be accomplished by the working class (Germaná, 1977: 165–6).

Mariátegui also gave prominence to the analysis of the Indian population, a marginal topic at the time both academically and politically. From his Marxian perspective Mariátegui challenged the prevailing view that the 'indigenous question' was a racial and cultural issue. He considered that the problem of the indigenous population and of their emancipation was rooted in the land question, i.e. in the system of private land ownership and the predominance of feudalism in the countryside. The concentration of land in the hands of landlords had given rise to '*gamonalismo*', i.e. to a system of local political domination and control by landlords over the indigenous population. Furthermore, finding a solution to the Indian problem was not only necessary for emancipating the Indian population but also for solving the national question and achieving national integration (Angotti, 1986: 39, 45).

Haya de la Torre foreshadows some of the central issues of structuralism and the reformist dependency position, while Mariátegui does likewise for the neo–Marxist and revolutionary dependency view.

Similarly, throughout the book I distinguish broadly between a structuralist–reformist and a revolutionary–dependency position but there are also common threads which allow me to speak of a distinct Latin American school of development.

COMMON CONCERNS OF THE LATIN AMERICAN SCHOOL

In this book I focus on four major contributions of the Latin American development school: structuralism, internal colonialism, marginality, and dependency. The presentation of these topics follows a chronological order starting with structuralist ideas, which were first presented during the 1950s, and ending with the dependency debate of the late 1960s and 1970s. As already mentioned a central concern of the Latin American school is to discover and highlight the peculiarities and distinctiveness of the Latin American economic, social, and political dynamics as compared with those of the developed capitalist countries. Another major preoccupation is to uncover the external and internal mechanisms of exploitation and domination in order to elaborate a path of development free from exploitation and oppression. While structuralism and dependency analyses give primacy to external factors as conditioning the periphery's development process, internal colonialism and marginality analyses focus on internal factors. However, all examine to a greater or lesser extent the interconnections between internal and external factors in development, the difference being largely one of emphasis.

A further common thread running through most of the contributions is the adoption (with some qualifications) of an anti–dualist stance which challenges the traditional–modern dichotomy of modernization theory. [13] The clear exception in the Latin American school is the modernization version of marginality, which overtly follows a dualist paradigm. In addition, the case of structuralism is not so clear cut. On the one hand, structuralist theory is anti–dualist as it regards the centre and the periphery as being interlinked and forming one world economic system in which both poles are reproduced as a consequence of those links. On the other hand, by positing the possibility of an autonomous and self–sustaining process of capitalist development in the periphery similar to that existent in the centre it assumes a dualist position.

The Latin American school is also concerned, to a greater or lesser extent, with identifying the social groups or classes which will carry through the reform or revolution. Structuralists locate the key agents for their reformist change as a coalition of the industrial bourgeoisie, the middle class, and the urban working class, under the umbrella of a technocratic and developmentalist state. In the more progressive versions of structuralism it is the developmentalist state which is the main agent of change as it is seen as the only institution capable of transcending sectional interests and thereby able to pursue the national interest. Under state capitalism the state would be able to achieve a certain degree of autonomy from class as well as foreign interests and promote autochthonous economic development. The thesis on internal colonialism highlights the importance of the Indian peasant population, particularly in countries which have large indigenous communities, and thus, any process of reform or revolution has to address this particular problem if it hopes to succeed. In turn marginality analysis brings to the fore a new product of internal colonialism which is of more recent origin: the shanty–town dwellers. Again the implication of marginality analysis for reformists and revolutionaries alike is that such a major social force cannot be ignored in any process of change, particularly in countries which experienced or are experiencing a rapid process of urbanization.

Dependency analysis take on board these lessons of the studies on internal colonialism and marginality which were absent in structuralist analysis. There are thus new elements considered by the *dependentistas* and there is a major difference between the two variants of dependency theory which are distinguished in this book: the structuralist and the neo–Marxist. The structuralist *dependentistas* differ from the old structuralists in no longer believing that those sectors of the industrial, middle, and working class which are now integrated into the dependent transnational corporate system will favour reforms. It is therefore the non–integrated sectors which are called upon to undertake the reforms: including those urban and rural groups which have been marginalized by the process of dependent development.

The neo–Marxist dependency position evolved in Latin America under the impetus of the Chinese and especially the Cuban revolutions, which affirmed the importance of the worker–peasant alliance in the revolutionary struggle for socialism. Neo–Marxist *dependentistas* argue that Latin America does not have to wait for the bourgeois revolution before proceeding to socialism as the existing mode of production is capitalist. Such a bourgeois revolution is unlikely to occur in Third World countries in any case owing to the dependent nature of their bourgeoisie. It thus falls to the socialist revolution, spearheaded by the worker–peasant alliance, to undertake or complete the required progressive transformations which the dependent bourgeoisie is unable or unwilling to carry out. Meanwhile orthodox Marxists, who characterize Latin America's existent mode of production as dominated by feudalism or strongly handicapped by its vestiges, insist that it is essential for the working class to form an anti–feudal and anti–imperialist alliance with the progressive sectors of the bourgeoisie so as to complete and hasten the process of transition to capitalism. Thus, the socialist revolution is not yet on the agenda. This position is similar to that of the structuralists except that for the orthodox Marxist the coalition would be headed by the working class and the ultimate aim of the process of change would in the long run be socialism.

AN OVERVIEW

In this section I give a brief overview of the book and implicitly draw attention to the continuity between the Haya de la Torre and Mariátegui debate and the contribution of the Latin American school in the post–1945 period.

In Chapter 2 I examine the manifold ideas of the structuralist position on economic development. Prebisch (1949; 1981a), the first and most original of the Latin American structuralist writers, courageously challenged neoclassical theory, attacked the prevailing pattern of international trade, and boldly proposed a theory of peripheral capitalism. He argued that, while prevailing orthodox economic theories might be valid for the centre countries, they could not explain the functioning of peripheral economies with their different structure. In particular he castigated neoclassical policy prescriptions for their negative effects on the pattern of growth, income distribution, and employment. Among the issues tackled by the structuralists are the terms of trade between the centre and the periphery, the process of import–substituting industrialization, and the inflationary phenomena in Latin America. The centre–periphery paradigm and the advocacy of the periphery's industrialization represented a major shift in development thinking at the time. The discussion on inflation is of interest because it was one of the first coherent rebuttals of the monetarist and IMF type anti–inflationary packages, and because it incorporated socio–political variables in the analysis of inflation, all of which had been ignored by monetarists.

These structuralist ideas were largely formulated by staff working within the Economic Commission for Latin America (ECLA), a United Nations agency. This may help to explain the fact that their social and political analysis is rather limited and couched in an anodyne, inoffensive way. The strength of the structuralist analysis lies in the methodology espoused and the approach to economic development. Structuralists believe it is possible to achieve a self–centred and more dynamic development process by reforming the peripheral capitalist system.

Structuralists proposed to replace the externally propelled development path inherited from the colonial period with an inward–directed development strategy on the basis of an import–substituting industrialization process. To bring about, or accelerate, such a shift structuralists called for a far greater role for government in development. The structuralist scenario implied a developmentalist state which actively intervened in the economy and the market through planning, protective tariffs for industry, price controls, state investment, joint ventures with foreign capital, the establishment of regional common markets, and so on.

However, structuralists did not advocate the nationalization of major foreign–owned primary commodity–producing and commodity–exporting companies but called for a shift of foreign investment towards manufacturing industry. The central concern was with the unequal distribution of the fruits of international trade between the centre–industrial exporting countries and the periphery–primary commodity exporting countries. As a consequence structuralists proposed an industrialization and development strategy which would favour the creation of a political alliance between the national and foreign industrial bourgeoisie, the middle class and the industrial working class. Such a multiclass alliance would displace from power the old coalition between landlords, the agro–mineral foreign bourgeoisie, and the traditional export–import commercial class. Structuralists anticipated that industrialization would not only replace the old oligarchical order but lead to the development of a modern and efficient bourgeois democratic state and society.

Chapter 3 examines the thesis of internal colonialism. This thesis draws much inspiration from theories of colonialism (or external colonialism) and imperialism but applies them to examine the forms of domination and exploitation within a particular country. This thesis was put forward in countries with a significant indigenous population to explain the internal mechanism of oppression and exploitation of one ethnic or racial group by another. In the Latin American case it refers to the relationship between the descendants from the Spanish and Portuguese conquerors (the *conquistadores*), including the *mestizos* (i.e. those of mixed white and native blood) and the Indian population. One motivation for this thesis is the criticism of dualist theories. According to internal colonialism the 'Indian problem' arises from the manifold links of domination and exploitation established by the expanding capitalist system. The 'Indian problem' is thus not a pre-existent state of affairs pertaining to some traditional stage but is the consequence of the integration of the Indian communities into the world capitalist system. Another reason for the emergence of the internal colonialism thesis is the desire to overcome a shortcoming of Marxist theory by examining social divisions other than those of class.

In some ways the internal colonialism thesis anticipates the discussion on the articulation of forms or modes of production which captivated Marxists from North and South in the mid–1970s. The internal colonialism thesis recognizes that although the Indian communities are integrated and exploited by the dominant capitalist mode of production, it does not necessarily follow that their relations of production are capitalist.

In Chapter 4, I discuss marginality, a concept which emerged as concern grew about the rising problem of structural unemployment. The coexistence of rapid industrialization and rising permanent unemployment was considered paradoxical and contrary to what was thought to have been the case in the developed countries during their industrialization. Orthodox Marxist analysis also seemed to be at a loss to explain such a situation and thus neo–Marxists felt justified in revising and extending Marx's surplus population theory to account for this novel fact in some Third World countries.

I distinguish between a modernization and neo–Marxist version of marginality. The modernization view on marginality argues that it is possible to reform the economic, social, and political system so as to incorporate the marginal population. In the neo–Marxist view this is not possible as the particular pattern of dependent capitalist development in the periphery itself engenders marginality. Thus, it is only by breaking out of such a situation through a socialist revolution that the problem of marginality might be resolved.

The debate on marginality and the 'marginal pole' of the economy undoubtedly influenced the subsequent formulation of the concept of the 'informal sector', although this has not always been acknowledged. The discussion on the relationships between the formal and informal sectors of the economy, which started in the early 1970s and to some extent still continues, also echoes the debate on the articulation of modes of production which took place at the same time.

The analysis of marginality also expresses an implicit concern with the insufficiency of class analysis as the marginal population is difficult to classify within the existent class categories. Do the marginals constitute a new class? Furthermore, what is their revolutionary or counter–revolutionary potential? These questions still remain unanswered, despite their relevancy.

Chapter 5 addresses the rich and multi–stranded dependency analysis, the best–known Latin American contribution to development theory. Dependency analysis can be considered the culmination, or at least the most sophisticated elaboration so far, of the ideas of reformists and revolutionaries on the problem of underdevelopment and development. In Chapter 5 I try to correct some inadequate, partial, and sometimes false readings of dependency analysis by exploring the ideas of some lesser known dependency writers. There exist various currents within the dependency school but it is possible to reduce these to essentially two: structuralist–cum–reformist and neo–Marxist–cum–revolutionary.

Chapter 6 tackles the complexities of the varied critiques of dependency analysis. Given the polemical, wide–ranging, inter– and multidisciplinary nature of dependency studies, the critiques likewise have been from a variety of perspectives and disciplines within the social sciences. In Chapter 6, I present a little known but illustrative and significant debate between some of the most prominent dependency authors. I then comprehensively survey the main criticisms, hoping to clarify some of the confusions which a bewildering critical literature has generated.

Chapter 7 highlights some contemporary development problems and examines to what extent the Latin American school of thought is still able to provide relevant insights and answers. I note the resurgence of neoclassical and neo–conservative ideas as well as the concomitant eclipse of development studies over the last decade. I examine the implications of these events for Latin American development theories and pinpoint some issues which these theories need to re–examine or develop further if they are to continue to make a contribution to, and assist in the process of, the renewal of development studies. It is my conviction that the crisis in development studies to which I referred at the beginning of this chapter can be overcome, especially if development thinkers and practitioners of the North take more fully into account the contributions from their counterparts in the South. Out of such a fusion of ideas a powerful and credible alternative to neo–conservative ideas and policies might emerge.

The structuralist school of development

The propositions which can be grouped together under the banner of the structuralist school of development were mainly put forward by social scientists working for the Economic Commission for Latin America (ECLA), a United Nations agency established in 1947 and located in Santiago, Chile. [1] Latin American structuralism emerged haphazardly as ECLA's initial concern lay in discovering the major obstacles to development in Latin America and suggesting policies to overcome these. Thus, the concern was more practical than scholastic. By this I do not want to imply that they dismissed theory. On the contrary, their original contribution to development studies grew out of their profound dissatisfaction with prevailing orthodox and neoclassical theories. In their view neoclassical economics had, at best, little to contribute to the understanding of the development problems facing the peripheral countries and, by perpetuating the income disparity between the centre and periphery, at worst, legitimized a development pattern in the periphery which was detrimental to growth. Latin American economists and a few sociologists working largely in ECLA aimed to construct an alternative autochthonous analysis. ECLA provided the institutional infrastructure and the inspiration for this alternative project, particularly under its well–known Executive Secretary, Raúl Prebisch. [2] Thus, structuralism can also be referred to as the ECLA school of thought or the ECLA theory of development.

Prebisch assembled an excellent team of social scientists who were similarly concerned with the question of Latin American development. [3] Never before had such an outstanding group of intellectuals from various Latin American countries been brought together and been driven by a common purpose and problematic. As a consequence a major regional perspective on development problems confronting Latin America was formulated, overcoming to some extent purely nationalist views. The UN's financial underpinning of ECLA helped to provide a propitious environment for research. The location of ECLA's principal office in Santiago de Chile was also a good choice as Chile provided a stable democratic setting at that time and became a testing ground for many of ECLA's propositions. During the 1950s and early 1960s ECLA's views on Latin America were informed by the experiences of those countries with which the principal contributors were most familiar, mainly the Southern Cone countries (Argentina, Chile, and Uruguay) and Brazil. Notwithstanding the predominance of this initial Southern Cone view, ECLA's propositions on the centre–periphery are of direct concern not only to Latin America as a whole but to the Third World in general. In this sense the ECLA school can claim to be the first genuine Third World development school.

While various writers developed the structuralist paradigm, Prebisch's original ideas were pivotal in launching this perspective, whose influence has extended beyond Latin America. ECLA's (1951) pioneering *Economic Survey of Latin America 1949* was authored, if not signed, by Prebisch, and Prebisch's (1950) *The Economic Development of Latin America and its Principal Problems* has been labelled as 'ECLA's manifesto' by Hirschman (1961: 13; 1971).

> The perception of the international economic system as one of industrial center and agrarian periphery, in which the former dominates the latter, has had a tremendous influence in the analysis of underdevelopment; the significance of the idea is impossible to gauge because its acceptance is still expanding. Raúl Prebisch's analytical terms, and the concomitant theory of trade relations, now known as unequal exchange, have been adopted not only by the followers of a dependency theory tradition in Latin America, stemming directly from Prebisch, but also by non–Latin American writers (assuredly, with extensive modifications) such as Arghiri Emmanuel, André Gunder Frank, Immanuel Wallerstein, Johan Galtung, and Samir Amin.
>
> (Love, 1980: 45)

The originality of the structuralist paradigm lies in the proposition that the process of development and underdevelopment is a single process; that the centre and periphery are closely interrelated, forming part of one world economy. Furthermore, the disparities between the centre and periphery are reproduced through international trade. Thus, the periphery's development problems are located within the context of the world economy.

The structuralists' perspective is both holistic and historical. It probes into the origins of the integration of Latin American economies into the dominant capitalist system from colonial times as producers of primary products (Pinto, 1961a; Sunkel and Paz, 1970). ECLA termed this pattern of development in the periphery the 'primary–export model' or the 'outward–oriented development model'. ECLA's approach is not narrowly economistic but emphasizes the institutional and social factors in the functioning of an economy and particularly the role of the state as a key agent in the development process. [4] Through this approach ECLA aimed to pinpoint those internal transformations of the peripheral countries which were brought about by the external impact of the centre countries, such as those resulting from the Great Depression and the Second World War.

The ECLA school strongly advocated an import–substituting industrialization policy which would help peripheral countries to switch from the 'outward–looking development' process (*'desarrollo hacia afuera'*) to an 'inward–directed' one (*'desarrollo hacia adentro'*). [5] ECLA initially pinned many hopes on this inward strategy but later realized the limitations of such a model and presented a series of novel propositions about its negative characteristics.

This model of development created by the import–substitution process was later characterized by the structuralists as both concentrating and exclusive (*concentrador y excluyente*) in that the fruits of technological progress brought about by industrialization were concentrated in the hands of the owners of capital, excluding the majority and exacerbating inequalities in the distribution of income (Pinto, 1965). At the same time this development process failed to absorb the surplus labour and even contributed to its size by destroying pre–existing labour–intensive artisan, craft, and simple manufacturing activities. Thus, the structuralists made an early contribution to the analysis of marginality, which it viewed as a new phenomenon created by the import–substitution model. Furthermore, this model resulted in 'structural heterogeneity' as differences between economic sectors (such as those between a backward agriculture and a modern capital–intensive industry) and those within economic sectors (such as those between the 'informal' and 'formal' parts of any one economic sector) were exacerbated. Finally, the ECLA school characterized the import–substituting industrialization strategy as leading to a 'perverse style of development'. In their view, industrialization in the periphery created a different development process altogether from that which had occurred in the centre countries.

The structuralist school also played a prominent part in the ideological current, known as *desarrollismo* or developmentalism, which swept through most of Latin America from the end of the Second World War until the early 1970s. [6] *Desarrollismo* has a certain Keynesian flavour as it entailed a major increase in government expenditure for development purposes but it went even further as it regarded the state as the crucial agent for economic, social and political change. Through economic planning, the state was seen as modernizing the developing countries by spearheading the industrialization process. ECLA influenced government policy in many Latin American countries through its writings, speeches, and press reports, its technical advice to governments, and the courses and seminars it provided for top civil servants. Its influence was particularly strong where governments intended to undertake major reforms, such as land reform, and where they aimed to work towards economic integration as a way of proceeding towards industrialization. When linked to populism, *desarrollismo* became a powerful, though elusive, political force. Its ideology was anti–feudal, anti–oligarchical, reformist, and technocratic. It questioned the perverse effect of capitalism in the periphery and the resulting inequities in the institutional economic arrangements but it did not advocate socialism or revolutionary change. In today's parlance it proposed a 'redistribution with growth' strategy. The heyday of *desarrollismo* was in the 1960s when several reformist governments came to power in Latin America and the US launched its New Deal with Latin America known as the Alliance for Progress. [7] Its downfall came with the establishment of military–authoritarian regimes in the Southern Cone in the 1970s and their pursuit of radical monetarist policies of the 'new right' or 'neo–conservatives'.

As mentioned earlier ECLA did not set out to construct a systematic and coherent development theory. The task of theorizing and systematizing came late in the day and was only partly undertaken by ECLA, being largely confined to the book by Osvaldo Sunkel and Pedro Paz (1970). Celso Furtado (1965; 1974a) made his major contribution to the theorizing of 'structuralism' while no longer working for ECLA. The most ambitious and comprehensive attempt to formalize ECLA's theory of development from a critical perspective has been undertaken by Octavio Rodríguez (1980). [8] The structuralist school of development has many detractors and has been criticized from various angles. However, ECLA did become aware of some of its own limitations and revised some of its own ideas as it gained experience and as its policies were tested over time. Some of these critiques are dealt with in this chapter whilst others are presented in the chapter on dependency as this partly developed as a critique of the ECLA school (see Chapter 5).

THE CENTRE–PERIPHERY PARADIGM

The cornerstone of structuralism is the centre–periphery paradigm (O. Rodríguez, 1977). This paradigm attempts to explain the unequal nature of the world economic system. It also suggests a series of policies to narrow the gap between countries of the centre and those of the periphery. According to this paradigm the duality in the world economy originated with the industrial revolution in the centre when the possibilities for increasing the productivity of the factors of production rose dramatically. The diffusion of this technical progress was, however, very uneven throughout the world. The centre countries internalized the new technology by developing an industrial capital–goods sector and by spreading the improved technology to all economic sectors. This resulted in the development of an homogeneous and integrated economy. In the periphery, by contrast, new technologies were largely imported and mainly confined to the primary–commodity–producing export sector. The industrial sector was small or insignificant and the capital goods sector was rudimentary or non–existent. As a consequence, the peripheral economy became both disarticulated and dualist: disarticulated because it had to import the advanced technology from the centre; and dualist because a large gulf in productivity developed between the export and subsistence sectors. A sizeable low–productivity pre–capitalist sector continues to survive in the periphery producing a continuous surplus of labour. [9] This large surplus of labour keeps wages low and prevents the periphery from retaining the fruits of its own technological progress as productivity increases in the export sector are largely transferred to the centre owing to the deterioration of the terms of trade (ECLA, 1951). Thus, in ECLA's view international trade not only perpetuates the asymmetry between centre and periphery but also deepens it.

The assertion that the central and peripheral countries are linked by a series of asymmetric relationships which reproduce the system represented a key departure from the evolutionist and mechanical stage theories of development (Furtado, 1974a: Chapter 10). Stage theories, such as Rostow's (1960), maintain that all developed countries were once underdeveloped and that the present underdeveloped countries will, like their predecessors, evolve through a series of stages into developed countries. Such theories are considered ahistorical by structuralists as they do not take into account the different structure and dynamism of the peripheral economy. The industrial revolution transformed the centre countries into industrial economies while the peripheral countries were assigned the role of primary–producing countries. While industry became the most dynamic economic sector in the centre, the most dynamic sector in the periphery was the primary-producing export sector – either agricultural or mineral. ECLA characterizes this export–led growth of the periphery as the 'outward–looking' development model. This model retains its dynamism so long as export earnings grow quickly enough to sustain an adequate rate of growth in the economy. For this to happen exports must grow faster than national income as the economic transformation brought about by export–led growth increases demand for foreign exchange. As incomes rise in the periphery, for example, the demand for imported industrial products rises at a faster rate than incomes, i.e. the income elasticity of demand for industrial commodities is larger than one.

The world depression of the 1930s dealt a major blow to this outward–oriented growth model as exports from the periphery fell dramatically. This brought severe internal consequences for income and employment and led to this model being increasingly questioned as a development strategy. However, in ECLA's view this outward–directed growth model was already beginning to be exhausted by the turn of the century and more particularly since the First World War when the USA gradually replaced Britain as the principal centre of the world economy. The US economy was far less open at this time than the British so that the dynamic impulses irradiated from the centre throughout the world economy weakened continually. The import coefficient of the US was far smaller than that of the UK and the growth of the US economy accordingly created a lower level of demand for imports from the periphery (ECLA, 1951: Chapter 2). The resulting disparity between the periphery's rate of growth of exports and imports led to an increasingly severe foreign exchange constraint strangling the growth potential of the periphery. In ECLA's view an important contributory factor to the foreign exchange crisis was the deterioration in the terms of trade suffered by the periphery. In order to overcome the constraining effects of this outward–oriented process ECLA proposed an 'inward–oriented' development model for the periphery. ECLA's thesis of the deterioration of the terms of trade will be discussed first as this provides the main argument for its advocacy of an inward–directed development process.

THE TERMS OF TRADE BETWEEN CENTRE AND PERIPHERY

The terms of trade analysis reveals ECLA's distinctive approach to the problems of development and underdevelopment as compared with neoclassical theories. This topic is the subject for which ECLA is best known and which has generated the most controversy, especially its thesis on the deterioration of the periphery's terms of trade. [10] By focusing on the analysis of the terms of trade, ECLA sought to challenge conventional economic theories of international trade and, by questioning the international division of labour, to propose a completely different development strategy for the periphery which they dubbed 'inward–directed'.

According to conventional international trade theory, the economic specialization of the centre in the production of industrial commodities and of the periphery in primary commodities worked to their mutual benefit as each enjoyed comparative advantages in these respective areas. Furthermore, this theory argued that the income gap between centre and periphery would diminish as perfect mobility of labour, capital, or products would equalize prices and distribute the benefits of technical progress more equally between trading countries (Bhagwati, 1965; Chenery, 1965). [11] In ECLA's view, however, specialization in raw materials limited the periphery's growth prospects, as evidenced by the exhaustion of export–led growth in Latin America. Prebisch (1949) observed that incomes grew faster in the centre than in the periphery. This widening gap was due, in Prebisch's view, to the prevailing international division of production and trade which confined the periphery to the production of primary commodities.

Prebisch set out to investigate the discrepancy between the predictions of conventional theory and reality. He argued that the commodity or net barter terms of trade – i.e. the relationship between the price index of the periphery's exports and the price index of its imports – had turned against the periphery since the 1870s. These terms of trade, needless to say, fluctuate continuously but the long–term trend identified by Prebisch was clearly unfavourable to the periphery. There was, therefore, a long–run tendency for prices of primary products to deteriorate relative to the prices of manufactured goods. This meant that the periphery had to export an increasing quantity of raw materials in order to continue importing the same amount of industrial commodities. ECLA was not only concerned with the evolution of the commodity terms of trade but with the income terms of trade as well. The latter are arrived at by dividing the value of exports by the price of imports, which is the same as multiplying the commodity terms of trade by the quantum index of exports. This means that the income terms of trade take the volume of exports into account and express the purchasing power of export earnings (*poder de compra de las exportaciones*) or the import capacity (*capacidad para importar*). Although the periphery increased the physical volume of exports this was partly offset by the deterioration in the terms of trade so that the growth in export earnings was insufficient to obtain the required rate of growth in national income. A study by ECLA (1951) pointed out that the rate of growth in Latin America's capacity to import between 1925 and 1949 was not even sufficient to keep pace with the rate of population growth.

Prebisch's analysis of the deterioration of the terms of trade deals both with demand and supply conditions of commodity markets. His demand analysis is, in my view, not necessarily incompatible with neoclassical economic thinking, while his supply arguments, which are given more weight, are typically structuralist. Hans W. Singer (1950) also discovered a deterioration in the terms of trade against the 'borrowing' (i.e. underdeveloped) and in favour of the 'investing' (i.e. developed) countries, advancing similar arguments to those of Prebisch. Singer, like Prebisch, was a United Nations functionary but at the New York headquarters. He reached his conclusions independently from Prebisch and around the same time (Love, 1980: 58; H. W. Singer, 1982: 13). Thus, the thesis on the deterioration in the terms of trade is known in the economic literature as the 'Prebisch–Singer thesis'. However, Prebisch specifically deals with the economic cycle and highlights to a greater extent than Singer the reasons for the different behaviour of wages in developed and underdeveloped countries.

On the demand side Prebisch (1959; 1964) argues that the terms of trade deteriorated against the periphery because of the different income–elasticity of demand for imports by the centre and periphery or, as he put it, due to the 'dynamic disparity of demand' between centre and periphery. This means that the centre's imports of primary products from the periphery rise at a lower rate than its national income, while the periphery's imports of industrial commodities from the centre grow at a faster rate than its income. The low income–elasticity of demand at the centre, which is well below unity, is explained by a number of factors. As income increases a smaller proportion is spent on food (the 'law of Engel'), technical progress develops new ways of producing commodities requiring fewer raw materials and/or substituting synthetic for natural products, and protectionist policies pursued by some centre countries restrict the market for exports from the periphery. In the periphery, by contrast, the income–elasticity of demand for imports is generally high (well above unity) as they mainly import industrial products the demand for which rises proportionally more than income.[12]

With respect to the supply arguments, or the 'cycle version' of the periphery's deterioration of the terms of trade, these are related to the differential effect of the world economic cycle on centre and periphery (ECLA, 1951). The capitalist economic system evolves in a cyclical fashion with the centre being the initiator of these cycles which provoke an adaptive cyclical response by the periphery. During an economic upswing the terms of trade generally turn in favour of primary producers but during a downswing they turn against them to an even greater degree. This results in the long–run deterioration of the periphery's terms of trade, especially as the downswings tend to last longer than the upswings.

This differential impact of the world economic cycle on centre and periphery is explained by the differential behaviour of prices, profits, and wages in the centre and periphery during the phases of the cycle. During an economic upswing wages grow substantially in the centre while they hardly rise in the periphery because of the availability of surplus labour. Meanwhile during a downswing the fall in centre wages and prices is limited due to the existence of trade union power and the oligopolistic structure of industry. In the periphery, by contrast, the downswing greatly reduces prices and wages as producers are able to compress wages substantially on account of surplus labour and the non–existence and/or weakness of trade unions. In addition the greater degree of competition between peripheral countries forces them to reduce prices of their exports to a greater extent than centre countries (ECLA, 1951). Thus, the greater the resistance is in the centre to a fall in wages and profits, the greater is the pressure on the periphery to reduce its wages and perhaps even profits (Prebisch, 1950).

Hans W. Singer (1975), like Prebisch, is also concerned with the international redistribution of the 'fruits of technical progress'. Both argue that an increase in productivity can result in either a fall in the price of a commodity where this technical progress has occurred, thereby benefiting the consumers; or in a rise in the payment to factors of production (i.e. wages and profits), thereby benefiting the producers; or in a combination of both. According to Prebisch the existence of trade union power and oligopolies in the centre means that prices have not fallen, or have fallen to a lesser extent than the increase in productivity. Thus, workers and capitalists in the centre are able to gain the fruits of their technical progress via rises in wages and profits. Meanwhile the opposite has happened in the periphery due to the weakness or non–existence of trade unions and the greater competition facing producers. However, the main argument put forward by Prebisch to explain the inability of workers to capture a significant part of the increase in productivity is the existence of a large surplus labour force. An additional factor is the low productivity of the pre– and semi–capitalist sectors with their low subsistence incomes and wages which act as a restraint on wage increases in the export sector where most of the productivity increases in the periphery occur (ECLA, 1951).

Although the periphery's terms of trade might deteriorate, this does not necessarily mean that it is unable to reap any gains from trade. What it does mean is that any gains resulting from international trade are distributed unequally between centre and periphery. It is essential to analyse additional factors before determining whether international trade is beneficial or detrimental to the economic growth of a country. In condemning the deterioration of the commodity terms of trade, Prebisch (1984) is not arguing against international trade, nor has he ever suggested delinking. On the contrary, he sees international trade and foreign capital as essential elements for raising productivity and growth in the periphery. However, Prebisch never explicitly set out his views on what he would consider a fair distribution of the gains from trade to be.[13]

In conclusion, the greater scope for productivity increases in industrial production and the maldistribution of gains from trade explain the rising gap in incomes between centre and periphery. If the product and factor markets were fully competitive in the centre, then the terms of trade should in fact move against the centre as technical progress proceeds at a faster pace in the industrial countries than in the primary producing countries (Pinto, 1983: 1049). In reality, the opposite has occurred, as the neoclassical assumptions do not hold for the reasons already mentioned. Thus, as H. W. Singer (1978: 51) put it, the industrial countries enjoyed the best of both worlds as they retained both the fruits of their own technical progress and captured part of the underdeveloped countries' productivity increase as well.

Prebisch proposed a variety of policies to counteract the negative tendency of the periphery's terms of trade. He suggested a tax on primary exports and a set of duties on manufacturing imports to help switch resources within the periphery from primary export to industrial activities (Prebisch, 1959: 263). He also proposed to allow union activity in the primary export sector to push up wages, to defend primary commodity prices through concerted international action, and to press for the reduction or elimination of protection for primary commodities in the centre. Thus, Prebisch was not against expanding the periphery's exports so long as these helped to reduce its labour surplus and thereby drive up wages and export prices (ibid.: 263). However, the main thrust of his argument was aimed at changing the periphery's structure of production and developing an industrial sector through a series of measures which would encourage the allocation of additional productive resources to the industrial sector. This would help the periphery to retain its productivity increases.

In short, structuralists argued that while the unequal terms of trade were not the cause of the periphery's poverty, they reduced the surplus that could be available to overcome it. They thus proposed a radical change in the outward–looking development path which most peripheral countries had been following. In its place they argued for an import–substituting industrialization policy as the centre–piece for a new inward–directed development strategy.

IMPORT–SUBSTITUTING INDUSTRIALIZATION

During the outward–looking development phase, which predominated until the crisis of the 1930s or in some instances until the post–war period, exports accounted for about 25 per cent of the region's gross national product in the 1920s, a fairly high export coefficient. This rapid growth of the export sector induced an incipient industrialization process in some Latin American countries. By the beginning of the century the industrial sector accounted for 18 per cent of the Argentinian and 14 per cent of the Mexican gross national product

(Furtado, 1970). The great crash of 1929 approximately halved Latin America's import capacity as export earnings fell sharply. This forced reduction of the import coefficient provoked a restructuring of the Latin American economies. Those smaller countries which had no significant industrial base adjusted by drastically depressing internal economic activity. By contrast governments of some larger, more industrialized countries took measures to reduce the harsh effects of the crisis by stimulating the industrial sector. The Second World War also stimulated industrialization in these Latin American countries owing to the inability of the centre countries to supply industrial products to the periphery.

Arguments for industrialization

ECLA's analysis merely provided a scientific rationalization for an ongoing process and a justification for government to adopt import–substituting industrialization policies more overtly and vigorously. Such a policy was pursued through a variety of means such as easy credit, infrastructural support, and favourable foreign exchange measures, but chiefly through protectionism. Tariff barriers were imposed or increased on all those industrial imports whose production was to be substituted (ECLA, 1966).

Prebisch's (1968; 1969) argument for industrialization rests on his analysis of the periphery's deterioration of the terms of trade and the limited international mobility of factors of production. By this he probably had in mind the restrictions put upon the international migration of labour. However, he also favoured industrialization because he believed that this would avoid a repetition of the disastrous effects of the 1930s world crisis, that it would lead to greater increases in productivity and incomes, and that it would reduce unemployment, thereby removing one of the causes of low wages in the periphery. In addition it would help the retention of productivity increases in the periphery and avoid further deterioration in its commodity terms of trade.

In Prebisch's view industrialization is justified in the periphery even where the cost of production of local industry is higher than the international price, as otherwise some factors of production would remain unemployed or would be used to produce export commodities with further adverse consequences for the terms of trade. For Prebisch (1959: 257) the relevant comparison is not between industrial costs and import prices but between the increase in incomes obtained by employing the factors of production in industry and their alternative employment in the export sector. This is the key criterion for determining the type and degree of industrialization in the periphery. Once this has been established a corresponding protectionist policy must be implemented to allow for the establishment, survival, and growth of the chosen industries. Protectionism is required so long as the productivity of the periphery's industry falls below that of the centre countries and so long as this productivity differential is not compensated for by wage differentials. [14] Prebisch is clearly not in favour of lowering wages as an alternative to protectionism as this would reduce the price of export commodities and lead to a further deterioriation in the periphery's terms of trade. He was also against excessive protectionism as this would discourage agricultural production and weaken industrial efficiency. Thus, he was in favour of balanced growth (ibid.: 252, 257).

Reflecting back on his early ideas, Prebisch recently wrote:

> Theoretically, the problem was put in the following dynamic terms. What is to be done with productive resources when further expansion of primary exports would bring a fall in prices? Should these resources be used to generate additional exports, or should they be allocated to industrial production for domestic consumption? The most economically advantageous solution depends on the proper combination between these two compatible options. Additional primary exports would be more advantageous provided the export income lost through the fall in prices was no greater than the income lost because of the higher cost of domestic industrial production in relation to imported industrial goods. Once beyond the point where such income losses were the same, the option in favour of industrialization was quite obvious.
>
> (Prebisch, 1984: 178)

As mentioned earlier ECLA set development problems within what today would be called a world economy perspective. ECLA observed that the export-propelled growth of the peripheral countries began to lose its dynamism as hegemony of the world economy passed from the UK to the US. As the US economy is far more self–sufficient than that of the UK, its import–coefficient was smaller, thereby limiting the export possibilities of the peripheral countries. As a consequence the per capita import capacity of the Latin American economies diminished, limiting the rate of growth of the gross national product. This insufficient growth of the periphery's export earnings, which placed an increasing stranglehold on its growth process, is one of the key reasons why ECLA advocated switching to a growth pattern via the domestic market.

ECLA hoped that an import–substituting industrialization strategy would transform industry into the most dynamic economic sector and lead to a higher rate of economic growth than that achieved by the export sector. Thus, it was expected that this substitution process would lead to two types of structural transformation: changes in the structure of production as industry's share of national income increased, and changes in the structure and composition of imports as these would form a smaller proportion of national income.

The employment argument for industrialization does not figure prominently in ECLA's writings although it was hoped that rapid industrial growth would help to absorb surplus labour. However, as early as 1952 Prebisch (1969) had doubts about the periphery's capacity to absorb this surplus labour because of the high capital density of the prevailing technology. As long as it lacked a capital–goods sector of its own the periphery had little alternative but to import technology from the centre, even if inappropriate. This penetration of a technology, which corresponded to a high wage, capital–intensive economy, intensified the problem of structural unemployment in the periphery as became evident later on. Furthermore, owing to the prevailing low incomes, savings in the periphery were insufficient to finance a high enough rate of capital accumulation to absorb the surplus labour because of the high capital density of technology, high rates of population growth, and investments which displaced labour from less productive activities.

It is remarkable that Prebisch had already perceived in 1952 the economic disadvantages which a small or absent capital–goods sector represented for the periphery. Not only did such a situation lead to the adoption of inappropriate technologies but to the periphery's inability to benefit from the growing demand for capital goods brought about by industrialization. Such a demand leaked abroad, benefiting the centre and depriving the periphery of one of the most important sources of productivity growth. However, Prebisch was aware that many of the technologies produced by the centre are superior to the pre–existent technologies employed by the periphery. Therefore, it is in the periphery's advantage to adopt the centre's technology as it raises economic efficiency. Owing to the structural difference between centre and periphery, the introduction of capital–intensive technology into the periphery's labour surplus economy will result in technological unemployment as many low–productivity industrial enterprises will go bankrupt and the displaced labour will only partly be absorbed by the more capital–intensive industry, if at all. [15]

With respect to foreign capital, ECLA initially welcomed this as contributing to raising investment and efficiency. Their early view of foreign capital was uncritical and they even encouraged its investment in the import–substituting industrialization process instead of in the old primary–export–producing sector as in the past. In general, ECLA was initially optimistic about the benefits industrialization would bring to the periphery. It was regarded as the panacea which would not only overcome the limitations of the outward–directed development process but would also provide social and political benefits such as enhancing the middle and working classes and democracy.

Notwithstanding, one of the first criticisms to emerge of import–substituting industrialization policy came from within the ECLA fold itself. 'ECLA's Manifesto' of 1949 (Prebisch, 1950) had already voiced misgivings about Latin American industrialization, and by the early 1960s ECLA published a series of critiques of the import–substituting industrialization process. These have often been overlooked by both neoclassical and dependency critiques undertaken in the late 1960s and early 1970s, as will be seen later. The 1949 Manifesto already considered the technology adopted to be too capital–intensive and the internal market too limited for industry to take full advantage of economies of scale. It also pointed to technological inefficiency arising from the limited abilities of both management and labour, even where the most modern technology was employed. Furthermore, consumption patterns were seen as too diversified and savings too small (ibid.).

By the early 1960s there was an increasing awareness in ECLA's writings that import–substituting industrialization had aggravated some of the earlier economic problems instead of resolving them. ECLA did not deny that import substitution had achieved some successes, notably that of reducing the region's import coefficient from 30 per cent in 1928–9 to 9 per cent in 1963–4 and the export coefficient from 31 per cent to 14 per cent, and of increasing industry's share in gross national product from 13 per cent to 23 per cent over the same period (CEPAL, 1969: Chapter 5). However, ECLA also pointed to an 'exhaustion' of the import–substituting industrialization process. ECLA acknowledged that this inward–directed development strategy had not led to a diversification of exports as anticipated, as the region continued to depend heavily on the export of primary products. The external bottleneck became even more problematic as, despite substitution, the volume of imports continued to increase rapidly. Furthermore, changes in the composition of imports towards raw materials, spare parts, and capital goods made them more, not less, crucial for sustaining industrial growth. In order to cover the resulting chronic deficit in foreign exchange, Latin American countries had continually to increase their foreign debt, the servicing of which became a major economic burden.

ECLA realized that if the foreign exchange obstacle were to be overcome, industrialization could not remain enclosed within the national market. ECLA therefore vigorously promoted the idea of regional integration by encouraging the setting up of a Latin American common market (CEPAL, 1975). It was hoped that the formation of a free trade association with its larger market would increase exports and encourage greater industrial efficiency. Regional economic integration was also regarded as strengthening the bargaining power of Latin American countries with regards to the centre. In order to ameliorate the new external vulnerability created by import–substituting industrialization, Prebisch (1971: 354–5) suggested in 1961 that industrial exports should be stimulated with special subsidies. It had become evident to ECLA that the small size of the internal market and the exaggerated and indiscriminate protection to local industry had resulted in the formation of an inefficient monopolistic or oligopolistic industrial structure.

ECLA further argued that industrialization was impaired by governmental delays in introducing the necessary structural and institutional reforms such as land reform. The stagnation of the agricultural sector limited industrial development not only because agriculture failed to provide sufficient cheap raw materials and food-stuffs for the internal market but also because the low purchasing power of the rural population limited the internal market for industrial commodities.

Thus, by the early 1960s the initial optimistic outlook had turned to a more cautious and self–critical stance. Import–substituting industrialization had proved incapable of diffusing its benefits to other economic sectors due to 'the concentration of technical progress and its fruits' (using ECLA's phrase, i.e. *la concentración del progreso técnico y de sus frutos*). It could not change the skewed distribution of income or create sufficient employment opportunities. Furthermore, it had aggravated the economy's external vulnerability (Prebisch, 1963) and led to an increasing denationalization of the industrial sector.

This disenchantment with import–substituting industrialization became more apparent as industrialization began to lose impetus. A series of studies by ECLA economists such as María da Conceição Tavares and Celso Furtado argued that once the so–called 'easy phase of import–substitution' (i.e. consumer–goods industries) had passed and industrialization advanced to the substitution of intermediate and capital goods which required more capital and foreign exchange, the process became stuck and industrial growth declined. This was contrary to the historical experience of the centre countries for structural reasons which will be discussed in the following sections.

Industrial stagnation or 'exhaustion': lack of profits or foreign exchange?

Tavares was one of the first ECLA writers to undertake a comprehensive review of the problems arising from import–substituting industrialization. In a well–known essay Tavares (1964) argued that external and internal problems had accumulated to the point where they acted as a brake on the dynamism of the import–substituting industrialization process. In her view, the main contradiction of this process was that the import–substituting strategy, which was largely adopted to relieve the foreign exchange bottleneck, ended up by aggravating it and constraining further economic growth. The economy had become far more vulnerable to balance of payments problems as an increasing proportion of imports consisted of raw materials, spare parts, and capital goods which were essential for sustaining industrial production. In addition, import–substituting industrialization, in her view, had failed to absorb the surplus labour and to improve the distribution of income (personal, sectoral, and regional), thereby aggravating the phenomenon of 'structural duality' (*dualidad estructural*). The widening gap between the subsistence sector and the capitalist sector constrained the development process.

One of the internal obstacles to which Tavares refers is the lack of growth in rural incomes, which meant that the majority of the population was excluded from the industrial consumer market. It is largely for this reason that she argues for an agrarian reform, as the resulting increase in peasant incomes would provide a mass market for industrial commodities. She also highlights the lack of labour absorption capacity of import–substituting industrialization, which she sees as arising from the fact that relative prices of factors of production did not correspond to their social opportunity cost – for example, industrial capital was subsidized and industrial wages were too high. Apart from the agrarian reform to ease the unemployment problem, Tavares proposed a public works programme to create employment opportunities.

Celso Furtado (1965) is the structuralist who has most forcefully put forward the thesis of structural stagnation in relation to the inward–directed development process. According to Furtado (1974a), the main distinguishing feature of underdeveloped countries is the existence of a pre–capitalist sector. This acts as a labour reserve for the capitalist sector, thereby maintaining low wages. The industrialization process employs a technology which rapidly increases in capital density, leading to further income concentration as wages remain stable. This increasing concentration of income creates and reproduces a pattern of demand biased towards consumer durables and non–essential industries which tend to be capital intensive. The inefficiency of such an industrial structure becomes worse because the small size of the internal market does not enable all the benefits of the economies of scale to be reaped. A mechanism similar to Myrdal's (1957) 'circular and cumulative causation' comes into operation whereby the increasing inequality in income distribution reproduces an increasingly inefficient and diversified industrial structure which in turn further concentrates income. It is this increasing economic inefficiency which leads to stagnation. Like W. Arthur Lewis's dualist model, Furtado's model is steeped in the classical tradition but his conclusions differ radically from Lewis's. In Furtado's model industrialization within a dualist structure reproduces this dualism and underdevelopment, leading to stagnation, while for W. Arthur Lewis (1954) industrialization – or more precisely the transfer of labour from the subsistence to the capitalist sector – facilitates high rates of capital accumulation and growth as the unlimited supply of labour keeps wages low, leading to high rates of profit in the industrial sector.

Furtado's model of stagnating underdevelopment has been challenged in a joint article by Tavares and Serra (1973). [16] They do not deny that import–substituting industrialization experiences problems of 'exhaustion' but they differ as to its causes and are less pessimistic about the problems of overcoming stagnation. It is true that once import–substituting industrialization has satisfied the demand for consumer goods it must advance to the production of consumer durables, intermediate, and capital goods which require larger amounts of investment. Furtado argues that, owing to the small size of the internal market, the intermediate– and capital–goods industries cannot take full advantage of economies of scale and are therefore inefficient as they do not operate at their optimal level of output. Thus, as the industrialization process advances to the production of intermediate and capital goods, the rate of profit falls, the productivity of capital in these capital–intensive industries being low. This fall in profits leads to an insufficient level of savings to finance the next stage of the import–substitution process. In Furtado's view it is the severe inequality in the distribution of income which explains the structural nature of industrial stagnation once the easy phase has been exhausted.

However, Tavares and Serra argue that, given the monopolistic or oligopolistic position which the intermediate– and capital–goods industries enjoy in the national market, the rate of profit is unlikely to fall even if economic inefficiency increases. Tavares and Serra also dispute Furtado's assertion that the productivity of capital is necessarily lower in the intermediate– and capital–goods industries. In their view the larger capital–labour ratio in these industries is compensated for by a higher productivity of labour. In algebraic terms the average productivity of capital (Q/K) is identical to the average productivity of labour (Q/L) divided by the capital–labour ratio (K/L), i.e. $Q/K \equiv Q/L \div K/L$ where Q stands for output, K for capital, and L for labour. As the capital–labour ratio (K/L) rises, the average productivity of capital (Q/K), or rate of profit, does not necessarily need to fall as the final outcome depends on the amount by which the average productivity of labour (Q/L) rises, as can be seen from the identity presented above. As labour productivity usually rises faster than capital productivity, it is unlikely that profits will fall.

Thus, Tavares and Serra do not regard the problem as one of insufficient profits but one of transforming profits into investment. Most of the machinery, equipment, and raw materials required by the intermediate– and capital–goods industries have to be imported, requiring large amounts of foreign exchange. Tavares and Serra see the lack of foreign exchange as the main constraint on the further development of the industrial sector. In this way the analysis has turned full circle as ultimately the rate of economic growth is seen to depend on the rate of growth of exports, as was the case before the process of import–substituting industrialization commenced.

Structural heterogeneity and the smallness of the internal market

Aníbal Pinto, a leading ECLA economist, argues that the stagnation of the import–substituting industrialization process is due to the lack of a mass market. However, he is not so pessimistic as Furtado as he sees the solution for the smallness of the internal market as lying in industrial exports and agricultural modernization. Pinto (1965) argues that it is paramount for the industrial sector of small economies (such as those of Chile and Uruguay) to seek export markets in order to maintain or accelerate their rates of economic growth. Like Furtado he blames the structural duality of the peripheral economies for blocking the dynamics of development and like Furtado he arrives at opposite conclusions to those reached by W. A. Lewis. However, Pinto's duality is more complex than Furtado's. Pinto holds that the inward–directed development model creates a new duality or, as he puts it, 'structural heterogeneity'. This structural heterogeneity is not just the simple duality between economic sectors but an internal division within sectors between modern and traditional strata. Instead of a 'trickle down' process of development, as sustained by neoclassical economists, a polarization takes places both between and within sectors.

This new polarization is brought about by the uneven distribution of the fruits of technical progress. Their concentration arises from the biased allocation of government funds (credit, investment, and so on), and from taxation and foreign exchange policies which favour the modern capitalist sector. Furthermore, the import–substituting industrialization policy turns the internal commodity terms of trade in industry's favour. Given this panorama, Pinto proposes a policy of income redistribution and particularly a policy of re–allocation of technical progress. In some ways he is an early proponent of a 'redistribution with growth' development strategy, which the World Bank proclaimed in the mid–1970s. Pinto urges the dissemination of technical progress, particularly to traditional agriculture, through state investment. This would lead to a reduction of surplus labour as agricultural technologies are less capital–intensive than those employed by industry. As a result not only would agricultural productivity and living standards increase but the internal market for industrial commodities would also expand. Thus, a key objective for development policy is to overcome structural heterogeneity by de–concentrating technical progress.

Structuralist critique of import substitution

As mentioned earlier the import–substituting industrialization process has come under heavy criticism from both neoclassical and dependency theorists. However, structuralists themselves were among the first to analyse the limitations of import–substituting industrialization. In this respect it is important to distinguish between the structuralists' argument for import substitution and the actual way in which the policies were implemented and industrialization took place in Latin America. Thus, for example, Prebisch wrote in 1961:

> Although the volume of industrial production is not arbitrary, its composition has proved to be so in Latin American experience. From this point of view, the process of industrialization suffers from three flaws which have weakened its contribution to improving the standard of living. These are: (a) all industrialization activity is directed towards the domestic market; (b) the choice of industries to be established has been based more on circumstantial reasons than on considerations of economic yield; and (c) industrialization has failed to overcome the external vulnerability of the Latin American countries....Development policy has been discriminatory as regards exports. Assistance has been given...to industrial production for internal consumption but not to industrial production for exports. The production of many industrial goods has thus been developed at a cost far above the international level, when they could have been obtained with a much smaller cost differential in exchange for exports of other industrial products which might have been produced more profitably. The same could be said of new lines of primary commodities for exports and even traditional export commodities within certain relatively narrow limits.
>
> (Prebisch, 1961, as quoted in Prebisch, 1986b: 213)

By 1965 other ECLA studies were also critical of the import–substitution process because of its failure to diversify exports (ECLA, 1970a: Chapter 5). This inability to transform the export structure was seen as a major contradiction of the inward–directed development process (CEPAL, 1969: 35). However, Pinto sees this as an example of a failure in policy rather than an inherent flaw in the inward–directed development model as such. In his view ECLA's advocacy of industrialization was never meant to be interpreted as disregarding the export sector (Pinto, 1983: 1,071). While import substitution had greatly changed the composition of imports in Latin America, their volume continued to increase owing to the substantial growth in incomes. Furthermore, export earnings did not rise rapidly enough because of the deterioration in the commodity terms of trade.

Therefore, the problems already identified in the ECLA Manifesto of 1949 persisted, although at a different level. On the one hand, the limitations of the capacity to import continued and even became more problematic owing to the higher capital–density of the intermediate– and capital–goods technology which was largely imported. On the other hand, the limitations of the internal market made the transition to higher stages in the industrialization process difficult. As a consequence the Latin American economies incurred large foreign debts which in ECLA's view merely postponed the foreign exchange problem.

As mentioned earlier, to solve this problem ECLA proposed the formation of a Latin American common market in order to increase industrial exports and efficiency. Compared with earlier writings, ECLA increasingly identified the cause of 'strangulation' of the foreign sector as the inability to expand industrial exports rather than the deterioration in the terms of trade (ECLA, 1970a: Introduction). Indeed, ECLA had a major influence in the creation of the Latin American Free Trade Association, or LAFTA (*Asociación Latinoamericana de Libre Comercio*, or ALALC) in the 1960s. As it turned out this did not, however, solve the foreign exchange problem and the experiences of economic integration have had limited success in Latin America.

ECLA's tone became more self–critical as it was clearly dissatisfied with the failure of the inward–development process to live up to expectations. Six reasons were given for this dissatisfaction: the persistence of foreign exchange problems, the inability of industrialization to diffuse its benefits or give impetus to other economic activities, the limited absorption of labour, the continued existence of marked inequalities in the distribution of income, and, finally, the increasing control exercised by foreign capital over the most dynamic and strategic industries and over the complementary financial and commercial activities, thereby reducing the degree of internal autonomy (CEPAL, 1969: Introduction). This last point was to become one of the major strands of dependency theory, as will be seen in Chapter 5. In addition, ECLA's reference to the inability of import–substituting industrialization to absorb surplus labour drew attention to the growing problems of the shanty towns, an issue which is taken up by the 'marginality' writers discussed in Chapter 4.

THE STRUCTURALIST ANALYSIS OF INFLATION

The monetarist–structuralist controversy

During the mid–1950s a group of Latin American economists started to challenge the conventional wisdom on the nature and cures of inflation. This gave rise to a long debate between 'monetarists' and 'structuralists' which was partly responsible for the development of the structuralist school of thought. [17] It is therefore important to examine this debate as it brings to the fore major contrasts between the neoclassical and structuralist ways of thinking. It is also useful because it highlights elements of the structuralist paradigm and method of analysis. [18] These two camps were engaged in a fierce polemic on inflation which took place mainly from the mid–1950s to the early 1960s and has sporadically resurfaced since. The labelling of one group as structuralists later gave the name to what came to be known as structuralism or 'the structuralist school of thought' regarding the analysis of development problems and processes in Latin America.

Several Latin American countries (notably Argentina, Brazil, and Chile), which were at the time vigorously pursuing an import–substitution industrialization policy, had been experiencing persistently high rates of inflation for decades, and particularly since the Second World War. Thus, it is not surprising that ECLA began to enquire into the causes of and cures for inflation, as it had implications for the development of the region (ECLA, 1955; 1962). The structuralist position on inflation also emerged as a reaction to the stabilization policies pursued by some Latin American governments and/or proposed by the International Monetary Fund (IMF). Such policies were seen by the structuralists as doing more harm than good to the economies concerned (Pinto, 1960b; Sunkel, 1963).

The monetarist–structuralist controversy first took hold in Chile in 1955 when the Chilean government contracted the services of a firm of US consultants, who became known as the Klein–Saks mission, to devise a stabilization programme to deal with the alarming increase of inflation over the previous couple of years. The Klein–Saks mission was strongly attacked by centre and left–wing politicians as well as by economists who argued that the proposed stabilization plan would have detrimental effects on growth, employment, and wages, and fail to deal with the fundamental causes of inflation (Felix, 1960). In the late 1950s the Chilean government, again at the instigation of the IMF, pursued monetarist stabilization policies which provoked a similar reaction to those of the Klein–Saks mission (Sierra, 1969; Ffrench–Davis, 1973).

The talented Mexican economist Juan Noyola is generally credited with putting forward the first elements of the structuralist position on inflation (Martner, 1970; Bazdresch, 1983). [19] He worked for ECLA from 1950 to 1960 and several ECLA studies on inflation are strongly influenced by his thinking (Paz, 1984: 314). The debate on inflation was particularly fierce in Chile and many Chilean economists, some of whom were working in ECLA, such as Pinto, Sunkel, and Martner, contributed to it. According to Seers (1962: 193) Aníbal Pinto is considered as 'the Pope of the structuralists'. Although Pinto (1960a; 1961b; 1968) has written much on the topic, Sunkel (1960; 1979) presented the most elaborate version of the structuralist position on inflation. Prebisch (1971), having been a former head of the Central Bank in Argentina and at the time heading ECLA, could not fail to intervene in the debate.

This section aims to illustrate the approach taken by the structuralists to analyse a particular economic problem, in this instance inflation. My concern is, therefore, not to test the validity of the various propositions made by protagonists in this controversy, especially as this has already been done by others. [20]

At the heart of the controversy between structuralists and monetarists are different economic philosophies. Structuralists give far greater weight, and devote far greater attention, to the social and political origins of economic events than monetarists. They also place greater emphasis on the state in promoting economic development and in overcoming the deficiencies of the market. For the structuralists the removal of the main obstacles to development requires structural reforms of a social and political as well as an economic kind. While structuralists favour an inward–oriented and, to some extent, a self–reliant development strategy, monetarists advocate an outward–oriented development strategy driven by a closer reliance on the international market. Important political differences also exist: structuralists are considered to be broadly on the left while monetarists are seen to be on the right. Structuralists are largely reformist although a few may also favour revolutionary change.

Structuralists situate the problem of inflation within the context of the problem of development of the Third World while monetarists are less prone to do so. Thus, structuralists would forego price stability for development while the monetarists' attitude is the opposite (Noyola, 1984: 362; orig. 1956). This difference arises because for the structuralists, inflation in Latin America arises from the socio–political tensions, sectoral imbalances and expectations generated by the process of development itself. Meanwhile, for the monetarists it is the inflationary process which is the major obstacle to growth.

Structuralists also situate the problem of inflation within an historical and world economy perspective which is often disregarded by monetarists. Thus, for example, the structuralists locate one of the origins of the persistent inflationary phenomena in Latin America in the transition from an outward–oriented to an inward–oriented development process and in the stagnation of the purchasing power of primary exports resulting from the long–term deterioration in the region's commodity terms of trade and the insufficient growth in demand from the countries of the centre for primary products from the periphery. This foreign exchange constraint, and particularly the 1930s world economic crisis, stimulated an import–substitution industrialization process in the larger Latin American countries, especially in those countries where governments pursued various expansionary policies to ameliorate the disastrous effects of the Great Depression of 1929, which had inflationary consequences. As the new local industries were less efficient and produced at higher costs than those foreign industries which had previously supplied imported industrial goods, internal prices rose. Thus, this industrialization process had inflationary consequences and reproduced Latin America's structural vulnerability to inflation.

The fundamental disagreement between monetarists and structuralists is over the causes of inflation. Monetarists regard inflation as a monetary phenomenon arising from excessive demand (too much money chasing too few goods) while for structuralists inflation arises from structural maladjustments and rigidities in the economic system. In the words of Noyola: 'inflation is not a monetary phenomenon, it is the outcome of disequilibria of a real character which manifest themselves in the form of increases in the general level of prices' (ibid.: 353). Simplifying, it could be said that monetarists stress demand conditions while structuralists emphasize supply factors.

Structural causes and propagating mechanisms of inflation

Structuralists make an important distinction between the 'basic' or 'structural' pressures and the 'propagating mechanisms' of inflation. These 'structural' pressures and 'propagating mechanisms' can vary from country to country. Among the 'basic' or 'structural' pressures of inflation two major inflexibilities are generally singled out: those of the agricultural and foreign trade sectors. The agricultural sector is unable to meet the increasing demand for food, arising from the population explosion and growing incomes, due to supply rigidities. It is thanks to industrialization that incomes have grown significantly. This structural imbalance between the agricultural and industrial sectors leads to a relative shortage of agricultural commodities. The resultant rise in food prices fails to stimulate a sufficient increase in agricultural output. This supply inelasticity of the agricultural sector originates in the traditional and unequal land tenure structure characterized by the latifundia–minifundia complex. Most of the agricultural land is concentrated in the hands of estate owners (the *latifundistas*), who are largely absentee rentiers and unresponsive to market stimuli, fail to modernize their methods of production, and hold land for reasons of social prestige and political power rather than for profit maximization. Meanwhile, the owners of small subsistence farms (the *minifundistas*) do not have the resources to expand production and have weak links with the market.

The other basic source of inflation arises from the foreign exchange gap and major fluctuations in export earnings. On the one hand, foreign exchange earnings have not grown enough due to the inelastic supply of the export sector and the deterioration in the commodity terms of trade. On the other hand, imports have become inflexible because they are mainly raw materials, spare parts, and capital goods which are necessary for sustaining the import–substitution industrialization process and essential food imports. The resultant foreign exchange gap and its fluctuation lead to periodic devaluations and thus rising internal prices.

These are the two main structural inflationary pressures. However, in his seminal article published in 1956, Noyola (1984: 359; orig. 1956) mentions that in Mexico the agricultural sector was not a structural source of inflationary pressure. However, he considered Mexico to be the exception which proves the general rule: exceptional because it was the only Latin American country which until then had implemented a far–reaching land reform. Other bottlenecks which are deemed to be structural and have inflationary consequences can be included according to the particular circumstances of the country analysed. Sunkel (1979: 58–9; orig. 1959), for example, writing in the late 1950s, mentions the following contributory factors in the Chilean case: the inability of the Chilean economy to raise its rate of capital formation or to increase its export earnings by diversifying its export structure; the instability, inflexibility, inefficiency, and regressiveness of the tax system; and the fact that tax revenues did not keep pace with the government's growing commitments and expenditure, resulting in budget constraints.

The distinction between the basic or structural factors and the propagating mechanisms of inflation is important in the structuralist analysis and sets it apart from that of the monetarists. According to the structuralists, the monetarists fail to discover the ultimate causes of inflation. Those factors which the monetarists regard as the origins of inflation are seen by the structuralists as solely propagating mechanisms of the basic inflationary pressures. Thus, they cannot constitute causes of inflation.

What, according to the structuralists, are the main propagating mechanisms? First, the fiscal deficit. This fiscal deficit arises, on the one hand, from the dependence of government revenue on foreign trade and from the regressiveness and inefficiency of the tax collecting system. On the other hand, government expenditures face a continuous upward pressure owing to the need to expand the public sector to create new employment opportunities and some basic social services such as education, health, and housing in the face of rapid population growth. In order to finance this deficit, governments resort to borrowing, revaluation of monetary reserves, and issuing new money, as well as raising taxes, public enterprise charges, and social security contributions. These various means of financing the fiscal deficit have, to a greater or lesser extent, inflationary consequences as they lead directly (through price increases in public goods and services) or indirectly (through an increase in money supply) to higher prices. They are thus means which propagate inflation.

A second propagating mechanism relates to the readjustment of salaries and wages. Given the increase in the cost of living, employees and workers demand higher salaries and wages so as to retain, if not increase, their purchasing power. The real incomes of employees and workers are constantly eroded as a consequence of increases in the price of foodstuffs, public goods and services, taxes, and so on. The devaluations of the currency also increase prices of imported goods, such as foodstuffs and petrol, which hit the low–income groups particularly hard. Where employees and workers are organized in trade unions they can exercise pressure on employers for a readjustment in their salaries and wages, thereby propagating inflation.

A third propagating mechanism derives from the readjustment in prices arising from cost increases. Faced with higher wage costs, higher input prices, and higher taxes, entrepreneurs in turn put up the prices of the commodities they produce. Given the high degree of protection and the monopolistic or oligopolistic character of industry, entrepreneurs can pass on increased costs of production to the consumer by raising prices.

The propagating mechanisms might differ between countries and vary in their intensity: for example, Noyola (1984: 359–62; orig. 1956) contrasts the cases of Mexico and Chile. In Mexico a far greater labour surplus existed and trade unions were weaker than in Chile, at the time he was writing in the mid–1950s, and therefore the second propagating mechanism was much less intense in Mexico as compared with Chile. The propagating mechanisms are interpreted by some structuralist writers in sociological terms as the outcome of a struggle between capitalists, workers, and the state to defend or increase their relative share of the national income. [21] This conflict over the distribution of the national income between different social groups and between private and state sectors fuels the inflationary process.

Sunkel (1959: 59) introduces a second type of inflationary pressure which he calls 'cumulative', being induced by the inflationary process itself and intensifying it. Among these cumulative pressures he mentions a series of factors which monetarists also regard as furthering inflation – for example, the distortions in the price system, some of which are due to price controls and protectionist measures arising from import–substitution industrialization. Other factors include the development of inflationary expectations and the erosion of productivity due to the proliferation of strikes and stoppages, as well as the speculative behaviour of entrepreneurs.

Anti–inflationary policies

What, then, are the cures for inflation? For the structuralists these are necessarily long term as they involve structural changes in production systems, sectoral composition of the economy and distribution of income. Among the radical changes proposed are reforms in the agrarian structure and in the taxation system (Seers, 1962: 189). In addition, an increase in and diversification of exports is called for (Sunkel, 1979: 62; orig. 1959). Prebisch (1971: 354) also proposes boosting industrial exports. With regards to tackling agriculture's supply problem, most structuralists at first shied away from endorsing an agrarian reform programme and only proposed measures to boost agricultural investment and raise productivity and output (Sunkel, 1967a: 47). Such an increase in investment was to be obtained through removing some of the discriminatory measures against agriculture, which had led to higher costs of production, as well as by special state support programmes and major public investments (Prebisch, 1971: 366).

Structural policies are longer–term measures designed to remove key supply bottlenecks in the economy. However, structuralists also propose shorter–term measures to deal with the propagating inflationary factors. These involve curbing demand factors of inflation through fiscal and monetary policies and acting upon cost factors by, for example, a prices–and–incomes policy. However, the stress of the structuralists' policy measures is on the basic inflationary pressures. They strongly attack the monetarist and IMF–type anti–inflationary policies for not tackling the roots of inflation and for leading to stagnation, unemployment, and income inequality. They are policies whose consequences are 'neither stability nor development', to quote the title of a book by Pinto (1960b). In the structuralists' view, monetary stability is compatible with economic development (Pinto, 1960a: 268; Prebisch, 1971: 380) and, to paraphrase Prebisch, to pose the question in terms of economic development or monetary stability is a false dilemma. However, to achieve this compatibility requires acting not just on demand factors as proposed by monetarists but above all on supply factors (Pinto, 1960a: 273). However, if a conflict between stability and economic development exists then the structuralists would prefer the latter (Noyola, 1984: 362).

As structural changes take a long time to implement and bear fruit, structuralists do not aim to reduce inflation drastically within a short period of time but to reduce it gradually over a period of time. Structuralists are aware that a national consensus is required to achieve stability and economic development. Only the strong will of a political majority in a democratic society can carry through the reforms and curtail the distributionist struggle. Favourable external conditions would, of course, ease this task (Sunkel, 1967a: 52).

Despite the fundamental disagreements between structuralists and monetarists over the causes of inflation, there are some areas of agreement. Both hold that inflation does not pay in the long run and that it is necessary to combat it. Some monetarists, as a consequence of this debate, acknowledge the influence of structural factors on inflation. However, in their view they are not the cause of inflation but a consequence of it (Campos, 1961a; Kahil, 1973). They thus turn the structuralist argument on its head. What structuralists consider as the causes of inflation this brand of monetarists sees as 'propagating mechanisms' – to use a structuralist expression. These monetarists argue that the supply rigidities arise from the distortions which inflation creates in the price and market system. What monetarists regard as the causes of inflation, structuralists see as propagating mechanisms.

Within the structuralist position it is possible to distinguish between moderate and radical structuralists although the difference is one of emphasis rather than substance. Noyola, a radical structuralist like Pinto, stresses the class struggle in his analysis of inflation: 'inflation is but a particular aspect of the much more general phenomenon of the class struggle' (Noyola, 1984: 354). He is also more willing to consider agrarian reform as a policy measure for dealing with inflation in comparison with moderate structuralists like Prebisch. (Sunkel falls between these two positions.) The position of moderate structuralists comes close to that of some monetarists – such as Campos and Kahil – who are willing to take structural factors into account. This can be gleaned from the following statement by Prebisch (1971: 370): 'in certain cases, inflation is not merely the outcome of structural factors but can become an agent in bringing about structural maladjustments'. However, Campos (1970: 242) goes too far and fudges the issue when he writes: 'The truth is, that in the short run, all structuralists when entrusted with policy–making responsibilities become monetarists, while all monetarists are, in the long run, structuralists.' While monetarists stress monetary and fiscal measures, which largely aim to reduce demand, structuralists emphasize development measures, which tackle specific supply bottlenecks, to deal with the inflationary problem. Structuralists do not disregard monetary and fiscal policies but these are subordinated to their programme of structural change. A more accurate and appropriate conclusion is that of Seers (1981a: 9) who reasons that 'neither structuralist nor monetarist explanations are adequate by themselves, and we need to draw on both to explain inflation'. [22]

Critical comments

While the structuralist analysis of inflation broke new ground and made a positive contribution to the debate, it is necessary to point out a number of pertinent criticisms.

First, the structuralists pay too little attention to monetary and fiscal factors of inflation, in particular the money supply. While structural factors may ultimately be responsible for inflation, this does not mean that their removal is a sufficient condition for achieving price stability. Appropriate monetary and fiscal policies are required as well and structuralists have little to say on what these policies should be, considering them to be of secondary importance. Thus structuralists need to give greater consideration to short–term macroeconomic management factors.

Second, and following from the above point, by focusing on long–term measures structuralists overlook the importance of short–term measures to combat inflation. To break the inflationary spiral it is necessary to reduce inflation in the short run so as to lower inflationary expectations. Monetary and fiscal measures have the advantage of showing results in the short run. While these measures are not a sufficient condition for eliminating inflation they are a necessary condition for it.

Third, in the long run some of the propagating mechanisms of inflation might become structural in countries with persistent inflation. In these countries various social groups have learnt to live with inflation (and some even benefit from it) by organizing themselves into pressure groups. These pressure groups have been able to develop a series of defensive measures against inflation such as continual price and wage readjustments which in some instances tend to anticipate inflation. It is thus necessary to reduce these expectations through an anti–inflationary programme which deals simultaneously with the structural causes and the (structurally embedded) propagating mechanisms of inflation.

Fourth, structuralists fail to distinguish between autonomous structural rigidities and induced rigidities resulting from government policies such as price and foreign exchange controls (Campos, 1970:247).

Fifth, the inadequacies of purely monetary policies are no guarantee that structuralist measures will be successful in solving the inflationary problem. Thus, it is certainly possible (as happened in Chile during the Allende government) that the structural transformations aimed to remove the basic causes of inflation might themselves fuel inflation in the short and medium run. Structural transformations tend to cause, at least initially, major disruptions in the production system which affect output negatively and thus aggravate inflationary pressures. Structuralists, before the failure of Allende, were either too optimistic or did not analyse the implications of structural transformations in the short and medium run sufficiently and thus lacked detailed policy proposals for taking effective counter–measures to avoid an acceleration of inflation.

Sixth, structuralists fail to study the social and political requisites for implementing a programme of structural transformations. (Monetarist studies display a far greater dearth of social and political analysis and tend to confine their analysis to economic variables.) It might not be politically realistic to achieve structural changes whilst maintaining stabilization of prices within a democratic and market economy setting, as implicitly proposed by structuralists. Major structural transformations are likely to intensify class conflict and might lead to a withdrawal of foreign capital, loans, and credits, with negative consequences for capital formation and growth. The outcome of such a heightening of the class struggle might end with the government either abandoning – wholly or partly – their programme of structural transformation or with the overthrow of that government. In either case the structural changes are thwarted.

This is perhaps the reason why governments in the past have learned to live with inflation as the achievement of price stability is not feasible politically or requires a higher social cost than those democratic governments are willing to contemplate. Thus, Hirschman states that: 'Inflation...is a remarkable invention that permits a society to exist in a situation that is intermediate between the extremes of social harmony and civil war.' (Hirschman, 1981c: 201.) Inflation can be seen as defusing the distributional conflict as no social group is powerful enough to impose its stabilization plan. Such plans always raise the awkward question of who pays for it and at what price? Is it the wage earners through a reduction in their real wages, or is it the capitalists through price controls, or both through credit restrictions, and so on? Powerful inter– and intra–sectoral struggles take place in society, and shifting political alliances are formed which need to be analyzed if a full understanding of the inflationary phenomena is to be attained (see, for example, Hirsch, 1978 and Rowthorn, 1980).

Ultimately the cause of inflation is political. It is thus necessary to undertake an analysis of the state but above all of the class struggle over the appropriation and distribution of the economic surplus. It is the outcome of this class struggle which determines the extent of the inflationary process. While most structuralists refer to the various pressure groups making competing claims over the national income, they relegate this distributional struggle to the propagating mechanisms of inflation. Only Pinto (1956; Sierra, 1969: 36–7) and to some extent

Noyola (1984) place these socio–political factors in the forefront of their analyses of the structural causes of inflation. However, even in their case a more detailed analysis of the class basis of inflation is required.

3

Internal colonialism: ethnic and class relations

This chapter analyses the theory of internal colonialism and examines its usefulness for studying Third World societies. Although the term internal colonialism was sporadically employed by earlier authors, its modern conceptualization was developed during the early to mid–1960s, principally by the distinguished Mexican sociologists Pablo González Casanova and Rodolfo Stavenhagen (who is also an anthropologist). This chapter starts by presenting the historical and *indigenista* (indianist) roots of the theory of internal colonialism. It continues by examining the main body of the theory such as the definition of, and variety of forms assumed by, internal colonialism, the specific rural–urban, class, regional, and socio–economic relationships which characterize it, and the factors which lead to its demise. Running through the analysis are the distinctive relations of exploitation and domination which characterize situations of internal colonialism in the Third World. The chapter then continues with a critical analysis of the theory. Finally, reference is made to the use of the theory of internal colonialism for studying ethnic minorities in developed countries and of regional relationships in developed and underdeveloped countries.

HISTORICAL ROOTS

National liberation struggles and the post–war decolonization process influenced the formulation of the concept of internal colonialism as well as theories of imperialism and colonialism. After independence the persistent poverty and exploitation found in Third World countries could no longer be fully blamed on the imperialist countries. The internal domination and exploitation of indigenous groups by other local groups was particularly evident in Latin America as most countries had gained national independence during the first decades of last century. 'With the disappearance of the direct domination of foreigners over natives, the notion of domination and exploitation of natives by natives emerges.' (González Casanova, 1965: 27.)

Some social thinkers began to draw parallels between the former external colonial relationships and the new internal relationships of domination and exploitation. Colonialism is then seen as not only an international but as an intra–national phenomenon as well. Furthermore, 'internal colonialism is part of, and intimately linked with, external colonialism, that is, imperialism' (Cockcroft *et al.*, 1972: xx). Existing concepts such as dualistic, rural–urban, class, caste, racial, and ethnic relations were judged by Latin American social scientists to be inadequate for explaining internal forms of domination and exploitation, thereby leading to the formulation of the concept of internal colonialism. It is argued that the phenomenon of internal colonialism is peculiar to those countries which have been conquered by the imperialist countries as part of a process of creating a world capitalist system and the concept is of particular relevance for those countries which have a large Indian or native population. Within the Latin American context internal colonialism is effectively a meaningful theory only in those regions which had a substantial pre–Columbian population, notably Mexico, Guatemala, Ecuador, Peru, and Bolivia.

The radical historical view

In the case of Ibero–America these relations of domination and exploitation arose from the Iberian (Spanish and Portuguese) conquest which divided society into two major cultural groups: the Iberians (including the *mestizos*) and the aboriginals, Indians, natives, or indigenous people. The *mestizos* (also referred to as *ladinos* in Mexico and Guatemala, *cholos* in Peru and Ecuador, and *caboclos* in Brazil) are of mixed European and Indian descent who speak the national language (Spanish or Portuguese) and who display a 'westernized' urban life–style. The Amerindians are of indigenous descent, speak indigenous languages, and maintain a 'traditional' life–style. While *mestizos* were mainly resident in the towns and villages, the Indians mainly lived in rural areas. Spaniards were the dominant group, *mestizos* occupied an intermediate position in colonial society, while the Indians were the exploited majority, being at the bottom of the social hierarchy. Colonial society was highly stratified with little social mobility. The Ibero–Americans monopolized the economic and political system, which strongly discriminated against the native Indian populations.

The theory of internal colonialism is informed by a radical interpretation of Latin American history. [1] The colonization of Ibero–America is seen as a military conquest arising from the expansion of the Iberian mercantilist system in search of gold and silver. In the initial period mining was the key economic activity which determined all others. At first agricultural activities were geared to supplying the mines with food for its labour, animals for transport, and wood for fuel and construction. Later, however, with the establishment of plantations Ibero–America also produced sugar, tobacco, coffee, rubber, and so on for the European market. The vast colonial administration which drained the economic surplus is seen by this historical school as oppressive, racist, and unable to curb the excesses of the Ibero–American elite.

Ibero–America was plundered of its gold and silver which ultimately benefited Britain and France as Spain and Portugal became in turn subordinate to them. 'Spain had the cow, but others drank the milk.' (Galeano, 1971: 46.) Britain in particular emerged after the period of transition to capitalism at the core of the capitalist world–system which it began to shape and dominate from the nineteenth century. Thus the pillage of Ibero–America's mineral wealth is seen as facilitating and significantly contributing to the capitalist development of Europe.

To operate the mines and the associated agricultural–ranching economy a variety of mechanisms of forced labour and tribute were imposed upon the Amerindian population. This ruthless exploitation of colonial labour based on the *mita, encomienda, obraje, diezmo*, and so on led to one of the most disastrous demographic declines in world history. The population was decimated through epidemic diseases, overwork, starvation, resettlements, and the reshaping, if not disorganization and destruction, of the pre–conquest economic, social, political, and cultural fabric of society by the establishment of luso–hispanic colonial relations.

The colonial period opened the veins of Latin America [2] through which its riches were, and still are, drained by the centre countries through a national and international chain of metropolis–satellite relations (Frank, 1966a). The wealth of Latin America is held to be the source of its poverty as the lure of its gold and silver led to the formation of the metropolis–satellite structure which continues to exploit its riches. The mechanisms of external and internal domination and exploitation are today different and more sophisticated than those of the colonial past but they still exist according to the radical view of Latin American history, particularly of the *dependentistas*.

Thus, the conquest created two or more distinct social, cultural, and ethnic groups. Two or more civilizations confronted one other, leading to a heterogeneous society. These social divisions continued after independence (which most Latin American countries achieved during the first half of the nineteenth century), changing over time but still persisting to the present day in many countries. González Casanova (1979: 47) estimates that today about 15–20 per cent of the population in Latin America is directly living in conditions of internal colonialism. This is largely the population living in indigenous communities, most of whom are subsistence peasants.

Indigenismo, Mariátegui, and critics

Another and more direct source of influence on the internal colonialism theorists are the writings of the *indigenistas* (nativists or indianists). The *indigenista* movement arose during the first decades of this century in various Latin American countries, especially Mexico and Peru. [3] It was a broad movement which encompassed novelists, painters, essayists, politicians, journalists, philanthropists, anthropologists, humanists, and so on. Their members were largely middle–class *mestizos*, who were pro–Indian and anti–hispanic in the sense that they attacked those who exclusively valued the hispanic heritage. At first many *indigenistas* had little knowledge about the Indians, did not speak their languages, and did not have much contact with them. Their attitude towards the Indian was charitable and one of benevolent paternalism. They had a romantic view of the Indian which depicted the pre–Columbian civilizations as idyllic. Such a view, which is still pervasive in some contemporary *indigenistas*, might be excusable at the time but is no longer so today given the far greater knowledge available about the Indian past and present.

Through their works of art, writings, or public meetings, and later through their positions in government, *indigenistas* aimed to change the prejudiced, racist, and negative view of the Indian in society. Through sporadic political agitation they called for social reforms in favour of the marginalized indigenous population who at the time constituted the overwhelming majority of the population in Mexico, Guatemala, Ecuador, Peru, and Bolivia. They campaigned for the integration of the Indian into national society. It is difficult to characterize the *indigenista* movement precisely as it had no clear ideology or political programme. Its composition, significance, and orientation varied in time and place and it is even questionable whether certain personalities considered themselves as *indigenistas* although some authors classify them as such.[4]

Mariátegui was critical of the *indigenistas*, with the exception of Luis E. Valcárcel whom he held in high regard because 'Valcárcel resolved his *indigenismo* politically in socialism' (Mariátegui, 1955: 28). He questions the effectiveness of organizations like the Pro–Indian Association which was founded by leading *indigenistas* in 1909 and considers their approach to the Indian question as erroneous. The Indian problem could not be solved through humanitarian and philanthropic actions because it is not a moral, cultural, or ethical question but is rooted in the socio–economic system prevailing in the country. Therefore, 'the resolution of the problem of the Indian has to be a social solution. Those who undertake it have to be the Indians themselves.' (ibid.: 27.) Despite his criticisms Mariátegui was influenced by the *indigenistas*. He might not have shared all their views but through his polemics with them he was able to define his own position on the Indian question (Castro, 1976). [5] In turn, Mariátegui, or 'the Amauta' (teacher in Quechua, the main indigenous language in Peru) as he is referred to today, influenced the *indigenistas*, especially after his death.

As in the case of Mariátegui, the internal colonialism theorists, like González Casanova, Stavenhagen, and Frank were influenced by the *indigenistas* although the thesis of internal colonialism grew out of a critique of the *indigenistas*. [6] Government organizations like the *Instituto Nacional Indigenista* (National Indian Institute) of Mexico published a series of studies on the indigenous population, some of which formulate ideas which come close to those of the internal colonialism studies. Frank, for example, cites approvingly from an Institute publication which presents ideas similar to his own:

> The Indians, in reality, rarely live isolated from the *mestizos* or national population; there exists a symbiosis between the two groups which we must take into account. Between the *mestizos* who live in the nucleus city of the region and the Indians who live in the agricultural hinterland there is in reality a closer economic and social interdependence than appears at first glance....The *mestizo* population, in fact, almost always lives in a city which is the center

of an intercultural region, which acts as a metropolis of an Indian zone, and which maintains an intimate connection with the underdeveloped communities which link the center with the satellite communities. (Our study found) the Indian or folk community was an interdependent part of a whole which functioned as a unit, so that the measures taken in one part inevitably had repercussions in the others and, in consequence, on the whole.

> (Frank, 1967: 133–4, citing from Instituto Nacional
> Indigenista, 1962: 33–4, 27)

This quotation reveals that not all *indigenista* writers fully adopted a dualist position so that the dualist charge levelled against them by some internal colonialism authors has to be qualified.

However, it is the far–sighted ideas of Mariátegui which exercise the key influence on the proponents of the internal colonialism thesis, being often cited by them. The following quotations from Mariátegui reveal the close parallels between their ideas:

> The problem of the Indian is rooted in the land tenure system of our economy. Any attempts to solve it with administrative or police measures, through education or by a road building program, is superficial and secondary as long as the feudalism of the *gamonales* continues to exist. *Gamonalismo* necessarily invalidates any law or regulation for the protection of the Indian. ...Unpaid labor is illegal, yet unpaid and even forced labor survive in the latifundium. The law cannot prevail against the *gamonales*.
>
> (Mariátegui, 1971: 22–3)

In the following paragraph Mariátegui explains what he means by *gamonalismo*. What is notable here is his idea that those Indians who become *mestizos* through upward mobility join in exploiting the Indians, an argument which is repeated much later by the proponents of the concept of internal colonialism. Thus, the exploitation of the Indian is not only a racial or ethnic issue but a class problem:

> The term *gamonalismo* designates more than just a social and economic category: that of the *latifundistas* or large landowners. It signifies a whole phenomenon. *Gamonalismo* is represented not only by the *gamonales* but by a long hierarchy of officials, intermediaries, agents, parasites, etcetera. The literate Indian who enters the service of *gamonalismo* turns into an exploiter of his own race. The central factor of the phenomenon is the hegemony of the

semi–feudal landed estate in the policy and mechanism of the government.

(ibid.: 30)

Despite the shortcomings of the *indigenistas*, as pointed out by Mariátegui, they helped to create a public awareness of the Indian problem and subsequently influenced the shaping of government policy towards the Indian communities (Marroquín, 1972; T. Davies, 1974: 55–6; Martínez and Samaniego, 1978). With the rise of populist governments from the 1930s onwards (which Mariátegui did not witness), many leading *indigenistas* became high government officials taking charge of newly established departments or institutes on Indian affairs. It was in Mexico that *indigenistas* had the greatest influence as a consequence of the Mexican revolution. The government party in Mexico (the Partido Revolucionario Institucional or PRI) has transformed *indigenismo* into an official ideology of the state. In Peru *indigenismo* has been less influential but it did play a brief but important role during the reformist government of Velasco Alvarado from 1968 to 1975. The anthropologist Carlos Delgado (1973; 1975) was instrumental in formulating the *indigenista* ideology and programme of that government. Much more recently, the populist Social Democratic APRA government of Alan García which came into office in 1985 has been tapping *indigenista* ideas for its political discourse and policy. [7]

A polemic with similar undertones to that between Mariátegui and the *indigenistas* in Peru [8] took place decades later in Mexico (Aguirre Beltrán, 1976). Gonzalo Aguirre Beltrán, one of the main and most enlightened figures of Mexican *indigenismo*, was criticized by a new generation of anthropologists and sociologists who largely followed a neo–Marxist or revolutionary socialist position. Essentially Aguirre Beltrán adopts a modernization approach as he argues that through a reformist government programme of action it is possible to integrate the Indian into the national system. The Indian cultures can only be developed by transforming the Indian as well as the *ladino* or *mestizo* regions (Aguirre Beltrán, 1967).

However, in Warman's view the accelerated capitalist development in Mexico since 1965 has worsened the conditions of the indigenous population. 'The growth of the "modern sector" of the economy has not only failed to absorb the "backward" sectors but has multiplied and impoverished them.' (Warman, 1978: 112.) This indicates to him the failure of developmentalist programmes and *indigenismo* which sheds a new light on the Indian problem. Contrary to the *indigenistas* the Indian problem 'is not due to the Indians' evolutionary backwardness but to their oppression by the dominant sectors: it is not a left–over of the pre–hispanic barbarism nor of colonial feudalism but a complex outcome of dependent modernization. The point is to define the Indians by their social position and not their culture' (ibid.: 113).

According to González Casanova (1979: 53) the *indigenistas* failed to pose the Indian problem in terms of the struggle against colonialism, imperialism, and capitalism. He charges Aguirre Beltrán with overemphasizing cultural and political factors and playing down relations of colonialism and exploitation.

> Aguirre Beltrán put forward a policy of 'modernization', 'integration' and 'development' of the 'indigenous communities'. His acknowledgement of the 'communities' did not lead him to state a policy for decolonization, defence of cultural or political autonomy, and even less to projects linked to the working class and their struggles for democracy and socialism.
>
> (ibid.)

González Casanova (1968: 479) agrees with Aguirre Beltrán that as a consequence of the revolution, 'Mexico has no racial discrimination per se', but points out that 'colonial discrimination against indigenous communities still survives'. In turn Stavenhagen (1965: 55, 75) finds the *indigenista* theoretical framework wanting or insufficient and is particularly critical of the *indigenistas'* and government's integration policies which seek to eliminate the Indians as cultural beings, instead of as colonized beings, by integrating them into the dominant *mestizo* national culture.

FUNDAMENTAL ASPECTS OF INTERNAL COLONIALISM

The theory of internal colonialism is one of the first challenges to modernization theory, particularly of the dualist thesis. [9] It also entails a critique of orthodox Marxist theory for its exclusive focus on class relations, thereby neglecting the ethnic dimension. The great strength and major contribution of the theory of internal colonialism is to explore the links between class and ethnicity. Modernization and Marxist theories had failed to explore such interrelationships.

Definition

rural pop. problem

One of the first explicit definitions of internal colonialism is provided by González Casanova, who writes:

composed of diverse elements

> Internal colonialism corresponds to a structure of social relations based on domination and exploitation among culturally heterogeneous groups. If it has a specific difference with respect to other relations based on superordination, it inheres in the cultural heterogeneity which the conquest of some peoples by others historically produces. It is such conquests which permit us to talk not only about cultural differences (which exist between urban and rural populations and between social classes) but also about differences between civilizations.
>
> (González Casanova, 1965: 33)

Dale Johnson, on the basis of his reading of González Casanova (1965), Stavenhagen (1965), and Cotler (1967–8) has elaborated one of the most explicit and comprehensive definitions of internal colonies:

> Economically, internal colonies can be conceptualized as those populations who produce primary commodities for markets in metropolitan centers, who constitute a source of cheap labor for enterprises controlled from the metropolitan centers, and/or who constitute a market for the products and services of the centers. The colonized are excluded from participation or suffer discriminatory participation in the political, cultural, and other institutions of the dominant society. An internal colony constitutes a society within a society based upon racial, linguistic, and/or marked cultural differences as well as differences of social class. It is subject to political and administrative control by the dominant classes and institutions of the metropolis. Defined in this way, internal colonies can exist on a geographical basis or on a racial or cultural basis in ethnically or culturally dual or plural societies. (Not all of these criteria need to apply in order to classify a population as an internal colony.)
>
> (D. Johnson, 1972: 277)

From these definitions it can be observed that internal colonialism pertains to a situation characterized by certain distinctive economic, social, and political relations. The relationships between these various characteristics and their relative importance are explored below.

Forms of internal colonialism

In his analysis of internal colonialism González Casanova lists a series of characteristics attributable to colonialism and finds that many of the factors which defined a situation of colonialism *between* countries in the past also exist *within* some present-day independent Third World countries. It is this similarity between the past colonial relations of domination and exploitation between countries with those which exist today within some countries which prompts him to use the term internal colonialism when referring to the latter. (The former could be renamed as foreign or external colonialism.)

González Casanova distinguishes thirty–seven mechanisms by which internal colonialism operates, under three general groupings: (1) monopoly and dependence, (2) relations of production and social control, and (3) culture and living standards. Whilst omitting any explicit ranking, it would appear from his brief examination of the post–colonial Mexican case that the most important mechanisms are as follows.

First, with regard to monopoly and dependence he points out that the dominant centres or major cities in Mexico, by exercising a monopoly of commerce and credit over the Indian communities, exploit them through unequal exchange and usurious interest rates, thus furthering the decapitalization of these areas.

Second, with regards to relations of production and social control the focus is on the exploitation and discrimination of the Indian population. The relations of exploitation are established by the different social classes of the *ladino* population and these are characterized by a combination of 'feudalism, slavery, capitalism, forced and salaried work, partnerships, peonage, and gratuitous "free" domestic services' (González Casanova, 1965: 34–5). Furthermore, the Indian population is discriminated socially, linguistically, juridically, politically, and economically.

Finally, the third category refers to the odd combination of culture and living standards. Under culture he lists the cultural peculiarities of the Indians and the stereotypes held of them by the *ladinos*. As for living standards this is a catalogue of characteristics of economic life of the Indian communities such as subsistence economy, low–quality land, backward technology, and lack of essential services (schools, hospitals, water, electricity).

Rural–urban and class relations

González Casanova explicitly distinguishes relations of internal colonialism from urban–rural and class relationships. Although urban–rural relationships are exploitative and marked by strong cultural differences, relations of internal colonialism in underdeveloped countries stand apart

> because cultural heterogeneity is historically different. It is the result of an encounter between two races, cultures, or civilizations, whose genesis and evolution occurred without any mutual contact up to one specific moment. The conquest or concession is a fact which makes possible intensive racial and cultural discriminations.
>
> (ibid.: 33)

With respect to the difference between internal colonialism and class relations, the former

> is not only a relation of domination and exploitation of the workers by the owners of the means of production and their collaborators but also a relation of domination and exploitation of a total population (with its distinct classes, proprietors, workers) by another population which also has distinct classes (proprietors and workers).
>
> (ibid.) [10]

In short, relations of internal colonialism differ from urban–rural relations in that they have a different historical origin and are based on discrimination. They also differ from class relations as they cut across class lines. Rural–urban and class relations cannot be fully understood without reference to internal colonialism, particularly in those Third World countries with a significant indigenous population.

Internal colonial and class relations

I fully subscribe to the comment by Torres–Rivas who writes that: 'The concept of structure of internal colonialism allows for the enrichment and completion of the class analysis.' (1971: 53, quoted by Stoltz Chinchilla, 1983: 157.) I will explore further the interplay between internal–colonial and class relations in this section and at various instances throughout the chapter.

Stavenhagen argues that during Mexico's colonial period and the first decade after political independence, colonial and class relations appear intermixed, with the former being dominant. Thus, the class relations between Spaniards (including *mestizos*) and the Indians largely took the form of colonial relations. 'As Spain was to the Colony, so the Colony was to Indian communities: a colonial metropolis.' (Stavenhagen, 1965: 70.) Nevertheless, within a wider perspective, colonial relations have to be considered as one aspect of class relations which were being forged by the mercantilist interests on a world scale (ibid.: 71).

With the subsequent development of capitalism on a world scale and its penetration into the remoter regions of Mexico from the second half of the nineteenth century, class relations increasingly entered into conflict with colonial relations as the latter primarily responded to mercantilist interests while the former met capitalist needs (ibid.: 70). As Stavenhagen puts it: 'The colonial relationships between Indian communities and the larger society tended to strengthen the Indian communities and foment their ethnic identity. ...Conversely, class relations contributed to the disintegration of the Indian community and its integration to the larger society' (ibid.: 71).

Thus, for Stavenhagen internal colonialism, by maintaining ethnic divisions, impedes the development of class relations. Indians and *ladinos* are not simply two antagonistic social classes as ethnic consciousness may override class consciousness in each group. Furthermore, the *ladino* regional dominant class may not be dominant at the national level, a factor which might not be perceived by the Indians (ibid.: 72).

With the development of capitalism the corporate structure of the Indian communities gradually breaks up and 'the Indian thus finds himself in the midst of diverse and contradicting situations: at times he is "colonized" and at times he is a member of a class (in the sense that he is in a typical *class situation*)' (ibid.: 73). Thus, internal colonialism gives a distinctive character to class relations and the class structure of those countries where this phenomenon exists cannot be properly understood without reference to it.

Coexistence of different modes and relations of production

Although internal colonialism does not directly address mode of production theory, it does illuminate some of the pertinent issues and to some extent foreshadows the subsequent discussion on the articulation of modes of production. Stavenhagen mentions that the Spanish conquest, by imposing systems of forced labour and serfdom in plantations, mines, and workshops, transformed the Indian communities into labour reserves of the colonial economy. González Casanova also draws attention to the coexistence and combination of different social relations of production during the colonial period, i.e. slave, feudal, and capitalist. This is contrasted with the classic European model where these relations of production are held by González Casanova to have succeeded each other, only coexisting during transitional periods. This combination of social relations explains, in González Casanova's view, the uneven development, and technical, institutional, and cultural heterogeneity of so many Third World countries. After independence, these colonial relations were gradually transformed into internal colonial relations (or endo–colonial relations, as Stavenhagen sometimes refers to them). Thus, the root of the uneven and heterogeneous nature of most present–day underdeveloped countries has to be sought in the colonial past.

Uneven development can be visualized by contrasting over time the dynamic economy of the *ladinos* or *mestizos* with the stagnant economy of the Indian communities. Moreover, the dynamism of the former is made possible by the exploitation of the latter. Many Indians are forced to sell their labour to the *ladinos* who own most of the means of production, receiving only a miserable wage in return. The *ladinos*, who are also the traders and creditors, are able to extract a further surplus from the Indians by selling them goods dearly and buying their produce cheaply, and by charging extortionate interest rates for loans.

Stavenhagen finds the concept of internal colonialism particularly useful because it enables him to criticize and discard the concept of dualism which was so influential during the 1950s and 1960s. He is one of the foremost and earliest critics of economic and social dualism as exemplified in a pioneering and concise article (1968). In his view the *ladino* and Indian economic and social systems, far from being independent of each other, 'are both integrated with a unique economic system, in a unique society' (Stavenhagen, 1965: 64).

Neither González Casanova nor Stavenhagen analyse the different social relations or their interaction in any detail. Furthermore, almost nothing is said about the process of capital accumulation or how this is linked to the diversity of forms of production and more precisely to internal colonialism. Through its mechanisms of monopolization, domination, and discrimination, internal colonialism facilitates and intensifies the process of exploitation of the Indian population by the *ladino* population, thereby enhancing the *ladinos'* process of capital accumulation. However, Stavenhagen opens the door for others to explore the links between the analysis of internal colonialism and the theory of modes of production further in a tantalizing series of remarks made at a seminar:

> In the majority of Latin American countries it is possible to speak of the coexistence in the same national territory of different modes of production, corresponding to different historical periods. ...It is beyond doubt that, especially in the countryside, vestiges of historically–surpassed modes of production still survive, while it is equally evident that the dominant mode of production (that is to say, dependent or peripheral capitalism) exercises its hegemony over others. This phenomenon is the one which we call internal colonialism, that is to say, the subordination of modes of production and forms of precapitalist accumulation to the dominant mode of production, which leads to the subordination and exploitation of certain economic and social sectors, of certain segments of the population from certain geographical regions, by others. Internal colonialism is a structural relation characteristic of the juxtaposition of modes of production corresponding to different historical periods within the global framework of dependent capitalism and the situation of underdevelopment.
>
> (Stavenhagen, 1973: 280–1)

Bonfil Batalla is one of the authors who has furthered the analysis of the articulation of modes of production in relation to the Indian population. In his view the specificity of the links of the Indians to society cannot solely be derived from an understanding of the dominant capitalist mode of production (Bonfil Batalla, 1978: 134–5). Thus, it is important to study the peculiar modes of production of the indigenous groups which, in the Mexican case, at least, he sees as non–capitalist. However, in Bartra's view it is not possible now to speak of an 'Indian mode of production' in Mexico, as the indigenous economy is no longer segmented from the national economy and is instead fully integrated into, and absorbed by, the national economic structure. Thus the Indian economy is best analysed in terms of petty commodity or capitalist production.

FROM INTERNAL COLONIAL TO CLASS RELATIONS

The demise of internal colonialism

From the above it would appear that *mestizos* or *ladinos* have a vested interest in maintaining internal colonial relations which are therefore continually being reproduced, albeit in modified forms. However, this is not always the case as the development of capitalism not only modifies internal colonialism but may also destroy it given certain conditions. Stavenhagen (1973: 76) points out that in some circumstances, when new opportunities for capitalist development arise, *ladinos* may be interested in strengthening class relations instead of internal–colonial relations as free wage labour may be more profitable and appropriate than serf or other forms of coerced labour. It is mainly those *ladino* producers whose enterprises can only survive on the basis of cheap labour, because their technology has fallen behind that of their competitors, who most actively seek to preserve internal colonial relations. Thus, the maintenance of internal colonialism depends ultimately on the degree of international and national capitalist development, and only secondarily on regional or local situations and decisions, even though endo–colonial relations largely prevail at the regional level.

The destruction of internal colonialism is not only brought about from above (i.e. through the actions of the dominant classes) but also from below. This can arise with the emergence of a new social sector in the countryside, such as the petty bourgeoisie. By forging a close relationship between the urban marginals and the Indians, this new group breaks down the vertical patron–client relationships which were manipulated in favour of the dominant class. In turn, horizontal class relationships may develop within the Indian population and a class alliance may be formed with urban workers (Cotler, 1968: 105). Quijano (1977b: 228) sees the demise of internal colonialism as resulting from the expansion of the petty rural bourgeoisie, the proletarianization of the peasantry, and the growing influence of urban culture on the Indian population. Consequently, situations of internal colonialism may be transformed into situations of class or marginality.[11] It is important to bear in mind that the class development of Indians is not only determined by their changing position towards the means of production but also by their articulation of class consciousness (Havens and Flinn, 1970: 14).

Once class relations come to the fore the demise of internal colonialist relations is accelerated through the political mobilization of the Indians. Internal colonialism prevents full political participation and González Casanova (1979: 56) points out that the struggle of the Indians is a complex struggle for ethno–cultural identity as well as for class–related goals. He (1968) calls for the destruction of internal colonialism as this will not only lead to the democratization of society but to higher rates of economic growth and a more equal development pattern as well. Cotler (1968: 104) refers to this struggle for the full political participation of all social sectors as pursuing the 'nationalization of society'. Decades earlier Mariátegui had already called for the 'peruanization of Peru'. As Stavenhagen (1965: 75) puts it in his critique of the *indigenista* Aguirre Beltrán, 'national integration may be achieved, not by eliminating the Indian, but only by eliminating him as a colonized being'. Thus, the achievement of democracy and greater development requires internal as well as external decolonization.

Despite the complexity of the political struggle of the Indians, Stavenhagen (1970: 189) considers that the emphasis of the Indian struggle in Mexico during this century has been on class. Thus, for example, they fought for land as landless peasants although this struggle is often proclaimed under the slogan of restitution of communal lands. Similarly when they organize themselves to defend their working conditions they fight not as Indians but as proletarians.

Worker–peasant alliance

The demise of internal colonialism may, however, be retarded by various factors. Unlike González Casanova, Stavenhagen (1968: 28–9) considers the forging of a worker–peasant alliance to be problematic as, in his view, the urban working class also benefits from internal colonialism. He gives as an example the case of agrarian reform which favours the Indian population and destroys some of the mechanisms of internal colonialism, but which might not be welcomed by urban workers because public investment might be diverted to rural areas and food deliveries to the cities might initially fall, leading to higher food prices. Conversely, urban working class demands for control of food prices might not be in the interest of the rural population.

Furthermore, Stavenhagen (1965: 77) argues that the lower strata of the *ladino* population also have an interest in retaining internal colonialism as a form of social exclusion to avoid competition for jobs with mobile Indians. This process of Indian upward mobility is often described as 'ladinization', i.e. the adoption by Indians of *ladino* cultural elements such as language and dress as a means of breaking out from the Indian communities in search of economic betterment. Ladinization usually means proletarianization, and it often requires rural–urban migration, thus contributing to the breakdown of internal colonialism.

However, despite Stavenhagen's reservations, it is likely that Indians, by stressing class factors in their political mobilization, have a greater chance of linking their movement to the wider and more significant struggle of the working class, thereby enhancing the attainment of their goals. Nevertheless, Indians might mobilize more readily and forcefully under an ethnic banner. A skilled leadership might resolve this dilemma by combining both ideological messages and thereby reinforcing the political outcome. Much, of course, will depend on the degree of proletarianization and class consciousness of the indigenous groups as well as on the concrete political and ideological circumstances prevailing in the country concerned. I leave the final word on this issue to Stavenhagen (1986: 90), who writes that

> it would be too simple to reduce ethnicity to class, just as it is equally simplistic to deny the class factor in so many forms of ethnic struggle. Sometimes, indeed, class interests are better served through ethnopolitics than through social class organizations.

REGIONAL DIMENSIONS

The theory of internal colonialism also incorporates a regional dimension. Stavenhagen (1968: 18) starts by affirming that:

> The kinds of relationships that were established between a colonial metropolis and its colonies were repeated within the colonial countries themselves, in the relationships that developed between a few 'poles of growth' and the rest of the country. As Spain was to her colonies, so the centres of colonial power in New Spain (and in the rest of Latin America) stood to the outlying, backward areas that surrounded them.

Thus, the colonial relationship leads to a process of economic and social polarization between different geographical units within a country. Stavenhagen (1971a: 66–7) distinguishes between dynamic zones and peripheral regions: the development of one leading to the underdevelopment of the other. Through a variety of mechanisms the dynamic zones extract a surplus from the peripheral regions, thereby contributing to their decapitalization. Furthermore: 'This metropolis–satellite structure within countries constitutes a kind of internal colonialism, which is strengthened by the political power structure and, in some nations, by the inter–ethnic relations between different segments of the population.' (ibid.: 67.)

For Stavenhagen (1968: 18), 'the backward, underdeveloped regions of our countries have always played the role of *internal colonies* in relation to the developing urban centers or the productive agricultural areas'. Furthermore,

> as long as there are areas fulfilling the role of *internal colonies* in the less developed countries, the relationships characterising their inhabitants tend to take the form of *colonial relationships*. These are strengthened where there exist...marked cultural differences between two sectors of the population.
>
> (Stavenhagen, 1965: 74)

These metropolis–satellite relations are similar to those formulated by Frank but in the theory of internal colonialism this regional dimension is not only subsidiary to, but is also closely linked with, relations of production, exploitation, and domination between social groups. It therefore avoids the (not always justifiable) criticism voiced against Frank's metropolis–satellite chain as being a mechanical formulation of regional relations lacking a class dimension. As if to underline this point González Casanova (1969: 193) entitles one of his essays 'Classes and regions in the analysis of contemporary society'. The regional dimension of internal colonialism is examined further on when the contribution of social geographers is reviewed.

RECAPITULATION

To summarize, the key elements of internal colonialism discussed so far are as follows. It is, on the one hand, a relation of domination of one ethno–cultural group by another largely through extra–economic coercion such as discrimination, violence, and so on. That is to say, political domination is exercised by excluding the subjected group from political participation, access to the state, and to civil society.

On the other hand, it constitutes a relation of exploitation which is based on non–capitalist forms. In other words, a surplus is extracted from the subordinate group through slave, serf, debt–peonage, and other non–free relations of production as well as through plunder and various forms of forced unequal exchange. Where wage relations exist they are secondary and wage rates are below subsistence level.

Thus, the relations of domination and exploitation which define internal colonialism differ from those typical of the classical capitalist mode of production exemplified by the developed countries. This does not mean that those underdeveloped countries which have, or until recently had, internal–colonial relations do not form part of the world capitalist system. What it does mean is that the capitalist development of some Third World countries continues reproducing internal colonialist relations of domination and exploitation which are absent or insignificant in the metropolitan countries. However, the capitalist development of the imperialist countries has led to the formation and reproduction of internal–colonial relations within the colonial countries, and which persist in the post–colonial world.

CRITIQUES OF INTERNAL COLONIALISM

The theory of internal colonialism has generated some critical debate but most of the discussion has taken the form of extending and applying it to new or different situations. One reason for this could be that the main exponents of the theory present rather general analyses which do not explore certain issues in sufficient detail or depth, and fail to study others altogether. Before dealing with specific critiques, however, let me first turn to a general critique which is also applicable to dependency theory and is explored further in Chapter 6:

> these approaches point to the conclusion that the ultimate burden of the development of the capitalist system falls on the more backward regions, since it is here that a surplus is tapped and transferred to the metropolis. Generally speaking, it may be accepted that in the first phase of capital formation this contribution of resources from the traditional sector was basic to the emergence of the modern sector. However, it has not been proved that the centres will always need this contribution from the domestic periphery in order to maintain their rate of development. That would mean disregarding the important part played by the development of productive forces in generating surplus–value, and the whole system would seem to be based on the sole consideration of the extraction of absolute surplus value.
>
> (Graciarena and Franco, 1978: 111)

Thus, the theory of internal colonialism may be guilty of giving too much weight to the extraction of the surplus produced by the native Indians and its appropriation by the *mestizos* and of exaggerating its significance for the process of capital accumulation, particularly after the historical phase of original capital accumulation has ended. The advanced capitalist centre of the economy, through continuous technical progress, is able to generate its own source of capital for accumulation. Thus, capitalist development increasingly relies on relative instead of absolute surplus value for its process of accumulation. [12] However, the focus in the theory of internal colonialism is on the various *relations* of exploitation and domination and not on the absolute amount of the economic surplus which is appropriated. Thus, the theory of internal colonialism goes beyond the above mentioned economic reductionism.

Turning to more specific critiques, Wolpe's (1975) contribution stands out from a theoretical point of view. He makes two main criticisms of internal colonialism: first, that it considers class relations as residual, and second, that it lacks historical specificity. Walton's (1975) critique focuses on the problems of identifying culturally homogeneous groups. The theory can also be criticized for not exploring sufficiently the differences between internal colonial and class relations, and for its idealized view of the development of the capitalist system in the advanced countries.

Class relations as residual

Starting with the critique that internal colonialism considers class relations as residual, Wolpe (1975: 240) writes that it

> presents society as a composite of class relations and ethnic, race, cultural or national relations. To this extent the theory may be distinguished from conventional analyses of race, ethnic or similar relations, since in the latter approach these relations are accorded sole salience. On the other hand, the theory of internal colonialism is unable to explain the relationship between class relations and race or ethnic relations. As a consequence, the latter relations come once more to be treated as autonomous and in isolation from class relations.

This criticism only partly stands up as both González Casanova and Stavenhagen examine the relationship between class and ethnicity although not as fully and adequately as one would have wished.

González Casanova regards internal colonialism as a complex of relations of domination and exploitation of one ethno–cultural segment of the country's population by another. Thus, all social classes belonging to one segment of society jointly dominate and exploit all social classes of the other. Although Stavenhagen explicitly states that the *ladino* working class benefits from internal colonialism it is quite another matter to argue, as González Casanova implies, that they exploit and dominate the Indian population. Even though *ladino* workers might benefit from unequal exchange they certainly do not own means of production or have sufficient extra–economic power with which to extract a surplus from the Indians. Whether *ladino* workers dominate Indians is more difficult to determine, but it is unlikely, as the former lack access to the system of domination. In short, *ladino* workers do not exploit and dominate Indians but are themselves exploited and dominated by the *ladino* or *mestizo* bourgeoisie.

Wolpe's first critique has some validity but in his attempt to sharpen it he does the internal colonialism thesis – particularly as presented by Stavenhagen – an injustice. His assertion that 'the conceptualization of class relations, which is present in the theory, is accorded little or no role in the analysis of relations of domination and exploitation which are, instead, conceived as occurring between "racial", "ethnic", and "national categories"' (ibid.: 230) is certainly a distortion of Stavenhagen's position. Stavenhagen, it will be recalled, stresses the changing relationships between internal colonial and class relations, and even considers colonial relations to be one aspect of class relations.

A more valid criticism of the theory of internal colonialism is that it fails to provide sufficient criteria for distinguishing clearly between internal colonial and class relations. This is a complex issue which requires the analysis of economic, social, political, and ideological elements. It is beyond the scope of this book to undertake such a task but it will be recalled that in my summary of the theory of internal colonialism I distinguished between two principal forms of exploitation which characterize internal colonialism. One mechanism of exploitation is through unequal exchange which occurs when the direct indigenous producers sell the commodities they produce below their value. [13] The other variant of exploitation is when the Indians sell their labour power, either on a seasonal or permanent basis, to *mestizos* for below its value. [14] In so far as the capitalist mode of production is predominant in the country which is being examined, and if these forms of exploitation are common and apply to non–Indian groups as well, then it is more appropriate to speak of class relations than colonial relations. It is only when these forms of exploitation are accompanied by extra–economic coercion and would not otherwise exist that it is valid to call the relations they engender as pertaining to internal colonialism. For this reason the political dimension of extra–economic coercion, which is not always stressed by the theorists discussed, is a key element defining a situation of internal colonialism.

According to Bartra (1974) relations of internal colonialism have been overtaken by class relations in Mexico. The process of capitalist development in Mexico has 'resolved' the Indian problem by erasing or redefining the economic peculiarities of the Indian communities. Furthermore, the bourgeoisie no longer has a direct interest in maintaining 'colonial–type' relations. However, 'this does not mean that inter–ethnic relations do not exist, but they function as an ideological apparatus of domination, which appear as supporting points of the powerful levers of class exploitation.' (ibid.: 481.) Thus inter–ethnic relations no longer have a distinct economic base but only an ideological function in Mexico.

Homogeneity of ethno–cultural groups

Another related weakness in the analysis of internal colonialism stems from its overemphasis on the homogeneity of the two (or more) ethno–cultural groups and its consequent failure to stress the emerging class divisions within the Indian communities. 'In other words, inside the "colony" there will be exploiters and exploited, and, the concept of colony tends to transpose primary contradictions to a secondary, and less significant, level.' (Foweraker, 1981: 188.)

By stressing cultural differences between groups González Casanova, in particular, blurs the social divisions within each ethno–cultural group. The major division in contemporary Latin American society is not between *mestizos* and Indians – important though this still may be – but between the bourgeoisie and the proletariat. Class divisions cut across both the *mestizo* population and, to a lesser extent, the Indian communities as well.

The penetration of capitalism in the Indian communities leads to the progressive development of private ownership of land and the gradual replacement of reciprocal exchange of free labour with wage labour. Communal land and use of labour is eroded – although in some communities they are still dominant – and exploitative relations within the Indian population come to the fore. Thus, the concept of internal colonialism fails to analyse the emerging class relations within the internal colonies. It also fails to explore the particular system of domination and exploitation which evolves within the Indian communities as a consequence of the process of socio–economic differentiation brought about by the penetration of capitalism. This oversight might be explained, although not excused, by the relative lateness of the development of class relations within the Indian communities, a process not yet complete in some Latin American countries.

Furthermore, Indian communities have often become little more than hatcheries for migrant workers. Overpopulation and the eroding land base of Indian communities means that an increasing proportion of Indians has to seek temporary or permanent wage employment through seasonal or permanent out–migration. Thus, a process of proletarianization has developed as increasing numbers of Indians have become full, semi– or sub–proletarians working as stable plantation or *hacienda* workers, as migrant labour gangs, and so on.

Nor does internal colonialism acknowledge sufficiently the diversity of ethno–cultural and linguistic groups within the Indian population. It is perhaps not without irony that the concept of internal colonialism was proposed at a time when the phenomenon under discussion had clearly lost importance as the majority of the Latin American population was by then *mestizo* or *ladino* and urban, and the industrial bourgeoisie and proletariat had become the main protagonists in the class conflict. It is as if the demise of internal colonial relations and the political struggles of the Indians awoke the consciousness of progressive intellectuals who then attempted to make sense of the distinctiveness of the Indian's class struggle.

Lack of historical specificity

Wolpe's second critique refers to the vagueness and lack of historical specificity of the internal colonialism thesis. He writes:

In part, this is due to the failure to distinguish between forms of colonial, political, ideological and cultural domination and modes of imperialist economic exploitation. In turn this conflation stems from the failure to distinguish differing modes of imperialist economic exploitation with the result that different forms of colonial domination cannot be explicitly related to different modes of exploitation. More specifically, much of the analysis of imperialism and underdevelopment (and of internal colonialism) has been based on the assumption that in the era of capitalist imperialism, exploitation everywhere takes place according to a single, invariant mode.

(Wolpe, 1975: 241)

While this may hold true for Gunder Frank, both González Casanova and Stavenhagen point out the various forms of non–capitalist relations of production and exploitation and discuss how they differ from, and sometimes conflict with, typically capitalist ones in situations of internal colonialism. They are far from sustaining that the relations of exploitation have been capitalist since the conquest, as argued by Frank. [15]

Wolpe aims to rescue the concept of internal colonialism by reformulating it. While Wolpe's analytical effort is commendable and sophisticated, his redefinition does not differ fundamentally from the original. As part of his reformulation Wolpe makes the following interesting point, a point with which González Casanova and Stavenhagen would probably concur.

In certain circumstances capitalism may, within the boundaries of a single state, develop predominantly by means of its relationship to non– capitalist modes of production. When that occurs, the mode of political domination and the content of legitimating ideologies assume racial, ethnic and cultural forms and for the same reasons as in the case of imperialism. In this case, political domination takes on a colonial form, the precise or specific nature of which has to be related to the specific mode of exploitation of the non–capitalist society.

(ibid.: 244)

Wolpe concludes his analysis by emphasizing that:

In particular, the point has been stressed that specific modes of political domination which assume a racial or ethnic and, therefore, a colonial rather than a class form have to be analyzed in terms of the specific relations of economic exploitation.

(ibid.: 250.)

The theory of internal colonialism certainly needs to explore the particular relations of domination and exploitation pertaining to it further and to relate them more specifically to class relations and changing historical circumstances. However, Wolpe overstates his critique and even his own analysis of South Africa does not fully accomplish this.

Identification of culturally distinct groups

The concept of internal colonialism has also been criticized by Walton (1975: 32–3) for assuming that 'culturally distinct groups' can be unambiguously defined at the operational level. The question is raised as to whether the concept should be abandoned in cases where exploitation is blatant but cultural differences between exploiter and exploited are less visible. Although empirical problems exist, Walton overlooks the important ethnic dimension which should facilitate the operational use of the concept. I would also argue that even where cultural distinctions are more subtle the concept still retains its usefulness so long as the particular mechanisms of domination and exploitation characteristic of internal colonialism subsist.

The key to the theory of internal colonialism is the particular relations of domination and exploitation which characterize the relations between different ethno–cultural social groups. The ethnic, social, cultural, and geographical elements in the conceptualization of internal colonialism are not central but certainly facilitate the identification, establishment, and intensification of the phenomenon described as internal colonialism. Thus, the criticisms should focus on the theory's analysis of the relations of domination and exploitation. If these relations cannot be clearly defined, do not exist in reality, or are already part of a theory which has greater explanatory and predictive powers, then the theory of internal colonialism should be abandoned. At the time of writing, to do so is premature in those instances where class relations have not yet displaced internal–colonial relations.

Idealized view of capitalist development

It can be argued that González Casanova has an idealized view of capitalist development in the developed countries and its possibilities in the underdeveloped countries. He argues that internal colonialism prevents competitive capitalism, destroys the progressive egalitarian tendencies in capitalism, and blocks the full political participation of the population. Accordingly, democratic politics are held to lead to more development and not the other way round (Kahl, 1976: 91). As he puts it, besides the laws of the market which influence economic decisions, it is the political structure of the country [Mexico] which prevents breaking the dynamics of inequality both internally and externally and is constituting the true bottleneck of a development policy.

(González Casanova, 1967: 134)

He argues that political pressure exercised by organizations representing the interests of the working class (such as trade unions and political parties) brought about the egalitarian process of the capitalist democracies in the developed countries (ibid.). Similarly he believes that by reforming the political system in countries like Mexico, it is possible to eliminate internal colonialism and accelerate the (capitalist) process of development.

Apart from overlooking the major inequalities which remain in the capitalist developed countries, it is doubtful whether working–class organization is a sufficient condition for destroying internal colonialism and for bringing about an egalitarian pattern of development. It is likely that the laws of capitalist development will set the scene for the progressive dissolution of internal colonial relations and that political events – barring a socialist transformation – will only influence the pace of its demise. The demise of internal colonialism and the organization of workers and peasants might be considered a precondition for egalitarianism but, unless the capitalist system of domination and exploitation itself is overthrown, it may not be a sufficient condition. Thus, González Casanova's desire for a competitive, national, and fully democratic capitalism in Third World countries like Mexico might not only be considered as unrealistic, given the strength of the forces opposing such reforms, but also illusory.

NEW DIMENSIONS OF INTERNAL COLONIALISM

There have been a number of attempts to reformulate the concept of internal colonialism in order to accommodate it to new situations and purposes. These extensions of the theory of internal colonialism tend to distort the core of the theory and weaken its analytical sharpness through over–generalizations and over–inclusiveness. The concept can easily fall prey to political sloganeering given the emotional content of the word colonialism.

The concept of internal colonialism has most commonly been picked up by geographers tackling problems of regional inequalities and by social scientists working on race and ethnic divisions in society. These authors are almost exclusively from the developed countries and their analysis generally refers to those countries, although not exclusively so. Although it is pleasing to note that theories emanating from the Third World have an influence on theory building in the developed countries, it is necessary to be aware of the historical and social specificity of concepts like internal colonialism. Internal colonialism can at best be considered only a partial theory and even the most thoughtful attempts to transform it into a general theory have to be viewed with some trepidation.

Dependency

A worthwhile development of the concept of internal colonialism is that put forward by Havens and Flinn, who attempt to link it to dependency theory in their study on Colombia.

> For our purposes, internal colonialism refers to structural arrangements typified by a relatively small dominant group which controls the allocation of resources, and a large, subjected mass composed of various groups with unarticulated interests largely divorced from participation in the development process and blocked from means of social mobility. We differ from the more common usage of the concept as found in the writings of González Casanova in that the subjected groups are not necessarily of different racial origin than the dominant group. Our major focus is not on racial differences but on the nature of the dependency relationship.
>
> (Havens and Flinn, 1970: 11)

Although this formulation retains some of the essentials of the concept, it fails to specify the mechanisms of exploitation and domination which are peculiar to a situation of internal colonialism. Furthermore, in my view, the concept of internal dependency would be more appropriate for their purposes as they are particularly keen to examine the intra–national relationship of dependency and explore its links to the country's external dependency. [16]

Region and space

Social geographers are certainly justified in exploring the theory of internal colonialism as, particularly in the work of Stavenhagen, it incorporates a regional and spatial dimension. However, the regional dimension is only a subsidiary element of the concept of internal colonialism. It follows from this that geographers will find the theory of internal colonialism most useful if they use it within a geographical framework which is based on the notion of created space as opposed to contextual space. Created space views space as socially created and thus linked to historically specific social relations of production. In contrast, the contextual notion views space as merely physical and external to society, and as 'a context *for* society rather than a structure created *by* society' (Wyn Williams, 1983: 17).

Furthermore, the employment of the concept of internal colonialism by some geographers to analyse regional disparities and problems within developed countries is highly questionable. It is certainly possible to speak of core, centre or metropolitan, and peripheral or satellite regions, but these should not be characterized as involving internal colonial relationships within the developed countries, as pre–capitalist social relations of production and exploitation no longer exist in any meaningful sense there and because most have never been colonies of an imperialist country in modern history.

Race, ethnicity, and class in the British Isles and the US

Another way in which the theory of internal colonialism has been extended is for the analysis of ethnic and race relations in the advanced capitalist countries. Hechter (1975), for example, uses the internal colonialism model to study the Celtic fringe in British national development from 1536 to 1966. In his view the fact that the Celts are an internal colony within the very core of the world capitalist system, contrary to the Indians in Latin America, does not invalidate the use of the concept of internal colonialism. A similar position is upheld by the Brazilian social scientist Octavio Ianni (1970: 10–11) who argues that within the metropolitan country itself a sort of internal colonialism operates and that this is an internal manifestation of imperialism. Hechter's use of the internal colonialism theory has some validity for an historical analysis of the British Isles but, in my view, ceases to be valid once capitalist relations fully predominate within a country and pre–capitalist relations have virtually vanished.

Internal colonialism has more often been used to analyse the position of ethnic minorities within the US. The national liberation movements during the post–war decolonization period influenced and inspired the civil rights, black power, and student movements in the

US. introducing the vocabulary of imperialism and colonialism into their political discourse. One such study is by Barrera, who belongs to the Chicano ethnic minority. [17] He coins the term 'colonial labour system', which 'exists where the labor force is segmented along ethnic and/or racial lines, and one or more of the segments is systematically maintained in a subordinate position' (Barrera, 1979: 39). He explains how a labour repressive system exists in the US, based on a dual wage system whereby the wage paid to minority workers is substantially inferior to that paid to other workers who perform exactly the same tasks.

Barrera uses the theory of internal colonialism to study racial inequality resulting from discrimination in the US. As ethnic minorities are relatively dispersed throughout the US he completely discards the regional dimension of the theory. 'Internal colonialism is a form of colonialism in which the dominant and subordinate population are intermingled, so that there is no geographically distinct "metropolis" separate from the "colony"' (ibid.: 194). For him the key element in internal colonialism is the ethnic and/or racial subordination and not the locational aspect. Consequently, 'Wherever ethnic groups do not have a territorial base but are scattered among the larger society, ethnic demands may be couched in more cultural or economic, rather than in political or territorial terms' (Stavenhagen, 1986: 89), like demands for self–government or independence.

If Chicanos have already been incorporated *historically* to the capitalist, professional, managerial, and petty bourgeois classes albeit as a subordinate segment, as sustained by Barrera (1979: 211–12), then it is debatable whether they can be constructed as an internal colony, as he proposes. In this case, class relations have clearly overtaken any pre–existing internal colonial relations, making the use of the theory of internal colonialism for this situation inappropriate and confusing.

By rejecting Barrera's application of the theory of internal colonialism to contemporary US society I am not dismissing its usefulness for analysing that period in the US's history when pre–capitalist relations, such as slavery and debt–tenancy, were significant, especially as North America had been a colony like Latin America. However, while North America has become fully capitalist and the US is the centre of the world capitalist system, Latin America has remained part of the periphery of this system in which pre–capitalist relations still retain significance.

CONCLUDING REMARKS

Despite the various weaknesses of the theory of internal colonialism it does focus attention on aspects of capitalist development specific to some Third World socio–economic formations which had not been analysed before. It can also be considered a forerunner of the major debate on the articulation of different social relations and modes of production. In order to transcend fully the theory of internal colonialism, mode of production theory needs to take into account the contribution of internal colonialism analysis, which so far it has neglected to do. Mode of production theory is not itself without problems and it might well be that other theories are more appropriate. The theory of internal colonialism, for example, could be subsumed by dependency theory, the relationships which have been characterized here as internal–colonial ones being viewed as internal manifestations of the dependence experienced by Third World countries on the developed countries.

Finally, a central weakness of the theory of internal colonialism is its utopianism, as it contains a hope for liberation from oppression and exploitation through ethnic, cultural, and national autonomy. While this theory can be (and has been) used to raise political consciousness, it cannot fulfil the promise of liberation. In the first instance the structural conditions for proclaiming 'internal independence' and establishing a separate state do not exist in most situations of internal colonialism. Most internal colonies are far too enmeshed and dependent upon the national capitalist system for such a declaration of independence to be viable. Even if the struggle is limited to the abolition of the relations of exploitation and domination peculiar to internal colonialism, victory would still not entail full liberation as capitalism continues to prevail. Thus, internal colonialism as an ideological device is historically limited and has to give way to class consciousness as the final struggle for full liberation entails the long and difficult process of the construction of true socialism – which in turn may prove utopian.

4

Marginality: social relations and capital accumulation

What Mayhew, Marx and Booth and others achieved in the last century in legitimizing the study of poverty within the European 'proletariat–in–formation', the Latin American 'Marginality School' has similarly achieved in forcing contemporary social science to shift its perspectives from the narrow confines of microempirical research to the broader quest for an answer to the problems of mass (rather than individual) poverty.

(Bromley and Gerry, 1979: 4)

It is a sad commentary on contemporary social science that 'marginality' represents practically the first attempt in a century to develop a concept that is capable of theoretically analyzing (not just describing) the structural position of that sector of the population conventionally referred to as 'the poor'.

(D. Johnson, 1972: 274)

The concept of marginality, like all myths, exerts a magnetic attraction. It offers a compelling yet simple explanation of a complex social reality and an ideology that appeals to deep–rooted prejudices. Were it merely an illusion, marginality would not have attracted so much attention and energy...[as] the myth of marginality hides behind it something very real.

(F. Cardoso, 1976: xi)

The term marginality acquired widespread popularity and generated much discussion in Latin America, particularly from the mid–1960s to the 1970s. This chapter starts by tracing briefly the origins and evolution of the concept of marginality within the social sciences and then analyses how Latin American social scientists have reformulated and developed the concept. Two major strands of the Latin American marginality school can be distinguished – dualist or integrationist, and single system or class conflict – located within the modernization and Marxist paradigms respectively. A number of critiques levelled at both marginality perspectives are reviewed and the relevance of the concept is assessed. Particular emphasis is placed on the Marxist discussion on marginality and the relative surplus population. The variety of social relations of production and exploitation through which the marginal population is inserted into the dominant capitalist system, its complex and changing articulation to this system, and its significance to the process of accumulation are explored.

HISTORY OF THE MARGINALITY CONCEPT

The term marginality, or more specifically the concept of marginal people, was first used by the US sociologist Park (1928: 881–93) to describe the psychological disorientation experienced by individuals situated on the edge of two conflicting cultures as a result of intermarriage or migration. Park describes how in the US the clash takes place between the dominant Anglo–Saxon culture and a multiplicity of diverse ethnic groups. Stonequist (1937) followed Park's lead in defining marginal people as suffering from psychological uncertainties arising from their unclear membership of two major racial or cultural groups whose codes conflict. Not being a full member of either group the individual 'falls between two stools' and his or her dual social connections isolate him or her from both groups. Within this perspective marginality is viewed as an individual, psychological phenomenon where the social dislocation brought about by cultural change and the resulting uncertain status experienced by those in a problematic social position (social or cultural hybrids) give rise to a distinct marginal personality. The concept was later extended to include other types of cultural contact arising from social and economic mobility within a nation, particularly between rural and urban cultures. This view of marginality can be referred to as psycho–cultural, and can be clearly differentiated from its Latin American usage.

In the early 1960s the concept of marginality was taken up by Latin American social scientists working within a modernization paradigm to refer to certain social consequences arising from the rapid and massive post–war urbanization process in Latin America. Rapid urbanization arose from a 'population explosion' and an unprecedented high rate of rural–urban migration resulting in sprawling shanty towns, slums, and squatter settlements variously known as *barrios marginales* (marginal neighbourhoods), *poblaciones callampas* (mushroom or makeshift townships), *barriadas* (slum quarters), *villas miserias* (squalid or destitute boroughs), *colonias proletarias* (proletarian colonies), *favelas, pueblos jóvenes* (young towns), *ranchos* (camps), *poblaciones marginales* (marginal townships), *campamentos* (settlements), 'pirate' or 'parachute' settlements, and *ciudades perdidas* (lost cities). [1]

Initially the term marginality was used to refer to the physical location of these dwellings on the periphery of the city, then to the substandard quality of the housing and the absence of communal services such as water, electricity, sewerage, and schools (Rosenblüth, 1968; Rabinovitz and Trueblood, 1971). Marginality was later used to refer to the social conditions experienced by shanty–town dwellers who were labelled as marginals such as high rates of unemployment, poor working conditions, and miserable living standards (Hoffman *et al.*, 1969). This approach can be called urban socio–ecological or urban social–geographical (Miller and Gakenheimer, 1971; Friedmann, 1973). [2] Incorporating the above, marginality was then perceived in relation to participation in both the system of production and consumption (Beyer, 1967; DESAL, 1969). This has been called the DESAL participation ideology approach, defining marginality as a group's lack of socio–economic integration and exclusion from political participation (Perlman, 1976: 98). [3]

Structuralist and neo–Marxist writers used the term marginalization with reference to the import–substituting industrialization's inability to absorb the growing contingent of the labour force and to its tendency to expel labour. This capital–intensive industrialization process led to further income concentration and marginalization of sectors of the population from the fruits of technological progress. As industrialization came to be dominated by foreign transnational corporations, this approach to marginality was linked to dependency theory (Nun, 1969; Sunkel, 1972a; Schteingart, 1973; Castells, 1974).

Finally, at its most general the concept was extended by some authors to include rural groups with similar problems and more broadly still to any group suffering from poverty and located on the lowest rung of the social hierarchy (DESAL, 1968; Arroyo and Gross, 1969; Stavenhagen, 1970). However, studies on rural marginality are few and most of the marginality literature tends to view the problem as urban and resulting from excessive rural outmigration (Margulis, 1968; Germani, 1973; Gilbert and Gugler, 1982).

Marginality studies mushroomed in Latin America during the 1960s largely for political reasons. As shanty towns began to encircle many Latin American cities they were perceived as a threat to political stability, especially where left–wing political organizations mobilized the inhabitants against the established social system (Franco, 1974: 520–1). Many shanty towns had their origin in illegal land invasions and violent confrontations sometimes ensued between the police (or the army in some instances) and the squatters at times resulting in eviction, imprisonment, injury and death. Thus, public awareness was aroused to this tragedy and many studies were commissioned by reform–minded governments enquiring into the origins and characteristics of the squatters with a view to taking prophylactic action and designing more effective policies for national political integration (Goldrich *et al.*, 1967–8).

Amongst social scientists, two theoretical interpretations of marginality came to the fore, mirroring wider political divisions and debates. One group, working within a modernization paradigm, viewed marginality as lack of integration of certain social groups in society; the other, working within a Marxist paradigm, viewed marginality as arising from the nature of the country's integration into the world capitalist system. Lloyd (1976: 13) calls these two views the integration and conflict perspectives respectively. The policy recommendations differed: while the former group argued for measures aimed at integrating the marginal groups into a reformed capitalist system, the latter argued that marginality was a structural feature of capitalist society and that only a socialist development option could solve the problem of marginality.

As representatives of the first theoretical position I will review the body of work emanating from DESAL and in particular the writings of the Argentinian sociologist Gino Germani. For the second position I will discuss the writings of José Nun and Aníbal Quijano, and their main Brazilian critics, Fernando Henrique Cardoso, Francisco de Oliveira, and Lucio Kowarick (the 'CEBRAP school').

MODERNIZATION THEORY AND MARGINALITY

The modernization or dualist perspective on marginality was largely developed by Gino Germani and the DESAL school. Roger Vekemans, a Belgian Jesuit priest, was the main driving force behind DESAL which was set up in the early 1960s in Santiago, Chile. DESAL undertook a series of studies on marginality, national integration, and development in Latin America. Although based in Chile, DESAL set up small research groups in a number of other Latin American countries to undertake country studies within the general theoretical framework elaborated by Vekemans and his associates, largely Chileans with reformist leanings.

Germani and the multidimension of marginality

Gino Germani is probably the most outstanding proponent of modernization theory in Latin America. [4] His writings on marginality are theoretically sophisticated and well–informed (Germani, 1972; 1980). He considers marginality to be a multidimensional phenomenon and his analysis starts by defining marginality as 'the lack of participation of individuals and groups in those spheres in which, according to determined criteria, they might be expected to participate' (Germani, 1980: 49). Furthermore,

> it is essential to note that the marginal sector is not located (socially) outside society but within it, eventually to be utilized or exploited by some of the participating sectors. It remains excluded from the exercise of its corresponding roles and rights according to the normative schema in use.
>
> (ibid.: 83).

In his multidimensional analysis of marginality Germani distinguishes between different types of insertion: in the productive sub–system (from total unemployment to low productive self–employment), in the consumption sub–system (access to goods and services), in the cultural sub–system, in the political sub–system, and so on. Thus, global marginality is made up of several distinct forms of marginality and individuals or groups experience different combinations or configurations of these forms (ibid.: 55–64). It is only when all dimensions are experienced to a high degree by a particular individual or group that it is possible to speak of absolute marginality (ibid.: 8).

According to Germani, marginality usually arises during the process of transition to modernity (which he defines as an industrial society) which can be asynchronous or uneven as traditional and modern attitudes, values, beliefs, behaviours, institutions, social categories, regions, and so on, coexist (ibid.: 26–8). This asynchrony means that some individuals, groups, and regions are left behind and do not participate in, nor benefit from, this modernization process. They, thus, become marginal.

Germani maintains that 'the discussion on marginality developed among Latin American social scientists has a general relevance not only for developing areas, but also for highly modernized nations' (ibid.: vii). While marginality is currently more acute in the developing world, he regards the situation as not being very different in the early stages of industrialization of the advanced countries. However, he acknowledges some differences arising from the higher rate of demographic growth in today's developing countries, the greater possibilities of emigration for European countries during their industrialization period, and the lower labour absorptive capacity of today's technology (ibid.: 34–6). [5]

The DESAL school: active and passive participation

According to the DESAL school the origins of marginality in Latin America lie in the Spanish conquest of the continent in the sixteenth century when the Spanish conquistadors subordinated the indigenous culture to their own. They define as marginal those people or groups who are located at the inferior end of the social scale or, more precisely, outside it, as they are not integrated culturally, socially, or economically to society. Marginals do not belong to and have even been rejected by the economic system.

> It can be said that the marginals are not socially and economically integrated into society or into a class system, because they do not belong to the economic system. ...They are not found in the countryside, which expels them, nor in the city, which does not receive them:...they are *nobody*, they are only *there*; they *populate* a piece of land which is *no–man's* land.
>
> (Vekemans and Silva Fuenzalida, 1969: 44)

Marginality is also used to refer to social groups which, although they are members of a nation, have been left on the sidelines of the modernization process (DESAL, 1969: 49). In this sense the DESAL view differs from those prevailing modernization theories which argue that economic growth leads to social integration and political participation. Indeed, 'The DESAL thesis changes the emphasis of past theories of dualism away from the problems of economic transformation and toward aspects of cultural transformation and social–political participation.' (Perlman, 1976: 120.)

Nevertheless, DESAL's modernization approach to marginality still encompasses a dualist perspective in which society is dichotomized into an incorporated and a marginal stratum. The defin- itive characteristic of the marginal group is its lack of participation in society. Two types of participation are distinguished by DESAL: passive or receptive, and active or contributive. Under passive participation the individual is considered to be the object of social processes. Marginals do not participate, or only minimally so, in the social and economic benefits brought about by development. Thus, for example, they have little or no access to education and culture, to the media, to housing, to health services, to the social security system, to regular and productive employment, to income, credit, technical assistance, and so on (DESAL, 1968: 30; DESAL, 1969: 54–5).

Under active participation the individual is considered to be the subject of the social process. The level of active participation by marginal groups is measured by examining their membership of representative organizations and participatory structures. In most cases their low level of participation debars them from engaging in decision–making processes, even on matters which directly concern them. Marginals are held not to participate, or only occasionally, in political elections, and not to join pressure groups or belong to organizations in general. Thus, they are regarded as not actively contributing to the society's institutional and policy–making processes.

In sum, while marginal groups are juridically members of a nation, they lack direct involvement or participation in its affairs. According to this school of marginality thinking, society is dichotomized into those groups which constitute the modern national community (the integrated groups) and those groups which are outside it, i.e. the marginal groups (DESAL, 1969: 242).

The assumption is made that as marginal groups gain access to resources and thereby become passive participants, an increase in active participation will ensue. As living standards and educational levels improve, so marginals will begin to intervene in social and political affairs which directly concern them (Mattelart and Garretón, 1965: 14). As will be seen later, this crucial assumption explains the emphasis the modernization school puts on *asistencialismo* or social–assistance–type policies. In this case lack of passive participation is held to be the cause of a group's lack of active participation. It can be argued, however, that the causality should be reversed, i.e. lack of passive participation in the social and economic benefits is a direct consequence of a group's low level of active participation. In this case the policy implications would differ.

According to DESAL the marginal sector's lack of active participation arises from their exclusion by other social groups and from their own 'inability to make a decisive contribution to the process of development' (DESAL, 1968: 30). This inability arises because marginal groups do not possess the psychological and psycho–social attributes for example, an instrumentalist rather than an affective orientation in the fields of economics, labour, politics, a universalistic rather than a particularistic value–orientation pattern) necessary for participating in modern society (ibid.: 31).

These values, norms, and perceptions of the marginal strata are identified by DESAL as obstacles to social incorporation. Thus, the marginals are portrayed as passive victims unable to react to their predicament and take positive action to overcome it. Furthermore, marginals are deemed to be guilty and ungrateful victims as governments who attempt to promote their interests often have to overcome their deep–rooted suspicions of the state. Thus, besides the economic and social power structures, marginals themselves are held to conspire against their incorporation into society – albeit unwittingly (ibid.). [6]

The DESAL studies aim to locate the problem empirically, by identifying marginal groups and measuring degrees of marginality through a series of economic, social, political, and cultural indicators (DESAL, 1969; Vekemans, 1970). Their methodology relied mainly on questionnaires, fieldwork, and the use of official statistics. [7] Many typologies were constructed, differentiating degrees of marginality and integration by social group and geographical region. In this way a diagnosis of marginality in several Latin American countries was made and target groups and areas identified with a view to facilitating remedial action by governments.

Who are the marginals?

Through these empirical analyses DESAL aimed to locate the marginal groups, to elucidate their internal characteristics and their relationship to the global society, and to measure their degree of marginality. Their findings showed that the great majority of the peasantry in Latin America is marginalized from modern society. Within the urban sector marginality is concentrated in what DESAL calls two types of sub–proletariat: (a) the self–employed who work in such low productive activities as small handicrafts, street sellers, seamstresses, shoe–shine boys; and (b) low–qualified wage workers who find only occasional employment in low–paid jobs such as casual construction workers, porters, carriers, domestic servants, garbage scavengers, and night–watchman. Most urban marginals live in the suburban shanty towns (although not all shanty–town dwellers are marginals) and in the inner–city slums (the *conventillos*).

Marginality is often used by DESAL to be synonymous with poverty, either explicitly or implicitly (Bromley and Gerry, 1979: 4; Germani, 1980: 86–90). Thus, for example, their study of rural marginals includes all the poorest groups in rural society such as tenants, sharecroppers, agricultural wage workers, smallholders (*minifundistas*), and dwellers of rural hamlets and villages (*pobladores*) such as carpenters, cobblers, petty grocers, mechanics, blacksmiths, masons, small shopkeepers, itinerant traders, and market sellers (DESAL, 1968: 28–9). By using such a general characterization of marginality and linking it to poverty, it is not surprising to find that the majority of the rural population and a large proportion of the urban population is defined as marginal by DESAL.

Policy implications

Although the DESAL studies are mainly concerned with diagnosing and measuring the extent of marginality, they provide some guidelines for designing policies to overcome this problem. Mattelart and Garretón identify two major barriers to integration. The first is the rigid class structure which 'creates a certain value imagery which, together with the institutionalized norms, do not respond to the impulses and values of the whole population but are the reflection of the values and norms of the dominant classes' (Mattelart and Garretón, 1965: 22). The other barrier is the persistence of sectoral discontinuities or disequilibria such as those prevalent between the rural and urban worlds or between the capital city and outlying regions, reflecting the dualist nature of Latin American countries (ibid.: 22).

In DESAL's view policies should be adopted sequentially as one type of integration must be achieved before proceeding to the next integrative mechanism (for example, passive participation has to be encouraged so as to bring forth active participation). First, it is necessary to overcome the atomization of the individual by the formation of solidarity links around a common goal or function. This type of internal functional integration can be achieved by promoting the establishment of grass–roots organizations. The second stage involves designing institutional mechanisms to integrate marginal groups into wider society. Third, to achieve the full incorporation of the marginals, it is necessary to change radically society itself. As the dominant groups are seen as an obstacle to the incorporation of the marginal groups, they have to be dislodged and replaced by a social structure 'based on a new cultural ethos' (DESAL, 1969: 394) so as to achieve the 'equilibrated and articulated unity of the whole social body' (ibid.: 393).

The election in Chile of a reformist Christian Democrat government in 1964 with which DESAL was closely associated presented a unique opportunity to test some of their ideas. A National Council of Popular Promotion was set up by the government and staffed by some DESAL members with the aim to design and co-ordinate social assistance and promotional policies targeted at the marginal groups. Minimum wages were raised, more educational, medical, and social services were provided to the marginal regions and self-help housing schemes were promoted. Shanty-town dwellers were encouraged to set up neighbourhood committees (*Juntas de Vecinos*) and mother centres (*Centros de Madres*). [8] As for removing some of the barriers which prevented societal integration, the government introduced a mild land reform programme among other measures.

One of the chief purposes of DESAL was to provide policy and ideological support to governments and groups willing to counteract the influence of left-wing organizations in the shanty towns. According to rumours at the time its director, the Jesuit priest Roger Vekemans, received funds from the CIA to finance the activities of his centre. What is beyond doubt though is that:

> DESAL rejected from the start its initial role as a research group uncommitted to political action. Its views are now seen more clearly in the political platforms it has produced. In this practice, DESAL emulates development models nourished by the North American social sciences. At the core of DESAL's work is the model of popular participation, an amalgam of activist policies designed to combat marginality and fight the threat of communism.
>
> (Perlman, 1976: 121)

In the wake of the Cuban revolution many US administrations were haunted by the spectre of communism in Latin America and were willing to support reformist governments in the hope of avoiding revolutions. 'In a period of political reformism aiming at "change without revolution", many programs of social participation were formulated, the ultimate objective of which was to be "functional" to the *existing* systems of power relations in Latin America.' (ibid.: 122–3.)

The reformist military government led by General Juan Velasco Alvarado in Peru, which seized power in 1968, was also influenced by marginality ideas of the modernization school, as witnessed by the far– reaching land reform and the ambitious programme of social participation. The National System to Support Social Mobilization (*Sistema Nacional de Apoyo a la Movilización Social* or SINAMOS) was launched in the early 1970s for the organization and co–option into the state machinery of shanty–town dwellers, peasants, and workers. These state–sponsored schemes had a corporatist character. The activities of SINAMOS were drastically curtailed and it was finally disbanded in 1978 during the 'second phase of the Peruvian revolution' from 1975 to 1980 under General Francisco Morales Bermúdez.

The main ideologue and one of the directors of SINAMOS was the social anthropologist Carlos Delgado. [9] Delgado's views on marginality and participation are a combination of the 'integration' (or modernization) and 'conflict' (or Marxist) paradigms, a combination mirrored in his common rejection of the capitalist and socialist systems for being non–participatory (Neira, 1975: 29). Delgado considered base groups (*grupos de base*) to be too weak during the early stages of Velasco's revolution to articulate their own interests effectively, so he envisaged a strong, centralized redistributionist state expropriating and transferring self–managed and social property enterprises to newly formed peasants', workers' and artisans' co–operatives. These co–operatives and enterprises would then receive a sustained period of 'promotion' and technical assistance from state bureaucrats and above all from freshly recruited and motivated SINAMOS cadres. Finally, after a period of about five to ten years, the state would voluntarily retire from centre stage, allowing the new, strengthened grass–roots groups to articulate their views and needs directly to higher and higher levels of the national system (Delgado, 1973: 221–67). For this reason SINAMOS was always viewed as a temporary organization but its activities were discontinued far earlier then expected and without having accomplished their goals (Béjar, n.d.: 61–6). [10]

The demise of the modernization conception

By the late 1960s the modernization view on marginality was being challenged from various quarters. Stavenhagen (1974: 131) attacked its dualism by arguing that the problem of marginality is structural as it is embedded within Latin America's process of dependent capitalist development. Marginals, far from being 'out of the system', are an integral part of it, though at the lowest level. Their condition is that of a sub–proletariat as they suffer the most acute forms of domination and exploitation. Furthermore, as long as Latin American countries remain tied to their present dependent socio–political structures, the problem of marginality will become more acute (Stavenhagen, 1971a: 54– 5).

Sunkel also criticized the modernization and DESAL marginality analysis by arguing that the marginality problem has to be located within the dependency perspective. In his view the penetration of transnational capital into the Latin American economies leads to national disintegration by dividing society into two sectors: one which is integrated into the transnational system and one which is excluded from this system and which constitutes the marginal sector composed of the majority of the population. This leads him to the conclusion that 'neither partial policies of participation or popular integration, nor global policies such as demographic control nor the indiscriminate acceleration of economic growth, respond to the true nature of the phenomenon [of marginalization]' (Sunkel, 1972a: 36).

The eclipse of the modernization perspective of marginality in the early and mid–1970s was partly due to the difficulties which reform–minded governments experienced in overcoming marginality. Attempts to achieve national integration often led to increased conflict and repression instead of social peace as the theory had led them to expect. The theoretical weakness of the modernization position of marginality stems from its failure to emphasize the class character of society and the existence of major class conflicts, and from its adherence to a dualist position which precludes an exploration of the interconnections between the marginal and 'integrated' sectors as well as between the developed and underdeveloped countries within the world capitalist system.

The class issue can be illustrated by the Chilean and Peruvian cases. The policies of 'popular promotion' and 'social mobilization' met with little success or had unforeseen consequences. The paternalist position adopted by these governments underestimated the political consciousness of marginal groups and undervalued their ability to intervene massively and forcefully in support of political parties and groups advocating the overthrow of the power structure. In Chile the Frei government unintentionally paved the way for the election of the first Marxist president – Salvador Allende (1970–3). Significantly, Vekemans dissolved DESAL after Allende's election and set up offices in Colombia where he soon faded into oblivion (Perlman, 1976: 123).

In the Peruvian case the military governments' (1968–80) attempts to incorporate and co–opt had the unintended consequence of strengthening the class consciousness of marginal groups who tended to join organizations independent from government influence or sponsorship and which had links with left–wing parties in opposition to the government. As these groups and organizations increased their demands and broadened their actions, clashes with the government ensued. It is repression and the unfavourable power structure which limits the ability of the marginal groups to intervene in society and less so their lack of consciousness or resources as maintained by the modernization school.

The above critiques are fairly representative of what Perlman has called the 'structural–historical perspective', which displaced the modernization– or DESAL–type theories of marginality. In this new perspective,

> the situation of marginality arises from a peculiar form of integration of certain segments of the labor force into the main productive apparatus. Hence the defining characteristic of the marginalized sector is its role in the accumulation process characteristic of dependent nations.
>
> (ibid.: 258)

Within this perspective it is those authors who work within a Marxist paradigm who have made the most significant contribution and it is to them that I turn next. [11]

MARXIST THEORY AND MARGINALITY

The Marxist view on marginality partly originated in response to the modernization view and partly in response to a debate within Marxist theory. The ideas of the key figures in this debate – Quijano and Nun – are presented and then the various critiques they engendered will be analysed. [12]

When the Peruvian sociologist Aníbal Quijano started writing on marginality in the mid–1960s, the modernization view, which emphasizes the adaptive, integrative, and consensus requisites for the functioning of the social system, predominated. Quijano questioned such a theoretical framework and initially adopted an historical–structuralist approach which highlights the conflicts and contradictions between the various parts of a structured totality as well as the dynamics of change deriving from such conflicts. Only in his later writings did he shift towards a more overt Marxist position. He has certainly been the most prolific marginality writer working within the Marxist tradition. [13]

Quijano's (1966) key objective in his first seminal article was to criticize the modernization and dualist view of marginality. According to him marginality reflected a particular manner of social integration and participation rather than non–integration or non–participation as the modernization theorists claimed. Given his view of marginality as the expression and consequence of a certain social system, reformist measures as the modernization theorists advocated, were seen to be inadequate.

José Nun (1979), an Argentinian political scientist and sociologist, places the discussion on marginality within a Marxist theoretical framework mainly by exploring its relationship to Marx's concepts of the 'relative surplus population' and the 'industrial reserve army' of labour. In his view Marx's original conception needs to be modified to take account of the transition from competitive to monopoly capitalism and the peculiar forms which the development of capitalism takes in dependent countries. (Nun's two most important essays on marginality first appeared in 1969 and 1972 and to my knowledge have not been published in English.)

Nun (1969), in his seminal marginality article, aimed to clarify a concept which had acquired a multiplicity of often vague meanings. His main interest lay in creating a new category – 'marginal mass' – which he differentiates from the Marxist concepts of 'relative surplus labour' and 'industrial reserve army'. Likewise, Quijano in his later writings engaged in a conceptual exercise by proposing and defining the concepts of 'marginal labour' and the 'marginal pole' of the economy. He too wrestles with the relationship of his new concepts with existing Marxist categories.

Quijano's and Nun's preoccupation with marginality arises out of the disillusionment and critique of the post–Second World War industrialization process in Latin America which failed to absorb the rapid increase in the labour force. They pinpoint the problem of marginalization as originating from the increasing control of foreign capital over the industrialization process resulting in its monopolization. Thus, marginality is largely a recent phenomenon. It is also found in imperialist countries, though less widespread and pronounced, as monopoly capital first became dominant there. Thus, they seem to argue that marginality is due to monopoly capital in general rather than being specific to the situation of dependence. However, they do not elaborate further on this point.

José Nun and the marginal mass

In his review of Marx's analysis of relative surplus population, Nun points out the function that this population performs within the capitalist mode of production. First, it provides a plentiful reservoir of labour which can be drawn on during the upward swing of the economic cycle. Second, it forces those in employment to work harder for, and subordinate themselves further to, capital. Third, it exercises a downward pressure on wages. Thus, it is functional to capitalism even though they are a surplus population 'in relation to capital's average requirements for valorization' (Marx, 1976: 786).

Nun argues that the penetration of foreign monopoly capital (transnational corporations) into Latin America has created such a large relative surplus population that part of it is not only afunctional but even dysfunctional for capitalism. This part of the relative surplus population does not perform the function of an industrial reserve army of labour as it will never be absorbed into this hegemonic capitalist sector, even during the expansionary phase of the cycle. [14]

The arguments Nun presents for the inability of the industrial sector to absorb labour are similar to those given by the *cepalista* (i.e. ECLA) and dependency–analysis writers (Lessa, 1973). On the one hand, the inward–looking development strategy did not revolutionize agriculture and thus no internal mass market was created for industry. On the other hand, it has furthered economic dependence, which has prematurely led to industrial concentration and the adoption of highly capital–intensive technologies. As a consequence little extra employment has been created despite rapid industrial growth. The problem of employment has been aggravated by the high rates of population growth in the developing countries in recent decades, which have been more than two or three times higher than those of the developed countries. Furthermore, only a tiny fraction of the population in developing countries is able to emigrate due to a variety of immigration controls by the rich countries. Meanwhile, Europe was able to reduce its absolute overpopulation in the nineteenth century by massive emigration. Thus, for example, two out of every three rural migrants went abroad during the second half of the nineteenth century in Great Britain.

Thus, in Nun's view a new phenomenon, not foreseen by Marx, has emerged in the dependent countries. For this reason Nun (1969: 201) feels justified in coining a new concept of 'marginal mass' to refer to that part of the relative surplus population which is afunctional or dysfunctional for the monopoly sector. It is non–functional because it will never be employed by monopoly capital and because it has no influence whatsoever on the level of wages of the labour force employed by the hegemonic sector. [15]

The marginal mass is composed of: (1) part of the labour employed by competitive industrial capital; (2) the majority of the workers who take refuge in low income activities in the service sector; (3) the majority of the unemployed; and (4) all the labour force which is secured by commercial capital, thereby lacking mobility (ibid.: 224). Unfortunately, Nun does not explain these different categories of marginal mass in any detail. [16] According to him (ibid.: 224), part of the marginal mass can perform the function of a reserve army with regard to competitive industrial capital. However, owing to the decreasing ability of the competitive sector to absorb labour, Nun even questions this possibility, thereby extending the concept of marginal mass further by including part of the competitive sector as well. [17]

Aníbal Quijano and the marginal pole

Like Nun, Quijano is keen to assert the need to reconceptualize Marx's industrial reserve army of labour and to adopt a new term for the Latin American case.

> The manpower available in the [Latin American] market no longer constitutes a 'reserve' for the hegemonic levels of industrial production, but an excluded labour force which, as changes in the technical composition of capital progress, loses in a permanent and not a transitory way the possibility of being absorbed in the hegemonic levels of production.
>
> (Quijano, 1974: 418)

This excluded labour which Quijano defines as 'marginal labour' does not function as an industrial reserve army. Furthermore, Quijano predicts that labour will be excluded even from the competitive sector and become marginalized due to the long–run decline of the capitalist competitive sector, which is being squeezed out by the monopoly sector. The similarities with Nun are obvious. However, there are some differences too which will become apparent later on.

Quijano identifies various sources of urban and rural marginality: first, the development of a monopoly sector which generates unemployment by bankrupting some industries of the competitive sector; second, both hegemonic and competitive capital destroy part of the handicraft, workshop, small commerce, and small–service sectors, making that labour redundant; and third, capitalism penetrates agriculture, expelling labour. The question then arises as to how this marginal labour makes a living. Quijano (1973: 165–6) argues that an increasing proportion of Latin America's population seeks refuge in what he calls the 'marginal pole' of the economy. The concept of marginal pole enables him to avoid dualism by showing that the marginalized labour force is still part of the economic system. With the emergence of a marginal pole, the overall economic structure becomes even more uneven, more heterogeneous and more contradictory, thereby accentuating the disequilibrium between the various levels (monopolistic, competitive, and marginal) of the system (Quijano, 1977a: 124; 1974: 422).

The marginal pole is characterized to a large extent by not being directly linked to any productive function. Consequently, the production relations between the marginal pole and dominant nucleus of the system are fragmentary and indirect. There is a direct relationship with the lower levels of the productive structure, however, and this part of the marginal pole produces a small surplus value which is appropriated by the petty bourgeoisie. From the point of view of realization of surplus value, the marginal pole plays a more significant role as it provides a market for the lower and, to a lesser extent, middle levels of the productive apparatus. The marginal pole is the lowest level of the economy but one which is far from constituting a separate sector as it is directly linked to the process of realization of surplus value and, fragmentarily, to the productive process. However, these relationships are unstable and precarious (Quijano, 1977a: 125).

Quijano distinguishes between two types of marginal population: the 'marginal petty bourgeoisie' and the 'marginal proletariat'. The former is less numerous and less marginal, being self–employed. Their productive activities and services are largely geared towards the marginal population but they may find a market in the urban proletariat and the non–marginal petty bourgeoisie. Meanwhile, the marginal proletariat find only occasional temporary employment in the labour– intensive and non–technified activities such as construction, non– productive and manual services. They are unlikely to be employed by the marginal petty bourgeoisie as the latter lack the resources (ibid.: 198–9). These types of marginals heighten social differentiation by constituting a sub–class within the petty bourgeoisie and proletariat respectively (Quijano, 1974: 422).

Another important issue which Quijano examines is the contribution which marginal labour makes to capital accumulation. In its role as reserve army for the competitive sector, the marginal proletariat contributes by depressing the wage levels of those employed in the competitive level of the economy. They also contribute by purchasing products from the competitive and monopoly sectors as they are 'exploited' as consumers (ibid.: 424–5; Quijano, 1977a: 186). [18] These can be regarded as indirect contributions to capital accumulation. Quijano has little to say about direct contributions, i.e. the contribution made by the marginal proletariat when they are sporadically employed by capitalists and surplus value is directly appropriated by capital. As for the marginal petty bourgeoisie they manage to accumulate a small amount of capital directly through their activities in the marginal pole of the economy (Quijano, 1974: 425).

Marginals, class consciousness, and political action

Having located the marginal sectors in the economy and society, it is appropriate to examine their political consciousness and generation. Nun argues that as the marginal mass is not part of the industrial working class this weakens their class consciousness. They have difficulties forging solidarity links and little experience in organizing themselves owing to their social fragmentation and instability. Their ability to engage in political action is thereby limited. From the point of view of revolutionary political organizations, the marginal mass offers both risk and hope: a risk because it can easily fall victim to the manipulation of populist politicians and undertake desperate violent actions which are self–defeating; a hope because it may be mobilized by revolutionary groups given the potential contradictions which its existence embodies (Nun, 1972: 126).

Quijano (1977a: 228–9), in turn, highlights the anti–systemic behaviour of the marginal proletariat as its basic interest in a stable job and adequate wages cannot be met by the existent system, although some immediate interests such as food, clothing, and housing might be. However, not being directly exploited by the bourgeoisie, this sector has difficulty in perceiving its class enemy and may identify it as the state. Furthermore, Quijano (ibid.: 203, 213) observes that the so–called *barrios marginales* (marginal neighbourhoods) are also inhabited by non–marginals who often control local organizations. This diffuses the marginals' class consciousness and actions as they can easily fall prey to the paternalism and clientelism of state sponsored organizations.

Some analysts argue that the marginals are open to political manipulation by charismatic leaders from the right and the left as they are vulnerable to short–term promises. They are a disposable mass for political mobilization by the defenders of the established order and status quo as well as by those who wish to tear it down. In this way they are seen as being both a potentially reactionary and revolutionary explosive force (Perlman, 1976: 123–8; Touraine, 1977: 30; Roxborough, 1979: 83).

MARXIST DISCUSSION ON MARGINALITY

Quijano's and Nun's theory of marginality has generated a lively debate largely from a broad left–wing and Marxist perspective. A group of radical social scientists (F. H. Cardoso, V. Faria, L. Kowarick, Paul Singer and F. de Oliveira, among others) working in the Brazilian Centre for Analysis and Planning (*Centro Brasileiro de Analise e Planejamento* or CEBRAP), which was set up in the early 1970s and located in São Paulo, have made an important contribution to this discussion (Roberts, 1978: 165). The critics query the need for new concepts and hold that existent Marxist categories are adequate. The discussion has centred on three major issues, some of which are closely interrelated: (1) the extent to which the marginality concepts differ from Marx's industrial reserve army of labour; (2) the contribution of marginals to the process of capital accumulation and their articulation to the dominant mode of production; and (3) the relationship between marginality and dependency.

Marginality, surplus labour, and reserve army

Turning first to the question of overlap between the concepts of marginal mass or marginal labour and the industrial reserve army of labour (see Godfrey, 1977), the first critical shot was fired by Fernando H. Cardoso, who rejects the concepts of marginal mass and marginal labour on both theoretical and empirical grounds. He agrees that certain social structures and productive sectors are marginalized by the new forms of production brought about by the expansion of capitalism but points out that while the marginalized remained subordinate to capitalist relations, they in turn conditioned capitalist development. This, in F. H. Cardoso's (1972a: 195) view, serves to indicate the combined and uneven development of capitalism and to show that the process of marginalization can be accommodated within the existent notions developed for the study of the capitalist mode of production. He concludes by stating that:

> I do not want to endorse, without further qualifications, the notion of marginality, nor do I think that it is easy to substitute the concept of marginal sectors for that of reserve army. In my view to abandon the hypothesis that the so-called marginal groups originate from the contradictions between accumulation and misery and that their existence is pertinent and necessary for the process of accumulation is too bold a theoretical step to take without further empirical proof and without redoing the analysis of the capitalist mechanisms of accumulation.
>
> (F. Cardoso, 1972a: 198)

In a later critique, Fernando H. Cardoso completely dismisses Nun's concept of marginal mass and argues that the distinction which Nun makes between his concept and Marx's reserve army is unjustifiable. Theoretically Nun's concept is flawed, as the relationship between marginal mass and capital accumulation is not defined at the structural level. Furthermore, the concept is so unspecific as to be operationally useless, including under its umbrella people who are employed, unemployed or unemployable, and so on. Cardoso also disputes the existence of a marginal mass on empirical grounds, affirming that Nun holds too negative a view of monopoly capital's ability to create employment opportunities, either directly or indirectly, and that this assessment is not born out by the facts. Indeed, he sees no major difference on this issue between what is happening in the developed countries and the underdeveloped countries. For all these reasons Cardoso (1971: 74–6) concludes that the replacement of the concept of reserve army by marginal mass is unwarranted.

Many orthodox Marxists express similar criticisms. They argue that the terms marginal mass or marginal labour are superfluous as Marx's original concepts are adequate for comprehending the phenomena analysed by the *marginalistas*. In Pradilla's view the marginal population is part of the surplus population and the industrial reserve army of labour as it provides labour in periods of expansion and depresses wages.

> In synthesis, no population exists in Latin America which is in a situation of occupational, political or cultural 'marginality', but a considerable number of workers are converted by the capitalist development into a *relative surplus population* and which objectively functions as an Industrial Reserve Army.
>
> (Pradilla, 1984: 696).

Similarly, for Kowarick (1979: 70, 83) the marginal groups form part of the industrial reserve army.

In between these two extremes lie a number of writers who accept some aspects of the neo–Marxist marginality analysis but locate these more firmly within Marx's original contribution. Some of these authors introduce only slight variations or additions to Marx's original terminology, while others prefer new but different terms to those proposed by Nun and Quijano. Thus, Campanario and Richter (1974: 38–9) argue that the concept of marginality is unnecessary and propose instead the term 'mass of surplus population', and in place of marginalization, 'the growing mass of pauperized surplus population'. Cockcroft (1983: 87.) drawing on Marx's theory of immiseration and relative surplus population, proposes to replace marginalization with 'the immiserated fraction of the working class'.

> As a reserve army of labor, the immiserated masses constitute a necessary condition for the development of industrial capitalism. [They]...all defray falling profit rates, hold industrial wages down, and provide for labor's reproduction at almost no cost to capital.
>
> (ibid.:86).

Furthermore: 'They constitute a subproletariat in a double sense: first as a relative surplus population or part of the reserve army of labor and second as moving in and out of the agrarian, industrial, and service/commercial working class.' (ibid.: 87.) In Cockcroft's (1983: 91) view many of these sub–proletarians or immiserated join what

Marx called the floating segment of the relative surplus population, which only finds irregular factory employment. While most of the remainder 'work for a pittance as street vendors, artisans, subcontracted seamstresses, carpenters, hawkers, carriers, small–scale workshop employees or owners, messengers' (ibid.: 91), and so on. Thus, some of the immiserated own some minor and meagre means of production which allow them to be self–employed. As they make a poor living despite putting in many hours of hard work, Cockcroft (1983: 96) considers them to be disguised proletarians who are 'self–exploited' rather than belonging to the petty bourgeoisie.

Likewise, Dale Johnson (1972) attempts to situate marginality more explicitly within class analysis and he coins the term 'marginal underclass' which he differentiates from internal colony as follows:

> Marginal underclasses, then, are those populations that have not been integrated, or have been integrated under highly disadvantageous conditions, into the institutions of society, but are not located in what will be termed 'regionally based internal colonies' or of allegedly 'inferior' social or cultural origins.
>
> (ibid.: 276)

Last but not least, Portes and Walton (1981: 103) do not adhere to the notion of a totally excluded marginal mass, preferring to speak of 'casual wage labor, disguised wage labor, and self–employment in petty production and trade'.

Influenced by the discussion on marginality, Quijano's position with regards to the relationship between marginality, the relative surplus population, and the industrial reserve army began to shift. Initially, Quijano (1977a: 120) argued that the industrial reserve army and marginal labour were two distinct concepts and he viewed the concepts of relative surplus labour and reserve army as interchangeable. In contrast with the reserve army, marginal labour arises out of the dependency relationship. He argues that even though the present surplus population in Latin America has many similarities with the industrial reserve army of labour,

> the present surplus population as a labour force can no longer be just considered as another 'industrial reserve army', and is fund-amentally a 'marginalized' labour force. This phenomenon is one of the outcomes of the dependent character of the labour market which is part of the dependent character of the economy as a whole.
>
> (Quijano, 1977b: 223)

Later (1974: 427–8), he argues that strictly speaking the concepts of relative surplus labour and reserve army should be distinguished. While the relative surplus population is a general category which can refer to various modes of production, the industrial reserve army is the specific manifestation of the former under the capitalist mode of production (Quijano, 1977a: 271) – a distinction previously made by Nun. This allows Quijano to maintain the distinction between marginal labour and reserve army, while at the same time claiming that his concept of marginal labour can be incorporated within the theory of relative surplus population (Quijano, 1974: 428; 1977a: 271). By drawing on this difference, Quijano (1974: 416; 1977a: 272–3) takes issue with Fernando H. Cardoso's criticism that the concept of marginalized labour is excessive as it is already subsumed under the concept of industrial reserve army.

Quijano's changing position can be gleaned from his important introduction to his collected essays on marginality (1977a). In my view his position has shifted to the extent of largely replacing marginality by reserve army. Like Nun, Quijano originally argued that marginality is a different concept to industrial reserve army as the former referred to that part of the relative surplus population which was never going to be absorbed by capitalist enterprises, even during an economic upswing. He now claims that 'the term "marginality"...far from being an alternative concept to that of "industrial reserve army" is probably a new dimension of it, related to a new modality of existence of the industrial reserve army' (ibid.: 19). He then examines the various modalities of relative surplus population which Marx distinguishes. There are three constant forms (floating, latent, and intermittent) and those which dwell in the sphere of pauperism – the lumpenproletariat, which includes vagabonds, criminals, prostitutes, and so on – and the paupers, the orphans, the ragged, those unable to work, and so on. Quijano then focuses on a paragraph by Marx in which the latter predicts that the development of capitalism increases the relative mass of the industrial reserve army, with the consequence that 'the greater this reserve army in proportion to the active labour–army, the greater is the mass of consolidated surplus population' (Quijano, 1977a: 21).[19]

Nun, who had quoted the same paragraph of Marx, concluded that 'it is precisely for thinking through the specific problems which follow from the consolidation of a non–functional sector of the surplus population that I introduced the concept of *marginal mass*' (Nun,

1972: 110). Nun justifies the introduction of his concept because Marx was not a witness to the new monopolistic phase of capitalism and because in dependent countries the importance of the 'classical' effects of the surplus population are weakened, i.e. the non–functional part of the surplus population is more prevalent in dependent countries. Quijano follows a similar line of reasoning and thinks that Marx did not incorporate the 'consolidated' modality of the relative surplus population within the categories which he enumerates as it only existed as a potential at that time. Thus, Quijano (1977a: 21–2) provisionally concludes 'that "marginality" is a new modality, although foreseen, of the present existence of the relative surplus population...and which Marx called "consolidated"'.

Finally, Quijano (ibid.: 22) allows that, despite attempts by him and others to rescue the concept of marginality for the theory of social classes, the term marginality lends itself to misinterpretation, as the phenomena it describes, far from being 'marginal' to capitalism, are a necessary and fundamental part of its present–day dynamics and existence.

One could conclude from the above that the terms marginal mass or marginal labour should be abandoned and replaced by 'marginal industrial reserve army' or by 'consolidated relative surplus population'. However, one of the already enumerated categories of Marx's relative surplus population would provide a better alternative. In examining this alternative I draw upon Middleton's illuminating clarification of a translation error in the Spanish edition of Marx's *Capital* which was used by Quijano. [20]

As mentioned Marx distinguishes three constant forms of the relative surplus population: the floating, the latent, and the stagnant. The latter was inaccurately translated as intermittent in the Spanish edition of *Capital* (Middleton, 1980: 10). The floating surplus population are those workers who are expelled and re–absorbed by industry in accordance with the economic cycle. In short, they are now laid off and now employed by capital whenever required: they are readily available. [21] The latent form arises out of the penetration of capitalism into agriculture which threatens to or makes redundant the labourers employed in pre–capitalist agriculture. As the majority fails to find employment in the countryside it is ripe for migrating to the urban areas when the opportunity arises. While the population of the first two categories are unemployed or underemployed, those who belong to the stagnant category are part of the active labour army (as opposed to the reserve army), but with extremely irregular employment (Marx, 1976: 794–6). Marx characterizes the stagnant relative surplus population as follows:

> Its conditions of life sink below the average normal level of the working class...It is characterized by a minimum of wages...It is constantly recruited from *workers in large–scale industry and agriculture who have become redundant*, and especially from those decaying branches of industry where handicraft is giving way to manufacture, and manufacture to machinery. Its extent grows in proportion as, with the growth in the extent and energy of accumulation, the creation of a surplus population also advances. But it forms at the same time *a self–reproducing and self–perpetuating element of the working class, taking a proportionally greater part in the general increase of that class than other elements.*
>
> (Marx, 1976: 796; my emphases)

I agree with Middleton that Quijano's 'marginalized labour force' corresponds to the stagnant relative surplus population. I would go even further and propose that it also overlaps to a significant extent with Quijano's 'marginal pole' of the economy. The last sentence in the above quotation from Marx, together with Marx's analysis of domestic industry, lead me to make this proposition. Middleton (1980: 11) thinks that the translation error, together with a certain ambiguity in Marx, account for Quijano's failure to make the connection, but this is to speculate and I am no closer to solving this puzzle – which also applies to Nun.[22]

In exploring the similarities between Marx's analysis of domestic industry and Quijano's marginal pole of the economy, I will turn to the section of *Capital* in which Marx (1976: 590–2) studies the impact of the factory system on manufacture and domestic industry. He explains how with the spread of the factory system, old–fashioned domestic industry is transformed. The domestic industries might be located in the worker's private home or in small workshops.

> This modern 'domestic industry' has nothing except the name in common with old–fashioned domestic industry, the existence of which presupposes independent urban handicrafts, independent peasant farming and, above all, a dwelling–house for the worker and his family. That kind of industry has now been converted into

an external department of the factory, the manufacturing workshop, or the warehouse. Besides the factory worker, the workers engaged in manufacture, and the handicraftsmen...capital also sets another army in motion, by means of invisible thread: the outworkers in the domestic industries, who live in the large towns as well as being scattered over the countryside.

(ibid.: 590–1)

And he continues later on:

In the so–called domestic industries this exploitation [of cheap and immature labour–power such as the employment of women and children under poor and unsafe working conditions or environment, exposed to over–work and night–work, and receiving miserable wages] is still more shameless than in modern manufacture, because the workers' power of resistance declines with their dispersal,...because a domestic industry has always to compete either with the factory system, or with manufacturing...; because employment becomes more and more irregular; and, finally, because in these *last places of refuge for the masses made 'redundant' by large–scale industry and agriculture*, competition for work necessarily attains its maximum.

(ibid.: 591; my emphasis)

These extensive quotations from Marx suggest that Quijano's marginal pole of the economy has very similar characteristics to Marx's modern domestic industry.

Role of marginals in the process of capital accumulation

The second central discussion concerns the marginals' contribution to capital accumulation. The CEBRAP school has been influential in arguing that this contribution is far greater than suggested by the *marginalistas*. They also put greater emphasis on analysing the social relations of production of the marginal sector which they characterize as being largely non–capitalist but functional for capitalist accumulation. Finally, they stress that marginality theory exaggerates monopoly capital's inability to stimulate employment opportunities.

Many critics who examine the social relations of production of the marginal population consider that most marginals are labouring under pre–capitalist social relations (Kowarick, 1974; Oliveira, 1985).

However, these relations are held to be closely articulated to capitalist relations of production, forming one system where the logic of capital predominates (Kowarick, 1975; 61, 83). The development of capitalism thus not only destroys pre–capitalist relations but also reproduces and creates these relations. As expressed succintly by Oliveira (1973: 437), the main proponent of this argument: 'The expansion of capitalism in Brazil happened by introducing new relations in the archaic and reproducing archaic relations in the new.'

Quijano and Nun have been criticized for remaining within a dualist position as they divide the surplus population into those which are functional, and thus part of the industrial reserve army, and those which are non–functional and part of the marginal population (F. Cardoso, 1972a, 190; P. Singer, 1973; and Torranzo, 1977: 17). In particular, Quijano's marginal pole can be interpreted as implying that this is separate from and essentially independent from the central pole of the economy. Although this might not have been Quijano's intention, the term marginal pole is not a felicitous choice. Whereas marginal mass, labour, population, or occupations leave some ambiguity on this point, pole seems to be definitive in emphasizing a separate and special identity and organization.[23]

The key thesis to emerge from these critics is that pre–capitalist relations are subordinated to capitalist relations (both forming a totality) and that the pre–capitalist sector makes a significant contribution to the capital accumulation of the capitalist sector. Thus, the emphasis is on combined and uneven forms of development in Third World social formations. So–called 'marginal' workers and activities are far from being considered a dead weight on the economy as *marginalistas* tend to hold (Kowarick, 1978: 31, 52).[24]

The contribution of marginal workers to capital accumulation can take various forms.[25] First, by providing ample and continuous supplies of labour to the industrial sector, marginal workers exert a downward pressure on wage levels despite the rapid increases in labour productivity and the substantial rise in employment in industry. Much of this labour comes from rural out–migration. Oliveira, while endorsing the above, gives priority to politics as repressive labour policies are the key factor in maintaining low wages with regards to the Brazilian case. This 'immense' industrial reserve army, together with the coercive power of the authoritarian state, helped to create a 'super–economic surplus' which sustained the 'super–accumulation' of capital, particularly during the years of the so–called Brazilian miracle – mid–1960s to early 1970s. (The terms in quotation marks are taken from Oliveira, 1985.) Oliveira's analysis can be generalized to other countries which have or are pursuing repressive labour policies.

Second, the marginal peasant sector, whose tiny farms or mini-fundia largely operate under non–capitalist relations of production, provides a cheap food surplus to the urban sector. Food prices are low because the cost of reproduction of the subsistence peasantry is so low. Long hours of work by unpaid family labour lead to this 'self-exploitation' of peasant labour (Deere and de Janvry, 1979).

Third, a similar subsistence economy exists in the urban sector which provides goods and services at low prices to urban workers. Given the similarity of this subsistence urban economy to the peasant minifundia, Campanario and Richter (1974: 67) refer to it as the 'urban minifundia'. Both the rural and urban subsistence economy help to maintain the price of the urban labour force at low levels as the cost of subsistence goods and services which workers purchase from them remain cheap.

Fourth, and linked to third form just described, those marginal workers engaged in certain service activities such as retail trading, repairs, and so on, contribute to the realization of surplus value of the capitalist enterprises by selling to, or servicing products for, cons-umers. These marginals may own small shops but Oliveira (1973: 443) considers them as pseudo–owners as the capitalists use them to externalize the servicing and repair part of their industrial production. They can be considered, in my view, as a form of 'out–worker' or 'proletariat in disguise', even though they are not directly employed by the capitalists.

Fifth, the marginal petty producers also provide goods and services directly to the capitalist sector at a price below their value, thereby transferring an economic surplus in the form of surplus labour to them. An illustration of the last three forms of exploitation based on a detailed empirical study of *favelas* in Brazil is given in the following quotation:

> The cheap labour that the favelados provide in services, crafts, and inputs to the competitive sector serves to lower reproduction costs of all economic sectors, either directly or indirectly. For example, by doing repair work as part of their odd–jobbing, and by charging substantially less than the 'institutionally certified' electrician or plumber, favelados directly lower the living costs of those outside the favela as well as within it. By providing cheap inputs to certain

stages of the manufacturing or assembly activities of the competitive capitalist sector – by making buttons or sewing upholstery at home, for example – favelados reduce reproduction costs indirectly as well.

(Perlman, 1976: 258–9)

Sixth, marginal workers contribute to capital accumulation by transferring surplus value through the sale of labour at prices below the costs of reproduction of the labour force. The reduction of wages below the value of labour power transforms the labourer's necessary consumption fund into a fund for the accumulation of capital (Cockcroft, 1983: 92). This is possible due to the unpaid domestic work of women and children, and to the 'subsidy' provided by the rural and urban non–capitalist subsistence economy through the sale of commodities below their value to the marginal workers employed by the capitalist sector (de Janvry and Garramón, 1977). In their struggle for survival, marginal workers not only accept very low wages for long hours of work but are also willing to perform jobs which others reject due to health and safety hazards, and so on.

Finally, surplus value is extracted from the marginal sector because this sector pays a price for goods and services from the capitalist sector which is far above the value embodied in those commodities. This exploitation of marginals as consumers helps the reproduction of the capitalist sector. Given their weak bargaining and purchasing power, marginals paradoxically pay high prices for commodities which are of low quality and for which there are few buyers. Perlman (1976: 259) again provides a useful example: '[Favelados] will buy secondhand clothes and furniture, stale bread, or imperfect manufactured products, and they will use the services of outdated professionals, or trainees.'[26]

In fairness Quijano and Nun (and associates) do identify some contribution by the marginal sector to capital accumulation. However, Nun in particular regards its contribution to capital accumulation as insignificant or uncommon. Nevertheless, Murmis, in a most perceptive article, succinctly analyses the various forms of exploitation of marginal labour and reflects that:

The possibility is left open that an analysis which adequately defines the forms of motion of dependent capitalism or of capitalism in dependent areas, will find that these non–classical forms of insertion fulfil a constitutive function in the system. Their conceptualization as 'marginals' thereby loses legitimacy as these sectors turn out to be central in the process of exploitation and accumulation.

(Murmis, 1969: 416)

In overlooking this article by Murmis, an associate of Nun, the critics have overplayed their hand. Some of the differences between Nun, Quijano, and their critics lie in empirical evidence which leaves the door open to a variety of interpretations, as country experiences differ. Kowarick (1979: 83.) represents an extreme position when he argues that the marginal sectors 'emerge as one of the pivots on which the economy turns'. This statement turns marginality on its head.

A further aspect of the debate deals with monopoly capital's ability to stimulate employment and the role of the service sector in economic growth. The thesis that the process of capital–intensive industrialization displaces labour and is one of the main sources of marginality is questioned by some critics. Empirical data from Brazil, for example, show that the industrial sector created more jobs than the agricultural sector between 1950 and 1970. Although employment grew far less in the industrial than the service sector, a significant proportion of service jobs were stimulated by industrialization (Faria (1976), quoted in Roberts, 1978: 165–6). [27] Portes and Walton (1981: 98) make a similar point when they criticize Nun for arguing that the absorption of labour by the industrial sector is slow. As Nun fails to explore the linkages between what some authors now call the formal and informal economy, he underestimates the impact of industrialization on employment. Portes and Walton show how, in their effort to reduce wage costs, many manufacturing industries subcontract part of their activities to the informal sector, thereby indirectly employing labour on a piece–rate or similar basis.

In turn Oliveira argues that the service sector is far from being unproductive as argued by many *marginalistas* but performs important economic activities required by both capitalist enterprises and consumers. The marginal sector is considered to be closely articulated to the capitalist sector, as illustrated by the following rhetorical question:

What volume of the sales of certain industrial products...such as razor blades, combs, cleaning materials, cutting instruments and other small objects, is retailed by street vendors...? What is the relation between the rising number of cars in circulation and hand–operated car washes? Is the increasing volume of car production incompatible with the multiplying of small workshops devoted to vehicle repair?

(Oliveira, 1973: 435, as quoted in Kowarick, 1979: 83)

Such a reinterpretation of the marginal sector and, in particular, of the service sector has led to a questioning of the commonly held view that many Third World economies suffer from premature tertiarization and hyper–urbanization. F. H. Cardoso (1968: 91), for example, speaks of an 'overburdened tertiary sector', Córdova (1973: 88) of 'the deforming hypertrophy of the tertiary sector', Castells (1974: 71) of 'an urban population which exceeds the productive level of the system', and others of a 'metropolitan macrocefalia' (Schteingart, 1973: 100). Critics like Paul Singer (1973), Pradilla (1984: 651), and Portes and Walton (1981: 82) consider that such notions are misleading, as the myriad of activities performed by the 'marginal' sector (many of which are located within the service sector of the main cities) are closely linked to the formal capitalist economy, as discussed earlier. Furthermore, to characterize the process of industrialization and urbanization of Third World countries as deviant, or as some sort of abnormality, in contrast with that of the advanced industrial countries is to misinterpret the peculiarities of Third World social formations.

This is a critique which applies to many Latin American development theorists, who consider industrialization and the growth of the industrial labour force as constituting development, while 'premature tertiarization' reflects undesirable expulsion of workers from rural primary production and their absorption into the urban labour market (the underemployed, the marginals, and so on) so that the service sector is seen as 'surplus labour'. This reflects the industrialization bias underpinning most theories of development and marginality whereby it is assumed that incorporating the majority of the labour force into a rapidly expanding industrial sector is the norm. It could be argued, however, that such a process is unique to those countries which became industrialized in the nineteenth and early twentieth centuries, when industrial technology was still fairly labour–intensive. Given advances in technology since then, the pattern of development will differ as even some of the most highly industrialized countries are shedding labour from the industrial to the service sector.

Dependency and marginality

The third issue of controversy centres on the relationship between dependency and marginality. Touraine (1977) concurs with Nun and Quijano in arguing that marginality is a characteristic of dependent societies and a sign of its disarticulation. Despite some critical remarks he finds their analysis far more satisfactory than the culturalist–, modernization–, and DESAL–type explanations of marginality. However, Paul Singer (1973) criticizes the rosy picture which Quijano (and Nun as well) paint of the autonomous national industrialization which is said to have taken place before the 1950s in Latin America. He argues that, on the one hand, the unequal patterns of capitalist development were already established before the international industrial monopolies penetrated into the Latin American countries and, on the other hand, that the process of marginalization would have happened in any case, although perhaps to a lesser extent and degree. Marginality depends as much on internal as external factors. In many Latin American countries the hegemonic sector is controlled by state as well as foreign capital and both can create new activities for the competitive sector. He concludes that:

> Although there are significant causal relations between dependence and marginality, these relations can be better studied and analyzed at a more concrete level, in which dependence ceases to be the principal source of social determination so as to become one of many factors which influence development, urbanization and marginality in societies like the Latin American.
>
> (P. Singer, 1973: 312)

The above statement reflects the CEBRAP perspective in which greater emphasis is given to the internal dynamism of dependent countries. In this view Third World countries are credited with a greater capacity to shape their economic, social, and political structures as compared with dependency theory (see Chapters 5 and 6). Accordingly, marginality is seen as arising mainly from the internal contradictions of capitalist development in Latin America rather than from external forces and dependency. However, these critiques are only partly justified, as both Nun and Quijano imply that monopoly rather than dependent capital is the primary causal factor of marginality, but they contribute to this ambiguity by not spelling this out clearly.

MARGINALITY: MYTH OR REALITY?

Marginalistas have been criticized for constructing an ideological concept or theory:

> Marginality theory, then, can be criticized not only as a false statement about the nature of a social group but also as a myth in the full sense of the word – a manner of telling the history of humanity in such a way as to serve the interests of a particular class. The material force of the myth of marginality is to allow the perpetuation of favelados and squatters in general.
>
> (Perlman, 1976: 261–2)

The modernization– and DESAL–type theory of marginality is regarded by radical critics as a pseudo–scientific ideology of reformism. For Pradilla (1984: 705), the concept of marginality is a component of dualist ideologies which cover up the existence of real class relations. While he denies the existence of marginality, he acknowledges the myth (which needs to be destroyed) and the reality of the most exploited and oppressed segments of society (who need to be liberated). It can be concluded from the detailed critiques of the psychological, culturalist, modernization, and DESAL marginality theories that the accumulated evidence is overwhelmingly in favour of abandoning these versions of marginality theory.

Yet others extended their reservations to include the neo–Marxist views as expounded by Nun and Quijano. According to Esteva (1983), the marginality school emerged as a consequence of the greater social and political visibility of new social groups which were becoming a problem for the dominant groups. The ethnocentric ideological discourse of *marginalistas* is held to negate and marginalize the economic, social, and political dynamics of these emergent and vast groups (Esteva, 1983: 744). Esteva criticizes the term marginality for being a residual category which characterizes a large section of the population as 'un–employed, in–efficient, and under–developed' (ibid.: 733) and for the moralizing and accusatory tone adopted by many *marginalistas* to depict the misery and unemployment which capitalism creates.

A more directly aimed critique is provided by Carlos Johnson (1979: 85), who argues that Quijano's and Nun's analyses are ideological because:

> the active labour army is taken as a given, the ideal norm against which the marginals are measured; marginality is perceived as

something negative, dysfunctional, an obstruction to development and economic and sociopolitical participation; ...unlike the industrial reserve army, marginals are considered to be unnecessary for capital production directly; ...marginality is thought to be something new to capitalism, specifically to the stage of the monopolistic phase of capitalism and to deformed capitalism.

In other words the *marginalistas* are ideological because they characterize marginality as being pathological or deviant, the norm being given by the advanced capitalist countries. While Nun's and Quijano's marginality position can hardly be criticized for constructing a myth, it is more open to the charge of containing ideological elements.

Be that as it may, what cannot be denied is that the terms marginality, marginal mass, marginal labour, and marginal pole are misleading. Following the CEBRAP critics, the main weakness of marginality analysis is its tendency to underestimate the significance of the 'marginals' for the reproduction of the capitalist system. Many critics have pointed out how this 'underclass', 'sub–proletariat', 'immiserated fraction of the working class', or 'informal labour' are far from being at the margin of the national and international system of capital accumulation. However, there is still a need to develop a conceptual framework and terminology to refer to such an important reality. This the more recent discussion on the formal and informal sectors has attempted to do. Despite the influence of the marginality school on the formal–informal analysis, it is surprising to find that few writers have explicitly explored this relationship in any detail. [28]

Three positions can be distinguished with regard to the analysis of the informal sector. The pioneering formulation of the formal–informal sector conceptualization sustains a dualist and reformist position which has many similarities with the DESAL marginality analysis (for example, International Labour Office, 1972; Hart, 1973; Sethuraman, 1981). It views the informal sector as potentially complementary to, and supportive of, the formal sector and should therefore be encouraged through positive government policies. At the other extreme is the approach taken by neo–Marxists who emphasize the close articulation between the formal and informal sectors, the exploitative nature of this relationship, and prefer to use Marxist categories such as petty commodity production when referring to the informal sector (for example, LeBrun and Gerry, 1975; Bienefeld and Godfrey, 1978; Breman, 1985). In between these two positions is the view which maintains that the relationships between the formal and informal sector are neither benign nor exploitative but are of 'heterogeneous subordination' (for example, PREALC, 1978; Tokman, 1978a). This is the Latin American variant of the informal sector analysis which grows out of a mixture of ECLA's structuralism and Nun–Quijano–type marginality analysis. These three variants can be labelled the 'ILO/Geneva', the 'neo–Marxist', and the 'PREALC/structuralist' perspectives respectively. [29]

What is significant in the context of this chapter is that at least two of the three above mentioned approaches to the informal sector have, been influenced by the Latin American marginality school.

CONCLUSIONS

The authors working within the modernization paradigm have had the distinction of putting the analysis of marginality on the agenda. However, it soon became apparent that their theoretical analysis had fundamental flaws which were largely derived from their dualist position, their culturalist emphasis, and their lack of, or inadequate, class analysis. These fundamental flaws became apparent with the failure to resolve the problem of marginality by reformist governments in Latin America. They were also exposed by those social scientists who rooted their analysis in historical materialism and argued that marginality is due to particular forms of articulation between different relations of production within a social formation and its integration into the capitalist world system. Furthermore, marginality arises during a certain historical period in the process of capital accumulation and is intensified in Latin America by the dependent nature of its industrialization process. In turn the Marxist discussion on marginality gave special emphasis to the various mechanisms of exploitation of the marginal population and stressed their significance for the process of accumulation and reproduction of the capitalist system.

The marginality debate is far from being closed as many issues remain unresolved which can only be clarified by further theoretical analysis and empirical research. I would argue that the concept of marginality should be subsumed within the Marxist theory of relative surplus population. In my view Marx's specific categories of stagnant and pauperized relative surplus population provide a useful starting–point for characterizing the phenomenon of marginalization. Furthermore, the marginal pole or sector of the economy is best discussed within the Marxist analysis on modern domestic industry, petty commodity production, and articulation of different forms of production. The marginal mass or marginal labour, like the relative surplus population, originates from the expulsion of labour from agriculture and large–scale industry, and from those decaying branches of petty production and competitive capital which cannot compete with monopoly capital. Similar factors generate the surplus labour which finds refuge in Marx's modern domestic industry and in Quijano's marginal pole. As for the future development of the stagnant relative surplus population and the domestic industry, Marx envisaged their increase in absolute as well as in relative terms, as do Nun and Quijano regarding the marginal population.

Nevertheless, Marxist categories can only be regarded as a first step for further theoretical development of the analysis on marginality, as even the general concepts of relative surplus population, industrial reserve army, and articulation of forms or modes of production were not fully developed by Marx himself. Also, some of the phenomena analysed by Nun and Quijano were not explored by Marx, nor could they be, as they refer to aspects in the later stages of the development of capitalism which Marx did not and probably could not have foreseen. Thus, the contribution of other schools of thought should be considered as well, especially those linked with the analyses on the formal and informal sectors of the economy.

In conclusion, the analysis of marginality undoubtedly opened up a useful debate on an important issue for Third World countries and for the world economy as a whole, as Third World labour can be considered as the industrial reserve army for global capital (Quijano, 1977a: 120). Despite the theoretical and empirical shortcomings of the Latin American marginality school, its merit has been to draw attention to the plight of a vast and heterogeneous mass of impoverished Third World labour and to stimulate detailed research on how the poor make a living and cope with their poverty. It has also pointed to a gap in social theory which had so far failed dismally to analyse and theorize on a major world issue. However, it is necessary to go beyond marginality theory, for

Only when both the working poor and left–wing organizers recognize the role of the immiserated not merely as a reserve army of labor, but as an activated arm of capital accumulation productive of surplus value or its realization can the burgeoning mass movement of the immiserated be linked to the fundamental dynamic of class struggle: capitalist owners versus urban and rural proletarians. Both theoretical reconceptualization and recognition of the new reality – expansion of ostensibly noncapitalist forms of economic activity for the purposes of resolving economic crisis or defraying falling profit rates, of reproducing the labour force, and of capital accumulation – can help integrate the present social movements of the poor with the main class struggle which ultimately will determine the future of all proletarians.

(Cockcroft, 1983: 105)

5

Reformist and Marxist approaches to dependency

INTRODUCTION

The dependency writers, or *dependentistas*, more than any other group caught the imagination of students, teachers, politicians, and even the public throughout Latin America during the late 1960s and early 1970s. One of the reasons for this impact is that 'intellectuals in Latin America are important because they are the voices of those who cannot speak for themselves' (F. H. Cardoso, quoted in Kahl, 1976: 179). The political influence of the *dependentistas* was such that some were driven into exile when military governments seized power in their home countries. [1]

The advantage of hindsight should make it easier to distinguish and assess the key contributions of the various dependency positions and critiques. In particular, this chapter seeks to redress one imbalance in the English–speaking world regarding 'the consumption of dependency theory': the almost exclusive focus on the writings of André Gunder Frank, whose work, being written in English, was more accessible than the literature in Spanish or Portuguese. [2] A key dependency text – the book by Cardoso and Faletto – which first circulated in a mimeographed version in 1967, and then in published form in 1969, did not appear in English until 1979. [3] Other key writings on dependency still await translation.

A number of factors account for the widespread appeal of the dependency approach throughout Latin America. [4] Dependency analysis appealed to nationalist sentiment which partly blamed foreign capital for the state of underdevelopment and more specifically for the shortcomings of Latin America's industrialization. [5] The *dependentistas*' call for a greater degree of national control over the development process and the investment of foreign capital, and their offer of a way out of the misery of underdevelopment through reform or revolution also struck a sympathetic chord with many. Furthermore, dependency analysis captivated many intellectuals because it offered the possibility of making an autochthonous contribution to the social sciences by challenging both Marxist and non–Marxist orthodox theories.

Theoretically and politically, dependency analysis appealed to a broad church, as its formulations tend to be general and at times vague, allowing writers and students from different perspectives to espouse it. Many participants in the dependency debate have made the point that studies of dependency cannot yet be considered to constitute a theory as no coherent or generally accepted set of propositions has emerged from them. Instead, they characterize these studies as an approach, a vision, framework, perspective, paradigm, and so on. Some *dependentistas* consider the attempt to construct a 'theory of dependent capitalism' as futile as 'it seems senseless to search for "laws of movement" specific to situations that *are dependent*, that is, that have their main features determined by the phases and trend of expansion of capitalism on a world scale' (Cardoso and Faletto, 1979: xxiii). Instead, they suggest that existent theories of capitalism should be enlarged and made more specific so as to include the dependent countries' laws of development.

To present the main ideas of the dependency approach for the study of underdeveloped countries is a complex task owing to the vast quantity of literature produced on the topic (hundreds of articles and many dozens of books in Latin America alone), and to the fact that in the course of the debate authors have often revised their original propositions and arguments. Surveying the dependency literature is like being confronted with a Tower of Babel. Any attempt to give a fair account is fraught with difficulties as one is forced to be selective with respect to both issues and authors.

REFORMIST AND MARXIST *DEPENDENTISTAS*

Although some propositions are shared, many important differences remain between dependency writers. Two positions can be differentiated: reformist and Marxist. [6] As with any classificatory schema some degree of arbitrariness and simplification is involved. The following aspects distinguish the Marxist from the reformist view on dependence. First, the most obvious difference is that their analyses are rooted in divergent theoretical frameworks: Marxist in one case and a modified version of modernization–cum–developmentalist theory in the other. Second, the Marxist *dependentistas* are less guarded in their critique of conventional economic theory and the modernization paradigm than the reformist authors. Furthermore, not only are they more critical of ECLA's *desarrollista* or 'developmentalist' position, but they also criticize the reformist *dependentistas* for over–emphasizing the external causes of dependency (indicated by the reformists' use of the term 'external dependence') and for being unable to overcome a dualist position (Frank, 1977: 356). Third, there are political differences. The Marxist dependency writers argue that the failure of import–substituting industrialization and the increasing dependence of most Latin American countries indicate the non–progressive nature of the local bourgeoisie and the inability of the nationalist–populist alliance to achieve genuine development. As the local bourgeoisie tends to turn towards authoritarian solutions to deal with the crisis of the populist alliance, it becomes even clearer that the political choice facing these countries is either fascism or socialism. They thus reject as unviable the reformists' political alternative of a new populist alliance which seeks to reform the international economic system. For the Marxists only a socialist revolution can resolve the problems of dependence and underdevelopment. This, however, is seen as utopian by reformist *dependentistas*.

Among the main reformist dependency writers are: Fernando Henrique Cardoso and Enzo Faletto (1979), Osvaldo Sunkel (1969), Celso Furtado (1971), Helio Jaguaribe (1969), Aldo Ferrer (1975), and Aníbal Pinto (1972; 1973). Their ideas are best seen as a further development of the ECLA structuralist school as they attempt to reformulate ECLA's developmentalist position in the light of the crisis of import–substituting industrialization. Most writers within this current were, or still are, closely associated with ECLA or its sister organization ILPES. As well as being referred to as structuralists (O'Brien, 1975: 11) they can also be seen as nationalists (Evers and von Wogau, 1973: 422), as they seek to increase the degree of national autonomy over the internal development process. They are reformist because they maintain that it is possible to resolve the problem of dependence by reforming the capitalist system. Munck (1984: 10) labels them the conservative wing of the dependency approach, as compared with the radical wing represented by the Marxist camp.

Within the Marxist dependency camp are the writings of Ruy Mauro Marini (1965; 1972), Theotonio Dos Santos (1971; 1973), André Gunder Frank (1970; 1975), Oscar Braun (1973; 1984), Vania

Bambirra (1972), Aníbal Quijano (1971), Edelberto Torres–Rivas (1969; 1970), Tomás Amadeo Vasconi (1972; Vasconi and García, 1972), Alonso Aguilar (1973; 1974), and Antonio García (1972). They use a Marxist framework for the analysis of dependence and argue that only a socialist revolution can overcome dependence. However, they are not orthodox Marxists and are best considered as neo–Marxists as they query the progressive role of capitalism in dependent countries.[7]

These two dependency positions have mutually influenced each other, although this has largely gone unacknowledged. The Marxist wing, in particular, has tended to distance itself from the 'bourgeois reformism' of ECLA, failing to recognize its debt to the pioneering framework provided by structuralism. Indeed, the ECLA school, together with the theory of imperialism, is one of the forerunners of the dependency school.

In addition to the two approaches it is possible to distinguish a 'Caribbean dependency school'. While individual members hold either reformist or radical positions, these ideological differences never crystallized into reformist and Marxist wings as in the Latin American school and it was thus a far more coherent school. It was also a more tightly knit group, for which the University of the West Indies provided an institutional base. Given the more recent colonial history of the Caribbean countries and the high reliance on foreign trade and investment, it is hardly surprising to find that dependency analysis appealed to many Caribbean intellectuals. The specific features and historical background of the Caribbean countries, such as being small islands and plantation economies, sharing a history of African slavery and a British colonial past, meant that the Caribbean *dependentistas* developed their own novel brand of dependency writings (Cumper, 1974; Oxaal, 1975; Pantin, 1980; Blomström and Hettne, 1984: Chapter 5). [8]

Returning to the Latin American school, the few formal definitions of dependency given by both sides are surprisingly similar. Compare, for example, Sunkel's (for the reformist approach) with Dos Santos's classical definition (for the Marxist approach): both emphasize interdependence and the absence of autonomous or self–sustained capacity for growth in dependent countries.

Development and underdevelopment can therefore be understood as partial structures, but interdependent, which form a single system. A principal characteristic which differentiates both structures is that the developed one, to a large extent by virtue of its endogenous capacity of growth, is the dominant, and the underdeveloped, due in part to the induced character of its dynamic, is dependent.

(Sunkel, 1972a: 17)

Dependence is a *conditioning situation* in which the economies of one group of countries are conditioned by the development and expansion of others. A relationship of interdependence between two or more economies or between such economies and the world trading system becomes a dependent relationship when some countries can expand through self–impulsion while others, being in a dependent position, can only expand as a reflection of the expansion of the dominant countries, which may have positive or negative effects on their immediate development. In either case, the basic situation of dependence causes these countries to be both backward and exploited.

(Dos Santos, 1973: 76)

Both dependency positions also share the view that underdevelopment, or the pattern of development of dependent countries, is the particular form capitalist development assumes in these countries. They also agree that dependency originated when these countries were forcefully incorporated into the world capitalist system by the dominant countries, and concur that, in order to understand the internal dynamics of the Third World countries, it is necessary to examine their relationships to the world capitalist system. Thus, underdevelopment is in their view not an historical stage through which the present developed countries passed. As Sunkel (1972b: 520) puts it for the reformists: 'Development and underdevelopment... are simultaneous processes: the two faces of the historical evolution of capitalism.' Likewise, Frank (1966a: 18), for the Marxists:

The now developed countries were never *under*developed, though they may have been *un*developed...Contemporary underdevelopment is in large part the historical product of past and continuing economic and other relations between the satellite underdeveloped and the now developed metropolitan countries.

THE REFORMIST APPROACH TO DEPENDENCY

The failure of the inward–directed development strategy to achieve national economic autonomy, as discussed in Chapter 2, led to a reformulation of ECLA's analysis by the reformist *dependentistas*. In what follows the principal ideas of Sunkel, Furtado, and Fernando H. Cardoso – who have been singled out as representatives of the reformist structuralist position within dependency – will be presented.

Sunkel and national disintegration

Sunkel opens his analysis by criticizing Latin America's import–substituting industrialization process for its inability to reduce external dependence. On the contrary, external dependence increased for a variety of reasons. First, the vulnerability to fluctuations in foreign exchange increased. As Latin American countries failed to diversify their exports and continued to rely on the export of one or more primary products, foreign exchange earnings continued to fluctuate and did not grow fast enough to pay for essential consumer goods (food) or crucial capital goods, spare parts, and raw materials required by the industrialization process. Second, foreign exchange earnings became increasingly insufficient to sustain the development process. As a consequence countries greatly increased their foreign debt which made them financially dependent on their creditors. The deteriorating balance of trade was partly due to agriculture's failure to generate sufficient exports or internal food supplies, resulting in increased food imports. Furthermore, a large proportion of the industrial sector was foreign–owned, putting an additional strain on the availability of scarce foreign exchange as profits were repatriated and payments made for royalties, technical services, and so on transferred abroad (Sunkel, 1967b: 51–5).

This diagnosis bears some similarity to the Marxist position but there is a major difference over how this state of affairs can be overcome. Sunkel (1967b: 59–66) proposes a strategy of development which expands and diversifies exports, reforms the traditional agrarian structure, and redirects the industrialization process by developing a capital–goods sector and producing for exports. Sunkel initially (ibid.: 67–9) hoped that this could be achieved by national governments entering into joint venture agreements with multinational corporations.

He was optimistic about the possibility of implementing a 'national development policy' as proposed above, but pessimistic about the possibility of a radical socialist revolution taking place in Latin America (ibid.: 55). Such a national policy, however, does not imply breaking away from the world capitalist system but reforming it. Although aware of some of the difficulties, he nevertheless concluded that 'the changes in the international situation seem to have created sufficiently flexible and tolerant conditions so as to permit the application of national development policies' (ibid.: 75).

In the early 1970s Sunkel began to shift his position as his dream of joint ventures with transnational capital turned into a nightmare, with the transnational conglomerates emerging as the *bête noire*. His analysis now focused on the way in which transnational capitalism creates a new international division of labour leading to national disintegration in Latin America. As transnational conglomerates began to take over the commanding heights of the economy, particularly in the industrial sector, Sunkel saw them as driving a wedge into national society. While a minority of the country's population is integrated into the transnational system and receives some of the spoils, this is at the cost of national disintegration. Each social group is fragmented, with a larger proportion of capitalists as compared with the middle class, and in turn a larger proportion of the latter as compared with the working class, being incorporated into this system (Sunkel, 1972b: 80–5). As Sunkel puts it: 'This process of transnational integration tends to reinforce the process of cultural, political, social and economic underdevelopment in the peripheral countries, deepening even further their dependence and their internal disintegration' (ibid.: 78).

Thus, Sunkel holds that the nation state is in crisis in Latin America: at the level of production by the domination of transnational corporations; at the level of technology by the penetration of capital–intensive techniques; at the cultural and ideological level by the absorption of conspicuous consumption patterns; and at the level of development policies and strategies 'by the pressure of national and international interests in favour of an industrialization process aimed basically at providing consumer goods for the high–income groups' (Sunkel, 1972a: 528).

While Sunkel initially pinned great hopes on the entrepreneurial or Schumpeterian elements within the national bourgeoisie and in the middle classes, he later lamented their desertion into the hands of transnational capital: 'A significant part of the national bourgeoisie is being transformed into a private transnational technocracy, losing legitimacy as part of a national ruling class' (ibid.: 527). Sunkel agreed with Furtado that: 'The elimination of the national entrepreneurial class necessarily excludes the possibility of self–sustained national development, along the lines of the classical capitalist development' (Furtado, 1968, cited in Sunkel, 1972a: 527). Sunkel (1972a: 531), however, continued to believe at this point that development without dependence and without marginalization can be achieved by reforming the asymmetrical nature of the international capitalist system through hard bargaining and pragmatic negotiations. Thus, his position remains reformist although his optimism has become guarded.

By the late 1970s a new realism had crept into Sunkel's writings. He now argues that economic growth implies structural change and that this is a dialectical process which is full of conflict and takes place through confrontation. He criticizes the modernization paradigm for putting all 'the emphasis on the positive and ex–post aspects of capitalist development, treating its end products – high living standards, relative reduction in social inequality, urban–industrial life styles, political democracy – as the means of development' (Sunkel, 1977: 11). Following Schumpeter he argues that capitalist development is a process of creative destruction and that:

> Under present day conditions of the world–wide expansion of a highly innovative and capital intensive oligopoly capitalism, the destructive effects of the development are still more severe in the peripheral countries than they were in the central capitalist countries.
>
> (ibid.: 11)

Furtado and dependent patterns of consumption

For Furtado the imposition or transplantation of consumption patterns from centre to periphery is the key factor which explains the perpetuation of underdevelopment and dependence in the periphery. 'The ability of certain countries to control technical progress and to impose consumption patterns became the decisive factor in the structuring of the productive apparatus of other countries, which in consequence became "dependent".' (Furtado, 1973: 120.) Furthermore, a vicious circle of growth is operating in some peripheral countries, as the higher the rate of growth, the more intensive dependence becomes. As Furtado (1974b: 17) puts it:

Underdevelopment is rooted in a specific connection, created in a particular historical setting, between the internal process of exploitation and the external process of dependence. The more intense the inflow of new patterns of consumption, the more concentrated income tends to become. Thus if external dependence increases, the internal rate of exploitation has also to go up. Higher rates of economic growth tend to imply aggravation of both external dependence and internal exploitation. Therefore, higher rates of growth, far from reducing underdevelopment, tend to make it more acute, as it entails increasing social inequalities.

Furtado argues that in order to keep the industrialization process alive, particularly after the exhaustion of the easy phase of import–substitution, a continuous new stream of consumer goods has to be produced. However, this is only possible in larger peripheral countries such as Brazil or Argentina and where the political system is able to repress discontent arising from the resulting inequalities in income distribution (Furtado, 1973: 121). The implication of the above is that the smaller underdeveloped countries can transcend the easy phase of import substitution if they manage to export industrial commodities, a possibility which is not examined by Furtado.

This increasingly diversified consumption pattern geared towards the high–income groups structures an equally diversified industrial consumer–goods production pattern. The technology for producing these products comes from the centre countries and largely from multinationals. This capital–intensive technology perpetuates further the tendency towards income concentration and the structural surplus of labour (Furtado, 1972: 323). It is unlikely that the increases in productivity will be fully transferred (if indeed at all) to labour via increases in wages owing to the existence of a large surplus labour force. Furtado, however, omits to explain fully the need for permanent repression in order to keep the dynamics of dependent industrialization.

Furtado's notion of 'external dependence' is indeed very much an external relation as his analysis implies that economic growth in peripheral countries depends on changes in the centre. Furthermore, peripheral capitalism is seen as imitative as it copies the consumption pattern of the centre countries. This, in turn, determines the composition of output, the technology used, the allocation of resources and, finally, the distribution of income. The multinationals are seen by Furtado as the engine of growth and as the instrument which further tightens the links of dependence as they provide the new products and associated technology.

It would appear from the above that foreign firms will increasingly control the productive apparatus of the dependent countries. However, Furtado (1974b: 12) admits that this is not a necessary outcome, as the state bureaucracy or a strong local bourgeoisie could maintain a dominant position over, or share control of, production.

Cardoso and associated–dependent development

The Brazilian sociologist (and politician) Fernando Henrique Cardoso is one of the key contributors to the dependency vision. Together with Enzo Faletto he wrote one of the first major books on dependency in Latin America, a book which has since become a classic. Over the years he has also written numerous papers on the subject, some of which are critical of the writings of other dependency–analysis colleagues. Here I will focus on his key ideas on dependency, leaving his critical, and often polemical, contributions to the dependency debate for the next chapter.

Like many other writers on dependency, Cardoso's analysis of dependence arose out of an attempt to explain why many of ECLA's and the modernization theorists' predictions for Latin America did not materialize. The 1964 military coup in Brazil, which drove him into exile, marked a turning–point in Latin America as it showed that industrialization and the expansion of the middle classes did not necessarily lead to political democratization and self–sustained growth. ECLA had failed to realize the extent to which foreign firms would take over the local industrial sector, the problems import–substituting industrialization might face, and, above all, the political problems it might generate. Although an implicit political theory which rested on the premisses of modernization theory underpinned ECLA's analysis, there was no explicit social and political theory. ECLA's writings omitted class analysis and a theory of the state. Thus, the emergence of authoritarian states was an alternative which had not been foreseen or contemplated. The dependency writings emerged partly in response to this failure of vision.

In their pioneering book, Cardoso and Faletto analyse the changing relationship between internal and external factors which have determined the development process in Latin America from the early 'outward expansion' of newly independent nations to the present period of internationalization of the market and the 'new dependence'. During the period of 'outward expansion' two types of dependence are distinguished: those Latin American countries where the production system was under the national control of local enterprises; and those countries in which foreigners controlled the export sector, which they characterize as enclave economies. In the first case the accumulation of capital originates internally while in the latter it comes initially from abroad. The implications of this in terms of class formation, class alliances, and the political process and their impact on economic growth, employment, income distribution, and so on are explored. The emergent prominence and political role of the middle classes from the beginning of this century occupy their special attention.

The crisis of the 1930s inaugurated a period of consolidation of the domestic market. Cardoso and Faletto go on to examine the social and political forces arising from this crisis and, in particular, the nationalism and populism which characterize the first decades of this period. During the inward–oriented development phase after the Second World War, a third type of dependency is seen as emerging, based on the dynamism of multinationals. The domestic market becomes internationalized, setting the stage for 'the new nature of dependence' which another *dependentista*, Dos Santos, simply calls 'the new dependence'.

By grafting ECLA's historical periodization of 'outward– and inner–directed economic development' on to different types of dependency situations, Cardoso and Faletto intermarry ECLA's economic structuralism with dependency analysis. Their economic analysis remains very much within the ECLA mould but they add a social and political analysis. This ECLA influence is hardly surprising as they wrote the book when they were both employed by ILPES, an organization which originated from ECLA and is still closely associated with it. Their originality lies in the way in which they analyse the changing relationships between economic, social, and political forces during key conjunctures in post–colonial Latin America, and the manner in which they relate the changing internal relationships to external forces, i.e. their attempt to throw light on the question of how internal developments link to external changes and how the world system impinges upon different Latin American countries.

This interaction between internal and external elements forms the core of Cardoso and Faletto's characterization of dependence. They seek to explore diversity within unity of the various historical processes, contrary to Frank's search for unity within diversity. Dependence is not regarded simply as an external variable as they do not derive the internal national socio–political situation mechanically from external domination (Cardoso and Faletto, 1979: 173). Although the limits for manœuvre are largely set by the world system, the particular internal configuration of a country determines the specific response to the same external events. Thus, for example, the world economic crisis of 1929 provoked different political responses which were the outcome of local class struggles in each country (Kahl, 1976: 136, 162). Thus, they do not see dependency and imperialism as external and internal sides of a single coin, with the internal reduced to a reflection of the external. They conceive the relationship between internal and external forces as forming a complex whole by exploring the interconnections between these two levels and the ways in which they are interwoven (Cardoso and Faletto, 1979: xv–xvi).

Cardoso and Faletto's approach to dependence is best summarized in their own words:

> The concept of dependence tries to give meaning to a series of events and situations that occur together, and to make empirical situations understandable in terms of the way internal and external structural components are linked. In this approach, the external is also expressed as a particular type of relation between social groups and classes within the underdeveloped nations. For this reason it is worth focusing the analysis of dependence on its internal manifestations.
>
> (ibid.: 15)

The above approach can best be illustrated by Cardoso and Faletto's analysis of the 'new dependency' and particularly by Cardoso's original formulation of 'associated–dependent development'. With regards to the 'new dependence', they argue that during the early and easy phase of import–substituting industrialization a 'developmentalist alliance' emerged in various Latin American countries. This alliance took a variety of forms but generally involved the industrial bourgeoisie, the middle sectors, and the industrial proletariat. In a few countries this alliance was reinforced by a 'developmentalist state'. A national, populist, and developmentalist ideology emerged out of this conflicting alliance which favoured an industrialization strategy geared towards the national market. Their analysis of the crisis of the import–substitution industrialization process is similar to ECLA's as presented in Chapter 2. When the easy industrialization phase becomes exhausted the 'developmentalist alliance' breaks down as it can no longer deliver the goods. The structural limits of import–substituting industrialization are exposed by the crisis. During the easy phase foreign investment started to shift from the primary to the industrial sector, thereby opening the domestic market to foreign control.

The continuation of the industrialization process and its extension to the intermediate– and capital–goods industries required increasing capital accumulation, access to the centre's technology, increased foreign exchange, and the co–operation of the transnational corporations. These requirements meant that government policy had to shift radically from the welfarist and redistributist policies of the populist phase towards containing popular demands, compressing wages, and other measures which furthered income concentration and gave appropriate guarantees to foreign capital. In many Latin American countries the introduction of this package of policies led to the breakdown of democratic governments and the emergence of authoritarian–corporatist regimes in which a militarized techno–bureaucracy occupied a central position. Under this new regime social exclusion is enhanced and marginality accentuated (ibid.: 149–71).

However, in some cases authoritarian regimes managed to break out of the cul–de–sac which import–substituting industrialization had run into, and to overcome the problem of stagnation. The authoritarian–bureaucratic state, by restructuring the political system and redefining the links of dependence, was able to deal with the crisis (albeit temporarily). Thus, Cardoso does not adhere to the early stagnationist position initially adopted by Furtado and still retained by Frank.

In contrast to some other dependency writers, Fernando H. Cardoso does not regard dependency as being contradictory to development and to indicate this he coins the term 'associated–dependent development'. He (1972b: 94) therefore rejects Frank's idea that when the links of dependence are intensified, growth falters, and when they are loosened, domestic growth is enhanced. Cardoso has the Brazilian case very much in mind where a decade of spectacularly high rates of industrial growth followed the military coup of 1964. A new alliance was formed by the state between the multinationals, the state enterprises, and the local big bourgeoisie replacing the old populist democratic alliance. This new alliance was built around the articulation of politico–economic interests which Cardoso labels 'bureaucratic rings'. The relations between the state and civil society are weakened as in this new political system, party organizations independent of the state are discouraged (if not suppressed) and the dominant class limits the political mobilization of subordinate classes as much as possible (F. Cardoso, 1977b: 63). The cliques belonging to the bureaucratic rings become the key power brokers in the system which facilitated the new stage of highly enhanced capital accumulation. Thus, in Brazil, development has occurred – albeit of a dependent kind (F. Cardoso 1972b: 89).

While Cardoso highlights the dynamism of the associated–dependent development model he also recognizes its high social costs such as increased poverty, repression, and marginalization. Although the bureaucratic authoritarian state has ensured the viability of capitalist development, it has done so by strengthening the links of dependence and by separating the nation or civil society from the state. As the local bourgeoisie is unable to create an autonomous capitalist path of development, it marries itself even more firmly to transnational capital in this new stage. The local bourgeoisie have thus come to embody the anti–nation by controlling a state which excludes most of civil society from participation and which represents the interests of foreign capital. 'The contradiction of a state that constitutes a nation without being sovereign is the nucleus of the subject matter of dependency.' (Cardoso and Faletto, 1979: 200.) Such a state of affairs is dictated by internal forces as much as by external ones.

Despite Cardoso and Faletto's emphasis on political and social factors, economic factors are pre–eminent in the end. Given the periphery's lack of a capital–goods sector, in order to complete its cycle of capital accumulation it has to link itself to the centre's capitalism. Thus, the key to the periphery's dependence, despite major industrialization since the Second World War, is its failure to develop its own technology, forcing it to rely on the centre's multinational corporations (ibid.: xx–xxi).

However, Cardoso and Faletto (1979: xv) do not mechanically derive the major historical phases of dependent societies from the 'logic of capital accumulation', as for them 'the history of capital accumulation is the history of class struggles, of political movements, of the affirmation of ideologies, and of the establishment of forms of domination and reactions against them' (ibid.: xviii). Their analysis of the multinationals lacks the economism of Sunkel and Furtado, among others, as they place them within the political context of both the centre and peripheral countries and avoid subordinating the political to the '"logic of accumulation of multinational corporations" and therefore to "external factors"' (ibid.: 186). This leads them to argue that, as some centre countries have lost political power in the international sphere, the possibility arises for some peripheral countries to pursue marginally autonomist policies, despite the increasing economic power of transnational corporations (ibid.: 185). While there is room for some form of associated capitalist development the possibility of a transition to socialism is, in their view, remote in Latin America. The only hope for socialism is by forging 'alliances between popular movements, national–popular demands, and properly working–class struggles' (ibid.: 213). In their view a strictly proletarian route to socialism is unviable within the present–day conditions of dependency.

THE MARXIST *DEPENDENTISTAS*

The most consistent effort to develop a 'Marxist theory of dependency' (Bambirra, 1973: 7) was undertaken by a group of social scientists working in the Centre of Socio–Economic Studies (CESO) of the University of Chile in Santiago under the leadership of Theotonio Dos Santos. [9] Although the group shared certain theoretical premises and objectives, different views and political positions existed among them. While no coherent and single theory was forthcoming, they produced many theoretical insights and empirical studies, which will be examined in this chapter.

The goal of developing a Marxist theory of dependency arose out of a realization that Marx never fully tackled the colonial question, being concerned with developing a theory of accumulation and development for the then most advanced capitalist countries. Furthermore, Luxemburg, Hilferding, Bukharin, Lenin, Trotsky, and other Marxists who had worked on the question of imperialism hardly touched on the development problems of the colonial countries.

For this reason we consider the approaches of the authors of the theory of imperialism to be limited. Lenin, Bukharin, Rosa Luxemburg,...have not approached the theme of imperialism from the standpoint of the dependent countries. Although dependency has to be situated within the global framework of the theory of imperialism, it has its own reality which constitutes a specific legality within the global process and which acts upon it in a specific manner. To understand dependency, conceptualizing and studying its mechanism and historical legality, implies not only widening the theory of imperialism but also contributing to its reformulation.

(Dos Santos, cited in Caputo and Pizarro, 1970: 237–8)

Marxist theories of imperialism

The classical Marxist theories of imperialism emerged during the first two decades of this century to account for changes in the development of capitalism, above all the rise of monopoly capital. While Rudolf Hilferding and Nicolai Bukharin can be considered to have made the main contribution to the Marxist theory of imperialism, Lenin was its main popularizer. The Latin American *dependentistas* were more familiar with the writings of Lenin and perhaps Luxemburg than with those of Bukharin and Hilferding. I will next briefly point out certain elements of this theory of imperialism which are likely to have been of relevance to the Marxist *dependentistas*; but first a clarification:

It is easy to misunderstand the classical Marxist theories of imperialism, since the very word 'imperialism' has expanded and altered its meaning since then. Today, the term imperialism is generally taken to refer to the dominance of more developed over less developed countries. For the classical Marxists it meant, primarily, rivalry between advanced capitalist countries, rivalry expressed in conflict over territory, taking political and military as well as economic forms, and tending, ultimately, to inter–imperialist war.

(Brewer, 1980: 79–80)

Luxemburg (1963) argued that capitalism in the advanced industrial countries faced a problem of capital realization, which meant that to reproduce itself it needed to find markets for the commodities it produced. These were initially found within the non–capitalist sector of the advanced capitalist country, but as these gradually disappeared, they were later found in the non–capitalist areas of the world largely located within the Third World. The advanced capitalist countries also needed to trade with the Third World so as to obtain access to cheap labour power and raw materials. Thus, capital accumulation in Luxemburg's view is impossible without the existence of non–capitalist modes of production. However, as capitalism enters into contact with non–capitalist areas it progressively transforms them into capitalist areas. This process reaches its limit, and the capitalist mode of production enters into crisis, when no non–capitalist forms of production are left. The merit of her analysis is to have drawn attention to the continuing existence of processes of primitive capital accumulation which rely on force and the power of the state, and to the continuing domination of capitalist over pre–capitalist forms of production, all of which assist the accumulation of capital (Brewer, 1980: 76).

Hilferding (1981) emphasizes the formation of joint stock companies and how this accelerates the concentration and centralization of capital. As small capitalists are driven out, the economy falls increasingly under the control of cartels or monopolies. In this process, financial, industrial, and commercial capital become bound together forming what Hilferding calls finance (as distinct from financial) capital, which he saw as dominated by banks. 'Since monopolies cannot yet control the world market, they need the protection of tariffs and they then seek to extend their protected markets to the maximum possible extent, hence the support of finance capital for expansionist policies.' (Brewer, 1980: 100.) Hilferding also stressed the export of capital from the developed to the underdeveloped countries in search of profitable investment opportunities by taking advantage of low wages and land rents. Another reason for the export of capital is the drive to overcome the tariff barriers erected by some countries and to take advantage of them. As will be seen later on, *dependentistas* found this aspect of Hilferding's analysis particularly relevant for their study of the changing pattern of foreign investment in Latin America. However, contrary to the Marxist *dependentistas*, Hilferding stresses the progressive character of foreign capital although aware that this might lead to economic and political dependence, thereby anticipating some of the arguments of the *dependentistas*.

> Characteristically, however, he turns away from these issues to discuss the way in which small countries become the battlefield for the struggles of the major powers, and hence gets back to the subject of the advanced countries, his main interest.
>
> (ibid.: 95)

The key contribution of Bukharin (1973) is his focus on the growing international interdependence of the world economy and its division into national units, as well as on the international division of labour. Thus, a twin process of internationalization and nationalization of capital takes place.

Just as every individual enterprise is part of the 'national' economy, so every one of these 'national economies' is included in the system of world economy. This is why the struggle between 'national economic bodies' must be regarded first of all as the struggle of the various competing parts of world economy...Thus the problem of studying imperialism, its economic characteristics, and its future, reduces itself to the problem of analysing the tendencies in the development of world economy, and of the probable changes in its inner structure.

(Bukharin, 1972: 17–18)

'The exchange of goods between countries, international trade, is simply a version of the social division of labour essentially the same as the exchange of goods between different enterprises. It establishes *social relations of production on a world scale.*' (Brewer, 1980: 103.)

It follows that world capitalism, the world system of production, assumes in our times the following aspect: a few consolidated, organised economic bodies ('the great civilised powers') on the one hand, and a periphery of underdeveloped countries with a semi agrarian or agrarian system on the other.

(Bukharin, 1972: 74)

For Lenin imperialism is dominated by finance capital and expresses the monopoly and highest stage of capitalism. His analysis was influenced by the reformist economist John Hobson (1961) as well as by Hilferding and Bukharin. It is therefore not surprising that his ideas are similar. He considers the export of capital from the capital–rich advanced countries as the economic basis of imperialism. This export of capital is driven by inter–imperialist rivalry to gain control of, and secure access to, raw materials as well as to reap the benefits of high profits arising from investments in the capital–poor countries. 'In these backward countries profits are usually high, for capital is scarce, the price of land is relatively low, wages are low, raw materials are cheap.' (Lenin, 1969: 73.) Lenin also viewed the world as divided between great rival empires.

Within these, two tendencies operated; on the one hand, the export of capital led to the internationalization of capitalist production and the extension of capitalist relations of production to the furthest corners of the world, while on the other hand, power was

concentrated into the hands of great blocs of finance capital and
wealth channelled to parasitic rentier classes.

(Brewer, 1980: 117)

The purpose of this brief review of the Marxist theories of
imperialism is to provide a background to the ideas of the Marxist
dependentistas as these theories influenced their writings.

Despite having pointed out the shortcomings of the Marxist theories
of imperialism, Dos Santos argued that dependency analysis has to be
inserted within a reformulated theory of imperialism. In his view it
was only after the Second World War with the national liberation
movements that Marxists turned their interest to the Third World.
Orthodox Marxists had not attempted to uncover the laws of
development of the underdeveloped countries as they had not
questioned Marx's proposition that these countries would sooner or
later follow the same path as the advanced industrial capitalist countries and that the laws of capitalist development were valid for all
capitalist countries, i.e. developed and underdeveloped. As Marx put
it: 'The country which is more developed industrially only shows to
the less developed the image of its own future.' (Marx, 1976: 91.) [10]

While the classical Marxist theory of imperialism addressed the
new stages and aspects of capitalism, it was mainly concerned with
the imperialist countries (revealing a certain Eurocentrism) and had
little to say on the underdeveloped countries, a gap which the Marxist
dependentistas hoped to begin to fill. Furthermore, they are critical of
the classical theories' progressive view of capitalism and of foreign
capital in Third World countries. For these reasons the Marxist
dependentistas can be referred to as neo–Marxists.

Despite these critical remarks the Marxist *dependentistas* consider
the classical Marxist theory of imperialism to be a useful starting point
for their analysis of dependency as they share its world–economy
perspective, its view on the centrality of monopoly capital within the
world capitalist system, and its emphasis on the international division
of labour and unequal development in international economic relations
(Caputo and Pizarro, 1970: 238).

For the dependency writers the key theoretical problem is how to
explain the different development process of the underdeveloped
countries. A group of Russian revolutionaries, known as the populists,
were the first to confront the problem of applying Marx's theory of
capitalism to a different historical situation, i.e. that of Russia during
the late nineteenth century. They were encouraged in their efforts by

Marx himself, and the Marxist *dependentistas* have drawn inspiration from this precedent (Dos Santos, 1978: 340–2). Thus, Marini does not view himself as a revisionist but as an orthodox Marxist. He considers those Marxists who are unable to recognize the peculiarities of capitalism in Latin America (i.e. its dependent nature) as distorting Marx's methodology and theory by not applying it in the creative spirit in which it was intended. He accuses the dogmatic Marxists of merely transplanting Marx's propositions to a different reality without screening them first for their suitability (Marini, 1973: 13–16). Thus, labelling authors as orthodox Marxists, neo–Marxists, and so on might be a convenient shorthand expression but it is as problematical as any other form of classification.

Paul Baran has exercised a major influence on the Marxist dependency writers, as they adopted his thesis that underdevelopment is rooted in the capitalist development of the imperialist countries and that underdevelopment and development are the common results of a world–wide process of capital accumulation (Baran, 1973: Chapter 5; Sutcliffe, 1973: 99). Baran's analysis of the transfer of economic surplus from the backward to the advanced countries, of its wasteful use in both, and of the negative effects of foreign capital in the Third World also struck a sympathetic cord with *dependentistas*. From his analysis of the 'morphology of backwardness', Baran derived the view that capitalism is no longer a progressive force in the stage of imperialism and monopoly capitalism, and that the so–called national bourgeoisies of the underdeveloped countries are unable to uproot underdevelopment so as to overcome poverty, stagnation, and backwardness (Baran, 1952). As will be seen these ideas are key propositions of the Marxist dependency view and had a major influence on Frank in particular.

Marini and super–exploitation

Amongst the Marxist dependency writers Marini has made the most systematic theoretical effort to determine the specific laws which govern the dependent economies. Unfortunately his analysis is extremely succint and not always easy to follow, particularly when he employs Marxist categories which are problematic.[11] Although Marini is, in my view, the most outstanding Marxist *dependentista* he is almost completely unknown in the English–speaking world.

For Marini dependence means that one group of formally independent nations is subordinate to another group of countries in such a way that the relations of production of the subordinate nations are modified and recreated so as to secure the extended reproduction of dependence. Thus, the dependency relationship is continually being reproduced and can only be overcome by eliminating the relations of production which they engendered (Marini, 1973: 18). Marini's central thesis is that the basis of dependence involves the over–exploitation or super–exploitation of labour in the subordinate nations. By over–exploitation of labour he means that labour power is remunerated below its value (ibid.: 42, 92–3). This means that workers are underpaid as the value of labour power is the amount of goods and services (or money) required to replenish the worker's labour power.[12]

Given the importance of over–exploitation in Marini's schema, it is necessary to examine it more closely. According to Marini over–exploitation can take three forms: an extension of the working day, a reduction of the worker's wage below what is considered to be the socially acceptable subsistence level, and an increase in the intensity of work. The first two forms represent an increase in absolute surplus value, while the third is an increase in relative surplus value.[13] Thus, over–exploitation is not identical to absolute surplus value (ibid.: 92), but for Marini the important fact is that all three forms constitute a mode of production which is based exclusively on a greater exploitation of the worker and not on the development of its productive capacity through technological progress (ibid.: 38–40).

This over–exploitation of labour in the periphery arises out of the need of capitalists to recover part of the fall in profit rates as a consequence of unequal exchange. Unequal exchange means that the periphery's profit rate falls and the centre's rises as value is transferred from the former to the latter. Thus, over–exploitation helps to compensate for unequal exchange.[14]

In turn this over–exploitation of labour hinders the transition from absolute to relative surplus value as the dominant form in capital–labour relations and the accumulation process in the periphery, thereby underpinning their dependence (ibid.: 100). According to Marini, Latin American economies contributed decisively to the centre's capital accumulation by exporting increasing quantities of primary products to them from the mid–nineteenth century. This export of cheap food (wage goods) from the underdeveloped world helped to reduce the value of labour power in the developed countries and through unequal exchange they transferred part of their surplus value to them. In this way the primary producing and exporting countries enabled the industrial countries to shift their axis of accumulation from the production of absolute surplus value to relative surplus value, thereby blocking their own transition (ibid.: 16–23).

The origins of dependent capitalism are to be found for Marini in the fall of the centre's profit rate during its industrialization. This propels them to reduce the value of labour power (i.e. the necessary labour time) by importing cheaper food from the periphery and thereby increasing the worker's surplus labour time, the surplus value, and the profit rate.

According to Marini the circuit of capital in dependent countries differs from that of centre countries. In dependent countries the two key elements of the capital cycle – the production and circulation of commodities – are separated as a result of the periphery being linked to the centre through the over–exploitation of labour. Production in the Third World countries does not rely on internal capacity for consumption but depends on exports to the developed countries. Wages are kept low in the dependent countries because the workers' consumption is not required for the realization of commodities. Thus, the conditions are set for the over–exploitation of labour so long as a sufficiently large surplus population exists.

In the dominant countries, meanwhile, the two phases of the circulation of capital are completed internally. Once industrial capital has established itself in the advanced countries, capital accumulation depends fundamentally on increases in labour's relative surplus value through technical progress. The resulting increase in labour productivity allows capitalists to afford wage increases without a fall in their profit rate. This rise in the workers' income fuels the demand for industrial goods and so the cycle continues (ibid.: 49–55).

Industrialization does not fundamentally alter the model of capital accumulation in Latin America, which continues to rely on the over–exploitation of labour. This is because the import–substituting industrialization process is geared towards satisfying upper–income groups' demand for industrial consumer goods, particularly of a luxury kind. As the realization of capital does not depend on workers' consumption, the industrial bourgeoisie is not compelled to introduce technical progress to reduce the value of labour and increase surplus value as happens in the developed countries. In other words, industrial production does not require the creation of an internal mass market and industry's profit rate depends on the over–exploitation of labour and low wages.[15]

Under conditions of over–exploitation of labour, technical progress brings problems of realization which in the first instance are resolved by a further redistribution of income from lower to middle and higher income groups through state policies and inflationary measures. However, this process has its limits and the industrial sector then starts to expand into the export market. Thus, as from the mid–1960s, some Latin American countries, particularly Brazil, Argentina, and Mexico, joined the process of formation of a new international division of labour. This means that certain branches or processes of industrial production for the world market are transferred or relocated from developed countries to new sites in the Third World (Fröbel *et al.*, 1980). However, this redistribution of industrial production on a world scale and the related policy of export–oriented industrialization in some less–developed countries has continued the over–exploitation of labour (Marini, 1973: 66–7; Frank, 1981a).

Marini's sub–imperialism thesis

The Brazilian military *coup d'état* in 1964 brought to the fore a new type of state formation and political economy. This new state has been characterized by O'Donnell as bureaucratic authoritarian.[16] The background to these new forms of military intervention arose out of the need to resolve the crisis of the inward–directed development model. In order to overcome industrial stagnation it was necessary to increase the intensity of capital accumulation as well as to open up new markets. The increasing demands for higher wages and the growing strength of the working class jeopardized the requirement for a higher rate of capital accumulation. As populist governments were unable to contain the growing working–class pressures on the system, the dominant class called for repressive measures which only a military government could deliver (Marini, 1969: 111–16).

Marini argues that in Brazil this new political economy took the form of sub–imperialism – a form which can only be reached at the stage of monopoly and finance capital in big dependent countries (Marini, 1971: 1). Sub–imperialism attempts to resolve the market problem, arising from the insufficiency of the internal market through the following three policy measures: first, the promotion of industrial exports; second, the further concentration of income; and third, to increase the state's demand for consumer durables and capital goods by expanding, *inter alia*, the arms industry, the state and military personnel, and the country's infrastructure (ibid.: 1–11).

It is the economy's need to conquer export markets which gives it the sub–imperialist strain. It is sub–imperialist rather than imperialist because Brazil does not possess a technological base of its own and is not in a position to dispute the dominant countries' control over the world market. Consequently the Brazilian bourgeoisie enters into a partnership with international imperialism whereby foreign capital is provided with the internal conditions for expanding investment and profits in Brazil in return for access to advanced technology and the world market controlled by the monopolies of the developed countries (Marini, 1969: 115).

The purpose of deepening the regressive income distribution is to develop a *sui generis* 'consumer society' based on what in a Brazilian context are luxury goods as modern industry and technological developments in the developed countries are geared towards the production of these commodities. Marini calls this type of economy absurd and monstrous, but logical, as it does not require a popular mass market for its realization. It is absurd and monstrous because the workers, who produce the mass of surplus value, have almost no access to the market, while the bourgeoisie and middle class, who produce no surplus value, consume and/or accumulate it. Thus, the class divisions in this type of society are particularly profound, making it prone to military intervention and repression (Marini, 1971: 6).

The strengthening of the country's military apparatus is irrational in the sense that increasing quantities of the economic surplus are absorbed for unproductive purposes. However, it serves to stimulate internal demand and enhance the state's internal repressive power as well as setting the basis for external expansion (Marini, 1969: 116).

It can be seen that in Marini's schema sub–imperialism and the over–exploitation of labour are closely linked. Indeed, the whole edifice of sub–imperialism rests upon the over–exploitation of labour which is required to compete in the international market, to attract foreign capital, and to secure the deepening income inequality (ibid.: 88–9; Marini, 1978a).

Bambirra's view on sub–imperialism

Vania Bambirra also views sub–imperialism as a way out for the large dependent countries to resolve the internal contradictions of their particular process of capital accumulation. These sub–imperialist tendencies

would consist of exploitation by a more developed dependent country of other less developed dependent countries, in search of control over a substantial part of their market; by means, not only of exports but, above all, of investment in the basic economic sectors – natural resources or industry – which would assume a certain political and military domination by the sub–imperialist country.

(Bambirra, 1973: 153)

Bambirra puts more stress than Marini on the political and military domination of the sub–imperialist power over other Latin American countries and also highlights its investment in those countries. Like the imperialist countries, the sub–imperialist also extracts a surplus from the dominated countries. Consequently she regards the dominated Latin American countries as being subjected to a double exploitation, i.e. by both imperialist and sub–imperialist countries (ibid.: 155). According to Dos Santos (1970: 112–3) this would increase the subjected country's rate of exploitation to almost intolerable levels. The logical conclusion of Bambirra's and Dos Santos's analysis on sub–imperialism is to argue, like Marini, that it leads to over–exploitation of labour in the subjugated countries, but they themselves do not use the term.

Dos Santos: socialism or fascism

Theotonio Dos Santos is one of the most prolific *dependentistas* and his ideas present some interesting differences to those of Marini and Frank. Any endeavour to extract his key arguments is made difficult by the fact that his analysis is not always consistent, and he tends to shift from the economic to the political level and vice versa before giving an adequate explanation at one of the levels of analysis.

Dos Santos has since reformulated his original definition of dependency cited earlier by giving greater emphasis to internal factors in the dependent countries than previously. Thus,

The dominant social formations are the irradiating focus of the cycles and thus their analysis precedes or conditions the analysis of those dependent social formations which have to accommodate themselves to these international cycles reacting positively or negatively according to their internal characteristics. Among these characteristics are their own economic cycles which as they derive from their internal laws of accumulation do not necessarily coincide with the international conjunctures.

(Dos Santos, 1978: 26)

For Dos Santos dependence is firmly rooted in economic factors of which technological dependence is the key.[17] However, Dos Santos's and Bambirra's analyses are unique in that they entertain the possibility that economic dependence may disappear if the political factors blocking this very real possibility are removed. Thus, they appear to argue that dependence is ultimately determined by political factors although they do not say so explicitly.

The cycles of the industrial sector within the dependent countries become less dependent on the cycles of international trade as they are increasingly conditioned by the internal laws of capital accumulation. These, in turn, are influenced by the particularities of the labour market and the socio–political context of the dependent countries. Nevertheless, the development of the industrial sector continues to depend on the performance of the export sector, which provides the foreign exchange required to import capital and intermediate goods as well as generating some demand for local industry (Dos Santos, 1978: 389). However, those dependent countries which have started to develop an industrial capital–goods sector have a more significant internally induced economic cycle – which follows from the cyclical oscillations of the internal accumulation process – in comparison with other dependent countries whose economic cycles are still largely induced by the cyclical fluctuations of the export sector (ibid.: 32–3). However, dependency increases as foreign capital increasingly takes control over industry. This process is either referred to as 'the denationalization of the industrial sector' as foreign capital buys out national capital and an increasing proportion of industry is owned by foreigners, or as 'the internationalization of capital' as the transnational corporations are leading this process (Dos Santos, 1970: 31; 1972: 21.)

Thus, Dos Santos (1970: 30) argues that while the import–substituting industrialization process boosted the internal economic cycle it did not transfer decision-making to inside the country as industry is controlled by foreign capital. He therefore criticizes ECLA's view that an inward–directed development strategy would lead to greater national control over the development process and lessen the reliance on foreign trade.

Dos Santos develops the issue of the capital–goods sector in a novel and controversial manner. For him dependence is internally contradictory, as while its objective necessity diminishes as the industrialization process advances into the intermediate– and capital–goods sectors, the economy acquires the technical capacity to be self–sufficient. 'So, the process of internationalization [of the national economies] has two faces: a dependent face (the present) and a liberating face (the future).' (Dos Santos, 1972: 21.) Consequently it is possible to overcome economic dependence:

> If the dependent economies can obtain a high degree of productive autonomy and develop an important sector I [of machines and industrialized raw materials], foreign capital would lose its capacity to determine the character of its development, it would turn into a purely artificial expression which would soon be destroyed, terminating the dependence relationship.
>
> (Dos Santos, 1978: 100)

In Dos Santos's view (1972, 23; 1978, 100), this process of expanding productive autonomy is very limited for the present. International capital would be negatively affected by the full and integrated industrialization of the dependent countries because the export of capital goods and industrialized raw materials are an essential component of the dominant countries' own exports. These reasons are, in my view, unconvincing as they do not distinguish between the interests of multinational corporations and those of governments in developed countries, and they fail to acknowledge the competition between multinationals as well as the rivalries between nation states. Dos Santos's analysis assumes a collective political conspiracy by all dominant countries and multinationals to prevent the development of a significant capital–goods sector in the dependent countries.

The above notwithstanding, Dos Santos and Bambirra are the only Marxist *dependentistas* to raise the possibility of an autonomous capitalist development in underdeveloped countries. They have also shifted the analysis of dependence from the economic to the political level:

> From the economic point of view, once heavy industry has been installed and a functioning sector I exists within the economy, the process of accumulation does not need to go through foreign countries for its realization. This alters qualitatively the model of dependent reproduction and, therefore, makes dependency on foreign machinery–capital potentially unnecessary for the maintenance of industrial activities. To the extent that this process takes place, the maintenance of dependence gradually ceases to be an imperative historical necessity of industrial functioning and comes to be a growing political problem.
>
> (Bambirra, 1973: 101)

According to Dos Santos foreign capital is able to prevent the development of a significant capital–goods sector because of its political control over the dependent countries. Within the dominant power block 'big monopoly capital' has achieved supremacy over the old agrarian and export interests as well as over national competitive industrial capital by controlling the most dynamic branches of industry, now the key sector of the economy. This big monopoly capital exercises a major influence over the political system through its domination over the state and the military as well as the mass media, the educational system, key pressure–groups, and so on. As big capital is largely foreign, the interests of foreign capital ultimately guide government policy. Furthermore, as the multinationals are also able to influence government policy in the centre countries they have an additional lever of power over the peripheral state (Dos Santos, 1972: 24, 75, 90–1, 112).

As seen from the above, the political is very much determined by economic factors. Similarly, Dos Santos's explanation for the emergence of authoritarian military regimes in Latin America rests on economic considerations, i.e. a strong state is required to carry out anti–popular measures in order to meet the demand for a high profit rate and a high rate of capital accumulation arising from the high capital–intensity of modern technology and the establishment of heavy industry (ibid.: 25, 111).

In his analysis of the process of dependent capital accumulation Dos Santos argues that dependent capitalism requires super–profits or extraordinary profits (i.e. an above average profit rate), as the surplus has to be shared between the dependent and the foreign bourgeoisies. Foreign capital is able to appropriate part of the super–profits because it has the monopoly over technology (Dos Santos, 1978: 383–4). In turn, super–profits require the over–exploitation of labour which keeps wages at a low level (Dos Santos, 1970: 67; 1978: 398). Dos Santos's use of the term over–exploitation is ambiguous and lacks the detail of Marini's analysis. In some places the term is used synonymously with low wages, poverty, and misery while in others it is used to refer to a high rate of exploitation of labour power arising from high labour productivity in the capital–intensive industrial sector and the low level of wages paid to labour. Dos Santos does not specify if labour is remunerated below its value but he does suggest that the high rate of exploitation is due to an increase in relative surplus value (Dos Santos, 1970: 64). It is important to remember that a high rate of exploitation is not necessarily the same as over–exploitation. For Dos Santos low wages are caused by labour market conditions (i.e. a large supply of labour and few employment opportunities) while for Marini they are derived partly from political conditions – a repressive state holding down real wages below subsistence.

Although Dos Santos acknowledges the introduction of new technologies, he holds that in the long run the domination of the dependent countries' industrial sector by foreign capital will lead to stagnation. This is due to the limited growth of the internal market as a result of low wage levels and to decapitalization as a result of the appropriation of part of the surplus by foreign capital and its transfer abroad (Dos Santos, 1972: 63; 1978: 387). Like Frank's 'development of underdevelopment' thesis, Dos Santos argues that the development of dependent capitalism reproduces backwardness, poverty, and marginality generating more dependence and more over–exploitation (Dos Santos, 1970: 67).

The development of a sizeable capital–goods industry in some underdeveloped countries requires an explanation and challenges Dos Santos's conspiracy and technological monopoly theses. In his later writings Dos Santos recognizes the emergence of a new export–directed phase in the industrialization of some underdeveloped countries but he fails to explore the implications of this for his dependency analysis. He sees industrial exports as the third stage in the history of foreign investment and as part of a new international division of labour but does not explore how this export–oriented development strategy could ameliorate the developing countries' foreign exchange constraint and give further impetus to the industrialization process, stimulating the development of the intermediate– and capital–goods industries through backward linkages (Dos Santos, 1978: 104).

The development of a major capital-goods sector in some developing countries poses a major challenge to Dos Santos and other *dependentistas*, as much of their analyses assumes the virtual impossibility of such an occurrence in dependent countries. It will be recalled that Dos Santos strongly criticized ECLA and other reformists for having harboured the illusion that the inward–directed development strategy would lead to the consolidation of a national and autonomous bourgeoisie. In particular, Dos Santos regards the local bourgeoisie's inability to develop an integrated industrial sector with a capital–goods sector as its core, as epitomizing the failure of capitalism in the dependent countries. He sees the proletariat as the vanguard in resolving this crisis and embarking on the transition to socialism: 'The struggle for national industrialization, oriented towards the full integration of the productive sectors and of a heavy industry, remains in the hands of the proletariat and of sectors of the petty bourgeoisie.' (ibid.: 100.)

According to Dos Santos the political options facing Latin America are largely determined by the requirements of the process of dependent capital accumulation and by the contradictions this engenders. The nationalist and populist alliance between the industrial bourgeoisie and the proletariat loses its legitimacy, particularly for the proletariat, owing to its inability to launch an autonomous and integrated development process which would raise the standard of living of the poor, improve the distribution of income, and reduce unemployment. It also loses the support of big capital because it is seen as unable to confront the proletariat and introduce the harsh measures seen as necessary for tackling the new problems of capitalist development in Third World countries.

Dos Santos, writing in the late 1960s, and from experience of the 1964 military coup in Brazil, predicted a long period of social radicalization and political confrontation arising from deepening class conflict, which either paves the way for further repression and fascism or for popular revolutionary governments and socialism. Intermediate solutions have been shown to be utopian and unable to cope with this contradictory reality (Dos Santos, 1970: 68). Bambirra also reached the same political conclusion, and writes dramatically:

> The contradictions generated by dependent development will tend to become more profoundly accentuated and increasingly require more radical answers which will certainly lead to more acute confrontations between the dominant and the dominated classes, between the more radical bourgeois alternative, neo–fascism, and the proletarian alternative, the socialist revolution.
>
> (Bambirra, 1973: 156–7)

Writing a decade later, when military governments had spread further and when various Latin American countries were reorientating their industrial sector towards the world market, Dos Santos saw no reason to change his political prognosis:

> The option continues to be the same...[as] the profound Latin American crisis cannot find a solution within capitalism. Either one advances in a revolutionary and decisive manner towards socialism and a path of development and progress for the vast masses in our

countries is opened, or one appeals to fascist barbarism, the only alternative able to secure the conditions of political survival for capital for some time so that it can continue its dependent development, based on the over–exploitation of the workers, the denationalization of our economies, the exclusion of vast sectors of the petty–bourgeoisie, the export adventure in detriment of the consumption of the national masses. Such type of 'economic development' can only be imposed on the basis of the most barbarous tyranny.

(Dos Santos, 1978: 471)

Frank: a reluctant dependentista[18]

Although the concept of dependence is best–known to an English–speaking audience through the work of Frank, he was not among the first to use the term dependence. [19] Indeed, Frank's main contribution to dependency analysis occurs before he actually uses the term dependence, but is found in his central idea of 'the development of underdevelopment'. His notion of underdevelopment, in particular, explicitly states that it is the capitalist development of the now developed countries which engendered the underdeveloped structures in today's Third World and which continues to reproduce them. Through this approach Frank was influential in challenging the modernization and developmental paradigms which had dominated social sciences in Latin America and beyond (Booth, 1975; Foster–Carter, 1976).

Thus, it was easy for Frank to substitute the term dependence for his notion of underdevelopment: indeed, these terms become virtually synonymous in his writings during his dependency phase. How then does he view dependence?:

The point of departure for any credible analysis of Latin American reality must be its fundamental determinant, which Latin Americans have come to recognize and now call *dependence*. This dependence is the result of the historical development and contemporary structure of world capitalism, to which Latin America is subordinated, and the economic, political, social, and cultural policies generated by the resulting class structure, especially by the class interests of the dominant bourgeoisie. It is important to understand, therefore, that throughout the historical process, dependence is not simply an 'external' relation between Latin

America and its world capitalist metropolis but equally an 'internal', indeed *integral*, condition of Latin American society itself.

(Frank, 1972b: 19–20.)

In my view many of the critiques of dependency analysis which single out Frank have been misdirected, as Frank is a reluctant and short–lived *dependentista*. As he himself acknowledges: 'In using the word "dependence" I only just attach myself – I hope temporarily – to the new fashion, already so widespread that it has become equally acceptable to the reformist bourgeoisies and to revolutionary marxists.' (Frank, 1970: 19–20.) Indeed, by 1972 he already pronounced dependence as dead, 'at least in the Latin America that gave it birth' (Frank, 1977: 357).

In retrospect Frank's writings can best be considered as belonging to the world–system perspective to which he, together with Samir Amin and Immanuel Wallerstein, has made such a vital contribution.[20] In his first book, which many consider to be his key dependency text, Frank (1967) already viewed Latin America's economic, social, and political structure as being externally determined by the imperialist centres. The Latin American countries were regarded as mere satellites of the all–powerful metropolis. Thus, it was a small step for Frank to embrace fully the world–system approach where the unit of analysis is no longer a country but the world economy, society, and polity. Lehmann (1986: 39) gives a succinct view of the world–system approach:

Theories of development in the style of Frank and Amin lead one to treat 'country' as a mere territorial unit defined by the power of a state apparatus which provides the instruments of exploitation and of the conservation of privilege. Domestic ruling classes are portrayed as mere appendages of an 'international' or 'imperialist' bourgeoisie who would have no existence but for their control of the state apparatuses. They have no dynamism, they have no autonomous capacity to accumulate; they merely live as guardians of the portals of the hinterland, and the share of the 'surplus' accruing to them is merely a type of rent received in recognition of their control of the instruments of power and of the services they perform as policemen, praetorian guards and so on...For Wallerstein, ultimately, the only way out of underdevelopment, which he freely admits to be utopian, would be 'world socialism'.

As can be seen, there are similarities between the dependence and the world–system approaches. Some of the critiques aimed at the dependency school (which are the subject of the next chapter) also apply to the world–system analysis.

Of course, Frank's work has been extremely influential all over the world but it would be a mistake to consider him as the dependency writer *par excellence*. His prolific and polemical writings helped to popularize the dependency vision, but at the same time the identification outside Latin America of dependency theory with the work of Frank has led to a one–dimensional view of it. Readers in the English–speaking world thereby failed to perceive the variety and richness of the Latin American dependency school. It is only possible to speculate on what the reception, diffusion, and critiques of dependency analysis would have been if the works of other dependency writers had been published in English earlier. [21]

Frank and the mode–of–production controversy: production vs. circulation

Another aspect of Frank's contribution to dependence is his mode–of–production analysis. The debate over the feudal or capitalist nature of Latin America acquired a new life with the publication of Frank's (1967) book on Latin America in which he boldly and assertively argues that Latin America has been capitalist since the European conquest in the sixteenth century. Frank's capitalist thesis was immediately challenged by many intellectuals (see Dos Santos, 1970: 139–50; Frank *et al.*, 1973; Garavaglia, 1973; Bartra, 1975; Foster–Carter, 1976; Brenner, 1977), the most influential being the critique of the Argentinian historian and political scientist Ernesto Laclau (1971). The ensuing debate bears similarities to the Marxist polemic on the transition from feudalism to capitalism in Western Europe which took place in the early 1950s, and whose main protagonists were Maurice Dobb and Paul Sweezy (Hilton *et al.*, 1976). In both controversies the key points of dispute centre on the relative significance of relations of production and circulation in the transition from feudalism to capitalism and over how to define the capitalist mode of production. While Dobb argued that the transition from feudalism to capitalism was essentially determined by changes in the relations of production within each country's mode of production, Sweezy sustained that external trade and exchange relations were the principal driving force or prime mover (Hilton *et al.*, 1976).

Similarly, Laclau castigates Frank for overemphasizing the importance of commercial relations while underestimating production relations (Laclau, 1971). Thus, these polemics can alternatively be called the Marxist mode of production, or the productionist *versus* circulationist controversies. (The relevance of the issues raised in these controversies for the dependency analysis are explored further in the next section and in Chapter 6.)

Frank's attack on those who sustained the feudalist thesis in Latin America also derives from his eagerness to dismiss the dualist analyses of modernization theory and the position held by orthodox Communist Parties. Though Laclau also rejects dualism, he argues that the colonial mode of production was not capitalist and that while today's mode of production is capitalist, pre–capitalist relations of production are still prevalent in Latin America. Frank's errors stem from his definitions of feudalism and capitalism in which feudalism is understood as a closed economy and capitalism as production for the market. Furthermore, he 'totally dispenses with *relations of production*' (Laclau, 1971: 25) in these definitions. Laclau convincingly argues that 'the pre–capitalist character of the dominant relations of production in Latin America was not only *not* incompatible with production for the world market, but was actually intensified by the expansion of the latter' (ibid.: 30).[22] Thus, by analysing relations of production and circulation within the system as a whole he is able to dismiss simultaneously the capitalist and dualist theses.

The significance of Frank's intervention was mainly political, as, by arguing that capitalism was the cause of Latin America's underdevelopment and responsible for its continuation, he challenged the orthodox Latin American Communist Parties, who argued that Latin America was still feudal and that popular forces should support the bourgeoisie so that it can fulfil its revolutionary task of accelerating the transition from feudalism to capitalism. This progressive role of the bourgeoisie would in turn facilitate the growth of the proletariat, which would bring nearer the day of the triumphant socialist revolution. For Frank the Latin American bourgeoisie was only perpetuating the development of underdevelopment and therefore, following the example of the Cuban revolution, capitalism had to be overthrown as only socialism could eliminate underdevelopment.

The feudalism–versus–capitalism controversy generated much heat, which, from today's perspective, seems to have been exaggerated as political circumstances have changed. The debate also had a major influence on the subsequent discussion of the articulation of modes of production (Seddon, 1978; Taylor, 1979; Wolpe, 1980). In the end 'Frank was right about the unity of development and underdevelopment, but wrong to draw from this the conclusion that the mode of production in underdeveloped social formations was necessarily capitalist' (Lehmann, 1986: 22).

Internal and external determination in Frank and other dependentistas

Frank (1984: 306–7) is emphatic in rejecting the idea that dependence is only an external condition as '"external" dependence is indissolubly linked with the "internal" class structure' (ibid.: viii). He thereby rejects the thesis held by the modernization theorists, and initially by the reformist *dependentistas*, 'that the "national" bourgeoisie has objective conditions for offering a "nationalist" or "autonomous" way out of underdevelopment' (Frank, 1970: 15). Such a solution does not exist precisely because dependence is integral and renders the bourgeoisie itself dependent. He even dismisses the Latin American bourgeoisie as a 'lumpenbourgeoisie' because they are only capable of bringing about a 'lumpendevelopment' (ibid.: 16). The analytical value of these polemical Frankian formulations is limited as they are tautological.

The discussion about the relationship between external and internal forces is crucial for dependency analysis. Although most reformist *dependentistas* – with the exception of Cardoso and Faletto – began by characterizing dependence as an external phenomenon, the position of some (for example, Sunkel and Furtado) has shifted. Sunkel (1972b: 519) now argues that the international capitalist system has a determining influence on internal developments and 'foreign factors are not seen as external but as intrinsic to the system, with manifold and sometimes hidden or subtle political, financial, economic, technical and cultural effects inside the underdeveloped country'. Furthermore,

> The importance which is attributed to external conditions should not obscure the existence of internal conditioning structures as, even though in the long run process of change the influence of the former tend to prevail, the structural transformation is the outcome of the interaction between both.
>
> (Sunkel, 1972a: 14)

Fernando H. Cardoso (1972c: 17) fully concurs with the following critical reflection of a Marxist *dependentista* who wrote that

it is necessary to conceive dependence as a dialectical unity of the general determinants of the capitalist mode of production and the specific determinants of each of the dependent societies and, therefore, as a synthesis of the 'external factors' and the 'internal factors'.

(Quartim de Moraes, 1972: 11)

Cardoso (1972c: 18) regards these forms of articulation between the dependent countries and the imperialist countries as the germ for a possible theory of dependence which, in his view, should be seen as complementing the theory of imperialism rather than replacing it.

For Vasconi, a Marxist *dependentista*, external and internal factors jointly create what he refers to as a dependent capitalist social formation and have to be considered simultaneously. This dependent formation follows the general laws of capitalism but acquires specific characteristics (Vasconi, 1971: 16–17). Consequently, he is critical of both modernization writers, who focus exclusively on internal factors, and those Marxist writers on imperialism who consider the development of the Third World as an epiphenomenon of, or as fully explained by, the development of the advanced countries (ibid.: 15, 30). The fact that underdeveloped countries have their own internal dynamic which can only be comprehended within the matrix of the international system is the *raison d'être* of dependency analysis.

Returning to Frank, his earlier remarks on the issue of internal and external determination were prompted in part by his critics. Laclau (1971), amongst other, charged that, by focusing almost exclusively on exchange relations between the developed and less–developed countries, Frank failed to see the internal dynamics of the less–developed countries, leading him to reach the mistaken conclusion that external factors are all determinant. Likewise Arrighi argues that 'it is the "internal mode of production" that determines the "external exchange relations", and not vice versa' (Arrighi, quoted in Frank, 1978b: 13–14), i.e. circulation determining production in the periphery of the capitalist system.

Although Frank (1970) is justified in refuting the charge that he has not analysed internal relations of production, he certainly did not analyse these sufficiently or adequately. Whilst his position remained circulationist, he undertook a more detailed analysis of internal relations of production, characterizing them differently and placing them within a world–system perspective in which the relations of production and exchange are examined simultaneously world–wide during a particular historical period (see especially Frank, 1978a; 1978b; 1984: 295–6).

Since Frank has moved on from dependence to world–system analysis he now argues that:

> The analysis of a single process of accumulation and the development of a single world capitalist system renders the question of the internality or externality of the determination, at least of this process itself, irrelevant and unanswerable. The determination is, of course, geographically and sectorally internal to where this process takes place...The predominance of 'internal' relations of production over 'external' relations of exchange is rendered more questionable, in turn, if we consider the necessary connection of both of these relations for the realization of, and therefore for the expanded reproduction of, capital, with successive relations and modes of production.
>
> (Frank, 1978b: 253)

With regard to internal factors, his thesis that the closer the ties between the metropolis and the satellite, the more intense the development of underdevelopment, remains unchanged. Conversely, through his initial historical analysis of Chile and Brazil and later of other preripheral countries, he attempted to demonstrate that when these ties are weakened, as during the world crisis of the 1930s, the bourgeoisies in these dependent countries are able to pursue more nationalist and autochthonous policies which strengthen the process of development rather than of underdevelopment. [23]

Frank has revised his characterization of the social relations of production by holding that these have not necessarily been capitalist since the colonial period, as he first argued. Although continuing to maintain that Latin America's mode of production has been capitalist since the colonial period, he now specifies that a variety of pre–capitalist, non–capitalist, and even post–capitalist relations have contributed to, and to a lesser extent are still contributing to, the process of capital accumulation (Frank, 1978b: 241–6). His main thesis still stands: that the underdeveloped countries have made a crucial contribution to the process of capital accumulation and economic development in the now developed countries which, at the same time, 'developed the mode of production which underdeveloped Asia, Africa and Latin America' (Frank, 1978a: 172). However, Frank does not specify how significant the transfer of surplus from underdeveloped to developed countries actually is at the present day.[24]

Frank's work has generated much controversy and has been criticized from various political positions.[25] Although his contribution to Marxist theory proper is modest, he did nevertheless help to shift the focus of Marxist and other intellectuals on the Third World and indeed on the world economy as a whole.[26] Nor is there any doubt about Frank's political commitment towards national liberation and socialist revolution. Like Dos Santos, he regards the dilemma facing Latin America as being either 'capitalist underdevelopment or socialist revolution' (Frank, 1970: 170). Frank reached the following political conclusion in an essay he presented to the Cultural Congress in Havana in 1968: 'Tactically, the immediate enemy of national liberation in Latin America is the native bourgeoisie...This is so – in Asia and Africa included – notwithstanding that strategically the principal enemy undoubtedly is imperialism.' (Cockcroft *et al.*, 1972: 425.) Despite statements like these critics were beginning and still continue to charge that he neglects internal and class factors in his analysis. It is in the next chapter that the debates and critiques of dependency analysis will be examined.

6

Dependency: debates, critiques, and beyond

The weaknesses of the dependency debate are closely related to its strengths, namely its interdisciplinary approach and its orientation towards long–term strategic policy issues. The ambitious interdisciplinary orientation invites oversimplification while the concern with strategic policy creates intense pressures to draw broad conclusions quickly, and to become committed to the conclusions once drawn. These shortcomings neither excuse the weaknesses, nor invalidate the approach.

(Bienefeld, 1981: 81)

After presenting the main approaches to dependency analysis, it is appropriate to turn to the debates and controversies it has generated. While some critiques take issue with particular aspects of dependency analysis, a majority reject the approach altogether. In substance, critiques have been based on theoretical, methodological, empirical, and political grounds; in scope they may even outweigh the original dependency writings. This barrage of criticism led to the following assessment by one of dependency's key figures:

Unfortunately these criticisms have not contributed much to the study of the problem as they reveal not only a great ignorance of the recent literature but also of the classic works on the situation of the dependent countries. The resulting distortion has provoked a great deal of confusion over the concept of dependence, the relationship between dependency and imperialism, the existence of the dependency situation, the theoretical status of the concept, etcetera.

(Dos Santos, 1978: 359)

THE SERRA–CARDOSO VERSUS MARINI DEBATE

Inevitably any review of such a vast critical literature has to be selective. The most important debate within the dependency perspective is, in my view, that between José Serra and Fernando H. Cardoso, on the one hand, and Ruy Mauro Marini on the other. In a long essay Serra and Cardoso (1978) launch a comprehensive attack on Marini's dependency thesis, focusing on four main areas of disagreement: Marini's analysis of unequal exchange, his theses on dependent capital accumulation and on sub–imperialism, and his political conclusions. Marini's (1978b) rebuttal is equally thorough and fierce.[1]

Serra and Cardoso's critique

Turning first to the analysis of unequal exchange, in a complex critique Serra and Cardoso undermine one of the pillars sustaining Marini's thesis of the over–exploitation of labour. Serra and Cardoso take Marini to be arguing that an increase in unequal exchange means a further deterioration in the terms of trade, and thus a fall in the dependent country's profit rate, which is compensated for by resorting to an increase in the over–exploitation of labour. Marini's use of the terms of trade as a proxy for unequal exchange leads him to think that an increase in the price of the commodities exported by advanced countries means a rise in unequal exchange. Marini is criticized for confusing unequal exchange with deterioration of the terms of trade and for brushing aside many of the unresolved issues regarding the problem of the transfer of value through international trade – i.e. how is socially necessary labour time to be determined when labour is not mobile internationally? (Serra and Cardoso, 1978: 20–4).

According to Serra and Cardoso, Marini's main theoretical mistake is to argue that unequal exchange against the periphery necessarily leads to a deterioration in its commodity terms of trade and vice versa (ibid.: 15). Following from this, Marini unnecessarily assumes that 'the increase in productivity in the production of manufactured goods in the centre countries implies *the reduction in the rate of profit in the periphery*' (ibid.: 24) by arguing that the commodity terms of trade have turned against the periphery owing to an assumed rise in imported manufactured prices, thereby increasing costs in the periphery. However, as Serra and Cardoso point out, it is possible for unequal exchange to turn further against the periphery without the terms of trade deteriorating. An increase in the productivity of manufactures might not lead to a change in the price of manufactures although it does mean that prices will deviate from exchange values. Furthermore, an increase in productivity in the periphery – even if it does result in a fall in export prices and thus in a deterioration of its commodity terms of trade – does not necessarily imply a fall in its profit rate as unit costs may fall by the same proportion; i.e. the single factoral terms of trade could remain the same (ibid.: 24–5). In short, even if unequal exchange increases and the commodity terms of trade deteriorate further against the periphery, its profit rate might not fall. Consequently, Marini's argument that the dependent countries have to resort to super–exploitation of labour to maintain profit rates is not validated, and his deduction that there is an inevitable economic tendency towards super–exploitation of labour cannot be sustained (ibid.: 25).

Turning next to the issue of dependent capital accumulation, Serra and Cardoso further criticize Marini's thesis of the super–exploitation of labour for dismissing relative surplus value as an alternative form of exploitation in dependent countries. According to Marini, industrialists in the Third World are not interested in raising labour productivity as this does not reduce the value of labour power (v) given that workers consume few industrial products. Thus, the rate of surplus value (s/v) does not increase either. (The rate of surplus value is also called rate of exploitation, which is the ratio of s over v, where s is the surplus labour or surplus value, and v is the necessary labour or variable capital.) [2] However, Serra and Cardoso point out that capitalists are fundamentally interested in increasing the rate of profit ($s/(c+v)$) rather than maximizing the rate of surplus value. This goal is achieved by cheapening the value of constant capital (c) through technological improvements in the production of commodities which comprise constant capital, such as machinery and raw materials. [3] This aspect of technological progress and resulting increases in labour productivity are ignored by Marini. Consequently, even assuming Marini's hypothesis that workers do not consume industrial commodities to be correct, it does not follow that a dependent country's capitalist development is necessarily blocked, nor that the only solution is to over–exploit labour (ibid.: 43–5).

Furthermore, Fernando H. Cardoso (1977b: 57–8) argues that the specificity of the monopoly phase of 'internationalization of the internal market' in dependent countries rests precisely on the extraction of relative surplus value and increases in the organic composition of capital (c/v), i.e. the ratio of constant capital over variable capital. Cardoso does not deny that over–exploitation of labour or capital accumulation via absolute surplus value are still important in the competitive sector of the economy, but he rejects Marini's thesis that they are the principal form of accumulation in the industrial–monopolistic sector.

In addition, Cardoso refutes Marini's argument that the process of capital accumulation in the advanced capitalist countries requires the extraction of a surplus from the dependent countries, thereby leading to the over–exploitation of labour in the latter: 'central capitalism, *in what it possesses as specific and dynamic*, depends on the production of relative surplus value and the increase of productivity...and not on the exploitative basis provided by the exploited regions' (F. Cardoso, 1972c: 23). Although central capitalism benefits from unequal exchange and the over–exploitation of labour in the periphery, Cardoso sees them as not essential to the reproduction of capital in the centre.

Turning to Marini's sub–imperialism thesis, Serra and Cardoso disagree that, given the potential problems of realization (i.e. insufficient internal demand), the only alternatives open to dependent countries like Brazil are to achieve a rising export surplus (i.e. a positive balance of trade by exports exceeding imports) or to increase government expenditure on armaments. On the basis of data from Brazil they show that no major problem of internal demand exists as almost two–thirds of the economy's growth between 1965 and 1975 was due to an increase in private consumption by upper–middle groups, the expansion of employment, and so on. They do not deny the importance of the rapid growth of exports for the Brazilian economy but they see their significance as lying in securing vital foreign exchange rather than in increasing effective demand, as in Marini's sub–imperialism thesis (Serra and Cardoso, 1978: 41).

Finally, Serra and Cardoso take issue with Marini's political conclusion that the alternative facing Latin America is fascism or socialism, and they regard his analysis as economistic and voluntaristic. Marini's economism is seen to arise from his belief that capitalist development is impossible in the dependent countries owing to stagnation and underconsumption, from which over–exploitation and sub–imperialism offer only a temporary respite. This catastrophic view of dependent capitalism leads Marini to political reductionism, as the necessity of militarism and fascism is seen to derive from the economic need for sub–imperialism.

As mentioned earlier, Serra and Cardoso do not believe that peripheral capitalism is stagnating through underconsumption or that the only way to dynamize it is by pursuing a sub–imperialist policy and establishing a fascist regime. They do not deny that repression and the containment of wages were important elements of the so–called Brazilian 'miracle' from the mid–1960s to the early 1970s (ibid.: 51–2). However,

> The recent historical process [in Latin America]...shows that the dominant classes have increasingly militarized their political style of domination. But it is wrong to think that the authoritarian and bureaucratic regimes...will move in the direction of social apartheid or that they extol fascist forms of political organization.
>
> (Cardoso, 1977b: 61)

Indeed, most Latin American countries which were governed by the military have returned to civilian rule in recent years – although it remains to be seen for how long. For the time being, however, Marini's (and above all Dos Santos's and Bambirra's) prediction that 'the political path of the continent is at the cross–roads: "socialism or fascism"' (ibid.: 61) has yet to materialize.

Serra and Cardoso (1978: 53) regard the option of socialism or fascism as too simplistic a political analysis, as it denies the possibilities of a variety of class alliances and of taking advantage of existing political opportunities. It also fails to specify how the transition from fascism to socialism is brought about, assuming this to be direct. Marini's espousal of armed struggle is seen to be voluntarist and self–defeating.

Marini's reply to Serra and Cardoso

With regards to Serra and Cardoso's criticisms concerning unequal exchange and over–exploitation of labour, Marini (1978b: 66) argues that they formulate the relationship between value and price incorrectly, and confuse profit rate ($s/(c+v)$) with rate of surplus value or exploitation (s/v). Taking the first point, Marini argues that whether labour is internationally mobile or not neither validates nor invalidates the theory of value, as 'the socially necessary labour time is not determined by the *circulation* of labour, but is exclusively the function of the development of the productive forces, the degree of dexterity, productivity, and average intensity of the labour power in *production*' (ibid.: 64). Furthermore, Marini denies confusing unequal exchange with terms of trade, being well aware of the difference and of the fact that value is not the same as price. He defends the use of price indices as a proxy for values over the long run for practical reasons and regards it as valid to examine the evolution of the terms of trade when analysing unequal exchange (ibid.: 65). In taking issue with Serra and Cardoso, Marini sometimes misinterprets their arguments about unequal exchange. He criticizes Serra and Cardoso for assuming that *'movements in prices do not imply movements in value'* (ibid.) when in fact they argue the opposite, i.e. that movements in value do not imply movements in prices. Marini therefore persists with his argument that unequal exchange has intensified against the dependent countries, implying a fall in their profit rate and necessitating a rise in the over–exploitation of labour.

Marini also denies arguing that economic stagnation is inevitable in Latin America (ibid.: 73). He claims that when he speaks of stagnation or regression he does not refer to the absolute amount of production but to rates of growth.

On the issue of over–exploitation of labour, he argues (ibid.: 85) that, despite his earlier clarification (Marini, 1973: 92), Serra and Cardoso continue to confuse over–exploitation with absolute surplus value alone. Marini does not deny that accumulation on the basis of the production of relative surplus value occurs in dependent countries. He therefore rejects their critique that over–exploitation of labour plays a minor role in the present phase of Brazil's capitalist development. Far from decreasing, over–exploitation has been increasing in Brazil principally through the expansion of the floating industrial reserve army of labour, the stepping up of repression and the implementation of a harsh policy of wage containment which has made it possible to reduce wages below the value of labour power (Marini, 1978b: 89). Furthermore, the working day has been extended and work has been intensified, thereby increasing both the extensive and intensive magnitude of work (ibid.: 97). Thus, despite the fall in workers' real wages, the value of labour power has increased. The greater expenditure of physical energy demanded by the rise in the work's magnitude augments the amount of means for its replenishment, thereby reinforcing over–exploitation and making the situation even more dramatic (ibid.: 98).

Turning to his sub–imperialism thesis, Marini supports his position by referring to an empirical analysis of the Brazilian case just as detailed as that carried out by Serra and Cardoso. According to Marini's reading of the data, the state is an important factor in the country's process of commodity realization as the expenditures of government and of public enterprises are a major proportion of the total. More importantly, the public sector is responsible for most of the country's fixed investment, i.e. demand for capital goods (ibid.: 77). Furthermore, the rapid growth of exports (at an annual rate of 20 per cent between 1968 and 1976) and particularly of manufacturing exports (by over 50 per cent per annum) are a clear indication, in Marini's view, of the growing importance assumed by exports in the country's sub–imperialist realization scheme (ibid.: 81).

In short, Marini argues that

to pretend that the over–exploitation of labour does not contribute to the commodities' restriction of realization in the Brazilian economy and that it does not basically rest on the realization scheme characteristic of sub–imperialism (exports, luxury consumption and state demand) constitutes, therefore, a coarse mystification.

(ibid.: 95)

Finally, in this at times acrimonious debate, Marini rejects the criticism of economism, underconsumption, and neo–populism, and charges Serra and Cardoso with sociologism, political reductionism, and neo–developmentalism. In Marini's view, while economic life conditions social and political processes in a complex set of relationships, this does not mean that he upholds an economistic position (ibid.: 99). In his view Serra and Cardoso mistakenly believe that the class struggle constitutes a *deus ex machina* and that the political is autonomous, as they explain the various political options and decisions solely with reference to forces which operate at the political level (ibid.: 68, 99). As for his so–called underconsumptionism, he reiterates that he is merely following Marx's analysis with regards to the contradictions in capitalism between production and private consumption, which he regards as being even more profound in dependent countries (ibid.: 102). For this, and other reasons, he sees no similarity between the Narodniks' position and his own (ibid.: 100–4).

The differences between Marini and Serra and Cardoso are mainly political and ideological. Marini accuses Serra and Cardoso of surreptitiously eliminating the differences between the developed and the dependent countries within the capitalist system, thereby abandoning the dependency framework and embracing a neo–developmentalist position – i.e. of returning to the fold of ECLA (ibid.: 102). Even worse, in Marini's eyes, they – and Fernando H. Cardoso in particular – attempt to forge a class collaborationist alliance between the bourgeois opposition to the Brazilian dictatorship and the working class, an alliance subordinating the proletariat to a state programme directed at developing Brazil's sub–imperialism (ibid.: 104). Marini is not against class alliances *per se*, but only supports them when the hegemony of the working class prevails. The debate, therefore, forms part of a much wider discussion between those who advocate a peaceful road to socialism and those who advocate armed struggle.

Further comments on the debate

The polemic between Serra and Cardoso and Marini has attracted a number of contributions from other researchers. Henfrey (1981: 23) considers that while Marini dictates the terms of the debate, the empirical evidence supports Serra and Cardoso. He criticizes Marini's formulation of the relationship between base and superstructure in Marxist theory, as Marini deducts certain necessary and universal socio–political inferences from the economic contradictions, thereby precluding any specific analysis of the class struggle (ibid.: 23–4). Furthermore, he characterizes Marini's over–exploitation model as 'ideologically determined' and as being 'a post–hoc theory of armed struggle' (ibid.: 25). In turn, Henfrey sees Fernando H. Cardoso's inductive and empirical analysis and his view of dependence as a 'methodology for analyzing a concrete situation' in danger of ending up as mere description. 'These [analyses] may be much more accurate and yet fail to interpret what they describe in the absence of a clearly guiding theory and related analytic concepts' (ibid.: 25–6).

Like Marini, Henfrey criticizes Cardoso and Faletto for having an indeterminate conceptualization of class and for their political reductionism. In Henfrey's view, Cardoso and Faletto's definition of dependence prioritizes the political, as 'the internal becomes the political – as opposed to the primarily political expression of latently economic variables – and the external the economic' (ibid.: 30). Thus, their analysis makes it impossible to determine structurally the history of classes and particularly that of the exploited classes who are less visible politically than the dominant classes and are not rooted in specific economic and social relations (ibid.). However, Randall and Theobald give a different interpretation, as in their evaluation that:

despite Cardoso and Faletto's explicit commitment to dealing with the political level, politics is conceived entirely in terms of the class struggle. The notion that the State might have some degree of autonomy, be above social groups and classes, is nowhere apparent in Cardoso and Faletto's study.

(Randall and Theobald, 1985: 135)

In general they accuse *dependentistas*, and particularly Frank, of marginalizing the political by regarding nation states in dependent countries as pawns of international capital (ibid.: 115–19).

Henfrey draws wider conclusions about dependency from his reflections on the debate:

Hence the striking features of dependency writing as typified in this debate are its overemphasis on the external, its economism at the expense of an understanding of the *social* relations of production, and its repetitive generality, with the lasting dearth of substantive case studies.

(Henfrey, 1981: 27)

Marini's analysis of over–exploitation and his underconsumptionist position have come under fire from others as well. Arauco (1974: 89–90) argues that Marini uses the concept of over–exploitation in two senses, each of which needs to be analysed in its own terms. On the one hand, it is used to mean the reduction of wages below the value of labour power and, on the other hand, to refer to payment of labour below the minimum level of subsistence. A situation whereby labour power is remunerated below its value is seen by Marx as a temporary phenomenon and thus, according to Arauco, Marini errs in regarding over–exploitation as expressing a general law of capital. As for the payment of labour below subsistence, this, in Arauco's view, is not considered by Marx as over–exploitation but as the 'embezzlement' of labour. Furthermore, neither form of over–exploitation is peculiar to dependent capitalism as both were part of the advanced countries' process of capitalist development (ibid.: 91). Thus, these various forms of labour exploitation are common to capital–labour relations and are not unique to dependent countries (C. Johnson, 1981: 61). In turn, Henfrey makes the sensible point that 'even if his [Marini's] model affords some insights, their expression as "laws" blocks their empirical application and possibly fruitful implications' (Henfrey, 1981: 25).

Marini's over–exploitation model has also been criticized on empirical grounds. Cueva (1974: 74) draws on the Argentinian case to question the general applicability of Marini's model. Although Argentina exported cereals and meat to advanced countries like Great Britain, thereby helping to reduce the cost of reproduction or value of Britain's labour power, it does not follow that Argentina's labour power was remunerated below its value or that the development of its internal market was blocked. On the contrary, wages in Argentina rose to such an extent that they attracted European immigrant labour as well as giving a boost to Argentina's industrialization and its early development.

Whilst Oliveira's evidence is not conclusive, it appears that the over–exploitation of labour did make a substantial contribution to raising the rate of surplus value in Brazil, thereby lending some support to Marini's thesis. Oliveira (1973: 450–7) argues that the rate of exploitation in Brazil has increased substantially in the industrial sector since the Second World War largely as a result of investments and new technologies which greatly raised labour productivity. However, labour was also remunerated below its value (super–exploited) as the cost of reproduction of labour increased – owing to an increase in the worker's cost of living – while nominal wages remained roughly stagnant, thereby resulting in a fall in real wages. This was possible owing to the large–scale rural out–migration which created an immense industrial reserve army of labour. Thus, the rising differential between the growth of labour productivity and wages was an important source of finance for the process of capital accumulation.

Veltmeyer's analysis clearly bolsters Marini's thesis as well as furnishing additional reasons for supporting a super–exploitation position. His conclusion is that:

Peripheral societies share economic conditions not found to any significant extent at the center of the system; that in terms of these conditions it is possible to identify a class structure typical of peripheral formations; and that this structure is shaped by what Marx termed 'the general law of capital accumulation'. With reference to conditions specified by this law, I argue that the class structure of peripheral formations revolves around the production of a relative surplus population and that certain characteristic features of this structure [persistence of precapitalist relations, active semiproletarianization, proliferation of petty production in its various forms, the sexual division of labour, and so on] serve to expand capital under conditions of superexploitation.

(Veltmeyer, 1983: 204–5)

However, Carlos Johnson (1981: 69) dismisses those who argue like Marini (1973: 36) and Bambirra (1978: 111), that super–exploitation of labour arises out of unequal exchange and is a way for local capitalists to recover the surplus value appropriated by imperialism. He argues that exploitation takes place only once at the level of production and not at the level of exchange or circulation and thus 'double exploitation or superexploitation whereby workers are supposedly exploited by local dominant classes *and* by unequal international exchange relations' cannot exist (Johnson, 1981: 69). Although Carlos Johnson's critique is marred by his confusion of double exploitation with super–exploitation, he is correct in asserting that the notion of exploitation of one country by another is theoretically problematic, as exploitation is a class, and not a national, relation.

According to Weeks and Dore (1979: 69), Marini upholds an underconsumptionist position, as he argues that in dependent countries the development of capitalism is limited by the smallness of the internal market arising from the underpayment of labour. [4] The underconsumptionist thesis was first formulated last century by the Narodniks but reached its most sophisticated form with Luxemburg (1963). Marini's novelty is to have applied and restricted it to Third World countries and linked it to over–exploitation. Lenin (1972), in his attack on the Russian populists, rejected the underconsumptionist thesis and later Bukharin (1972) also criticized it (Dore, 1983: 116). Lenin and Bukharin pointed out

that there is in fact, no 'realization problem' (problem in converting surplus value into profit) since the major portion of the realization of value occurs not through workers' (or even capitalists') consumption of the means of subsistence (the products of Department II in Marx's schema), but through the productive consumption of the means of production (the products of Department I).

(Weeks and Dore, 1979: 69–70)

As mentioned earlier, Marini denies holding an underconsumptionist position. To resolve this issue also requires further analysis of the concrete and diverse situations pertaining to the Third World, especially as in many countries – but certainly not Brazil – the capital goods sector is insignificant.

CRITIQUES OF DEPENDENCY

Whatever its shortcomings, few social scientists in Latin America or beyond have remained indifferent to dependency. Indeed, the critical literature has become so vast that at times it loses sight of the original dependency authors. A shortcoming of many critiques is their tendency to pass off partial critiques as general ones. Critiques in the English–speaking world have focused on the work of André Gunder Frank, who is taken to represent the dependency school as a whole. The barrage of criticism directed at Frank has often been interpreted as a blanket condemnation of *all* dependency authors, with the unfortunate consequence of precluding exploration of non–Frankian dependency analyses.[5] Important differences between dependency writers have thereby been overlooked.

While many responsible and thoughtful critiques have been published, others are misplaced, sweeping, unfair, misinformed, and/or ideologically prejudiced (Bienefeld, 1980: 5).[6] Given the varied and wide–ranging nature of dependency analysis, it is hardly surprising that the dependency school has many weaknesses. Some of the harsher criticisms are illustrated in the following synoptic quotations: '[dependence is an] eclectic combination of orthodox economic theory and revolutionary phraseology' (G. Kay, 1975: 103); 'dependency theory neither can claim empirical verification nor theoretical validity' (Weeks, 1981: 118); 'the concept of dependence...is impossible to define and cannot be shown to be causally related to a continuance of underdevelopment' (Lall, 1975: 808); 'the meaning of dependence is ever more elusive, not to say mystical' and 'the concept of dependence is totally misleading' (Warren, 1980: 182, 184); 'it is becoming clear that "underdevelopment" and "dependency" theory is no longer serviceable and must now be transcended' (Leys, 1977: 92); 'the theory of dependence should be rejected' (Fernández and Ocampo, 1974: 39); 'the dependency position is vitiated by a variable combination of circular reasoning, fallacious inferences from empirical observation and a weak base in deductive theory...[and] has been shown to be untenable on a combination of logical, analytical and theoretical grounds' (Booth, 1985: 762, 764); 'the dependency theorists represent and reflect the class needs of local dominant classes' (C. Johnson, 1981: 66); and 'the most significant political impact of dependency theory has been to divert and dampen support for socialist revolution' (Angotti, 1981: 127).

Further, dependency analysis has been accused of being tautological, economistic, ahistorical, utopian, devoid of class analysis, populist or Narodnik, nationalist, myopic, one–dimensional, ideological, eclectic, mechanical, sophist, a negative teleology, idealist, anti–capitalist, a marxified structuralism, non–Marxist or non–materialist, careless in the use of Marxist theory, unable to break with bourgeois development theory, without empirical grounding, theoretically imprecise, unclear, contradictory, too global or holistic, deterministic, methodologically and conceptually eclectic – a tower of Babel, lacking in clear policy recommendations for overcoming dependence, stagnationist, circulationist, and so on. A long list of charges indeed!

In what follows only the principal and more serious criticisms will be examined. In assessing the extent to which dependency analysis is able to surmount these weaknesses, it is useful to bear in mind 'the need to discuss dependency in terms of the question it poses, rather than in terms of the answers some of its exponents have at times suggested. These questions are important, both politically and analytically, and they are questions which traditional approaches have frequently in practice ignored or treated as peripheral' (Bienefeld, 1980: 10).

Relationship between internal and external factors

A frequent criticism is that dependency analysis exaggerates the power of external forces and downgrades the internal forces which shape a Third World country's development (D. Johnson, 1981: 112–13). Kalmanovitz (1982: 534) attributes this overemphasis on external determination to the holistic perspective (*enfoque totalizador*) of the *dependentistas*, who assume the totality as given and as overdetermining the parts. Consequently, dependency authors tend not to search for 'internal laws' or to disentangle the dynamics of the parts within this totality. In Kalmanovitz's view the symbiosis between the external and internal, or the way they combine, needs to be specified more precisely (ibid.: 535). His own position privileges internal factors, as can be gleaned from his statement that: 'The capital accumulation is given endogenously and the flows of trade and foreign capital "articulate themselves with it and *modify it from within*, accentuating the internal changes going on, the productive structure and the historical pattern of accumulation"' (ibid.: 541, citing from Tavares, 1974: 116–17).

Other critics, like Brenner (1977), Weeks and Dore (1979), and Geoffrey Kay (1975), also see internal forces as defining the dependence relationship. Likewise, Oliveira (1973: 447) argues that the internal class struggle has had a greater influence on Brazil's capitalist development since 1930 than external circumstances. Cueva (1979: 91) goes even further and inverts the dependency thesis by arguing that it is the nature of Third World social formations which determines in the last instance the forms of their linkages with the world capitalist system.

Bernstein (1982: 231–2) argues that the very dichotomy of 'internal' and 'external' needs to be transcended. Frank aimed to achieve this by adopting a world system approach in which the question of internal or external determination becomes irrelevant as the analysis is concerned with 'a single process of accumulation and the development of a single world capitalist system' (Frank, 1978b: 253). However, for Bernstein unresolved issues persist in a world–system analysis: for example, the terms 'national economy' and 'world economy' remain problematic because they cannot be taken as 'given' entities. The question he poses is: 'Which conditions and aspects of the process of value formation and of the reproduction of capital are constituted within "national economies" and which are constituted within the circuits of world economy, and how do they bear on each other?' (Bernstein, 1982: 230). In his view the way forward for dependency and world-system analyses is 'to analyze *any* social formation in its specificity – as a complex ensemble of class relations and contradictions of the economic, political and ideological conditions and forms of class struggle' (ibid.: 232), as such diverse countries as Brazil, India, Bolivia, and Nepal cannot be lumped together.[7]

Similar points are raised by Petras and Brill who criticize the 'globalist dogma' in dependency and world–system theories. In their view,

A subordinate actor is never absolutely controlled, there is always a potential for resistance within the relation. The globalist perspective paints a picture of domination based on a 'passive receptacle' notion of the Third World in which the internal class forces are non–actors, or even blank surfaces ready to be shaped and exploited by the 'Core'.

(Petras and Brill, 1985: 405)

Instead of the 'iron cage' of globalism, they emphasize the emergence of new class forces and alliances which enhance the capability of Third World countries to redefine their relations with the dominant countries and the world economy. They do not deny the existence of a world economy but this does not preclude its heterogeneity and its combined and uneven development. They therefore conclude that: 'The process of altering relations at the global level *begins* through changes *within* the national class and state structure.' (ibid.: 408.) In my view, their pointed criticism of what they call 'the tyranny of globalism' is more appropriate to world–system theory than to dependency analysis.

Many of these criticisms mistakenly assume that most *dependentistas* hold the view that external factors are the prime determinants of underdevelopment and dependence, when it was mainly Frank and the 'external dependency' reformist writers, like Sunkel and Furtado, who argued this. Dos Santos distinguishes between 'conditioning' external factors and 'determining' internal factors and F. H. Cardoso constantly stressed internal relations as being crucial for the understanding of dependent development.

The dependency perspective has also been criticized for its failure to differentiate between Third World countries (Hoogvelt, 1982: 213; Staniland, 1985: 129). Substantial differences exist between dependent countries regarding their structural situation and development problems (Seers, 1979b). In some instances these differences might even be greater than those existing between some developed and developing countries. However, in my view, this criticism does not apply to F. H. Cardoso, as he seeks to examine 'diversity within unity', unlike Frank who emphasizes 'unity within diversity'. It is also less valid with regard to Bambirra, who analyses dependency in Latin America by grouping countries into three types of dependent situations. However, this differentiation needs to be further refined, especially when Asian and African countries are incorporated into the dependency analysis, as there are important regional as well as country–wide disparities. [8]

DEVELOPMENT OF UNDERDEVELOPMENT

A second important critique relates to Frank's thesis of the 'development of underdevelopment' and the tendency for *dependentistas* to regard capitalist development as deformed or unviable in dependent countries (D. Johnson, 1981: 111). Cardoso rejects the notion of 'development of underdevelopment', as it implies that Third World countries are either stagnating or that their development is distorted, making capitalist development unviable (F. Cardoso, 1972b: 94; 1977b: 54–5). He argues instead that rapid economic growth has taken place and that the forces of production have been developed, particularly since the new phase of dependence associated with Latin America's industrialization under the aegis of multinational corporations. Cardoso (1972c: 21–2) does not deny that capitalist development in Third World countries is highly uneven, unequal, and full of contradictions, but this does not signify that capitalism does not lead to development or that it is unviable. In place of what he sees as the mistaken notion of 'development of underdevelopment', Cardoso (1973b: 143; 1982: 125) proposes the term 'associated dependent development' as more accurately reflecting the process of both development *and* dependency which characterizes many Third World countries. Following Cardoso, Palma (1978: 903) argues that underdevelopment cannot be attributed to dependence *per se* as it is characteristic of capitalist development in general, although it takes specific forms in dependent countries. Consequently, 'It is more appropriate to view dependence as aggravating conditions of underdevelopment that are inevitable under capitalism than to view dependence as a major cause of underdevelopment.' (Weisskopf, 1976: 21, cited in Palma, 1978: 902.)

Weisskopf's research (1976) shows that no empirical evidence exists for the stagnationist thesis. On the contrary, some dependent countries had higher rates of growth than non–dependent countries (Palma, 1978: 902). Castañeda and Hett (1978) also stress the significant development of the forces of production in some Third World countries. For Lall (1975: 808), dependence 'cannot be shown to be causally related to a continuance of underdevelopment' and he accuses dependency writers of confusing the undesirable effects of capitalist development with the non–viability of capitalist development.

In opposition to the above, Bambirra (1978: 49–50) denies that *dependentistas* negate the development of the productive forces. She claims that their argument was directed against dualist positions as, for the *dependentistas*, the development of the productive forces in the dependent countries at the same time reproduced backwardness, which was a condition and consequence of their capitalist development.

The 'development of underdevelopment' and the Marxist dependency theses also argue that underdevelopment or dependence originates from the incorporation of subordinated or dominated countries into the world capitalist system and will continue as long as they remain tied to it. These propositions blame foreign trade and foreign investment for the underdevelopment and dependence of Third World countries. This directly challenges both neoclassical economic theory and modernization social theories, as well as revising certain classical Marxist tenets; so it is hardly surprising that this position has prompted a vigorous counter–attack, particularly from orthodox Marxists.

The position of the orthodox Marxists can be summed up by the view that it is the very lack, or insufficient penetration, of capitalist development in Third World countries – and not its presence – which creates and perpetuates underdevelopment (Blomström and Hettne, 1984: 85; Munck, 1984: 20–1). Thus, for example, 'The basis for Latin American backwardness cannot be attributed to the capitalist character of its economies and their integration within the world capitalist system, but rather the *lack* of capitalist development and the persistence of feudal forms in agriculture.' (Fernández and Ocampo, 1974: 36.) Furthermore, 'Latin American backwardness has a pre–capitalist character' (ibid.: 46). Geoffrey Kay (1975: 55), echoing Luxemburg and Joan Robinson, phrases his criticism neatly as 'capitalism has created underdevelopment not simply because it has exploited the underdeveloped countries but because it has not exploited them enough'. According to Warren, for whom imperialism is the 'pioneer of capitalism' and a progressive force, underdevelopment theorists 'exclude by definition the possibility that the less developed countries have been becoming progressively more developed, in terms both of the expansion of the productive forces and of material welfare, as a result of their rising integration into the world market, partially because of imperialism' (Warren, 1980: 169). These sentiments are also echoed by Castañeda and Hett (1978). In Bernstein's (1982: 228) view, Emmanuel (the Marxist unequal exchange theorist)

> goes much further than Warren in arguing that a major cause of the reproduction of 'underdevelopment' is not that Third World countries have been invaded by foreign capital (the dependency position) but that they have been *starved* of it. The essential issue is the scale and rate of accumulation, not the 'nationality' of the capitals involved.

Frank (1974: 100), however, dismisses the critiques by Warren (1973), Nove (1974), and others – who argue 'that foreign investment and capitalism offer the best of all worlds to all' – as 'backward–looking, downright reactionary critiques' which are 'part and parcel of a reactionary counter–offensive, not only from the right but unfortunately also on the part of much of the left' (Frank, 1974: 102). Unfortunately he does not examine these criticisms on their own merit but brushes them aside with a political comment.

Leys criticizes dependency for the causality it establishes between foreign capital and underdevelopment by stressing the primacy of the internal over the external. Thus,

> What produces *under*development is not the 'transfer of surplus' appropriated by metropolitan capital from the periphery of the metropole, significant though this may be. Rather, such a transfer should be seen as an *effect* of structures at the periphery which militate against the productive investment of the surplus at the periphery. Speaking generally these are class structures which permit absolute surplus labour to be appropriated, but prevent the realisation of relative surplus value.
>
> (Leys, 1978: 245)

In his view, it is the internal class structure of the dependent countries which impedes or conspires against the development of the productive forces by failing to provide sufficient incentives, such as adequate levels of profitability, for capital investment. (Here, Leys follows a point made by Brenner, 1977: 85.)

Inadequate class analysis

Third, *dependentistas* have been charged with economic reductionism for reducing the social, political, and ideological factors to the economic level in society, and for maintaining, either explicitly or implicitly, that the country's social and political structure is determined by, or derivative from, its economy (Staniland, 1985: 121–3; Leys 1977: 95; 1978: 245). Dependency studies are seen as failing to examine, or insufficiently so, the social relations of production and to lack an adequate conception of the theory of the modes of production, if any at all. Without an analysis of the social relations of production there are no class struggles, no classes, and consequently no revolution, according to Castañeda and Hett (1978: 82).

In Dale Johnson's view, (1981: 112), the *dependentistas'* excessive economic determinism reduces the internal social forces to impotence, thereby exaggerating the influence of external factors, as mentioned earlier. While Henfrey (1981: 35–6) criticizes most dependency writers – such as Frank, Dos Santos, Marini, and even Quijano – for lacking a class analysis, D. Johnson (1981: 109) argues that they do employ class analysis to differing degrees but of the wrong kind. Roxborough (1979: 90) finds particular fault with Frank's analysis of class because:

> unlike the Marxist view of class, the Frankian view of class conceptualises not merely exploiting classes and exploited classes, but also classes which are at one and the same time both exploiting and exploited. In Frank's framework, every class between the peasant at the bottom of the ladder and the metropolitan bourgeoisie at the top must simultaneously be exploited by the class above it (its metropolis) and exploit the class below it (its satellite).

One implication of this type of class formulation is that while the urban working class is exploited by the urban bourgeoisie, it, in turn, exploits the rural workers. The problem is that some dependency writers, particularly Frank, formulate dependency in regional (centre–periphery or metropolis–satellite) rather than in class terms (D. Johnson, 1983: 234).

Others, in turn, criticize the dependency view of the national bourgeoisie. F. H. Cardoso (1977b: 58), for example, disagrees with the dependency thesis that 'local bourgeoisies no longer exist as an active social force'. He is at odds with those dependency colleagues who argue that 'the local bourgeoisie become *lumpen*, incapable of national accumulation, dilapidated in their consumerism, blind to their "real interests"' (ibid.:58). In his view,

> the national bourgeoisies continue to play an active role in political domination and social control of the subjected classes. They lack nevertheless, aspirations for political hegemony and, instead of support for anti–imperialist struggles, the 'national' bourgeoisies (or better, *local* bourgeoisies) become part of the internationalized system of production.

> (ibid.: 59)

Some critics regard this deficient class analysis as deriving from the *dependentistas*' location of dependency in the sphere of circulation instead of in the sphere of production. By focusing on market and exchange relations, such a circulationist position neglects the analysis of social relations of production and consequently the configuration of classes and their characteristics. Another implication of this circulationist position relates to the stagnationist critique mentioned earlier. Dependency, by locating exploitation purely in the sphere of exchange relations, is seen to overlook the benefits of foreign investment to the internal economy (Kitching, 1982: 167–8) and the development of the forces of production (Castañeda and Hett, 1978: 49, 75, 171), as well as to fail 'to focus centrally on the productivity of labour as the essence and key to economic development' (Brenner, 1977: 91). Again, it is important to differentiate between dependency writers. Dos Santos, for one, does not adopt a circulationist position: on the contrary, he categorically states that 'one has to combat any tendency to explain underdevelopment and dependence through the mechanisms of exchange' (Dos Santos, 1978: 367). For him exploitation of labour does not take place at the level of exchange but at the level of production. However, he fails to undertake a detailed analysis of the relations of production, although he does employ a class analysis of sorts.

Another implication of this circulationist position relates to the wider debate between Dobb and Sweezy on the transition from feudalism to capitalism in Western Europe. Sweezy's circulationist position has been interpreted as meaning that the transition arose out of external forces while Dobb, who ascribes a central role to production relations, is held to view the transition process as determined internally (Frank, 1978b: 252; Dobb, 1980: 9–10). Similarly, it is argued that dependency's circulationist position is responsible for the overemphasis on external factors when studying the process of change in Third World countries. The internal class structure is also viewed by critics like Geoffrey Kay (1975: 117), Brenner (1977), and Weeks and Dore (1979) as being the main factor for explaining the underdevelopment of those countries where it blocks or retards the development of the forces of production (de Janvry, 1982: 20).

Autonomy or dependence: a false dilemma and the inadequacy of policy proposals

Fourth, the use of the category of autonomy to differentiate the characterization of dependency and the policy proposals following from it have been criticized. In Bernstein's view the advanced capitalist countries 'are no more "autonomous" than the underdeveloped economies' (Bernstein, 1979: 91) and thus the category of autonomy cannot be used as a central element in defining dependence. As he puts it (ibid.: 92):

Underdevelopment theory cannot have it both ways. If the field of analysis is world economy, if the centre needs the periphery for modes of exploitation that off-set the tendency of the rate of profit to fall, if the circuit of capital in general is realized on the international plane, then there is *no* capitalist formation whose development can be regionally autonomous, self-generating or self-perpetuating. 'Development' cannot be conceptualized by its self-centred nature and lack of dependence, nor 'underdevelopment' by its dependence and lack of autonomy.

Brewer (1980: 178) likewise criticizes the concept of dependency for implying that the process of development in the advanced countries is economically independent and self-sustaining. He prefers 'to speak of relations of interdependence and dominance rather than of dependence' (ibid.). Leys (1977: 95) also speaks of a complex set of interdependency, and Ray (1973: 4–20) argues that, as it is impossible to achieve a state of non-dependence, it is preferable to speak of degrees of dependence in an interdependent world. Brookfield (1975: 201) even argues that the advanced countries are more strongly dependent on the world economy than the underdeveloped countries. Ferrer (1979b: 875–85) argues that *dependencia* needs to be updated as in recent decades economic power has become more dispersed among the developed countries and the relative bargaining power of developing countries has improved. According to Brookfield, the US no longer imposes or dictates world events. Others argue that the power of organizations such as OPEC, displayed so effectively during the 1970s oil crises, and the rise of the newly industrializing countries means that Third World countries have acquired a greater influence in world affairs. Thus, many developing countries now enjoy greater freedom of manoeuvre than in the past.

Similar sentiments are expressed in a forceful manner by Warren who argues not only that interdependence between developed and underdeveloped countries has increased but also that the relationship has become less subordinate. Thus,

all the normal indicators of 'dependence' point to *increasingly* non-subordinate economic relations between poor and rich countries as regards to trade diversification (geographically or by commodities), control of foreign investment, structural change (in both inter-sectoral and intra-sectoral terms), and balance of payments accounts.

(Warren, 1980: 170)

Furthermore, in opposition to the autarchic strand in certain versions of dependency, he argues (ibid.: 184) that increased economic inter-action between developed and developing countries is a pre–condition for 'genuine equality among interdependent economies'.[10]

The dependency perspective has also been criticized for its failure to propose specific economic policies which would reduce the ties of dependence (Paz, 1981: 73; Seers, 1981b; Staniland, 1985: 138–40). It is seen to lack a political economy for achieving independence – if such a situation is possible in today's increasingly interdependent world (Ferrer, 1979b). Reformist *dependentistas* do, however, specify some general policy measures for enhancing the degree of autonomy in Third World countries. These include economic integration between developing countries, measures to restrict the abuses of multinational corporations and to encourage the transfer of technology and re–investment, and the call for a new international economic order (Sunkel, 1969; 1972a). Radical dependency writers, by contrast, have few policy recommendations beyond calling for the overthrow of capitalism and the establishment of socialism as if these were unproblematic.[11] While radical *dependentistas* have increasingly recognized that even countries committed to reducing dependence have faced far greater difficulties in this task than what they originally expected, it is still difficult to find any specific policy measures in their more recent writings. Some radical writers like Amin (1977b: 1–21), Senghaas (1974: 31–5; 1977), and Galtung (1980) propose a strategy of autocentric, self–centred or self–reliant development, and, in some instances, of selective dissociation, de–linking, and autarchy.

In his notable critique of dependency, however, Warren (1980: 252–5) argues against de–linking and similar strategies, favouring instead the full integration of Third World countries into the world capitalist system as well as supporting policies which remove pre–capitalist obstacles to development. In turn, Kitching (1982: 181) argues that to see the eradication of poverty and achievement of development in nationalistic and autonomous terms is to invite simplistic, illusionary, and ultimately dangerous policy conclusions. He disagrees with those who think that the more policies are nationally oriented and the greater their degree of delinking and self–reliance, so much the better. While some countries who have pursued self–reliant policies have seen them end in failure, other countries who have followed the opposite path of further integration into the world economy have achieved unprecedented high rates of growth. This invites rethinking dependency.

Despite the evident weaknesses of much writing on dependency, it should not be assumed, however, that dependency analysis is no longer relevant and that dependency is largely a pre–1973–OPEC–crisis phenomenon. As Ray Bromley writes:

> Before 1973 it was more clearly a dependency of poor capitalist nations on rich ones; now it's more a dependency of poor capitalist nations on the international capitalist system. Capital is increasingly footloose, but its power is evident, most notably in the flowering of the international debt crisis in the 1980s – surely making many Third World countries more dependent than ever. In my view the Third World debt, and most notably the Latin American debt, is the perfect illustration of the continuing importance of the dependency concept. It means that Latin American governments have very little bargaining power on the international scene, and that internal policies are imposed from outside by foreign governments, international organizations and the international banking community. Surely this 'loss of control' is the most classic manifestation of dependency.
>
> (Personal communication, 31 August 1987)

At first sight the unprecedented high growth rates of the East Asian newly industrializing countries would appear to disprove such a dependency thesis based on 'loss of control' as the spectacular development of their forces of production was achieved by further integration into the world capitalist system through the promotion of foreign investment and a vigorous export–oriented industrialization policy. What are the lessons for dependency analysis? In Bienefeld's view (1981: 94) the experience of these countries does not represent an adequate and desirable pattern of development as it does not ensure the diffusion of benefits and is not responsive to popular needs. Another commentator sees the lessons for *dependentistas* in the following terms:

> The East Asian experience clearly contradicts the caricature of dependency theory which purports to argue that stagnation and exclusion will follow in proportion to the extent of international connections; but so does Latin American experience. If East Asianists can speed the demise of some of the simplistic and mechanical propositions with which the dependency tradition has become burdened, so much the better. If, on the other hand, we confront the East Asian experience with an historical–structural or

Cardosian version of the dependency approach, we find the results for that approach more confirmatory than contradictory.

(P. Evans, 1987: 220–1)

A similar, but wider, conclusion is reached by Browett (1985: 789) who argues that:

> The failure of the neo–Marxist dependency perspectives to accommodate and come to terms with the possibilities of peripheral capitalist development in the four Newly Industrializing Countries (NICs) of East and Southeast Asia should not then result in the embracing of the stages approach espoused either by modernization theory or by Warren. Rather, consideration should be given to approaches which emphasize, within the backdrop of the changing internationalization of the self–expansion of capital, the historical specificities of capital accumulation, class struggle and the role of the state in the process of social reproduction.

In conclusion, the problem remains as to how to overcome dependency. For radical *dependentistas* the solution is revolution and transition to socialism. In addressing this issue *dependentistas* have to think through the various options open to a country. There are two alternatives: solidarity with the Soviet bloc or delinking from the world system and pursuing a strategy of self–reliance. Developing close links with the Soviet bloc has the danger that new links of dependence might arise based on aid, trade, investment, and above all on the (military) protection afforded by the USSR as a superpower. The problem with delinking is that this might not always be economically and politically feasible and might condemn the country to slow growth and technological inferiority. A further question is how much the size, location, resources, class composition, and so on of a country influence the viability of revolution, socialism, and either solidarity with the USSR or self–reliance. These crucial issues need to be explored further by *dependentistas*.

Empirical critiques

Fifth, *dependentistas* have been criticized for neglecting empirical analysis and for being factually inaccurate (Staniland, 1985: 126–8). Empirical critics often isolate a particular dependency proposition and subject it to a variety of statistical analyses, rejecting those dependency hypotheses where, in their view, the statistical tests conclusively show that they do not conform with empirical reality or simply with the facts. Some of these empirical studies, which have found particular favour with North American critics of dependency, are seriously flawed, for by reducing dependency propositions into testable hypotheses they often seriously distort them. [12] There are also problems with the data, the countries, years, and time–span selected, as well as with the statistical tests employed.

Some writers on dependency regard the main shortcoming of these empirical tests as methodological. As Cardoso and Faletto (1979: xii–iii) put it:

> The question is not whether to measure. The question is rather what and how to measure and also concerns the methodological status of measuring...[which] in a dialectical approach does not play the role of a fundamental device in the logic of demonstration, as if we were dealing with hypotheses to be accepted or rejected only after statistical tests...[as] the crucial questions for demonstration are of a different nature.

Thus, for example, they argue that the procedure of separating and submitting economic and political factors to independent tests goes against the essential characteristic of dependency studies – namely, its emphasis on global, dynamic, and interactive analysis (ibid.: xii). Similarly,

> Dependency, as a concept, does not possess a *specific empirical reference*. It is for this that it cannot be treated as a 'variable' susceptible to be attached to the existent analytical models. It implies a new perspective, a global reinterpretation of...underdevelopment.
>
> (Vasconi, 1971: 18)

According to sympathetic reviewers of the dependence perspective, 'It is meaningless to develop, as some social scientists have, a series of synchronic statistical indicators to establish relative levels of dependence or interdependence among different national units in order to test the "validity" of the model' (Valenzuela and Valenzuela, 1979: 44). Furthermore,

> The point of dependency analysis is not the relative mix at one point in time of certain identifiable factors, but the evolution over time of structural relations which are intimately related...The dependence

perspective is a historical model which cannot be 'tested' by doing cross national research at one point in time.

(ibid.: 57)

Some critics, particularly those of the Anglo–Saxon world, may be unaware of the large number of concrete regional and country studies undertaken from a dependency perspective. [13] *Dependentistas* are not averse to empirical studies *per se*, but for many, empirical analysis only makes sense where there are adequate theories and concepts underpinning the selection and interpretation of data and 'facts' (Cardoso and Faletto, 1979: xiii). The financial, institutional, and political constraints on undertaking research and field–work in Latin America have also to be borne in mind. Given adequate facilities, *dependentistas* are unlikely to eschew the opportunity to engage in further analyses of concrete situations of dependence. Thus, the plea for the study of specific social formations, which many critics have voiced, is likely to be welcomed by *dependentistas*.

Ideology, politics, and socialism

This sixth critique questions the political underpinnings of the dependency perspective and queries its notion of socialism. According to Mires (1978: 2), a critique of dependency analysis has to be above all a political critique. In his view, the dependency school performed a critical role as an 'ideology of rupture' for those searching for an alternative politics; and the original generalizations and simplifications of dependency analysis were eminently suited to this ideological task. Thus, Mires argues, it might be more appropriate to speak of an ideology of dependence instead of a theory of dependence. Castañeda and Hett (1978: 185) also argue that the theory of dependence is ideological but, unlike Mires, maintain that it is part of the dominant ideology and consequently an epistemological obstacle to understanding the contradictions in backward social formations. [14]

As mentioned earlier, both 'reformists' and 'revolutionaries' were searching for alternatives to the existing models of development. After the Cuban revolution, alarmed (but enlightened) bourgeois groups sought to locate this alternative in the ideology of the 'Alliance for Progress' and its related reformist dependency formulation. The 'revolutionaries', by contrast, looked to the Cuban revolution to endorse their thesis of the immediacy of socialist revolution and to discredit the Communist Party's 'reformist' thesis of the bourgeois–

democratic revolution. The Marxist dependency perspective provided them with such an ideology and paradigmatic break (Mires, 1978: 6–7). However, the failure of 'Che' Guevara's guerrilla campaign in Bolivia, the uncomfortably close links between Cuba and the Soviet Union, and the overthrow of Allende's socialist experiment in Chile dampened their early optimism. Furthermore, the 'success' of the Brazilian 'miracle' encouraged the non–reformist or dominant bourgeoisie. This set of events led to a re–appraisal of the dependency perspective by both left and right. Part of the left responded to the shortcomings of the dependency analysis by developing the theory of the modes of production; others advocate the study of the processes of class struggle in specific social formations. In Mires's view (1978, 31–3), the mode of production theory is not a theory of social classes which he regards as necessary for advancing the struggle for socialism.

Mires (1978: 6, 13) also criticizes the Marxist dependency perspective for its 'super–idealism' and for believing in capitalism's collapse. In a similar vein, others have found fault with dependency analysis for undervaluing the resilience and adaptability of capitalism in the Third World, and for its idealist and utopian conception of socialism (Leys, 1977: 98; Castañeda and Hett, 1978: 82; Bernstein, 1982: 227–8; C. Johnson, 1983). Radical or Marxist *dependentistas* are held to arrive at the notion of socialism by default and by despair. This is because for *dependentistas* the question of socialism arises out of the assumed non–viability of dependent capitalism which fails to lead to improved income distribution, full employment, a welfare state, a mass consumer market, high wage levels, and so on. Bernstein regards such a conception of capitalist development as embodying a conceptual delusion and a fallacy. Further it is a negative teleology and ahistorical as it defines underdevelopment and dependence with reference to an implicit 'model' of 'normal', 'autonomous', 'self–sustaining', (and so on) capitalist development followed by today's advanced countries under very different historical conditions (Bernstein, 1979: 93; 1982: 227). Thus, socialism is seen by default as the only alternative for achieving 'genuine' development: 'Revolution and socialism are now on the agenda as an effect of the failure of national capitalist development.' (Bernstein, 1979: 96.)

An adequate analysis of the prospects for socialism is held to require an understanding of the contradictions of capitalism, of the class struggle in specific social formations, of the identification of revolutionary forces, and of the formulation of the strategy and tactics for achieving power (Leys, 1977: 98). Such an analysis has in part been carried out by only a few *dependentistas*. Radical dependency analysts often overlook capitalism's ability to deal with crises and find non–socialist alternatives of change, seeing fascism or sub–imperialism as the only alternatives to socialism. In this way, socialism is held to result from the despair of the masses, who are only too ready to follow the revolutionary guerrilla *foco* which will ignite the fuse sparking off a mass uprising and heralding liberation.

Dependency's theoretical status and Marxism

Seventh, the theoretical status of the notion of dependency has been queried for a variety of reasons. Given the variety of theoretical approaches to dependency, some prefer to speak of a 'dependency school', 'paradigm', 'approach', or 'perspective' rather than of a theory (Palma, 1978: 911; Blomström and Hettne, 1984: 77). As mentioned earlier, Fernando H. Cardoso himself suggested that it would be more fruitful to undertake studies of 'concrete situations of dependency' rather than constructing a formal theory. However, he thinks it possible to formulate a theory of dependency provided it is part of a wider theory of capitalism or of socialism (Cardoso, 1972c: 17).

For Bernstein (1979: 93) a theory of dependency is impossible because it constitutes 'a negative teleology' – i.e. by stating what cannot occur in Third World countries (development *à la* advanced capitalist countries) it does not provide the means of investigating what does occur. Fernández and Ocampo (1974: 30–59), who dismiss dependency theory altogether, propose instead a theory of imperialism. Similarly, Castañeda and Hett (1978: 151, 175, 185, 191), who reject the notion of dependent capitalism, propose the concept of 'dominated imperialist social formation' (*sic*). In sustaining that the development experience of dependent countries differs fundamentally from that of the advanced countries, they accuse the *dependentistas* of 'inverted ethnocentrism' (ibid.: 151–2). Geoffrey Kay (1975: 104–5) also rejects the concept of 'dependent capitalism' as he regards the Marxist laws of capitalism as being applicable to all capitalist modes of production. While he agrees with the *dependentistas* that capital in underdeveloped countries does not create a developed world, his reasons for this differ. In Cueva's view (1979: 79), there is no qualitative difference between the laws of development of advanced and of backward capitalist countries. Thus, the orthodox Marxist theory of capitalist accumulation is sufficient for analysing the process of development in Third World countries. In denying that any specific laws are operative in dependent countries, Cueva challenges the very core of the dependency paradigm.

Cueva's analysis provides an entry–point into the discussion concerning the Marxist nature of the radical wing of the dependency perspective. He regards their writings as non–Marxist as, by criticizing orthodox Marxism, they absorb developmentalist notions from the bourgeois social sciences (ibid.: 64). Furthermore, as Cueva does not believe in the existence of a dependent mode of production, he regards traditional Marxist theory as adequately explaining the dynamics of the Latin American economy and society so that no neo–Marxist dependency is required (ibid.: 80–1). In Weeks's view (1981: 118), Marxist theory differs from, and is incompatible with, dependency theory. Booth (1985: 763) goes even further:

> A number of critics...have made much of the fact that dependency and underdevelopment theory is not rooted in a rigorous application of Marxist economic theory,...the point is surely that it is not rooted in *any* rigorous body of deductive–type theory.

However, Foster–Carter rejects the sectarianism of certain critics of dependency analysis. He disagrees with those who believe, like J. Taylor (1974), Leys (1977), Phillips (1977), and Bernstein (1979), 'that it is important to distinguish: (a) on the one hand, "Marxism"; and (b) on the other hand, something else; variously called "underdevelopment and dependency theory", or "UDT" for short (Leys) or "radical underdevelopment theory" (Bernstein)' (Foster–Carter, 1979–80: 214), as they all think for various reasons that the latter is neither Marxist nor useful. He claims that 'it is *not* on the whole necessary, true, useful or even possible to make a distinction between "Marxism" on the one hand, and "radicalism" or "dependency theory" on the other' (ibid.: 214). He forcefully argues against dogmatism and intellectual apartheid, concluding that, as for development theory,

> many, if not most of the key theoretical questions are and perhaps always will be contentious – there are no 'correct' answers; and...the sectarian example to exclude and foreclose debate by arrogating the label 'Marxist' to certain positions only, can have nothing but negative implications. On this basis, let a thousand debates proceed.
>
> (ibid.: 232)

In a similar vein, Edelstein (1981: 107) argues that the context of dependent capitalist development differs from Marx's analysis of the classical case of capitalism and that 'the sectarian critics' refusal to accept the significance of the differential loci results in an inadequate, rigidified analysis'. In his view *dependentistas* never pretended to develop a general theory and he blames the critics for upgrading it into a competitor with Marxist theory. In his opinion,

> the concepts used by left *dependentistas* do not sufficiently specify a set of relationships to constitute a theory. But if these concepts were to add up to a theory, it is a special rather than a general theory.... It is not an alternative to Marxist analysis.
>
> (ibid.: 107)

Similarly, Munck concludes from his exploration of the relations between Marxism and dependency that 'in the confrontation between dependency theory and the sterile dogmatic Marxists ("the ideological cops") we see many wilful distortions and an inability to learn from one's opponent' (Munck, 1981: 166).[15] Finally, who would quarrel with the claim that 'the dependency school's attempts, even if they were not Marxist, eventually resulted in a vitalized Marxist view of "underdevelopment"'? (Blomström and Hettne, 1984: 54).

NEW DIRECTIONS AND BEYOND DEPENDENCY

While Frank (1977: 357–8) had announced 'dependence' dead in 1972, Bambirra (1978) for one did not agree and published a vigorous defence. Similarly, Godfrey (1980: 4) is of the view that it would be premature to pronounce *dependencia* as dead, although he recognizes that it needs to be modified and extended for a theory of dependence to be successfully developed – a sentiment shared to some extent by Foster– Carter (1979–80), Chilcote (1981), Edelstein (1981), FitzGerald (1981), D. Johnson (1981), Munck (1981; 1984), Veltmeyer (1983), and O'Brien (1984), among others. By contrast, other commentators concur with Leys (1977: 92) that dependence should be transcended or abandoned. A similar assessment is made by Cueva (1974), Geoffrey Kay (1975), Semo (1975), Castañeda and Hett (1978), Bernstein (1979), Warren (1980), Weeks (1981), and Booth (1985), among others.

A number of refinements, modifications, or alternatives to the dependency framework have been proposed, some of which have already been mentioned. Thus, those who argue that the dependency perspective lacks a class analysis propose a class analysis; those who sustain that it marginalizes the political, that this should be brought into focus (Randall and Theobald, 1985), and those who criticize it for its lax use of Marxist concepts suggest that these should be applied more rigorously. Others argue that dependency analysis cannot accommodate these criticisms and that it should be abandoned. This position is generally adopted by those who argue that a theory of dependency is not required as it can be subsumed or replaced by the Marxist theory of imperialism. However, others argue that reverting to a theory of imperialism pure and simple does not provide an alternative as 'neither the classical theory of imperialism nor contemporary strains of orthodox Marxism provide ready answers to the problems of underdevelopment that dependency theory has addressed' (D. Johnson, 1981: 108). Yet others argue that the impasse can be dealt with by developing a theory of capital accumulation (Marini, 1972; Paz, 1981) or a theory of 'dependent reproduction' (Kalmanovitz, 1975; Munck, 1984: 31–5, 347–50).

As mentioned earlier, some *dependentistas* have shifted the focus of their analysis from the nation state to the international political economy and embraced or contributed to the development of a theory of the 'transnational system' (Sunkel and Fuenzalida, 1979) or to the 'internationalization of capital' (Barkin, 1981: 156; Marcussen and Torp, 1982) or to 'world system theory' (Frank, 1980; 1981b). However, for Petras and others, by focusing on circulation and losing sight of social relations and class formation, world system theory has its own weaknesses (Munck, 1981: 170; Petras, 1981: 149–53).

In Henfrey's (1981: 49) view, 'The task is of relating a theory of imperialism to the histories of exploited classes, not in dependent capitalism or articulated modes of production, but in Latin American social formations.' Chilcote (1984: 129–32) also calls for a theory of class struggle, endorsing Henfrey's resolution. For Howe (1981: 82, 86) neither class analysis nor a theory of imperialism are sufficient by themselves or adequate alternatives to dependency analysis. D. Johnson (1981: 112–14), while favouring class analysis, warns against sociologism by reminding those who might embrace such a position that 'people make history but only under circumstances that are objectively given' (ibid.: 114). He also argues against economism and determinism – be it internal or external.

Finally, several authors have suggested that the theory of the modes of production is a way out of the theoretical shortcomings of the concept of dependence as this focuses on internal social relations of production as well as on their articulation within a wider totality

(Sempat Assadourian, 1971; Laclau, 1971; Foster–Carter, 1978; J. Taylor, 1979). However, for Booth (1985: 768) the mode–of–production debate has led to an 'impasse within an impasse' as 'the concept of mode production is subject to multiple and in practice contradictory theoretical requirements which make it incapable of consistent application to the task of illuminating world development'. For D. Johnson (1983: 237) the mode of productionists, by defining capitalism far too narrowly, reproduce the error of those they criticize. Capitalism cannot be defined by a single criterion, be it commodity markets (Frank) or free wage–labour (mode of productionists). The widespread existence of unfree and non–wage labour 'are best understood not as modes of production in articulation but in their linkages with the capital accumulation process and the reproduction of cheap labor power' (ibid.: 236) in dependent countries.

In turn, Cueva (1979: 80–1) criticizes those who have tried to seek refuge in the concept of 'dependent mode of production', as no such *sui generis* mode of production can be constituted. Such a concept can be considered a contradiction in terms for in the Marxist conception, each mode of production has its own internal laws, while under dependence the laws of capital accumulation and realization cannot be fulfilled internally and are in dialectical relationship with another dominant mode of production. Bambirra (1978: 26) agrees with the above but holds that it is possible to speak of a 'dependent capitalist socio–economic formation'. In short, the mode of productionists do not appear to offer an alternative to the dependency perspective. Thus the debate continues.

What can be concluded from these debates and criticisms of dependency analysis? What is the final verdict on the contribution of dependency analysis to development theory? Any assessment is complicated by the fact that no systematic and coherent theory of dependency has yet emerged. There is no doubt that dependency analysis gave an enormous boost to the social sciences in Latin America and beyond by stimulating a wealth of theoretical reflections and empirical research on the Third World and its relationship to the world economy, and to the developed countries in particular. Many of the strengths and weaknesses of dependency analysis arise from the scale of its aim and ambition. *Depedentistas* had the vision and audacity to think big and to aim to create a new paradigm. They might not have succeeded, given that the interdisciplinary, historical, total, and multiple character of dependency analysis makes the creation of such a paradigm an almost impossible task, and one which is riddled with contradictions.

While dependency analysis did not succeed in creating a new fully developed theory, it did succeed in questioning the validity of modernization theory and hastening its demise. It also challenged orthodox Marxism by re-examining the validity of certain aspects for Third World countries in particular. By stressing the specific structures and development processes of Third World countries, dependency analysis has defied both modernization and orthodox (or Stalinist) Marxist theories. In this sense dependency analysis has also given a new sense of identity as well as commonality to Third World countries.

A key and valuable insight of *dependentistas* is to have emphasized that the dynamics of dependent countries have to be examined in relation to the dynamics of the dominant countries. Thus, internal and external relations are not seen as separate elements as in dualist modernization theory, but as forming a dialectical unity. Dependent and dominant countries have increasingly become interrelated since colonial times in a complex web of economic, social, political, and cultural elements which form a totality. Dependency analysis showed how the advanced or modern can reproduce the backward or traditional and, paradoxically, how the modern can even create new forms of backwardness or traditionality.

Undoubtedly there are many weaknesses of dependency analysis, the most important being its overdetermination of the external. By overstressing the dependency relationship, dependency analysis provided a convenient scapegoat for the development problems of Third World countries. Imperialism and the dominant countries are held to have generated them in the first instance and to be responsible for their continuance. This creates a distorted historical picture of conditions in the pre-dependence period, which is explicitly or implicitly idealized and seen as unproblematic. Second, by underemphasizing the internal causes of underdevelopment, dependency analysis does not pay sufficient attention to the class contradictions and obstacles to development within the country. Third, dependency analysis fosters the 'autonomist' illusion that if only the ties of dependence could be cut, all would be well: a genuine process of development would follow and underdevelopment would be conquered. The desire of *dependentistas* to revert to some sort of autarchic utopia inspired the battle-cry of many Third World leaders that, following political independence, their countries have now to go on to achieve economic independence. As dependency is identified as the source of all evil, it is small wonder that *dependentistas* are bereft of concrete policy proposals for development. Thus, dependency analysis has few specific proposals for raising the rate of economic growth, improving the distribution of income, diversifying exports, generating employment, reducing social inequalities, removing racial and sexual discrimination, and so on. By thinking in terms of creating a new international system, through either reform or revolution, they underestimate the room for manoeuvre of governments in Third World countries. Theirs is the grand historical and total vision which fails to perceive and seize the minor but immediate opportunities. It is an all or nothing illusion.

Nevertheless, whatever the deficiencies of dependency theory, the dependency of the Third World is certainly a reality and one which has much to answer for its predicament; but so have the internal structures of domination and exploitation. Structuralism, internal colonialism, marginality, and dependency analysis have certainly contributed towards an understanding of the relationships between the internal and external webs of domination and exploitation, although some of these analyses might have got the balance wrong. The continuing relevance of these Latin American theories of development, as well as some conclusions regarding their contribution to development theory in general, are explored in the next and final chapter of this book.

The Latin American contribution in perspective

This chapter examines the waning influence of structuralist and dependency analyses and the subsequent rise and fall of neo–monetarism. Neo–monetarism became the fashion from the mid–1970s onwards but ran into trouble in the early 1980s. Latin America has been going through a profound economic crisis since the 1982–3 world recession from which it has yet to recover. Neo– monetarist policies are partly blamed for this economic collapse, which in many Latin American countries is more severe than the Great Depression of the 1930s. It is possible that the loss of credibility of neo–monetarism will lead to a renewal of interest in structuralist and *dependencia* ideas. At present old debates are resurfacing under new guises, such as those on industrialization, the debt, inflation, and state intervention. Thus, the various contending theoretical paradigms have had their ups and downs, leaving a vacuum which still waits to be filled. The question I want to pursue here concerns the extent to which structuralism and dependency analysis can provide a framework for the study of Latin America's present–day predicament, and more generally provide a way out of Latin America's development crisis as well as of the crisis of development theory identified in Chapter 1.

THE RISE OF MONETARISM AND ITS CONSEQUENCES

The heyday of ECLA's structuralism was the 1950s to the mid–1960s. It began to lose influence with the exhaustion of the import–substitution industrialization process in the early 1960s, with the later crisis of reformist governments, and above all with the simultaneous challenge at the theoretical and practical levels of the dependency and monetarist critiques and the new development path pioneered by Brazil.

The significance of the 1964 Brazilian coup lies not only in the political blow it dealt to a populist reformist government, but in the distinctive nature of the military government which took over. It initiated a new development project which has variously been called 'bureaucratic authoritarianism' (O'Donnell), 'savage capitalism' (Castro de Andrade), 'sub–imperialism' (Marini), 'state capitalism' (Fishlow), the 'Brazilian miracle', and so on. This new Brazilian development strategy, based on a triple alliance between state capital, transnational enterprises and the local bourgeoisie, combined orthodox monetary policies with decisive state intervention and widespread political repression (F. Cardoso, 1973b; P. Evans, 1979). Foreign investment was encouraged and public corporations were given a key role in the economy. By overcoming Brazil's stagnation and exhaustion of the import–substitution industrialization process, this strategy challenged the structuralists' development path as it was achieved not via democratization of society, but by an authoritarian military regime. It threw overboard ECLA's reasoning that industrialization, with its concomitant growth of the middle class and skilled labour force, would enhance the democratization of society, and that these two processes were mutually reinforcing.

By following an 'income concentration with growth strategy' which achieved unprecedented high growth rates, the Brazilian military regime also overturned the structuralists' redistribution–with–growth strategy and the stagnationist thesis. Although Brazil did not reverse the import–substitution industrialization process (as the neo–monetarist model later did in some Latin American countries), it overcame the impasse reached by this process through a different route from that recommended by structuralists. Instead of widening the internal market through income redistribution and agrarian reform, the military government's policy was based on further income concentration as well as land concentration and proletarianization of the peasantry. A solution was also found to the problem of capital accumulation which combined a drastic process of 'primitive accumulation' with remarkable increases in productivity. Most, if not all, the increases in labour productivity were appropriated by capitalists and were not transformed into higher wages. The Brazilian military did not share ECLA's export pessimism, nor did a possible deterioration in the commodity terms of trade deter them from boosting traditional exports. However, the military government also eased the foreign–exchange constraint by pursuing a vigorous export drive in manufactures. This was a qualitatively new situation.

The implications of the challenge posed by the Brazilian model to structuralist and dependency theory were not fully appreciated at the time, especially as the development strategies pursued by some other Latin American countries continued to give encouragement. Political developments in Peru and Chile, for example, lent support to the structuralist–dependency model – one through a reformist military regime and the other through a democratically elected socialist coalition.

In Peru from 1968 to 1975, General Velasco's progressive military government drew inspiration from ECLA's development model in designing its own strategy (Booth and Sorj, 1983). The import–substitution industrialization process was enhanced through a variety of protectionist and state–interventionist measures. Many public enterprises were created (some by expropriating foreign companies), a comprehensive agrarian reform was set in motion, national and regional planning offices established and development plans elaborated, and a variety of workers' participation schemes and worker and co–operative enterprises introduced.

Even before its overthrow in a bloodless military coup led by General Morales Bermúdez in 1975, the Velasquista project had began to run out of steam. Morales Bermúdez inaugurated the so–called 'second phase of the revolution' which finally buried whatever revolutionary impulse might have been contained in Velasco's 'third road' to the Great Transformation, which was to be neither capitalist nor socialist. Morales Bermúdez's government made further concessions to the local and foreign bourgeoisie and gradually began to follow a mild version of the monetarist model.

More dramatically, in Chile the first democratically elected socialist and Marxist President, Salvador Allende, took office in 1970 on a platform of structural change. Some of Allende's ministers and high officials had previously worked in ECLA or other United Nations agencies, and Allende's policies were clearly influenced by a mixture of structuralist and dependency prescriptions. The copper mines, Chile's symbol of dependence and largest source of export earnings, were nationalized. The agrarian reform process was accelerated and extended. Banks were nationalized, along with many major (and in some instances lesser) industrial enterprises. This process of expropriations was propelled forward by pressure from peasants and workers who, in many instances, took over landed estates and industries, demanding their expropriation (O'Brien, 1976; Winn, 1986). In the international sphere Allende's government vigorously argued for improved terms of trade for Third World primary exports, a reduction or elimination of protectionist measures by the developed countries, greater controls on foreign capital and transnational corporations – in short, for a new international economic order.

Allende's 'Chilean road to socialism' pursued policies which could be described as combining elements of 'redistribution with growth', 'basic needs', and 'self–reliance'. The Chilean experiment was viewed and studied with great interest by international development specialists, as exemplified by the round–table jointly organized by ODEPLAN (the Chilean National Planning Office) and IDS (the Institute of Development Studies at the University of Sussex, England) (Zammit and Palma, 1973). Through redistribution of income the Allende government hoped to give a new boost to the import–substitution industrialization process, which was redirected from luxury goods to the production of mass consumer goods. This redirection of import substitution aimed to stimulate medium and smaller enterprises which used less capital–intensive technologies, thereby enhancing employment opportunities and saving foreign exchange. Politically, it was designed to win over or neutralize the petty and medium bourgeoisies. Thus, it was hoped that this new import–substitution industrialization model would overcome the market, employment, and foreign exchange constraints of the old 'exhausted' process.

During the first year the economy expanded, wages rose substantially, unemployment was reduced to an all–time low, and inflation was brought under control. However, problems mounted during the second year. Economic growth faltered owing to difficulties in financing investment, among other reasons. Private investment fell dramatically and public investment was unable to bridge the gap. Rents and monopoly profits of the expropriated enterprises turned out to be far less than expected. On the one hand, these surpluses had been grossly overestimated for political reasons and, on the other hand, wage increases and disruptions in production arising from take–overs made substantial inroads into them.

The financing of the Chilean road to socialism was not made easier by the boycott of the IMF, the World Bank, and the international banking community. Moreover, the socialist bloc's commitment or ability to finance this experiment was limited. Thus, the government increasingly resorted to deficit financing to avoid investment falling further. The rise in social expenditure (health, housing, education, and social security), the compensations paid to some expropriated owners, the withering of the economic surplus of state enterprises, the food subsidies, the highly overvalued local currency, and other factors further multiplied the fiscal deficit. Inflation escalated into three–digit figures and the economy became unmanageable. On the one hand, the inordinate growth in government expenditure and the steep rise in wages led to excessive demand. On the other hand, insufficient investment, foreign exchange shortages, and the political turmoil led to a fall in production. In the end neither redistribution nor growth could be sustained.

With the demise of the 'Chilean Road to Socialism' and Perú's 'Third Road', monetarism became the rising star, not only in Chile and Peru but in most of Latin America. This had profound consequences for structuralism and dependency theory but also for development theory in general. In many countries the class forces supporting monetarist neo–conservative market policies gained the upper hand by capturing the state. However, the neo–monetarist (often referred to as neo–conservative or neo–liberal) policies implemented in various Latin American countries from the mid–1970s to the early 1980s have also failed, opening a space for alternative projects (Felix, 1981). The main heritage of neo–monetarism is the daunting debt problem, and increased levels of poverty, inequality, and unemployment (Griffith–Jones and Sunkel, 1986). Neo–conservative monetarist theory in its extremism and globalism overlooks the structural peculiarities of individual countries and this has contributed to its failure. Its birth was marked by a profound antagonism to structuralist and dependency theory. To the developmentalist, statist, and national autonomy concerns of structuralism and dependency, it counterposed a view of international monetarism, free markets, and anti–statism.

Neo–monetarist policies can be seen as a reaction against the previous decades of import–substitution industrialization and the rising importance of the state in the economic affairs of those countries which had pursued an inward–directed development strategy (Foxley, 1983). The neo–liberals thus proceeded to dismantle the array of protectionist and interventionist measures which had been built up since the 1930s. In some ways their policies were the mirror image of those advocated by structuralists and *dependentistas*, in particular. Neo–liberals sought the complete integration of the national economies into the international economy by removing barriers on trade and capital flows. Thus, resource allocation was ultimately to be governed by international prices and comparative advantages. The rhythm and direction of development was to be determined by international market forces and not by government intervention. In the structuralists' terminology, the neo–liberals were pursuing an outward–directed development model.

There is an urgent need to find alternatives to neo–conservatism. Given the failure of neo–monetarist economic policies in most Latin American countries, especially those where they were introduced more radically – i.e. the Southern Cone countries of Chile, Argentina, and Uruguay – there are sound economic reasons for considering some new structuralist or dependency–inspired development strategies. The only success achieved by neo–monetarism has been a significant and, in some countries, spectacular growth in exports. However, the policies underpinning this success have also led to a dramatic rise in the foreign debt, which has more than cancelled out the rise in exports. The net effect has thereby been a marked deterioration in the foreign exchange balance to the extent that the debt problem has become the central economic problem in most Latin American countries today. As for inflation, one of the neo–monetarists' main policy objectives, after some initial success – in some instances inflation fell from three to two digits – inflation later began to accelerate (Ramos, 1987).

More importantly, neo–conservative policies have led to de–industrialization, unemployment, income inequalities, and poverty. There have been brief spurts of economic growth but as a result of greater income inequalities poverty has risen. Whatever growth has taken place has benefited only a minority of the population. Neo–liberal policies also greatly increased the vulnerability of a country's economy to changing external conditions. Thus, the international recession in the early 1980s led to a drastic fall in output and its overall effects on the Latin American economies have been worse than that of the 1930s. Per capita incomes have fallen, in some instances to below those which existed when the neo–monetarist policies were first introduced a decade earlier. The per capita gross national income of Latin America fell by 14 per cent between 1980 and 1985, and in the Southern Cone countries the drop was roughly twice as much (Marcel and Palma, 1987: 4; PREALC, 1987:2).

The debt crisis has certainly contributed to the discrediting of neo–monetarist policies in Latin America. Too much internal financial liberalization led to capital flight, speculative investment, and an enormous inflow of foreign capital (largely loans) which for a time created a false bonanza. When the bubble finally burst, the state rescued many private banks from collapse and, ironically, nationalized some as a way of ensuring their survival. Thus, neo–conservative governments bailed out bankrupt financial institutions so as not to antagonize national and international finance capital. The repressive measures against labour and the bail–out of finance capital illustrate the class nature of neo–monetarist governments (O'Brien, 1986). The collapse of many industries and rising unemployment resulting from the over–rapid and drastic reduction in protectionism have also contributed to the disrepute of neo–monetarism.

There are also strong political reasons in favour of some form of structuralist or dependency–type policies. The implementation of the neo–monetarist model took place within a context of military–authoritarian governments which had overthrown elected democratic governments. Indeed, in some Latin American countries, particularly those with strong trade unions and left–wing political parties, neo–conservative policies could only be implemented under repressive circumstances. Paradoxically economic liberalism has often been achieved through political anti–liberalism. (This does not mean to say that some elected governments in Latin America have not followed the trend and pursued some variant of neo–monetarism, although in a less extreme and more gradual manner.) A key component of the neo–monetarist model is the reduction of wages so as to bring down production costs and thereby prices. This would help to slow down inflation as well as allowing some industries to remain competitive in the face of the dismantling of protectionist measures. Although neo–monetarist governments profess to let market forces reassert themselves in the economy, they clearly intervened in the labour market. In many countries this intervention meant a series of repressive measures such as the curtailment or outlawing of union activities, obstacles to or prohibition of strikes, and the persecution, imprisonment, and 'disappearance' of activists. Thus, some authors have labelled this type of neo–monetarism as 'repressive monetarism' (Fortín, 1984) or 'militant monetarism' (Sheahan, 1987). In addition, the limited welfare state, which had been built up during the populist and developmentalist era, has largely been dismantled leaving no safety net for the poor.

Thus, repressive monetarism has severely damaged the social fabric of society and encouraged rampant and materialistic individualism. As a consequence the increasing and vociferous demand for civil liberties, human, and democratic rights has become associated with the overthrow of the military regimes and their neo–monetarist policies. Where military dictatorships have given way to civilian governments (for example, Brazil, Argentina, and Uruguay), the opportunity arises for new variants of structuralist and dependency policies to be formulated. The possibility that a reformulated neo–monetarism, adapted to democratic circumstances, might emerge has also to be borne in mind. At the time of writing (early 1988), the outcome of these democratic experiences is uncertain.

SHORTCOMINGS OF STRUCTURALISM AND DEPENDENCY ANALYSIS

These varying development experiences continually challenge established theories, leading to their revision or abandonment, and to the emergence of new theories. As mentioned earlier, the structuralist and dependency approaches need to be revised in the light of past experiences and new economic and social circumstances. Some major issues which need to be reconsidered are set out below.

First, the structuralists' and *dependentistas'* central emphasis on the deterioration of the terms of trade and unequal exchange respectively needs to be cast in a new light. The structuralists' almost obsessive preoccupation with the terms of trade conveys the image that poverty and underdevelopment are essentially due to the periphery's exploitation by the centre. This detracts from the fundamental issue of development and underdevelopment, which is the class struggle within each society, and it fails to draw some key lessons from the historical experience of those countries which managed to grow successfully over long periods of time.

Unequal exchange, by transferring part of the economic surplus generated in the periphery to the centre, undoubtedly diminishes the periphery's capacity for capital accumulation and growth. However, a country's development has as much to do with its ability to generate, as to retain, its surplus, and this is largely determined by its internal mode of production. A country's socio–economic formation is, in turn, the outcome of a complex interaction between economic, social, and political factors within which the class struggle assumes a major significance. By locating exploitation solely at the level between nations these analyses detract from the fact that exploitation is a class phenomenon. This primacy of relations between nations goes some way towards explaining why class is a category which is practically absent in structuralist thought and is not given a crucial place within dependency studies. As structuralists want to reform rather than overthrow the capitalist system they are unwilling to recognize the class nature of exploitation.

There is growing recognition that not all the Third World's problems stem from outside. Imperialism, unfavourable terms of trade, foreign capital, or transnational corporations are no longer uniquely blamed for all the ills besetting the Third World. Policy–makers in the Third World are increasingly learning that they can change internal policies so as to minimize negative effects, as well as exploit new opportunities which might arise from changing international circumstances (Senghaas, 1988: 42–7). The view on transnationals is also changing, as some Third World countries have negotiated improved deals from them and value their superior technological and marketing skills or power (Emmanuel, 1982). Even some socialist countries are beginning to establish links with transnationals. Warren's (1980) trenchant critique of dependency's nationalism, the rapid industrialization of the East Asian countries, and the growing economic links of the socialist countries with the developed capitalist world, all require that structuralists' and *dependentistas'* rethink their position on the world economy and foreign capital.

Second, Frank's influential thesis, that the development of the centre countries is due to the exploitation of the peripheral countries and that the underdevelopment of the peripheral countries is due to the development of the centre countries, has to be abandoned. Recent historical research has shown that the development of the centre countries was above all due to the internal creation, appropriation and use of the surplus and had less to do with the pillage or exploitation of the peripheral countries (Weeks and Dore, 1979: 63, Senghaas, 1985: 66–7). Thus, for example, the international trade between Europe and the Third World accounted for roughly 1 per cent and 3 per cent of Europe's gross domestic product (GDP) in 1830 and 1910 respectively (Senghaas, 1985: 66). The reasons for the successful development of the now advanced countries have to be sought principally in the particular economic, social, and political institutional framework which they created and which was amenable to capital accumulation and innovation. This is not to deny that an economic surplus was transferred from the less– to the more–developed countries and that this facilitated the development of the latter and created problems for the former.

What is being argued is that development and underdevelopment are primarily rooted in social relations of production and, thus, in class relations and not in relations of exchange. In Brenner's view (1977: 86), 'it was the class structure through which export production was carried out (based on ultra–exploitation/methods of absolute surplus labour) which determined that increasing export production would lead to underdevelopment rather than development'. For this reason the main flaw of the structuralist centre–periphery paradigm (and to a certain extent of some dependency writers) is its lack of class analysis. Those analyses which essentially focus on exchange relations between nations tend to underemphasize the internal obstacles to development and overemphasize the external obstacles. In addition, they fail to visualize the creation of more favourable internal and external circumstances or to seize opportunities as they arise. Furthermore, participation in the international division of labour can lead to development, while an autarchic development strategy does not ensure development and can even lead to disaster, as in the case of the Khmer Rouge government under the leadership of the notorious Pol Pot in Kampuchea over the period 1975–8.

In short, the crucial lesson which Third World countries can learn from the developed countries is that the essential condition for development is to undergo certain internal transformations. The type of internal transformation required if development is to be achieved will differ between countries and change according to historical circumstances.

Third, the role of the state in development needs to be redefined. Structuralists and *dependentistas* have to arrive at a more realistic appreciation of what the state can and cannot or should not do. Structuralists often take the rationality of the state for granted by following the enlightenment ideology. The early writings of ECLA, in particular, reveal an idealized picture of the developmentalist state as a liberating, equalizing, and modernizing force in society. If only the oligarchical state were in the hands of the industrial bourgeoisie and staffed by technocrats and professionals, all would be fine as the state would then become the main force for progress. This enlightened state would implement development programmes whose fruits would be distributed widely through a newly created welfare system.

Dependentistas also had an idealist vision of the socialist state. In this model, the exploited classes, and particularly the industrial proletariat, are to be in the driving–seat – the key problem being how to capture state power. The proletarian state would abolish exploitation and poverty. Through a comprehensive programme of nationalization and planning, a self–reliant and self–sustaining development process would be achieved, and underdevelopment and foreign exploitation would finally be overcome. Today both structuralists and *dependentistas* hold a more sober view of the role of the state in development and the feasibility of certain development strategies. The performance of the state during the import–substitution period disenchanted many structuralists; but in particular, the authoritarian and repressive role assumed by the state during the recent neo–monetarist phase is leading to a more realistic view of its role.

Guillermo O'Donnell (1973) formulated his theory of the bureaucratic–authoritarian state in the wake of the military coups in Brazil in 1964 and in Argentina in 1966. The coups in Chile and Uruguay in 1973, two Latin American countries with the longest record of continuous democratic government, lend further support to his theory. In his thesis O'Donnell tried to come to grips with the new nature of the state and provides a theory of the state which is missing from the structuralist literature. He argued that the era of the populist–democratic state based on a multi–class coalition between the industrial bourgeoisie, the middle classes, and sectors of the working class had come to an end.

O'Donnell's model of politics was strongly determined by economic factors, as he saw a close correspondence between the rise and fall of the populist state and the various stages of the import–substitution process. During the 'easy' phase of import–substitution the industrial bourgeoisie came to power. Rapid industrial expansion enabled new social sectors to be incorporated into the state. As has been analysed in Chapter 2 this 'easy phase' of import substitution was based on the production of basic consumer goods (such as textiles) which could and did reach wider sectors of society. However, once the import–substitution process moved into the production of durable consumer goods (such as cars) which catered for upper income–groups and intermediate and capital goods (such as chemicals, steel, and machinery), the process of capital accumulation changed. This capital–deepening import substitution called for increased income concentration to expand the market for this type of product and to obtain the increased finance, via the higher propensity of the high income-groups to save. Thus, contrary to the structuralists' predictions, the modernization process led to the establishment of a bureaucratic–authoritarian state which underpinned high concentration of income as well as widespread restructuring of the economy and society in favour of capitalist interests. [1]

Dependentistas have also become disenchanted (if they were not already) with the nature of the state in the contemporary (or so–called actually existing) socialist societies of Eastern Europe and elsewhere (Bahro, 1978). The state is far from withering away in these societies, as originally conceived by Marx, although the present political changes and economic reforms (for example, *glasnost* and *perestroika* in the Soviet Union) are opening up a greater space for local initiatives. The changes in the post–Mao era in China have been more drastic. Whether these herald a new phase in the transition to socialism or a new variant of capitalism only time will tell. Even the Cuban revolution, which many *dependentistas* saw as an example of how to break with underdevelopment and dependence, has not fully lived up to its original promise. The task of diversifying the economy and achieving a degree of self–reliance is a task which has turned out to be far more difficult and complex than originally envisaged. Even a committed revolutionary government in full control of the state cannot rapidly overcome dependence. Furthermore, centralized planning, while responsible for many achievements in Cuba, reveals its shortcomings, as the economy becomes more intricate and can even become an obstacle to further development. In such a situation economic reforms are called for which enhance decentralized planning, give greater authority to local enterprises, encourage participation from the bottom up, and provide a bigger role for the market. While the Cuban government has made some attempts since the mid–1970s to move in that direction, these have not gone far enough and are punctured with partial reversals like the recent 'process of rectification' (C. Kay, 1988).

Thus, far greater recognition needs to be given to the limitations of the state in overcoming underdevelopment and dependence and to the pervasiveness of such a state of affairs. Furthermore, more attention needs to be paid to the relationship between state interventions and market mechanisms in development in both capitalist and socialist countries (Nove, 1983; Helm, 1986; FitzGerald and Wuyts, 1988).

Fourth, the constraints and costs of a revolution have also to be considered more carefully. Revolutions certainly do not come on the cheap! An old order is destroyed, the new order takes time to bear fruit and often fails to deliver the goods, let alone live up to its original promises. While the Bolivian bourgeois revolution of 1952 can be judged a failure, the Cuban socialist revolution of 1959 can be considered a partial success. Despite the nationalization of the tin mines and the agrarian reform, the Bolivian workers and peasants have secured few permanent gains with the revolution, although at the time they managed to extract some short–lived benefits. The main organizations involved in the seizure of power were the alliance between the middle–class MNR (Movimiento Nacionalista Revolucionario) and the Trotskyst POR (Partido Obrero Revolucionario). Once in power the MNR opted 'for state–guided development within the international capitalist system, but failed in the event to achieve any reasonable degree of sound economic growth' (Roxborough, 1979: 151). The MNR resorted to repression in order to impose this option and also to prevent a possible challenge from the organized working class which might have radicalized the revolution.

As revolutions differ they tend to make new (and sometimes old) mistakes. The Cuban government, for example, under the influence of ECLA's structuralism, launched an import–substitution industrialization drive in the early 1960s which soon had to be abandoned as the country did not possess the necessary infrastructure, raw materials, and technology. In turn, the target to export 10 million tons of sugar in 1970 was an overambitious goal which put a severe strain on other economic sectors, jeopardized the political support for the revolution, and undermined the moral basis for future mobilization of voluntary labour. The vast mobilization of this unpaid labour was poorly organized and led to much waste and inefficiency. However, the Cuban revolutionary leadership did not make the mistake of the Soviet Union of squeezing the peasantry, nor of imposing a Stalinist collectivization process upon the peasantry which would have alienated their support (Ghai *et al.*, 1988).

In the case of Nicaragua, external aggression has diverted scarce economic resources and human manpower to fighting a war which has put severe strains on the economy. While US intervention has much to answer for the difficulties facing Nicaragua some problems are self–made, aggravating an already precarious situation. Thus, for example, the economic policy pursued before 1985 led to significant inefficiency in resource allocation and stimulated a 'parasitic economy' and the black market (Spalding, 1987: 9). In addition, the initial emphasis on export agriculture jeopardized food security and endangered peasant support to the Sandinista government, requiring a reorientation in development strategy (Vilas, 1987). In 1985 the government radically redirected its agrarian policy from the previous emphasis on state, co–operative, and some large–scale private export–agriculture towards favouring small and medium individual peasant production geared towards food production (R. Harris, 1987: 9).

In short, revolutions, while solving some problems, at the same time create new ones. The question remains as to which development policies should be pursued by those Third World governments intent on initiating a process of transition to socialism. There is also the question of where the line should be drawn so as to ensure the survival of the revolution as well as avoiding compromising its socialist character. Given today's increasingly interdependent world, most small peripheral countries simply cannot afford to disengage from the international capitalist system despite the misgivings they might have about it. Opting out of this system might increase the costs of the process of transition even further. A process of transition thus often entails changing alliances and concessions both internally and externally. The literature on these issues is still sparse and often too general to be of direct assistance to those Third World countries faced with such dilemmas in their quest for a socialist development. [2]

Fifth, structuralist and dependency analysis needs to give a more explicit commitment to civil society, especially in view of the recent traumatic experience of the authoritarian state in Latin America. It is necessary for civil society to strengthen the ability of exploited groups to organize and express their needs so as to influence and shape development processes as well as to resist further repression and exploitation (Touraine, 1987). New social movements, such as anti–authoritarian, religious, ethnic, feminist, regional, anti–institutional, and ecological movements, are emerging in Latin America (Slater, 1985). These differ from the old class–based movements, and politicians and social scientists can only ignore them at their peril. Furthermore, the spread of non–governmental organizations is a testimony to the crisis of the state as well as an expression of civil society's need of and desire for alternative forms of institutional representation.

In both structuralism and *dependencia* there is a need to rediscover civil society, to present proposals for strengthening the social participation and the social organizations of the weak, the voiceless, the oppressed, and the poor. It is also imperative to give greater recognition to the importance of cultural and ideological elements in the mobilization of society for development, the institutionalization of change, and the achievement of social cohesion and integration. In recent years ethnic and gender divisions have surfaced with renewed force, and the development literature is bereft of ideas regarding how best to deal with these issues and propose policies for overcoming the exploitation of ethnic groups, women, and what are often called 'minorities'.

Sixth, structuralist and dependency analysts have to undertake more studies of the smaller or micro units of a country. These micro studies have, of course, to be linked to the global or macro national and international theories. Dependency studies have a tendency to distort historical processes or to neglect the particular in their attempts to generalize. The specificities of certain experiences are simply abstracted away so as to conform to the general model and many small, but by no means insignificant, incidents are simply not recorded. It is often the distinct and unassuming small events which give diversity and richness to a theory. More importantly it leads to better theory, especially compared with those which are prone to dogmatic and unidimensional tendencies.

In this sense structuralist and dependency analysis would greatly benefit from studies on the development of local markets and their linkages with national and international markets; and investigations into the varied ways and means by which production is organized and the surplus is created in non-capitalist and capitalist enterprises, on estates and subsistence farms, and on foreign and national units. Research also needs to be undertaken into the varied processes of class formation and exploitation which are sensitive to the ethnic, gender, and cultural dimensions; and into the local forms of domination and political control, such as *caciquismo* and patron–client relationships.

Seventh, and last but not least, **structuralist and dependency writers have to consider the possibility and feasibility of a variety of styles and paths of development.** It is only at a very high level of abstraction and simplification that dichotomies such as capitalism and socialism are valid. Thus, for example, for Dos Santos (1969) the vital dilemma facing Latin America was fascism or socialism, and dependence or revolution. Similarly, for Frank (1969), the choice lay between capitalist underdevelopment or socialist revolution (and development). Structuralists, in a less dramatic fashion, spoke of outward– and inward–directed development paths. The former was considered as perpetuating underdevelopment and non–democratic forms of government, where this was already the case, and the latter as leading to development and democratization. However, not all authors thought in terms of dichotomies. Structuralists like Sunkel and Paz (1970), and *dependentistas* like Bambirra (1973) and, above all,

Cardoso and Faletto (1979) envisage multiple paths of development, although referring to Latin America's past and within a process of capitalist transformation.

A variety of development models have been pursued in the last few decades in Latin America but, with the exception of Cuba and Brazil, most have not endured. What these different cases show is that within both socialism and capitalism there are a variety of styles of development. This means that no rigid path or dogma needs to be followed and that it is possible to respond imaginatively to changing circumstances and new problems. This variety of roads of development has to be acknowledged by all development theories. Development theory needs to overcome its Eurocentrism or, more precisely, 'Centrecentrism', and give greater weight to the experiences of and theories from the Third World. The development experience of the centre countries is far too often viewed as the model which the peripheral countries should follow; but historical experiences can never be repeated, as circumstances in each country differ and the international context changes constantly. This is even truer today owing to the higher and increasing levels of interdependence, which limits certain options but opens others. This interdependence is, of course, asymmetric: for example, only six developed countries, which have only a tenth of world population, control two–thirds of world trade (Iglesias, 1987). Thus, a few developed countries obviously call the shots and it would be foolish to pretend otherwise.

Usually it is the centre capitalist paradigm which prevails in a distorted form to suit neoclassical or monetarist ideologies (Senghaas, 1985). However, dependency analysis, while rejecting the capitalist model, has in turn idealized certain aspects of Marxian economics and the Soviet–type development model. As mentioned in Chapter 5, a key aspect of the dependency situation for *dependentistas* is the absence or rudimentary nature of the capital–goods sector, or department I in Marxist terminology. They therefore advocate the development of a capital–goods sector, which they regard as not only a necessary but even a sufficient condition for achieving self–sustaining and autocentric development.

The question immediately arises as to whether it is advisable or indeed possible for all Third World countries to develop their own capital–goods sectors. It is fairly evident that the answer has to be in the negative. *Dependentistas* might agree that in small and sparsely populated countries it makes no sense to develop a capital–goods sector. The problem is that dependency writers do not specify under what conditions it makes sense to develop a capital–goods sector, how this could be done, and what the consequences are of so doing. The establishment of a capital–goods sector might only be possible by drastically raising the rate of capital accumulation. This in turn could lead those countries to adopt some sort of capitalist or socialist primitive capital accumulation measures (Marx, 1976: Part 8; Preobrazhensky, 1965). Few *dependentistas* would suggest such policies, especially in view of the consequences of Brazil's 'savage capitalism' and Stalin's collectivization, even though it is a logical consequence of their position which transforms the development of a capital–goods sector into a *sine qua non* condition for breaking with dependence.

Furthermore, the question arises as to whether an indigenous comprehensive capital–goods sector is necessary in today's interdependent world where it is relatively easy to purchase much of the advanced technology at relatively competitive prices. Thus, in today's conditions it is possible for a country to become an industrial exporter without developing the full range of capital–goods industries. Nor is the establishment of a capital–goods sector any guarantee that the country will achieve or retain technological dynamism, i.e. the capacity to revolutionize continually technology itself. In this respect the development experience of Soviet–type economies is illustrative. As the industrial sector becomes more complex and mature, and consumers more sophisticated, the centrally planned economies find it difficult to respond. The Soviet–type economies begin to lose their dynamism despite (or because of) the predominance of the capital–goods sector. Thus, even the existence of a large capital–goods sector is by no means a guarantee of sustained development. Finally, it could be argued that the development of a capital–goods sector in itself might not be a sufficient condition for achieving non–dependent development or symmetric interdependence. These are issues which still need to be explored by *dependentistas*.

Besides examining a variety of styles of development neo–structuralists and neo–*dependentistas* should include more specific macroeconomic models so as to achieve compatibility and dynamic equilibrium in the economy as well as more specific designs of short–term policies (L. Taylor, 1983; Rosales, 1988). The neo–*dependentistas* will also have to grapple with the problems of actually existing socialism. They will have much to learn from the difficulties which countries like China and Cuba have faced in their processes of transition.

CONTEMPORARY RELEVANCE OF THE LATIN AMERICAN THEORIES

Despite these criticisms and reservations, Latin American theories of underdevelopment and development provide a fertile starting–point for understanding and overcoming the Third World's, and particularly Latin America's, present–day predicament. This is especially the case if structuralism and dependency analysis are understood as methods of analysis, as frameworks, and as series of propositions rather than as fully fledged theories. A renewal of structuralist and dependency thinking is called for, and this could lead to a neo–structuralist and/or neo–dependency theory. Additionally, elements of the Latin American school of thought are being incorporated into other theories. The Latin American theories continue to challenge and to present an alternative to the neoclassical paradigm which has proved unable to tackle the problems of poverty, inequality, and underdevelopment (Bitar, 1988). As Prebisch (1981b: 153) reflected in his maturity:

> the root cause of the incapacity of neoclassical thinking to interpret peripheral capitalism lies above all in its failure to take into consideration the economic surplus, which is the hub of this system's basic characteristics. It disregards the structural heterogeneity which possibilitates the existence of a surplus; it bypasses the structure and dynamics of power which explain how the surplus is appropriated and shared out; it shuts its eyes to the monetary mechanism of production which allows the surplus to be retained by the upper strata; and it underestimates the waste involved in the ways in which the surplus is currently used.
>
> This shortsighted interpretation of the economic process predisposes neoclassical thinking to propose policy measures which do not succeed in promoting the development of the periphery; which increase and consolidate social inequality and which necessitate the establishment of authoritarian regimes, diametrically at variance with the ideas of democratic liberalism.

The curse of external vulnerability

In the late 1940s the structuralists argued that the key obstacle to Latin America's economic development was the foreign exchange constraint, and in the late 1960s the *dependentistas* expressed this central problem in terms of external dependence. The problem of capital accumulation and growth was above all a problem of insufficient availability of foreign exchange rather than a problem of insufficient savings. This statement has even greater validity today although the causes as well as the cures of the foreign exchange constraint may differ. As a consequence of the neo–monetarists' outward–directed development strategy, and more specifically the debt crisis, Latin America's external vulnerability is even greater than before (Thorp and Whitehead, 1987).

In addition, the structuralists' and the *dependentistas'* analysis of the terms of trade and unequal exchange retains some validity, but new factors, such as the debt, contribute to the region's external vulnerability. Although the deterioration in the terms of trade continues to create periodic problems, its negative impact has been curtailed in countries like Brazil, which have been able to diversify exports from primary products to industrial commodities. Furthermore, the reasons for a relative deterioration in the terms of trade may diverge from those originally put forward by the structuralists (Spraos, 1983; H. D. Evans, 1987: 657). In recent years the studies on the terms of trade between North and South have multiplied, most notably because of their drastic deterioration and negative consequences, particularly for some African countries (Thirlwall and Bergevin, 1985; Sarkar, 1986; Maizels, 1987). While in earlier decades neoclassical economists refuted or cast doubts upon the deterioration in the terms of trade, today at least they acknowledge that this has taken place. However,

> What can be said about the reasons for this apparent secular deterioration in the relative prices of primary commodities is...limited. The simple primary trends that we measured appear to go against the expectations of classical economists regarding the relative price movements of manufactured goods and instead to be consistent with the original Prebisch–Singer counterargument. It is not difficult, however, to show that these empirical findings can be theoretically explained outside both the classical and the original Prebisch–Singer framework. Neoclassical analysis of the effects of growth on relative trade prices offers numerous possible alternative explanations, and so does unequal development theory.
>
> (Grilli and Yang, 1988: 35–6)

Although the terms–of–trade debate continues to be relevant, it can no longer be sustained in the same way as in the past because of changing patterns of international trade. Some Third World countries, for example, are losing their traditional comparative advantage in primary production mainly because of rapid technological advances in, and subsidies to, the developed countries' agriculture. World trade in agricultural commodities is increasingly dominated by developed countries to the extent that some underdeveloped countries who used to be net exporters of food have now become net importers. On the other hand, some developing countries have acquired comparative advantages in certain manufacturing products. The so-called newly industrializing countries have made some inroads into industrial world–exports which were once exclusively dominated by the developed countries.

Continuing technological dependence also adds to the external weakness of the periphery, and one way in which this manifests itself is through the demonstration effect. As new and more sophisticated consumer products are developed in the centre, demand is created for imported products in the periphery through the imitative conspicuous consumption patterns of upper income groups (Wells, 1987). Some products may later be produced internally but this involves the importation of machinery, equipment, raw materials, and spare parts, as well as the payment of royalties, profit remittances, foreign management or consultancy fees, and so on, all of which require foreign exchange. Even in the unlikely event that a few developing countries may eventually succeed in exporting some of these new products, the net outcome is generally a further pressure on the already very fragile balance–of–payments position.

The structuralist terms–of–trade analysis has been transformed by Marxists and *dependentistas* into the theory of unequal exchange (Emmanuel, 1972; Braun, 1973). This theory, in turn, has generated some debate (Emmanuel *et al.*, 1971; H. D. Evans, 1981c; Raffer, 1987). While some authors emphasize the exploitation between countries, others stress the exploitation between classes. Some Marxists consider that those who focus on the North–South divide tend to erect a smoke screen which disguises the class exploitation within the developed countries and above all within the Third World. By presenting the Third World as victims of deteriorating terms of trade or exploitation by the developed countries, attention is diverted from the key issue – the exploitation between classes. For the unequal–exchange theorists, the nature of the commodities (primary or industrial products) exchanged between the centre and periphery countries is irrelevant (H. D. Evans, 1981a). So long as wage differentials are larger than the productivity differentials between the centre and the periphery, unequal exchange will continue to exist. Thus, according to the unequal–exchange theorists, the changing nature of international comparative advantages and trade might not necessarily mean that unequal exchange will diminish or even cease to exist.

In an attempt to mitigate the foreign–exchange problems of the Third World such as the wide fluctuations of primary commodity prices and their long–run deterioration, UNCTAD (United Nations Conference on Trade and Development) was established in 1964. Prebisch was the driving force behind the creation of UNCTAD and its first Secretary–General. UNCTAD became a major forum for debating North–South issues and was an inspirational force for those countries who were calling for a new international economic order. However, UNCTAD failed to achieve a major breakthrough in North–South relations and its attempt at global Keynesianism was not to be (Clairmonte, 1986). No agreement was reached, for example, on how to administer and finance the establishment of some key primary commodities' buffer stocks, an essential measure for reducing price fluctuations. Without such buffer stocks there was even less chance of finding a compromise solution to the commodities' terms–of–trade issue. The buffer–stocks scheme failed because some developed countries were reluctant to finance it and because they also suspected that it could be used by the Third World to raise primary commodity prices. In the neo–conservative climate of the 1980s, UNCTAD is making even less headway and its inefficacy is revealed with respect to the debt problem.

The foreign debt burden: financial and technological dependence

The debt crisis has added a new dimension to the region's financial dependence which has been considerably aggravated. It also reveals the limited options open to the debtor countries due to their technological dependence. In this way some aspects of dependency analysis are vindicated.

The problem today is not just one of insufficient growth of foreign–exchange earnings and capital accumulation: it has been made considerably worse as a result of the crippling foreign debt. In order to service this debt Latin America has become a net exporter of capital since 1982 (Payer, 1985: 19). This has meant that the rate of capital formation has fallen with the consequent stagnation or negative growth of the economy (PREALC, 1987: 2). Although the region's volume of exports has increased to service the debt, the value of total exports has remained roughly the same during the first half of the 1980s owing to the deterioration of the commodity terms-of-trade. With the rise in debt service, Latin American countries have had to reduce their imports by a staggering one-third between 1983 and 1985 (Marcel and Palma, 1987: 4). The brunt of the cuts in imports was borne by capital goods, as it is difficult to reduce the imports of essential consumer goods like food. Although Brazil, Argentina, and Mexico have acquired some technological capacity, capital-goods requirements for the region as a whole still have to be met from outside. Thus, the *dependentistas'* focus on the negative consequence of technological dependence continues to be relevant but has to be adjusted to the new circumstances.

The origins of the debt crisis also illustrate the *dependentistas'* claim of the pervasive influence of external factors on developments in the periphery as well as the interaction between external and internal factors. According to Prebisch (1986a), the ultimate origins of the debt problem lie in the abandonment of the Bretton Woods agreement by the USA in 1971, when dollar-gold convertibility was abrogated. This, together with the development of the Eurodollar market, allowed the US to run higher and higher balance of payments deficits, i.e. to import more and more in relation to its exports (Brett, 1985: 111-31). The 1973-4 oil shock is another factor which facilitated the debt crisis. Finally, the crisis erupted in 1982 when the largest debtor countries – Argentina, Brazil, and Mexico – technically defaulted on their payments. Among the more immediate causes for this were the sudden rise in US interest rates in 1979, the unusually high interest rates prevailing during the early 1980s, and the world recession. As a consequence the servicing of the Third World's debt (which is largely held in dollars) rocketed, while at the same time its export earnings declined. The US and world recession in the early 1980s meant that export markets dried up for the South at the same time as prices of primary commodities fell. Thus, many debtor countries ran into serious external imbalance difficulties and were unable to continue to service their debt.

The continuing structuralist-monetarist controversy: stabilization policies

The failure of recent monetarist stabilization experiments in Latin America has produced a search to understand inflation as something more than just a monetary phenomenon. This has rekindled the old monetarist–structuralist debate about the causes of inflation in Latin America.

(Baer and Welch, 1987: 989)

The debt crisis, together with the resurgence of inflation, has also led to a renewed interest in the old structuralist–monetarist debate on the IMF's adjustment and stabilization programmes (Petras and Brill, 1986; Ffrench-Davis, 1988). Many Latin American governments resent IMF interference in the formulation of their internal economic policies. However, most debtor countries have to come to terms with the IMF so as to acquire desperately needed loans and, above all, to reschedule their massive debts with foreign banks whose consent is only forthcoming if the debtor countries swallow the bitter medicine of the IMF. This policing role of the IMF is particularly disliked by Third World governments as it raises questions of sovereignty.

The IMF stabilization programme largely follows the neo–monetarist line. The diagnosis is always one of excess demand. Supply factors are largely ignored and structural factors are given short shrift. The same medicine is prescribed for all countries without acknowledging that the patients may differ in significant respects. The difference with past IMF prescriptions is that anti–inflationary measures are now intertwined with policies geared to reduce the debt burden. The purpose of some stabilization measures, like the reduction in internal demand, is to reduce imports and free resources for export. The IMF adjustment–programme usually requires the liberalization of foreign exchange and import controls, greater freedom of capital movements, and encouragement of foreign investment and exports. These measures largely aim to promote exports so as to ease the foreign debt. Policies designed to deal specifically with inflation include, *inter alia*, control of bank credit, increases in interest rates, reduction in government deficits, curbs on nominal wage rises, and dismantling of price controls. The effects of these austerity programmes are invariably a sharp fall in incomes of the poor due to cuts or abolition of food subsidies, reduction in real wages, rising unemployment, and so on (Ground, 1984).

In his last public address, made shortly before his death, Prebisch (1986a) exposed the essence of monetarism as he saw it. In his view monetarist policies were deliberately designed to increase unemployment (although this was often not admitted to by monetarists) so as to bring down real wages. Thus, the burden of adjustment falls on the shoulders of those least able to bear it. It is estimated that in 1985 per capita income in much of Latin America had fallen to levels prevalent ten years before (Frieden, 1985).

Furthermore, these IMF–inspired adjustment packages have so far shown little sign of success (Inter–American Development Bank, 1985). Seers (1981a) attacked the short–sightedness of IMF policies and, while castigating some developing countries who followed structuralist–type policies for financial irresponsibility, argued that economists in the developed countries could learn useful lessons from the structuralist– monetarist debate. He criticized those economists for not taking the structuralists' contribution on inflation into account and condemns their ignorance of it. In turn, structuralists need to consider short–term monetary and fiscal measures and to link these more closely to the debt problem when designing an anti–inflationary programme.

The new democratic regimes in Brazil and Argentina, as well as the populist government of Alan García in Peru, have adopted novel stabilization policies which combine structuralist and monetarist features (Bresser Pereira, 1987; Manzetti and dell'Aquila, 1988). These 'heterodox shock' stabilization policies comprise a whole set of economic and social measures enshrined in the Plan Cruzado (1986) in Brazil, in the Plan Austral (1985) in Argentina, and in the Plan Inti (1985) in Peru, for which the governments sought public support through a series of political campaigns (Flynn, 1986; Heymann, 1986; Epstein, 1987). (The name of these plans derives from each of their new national currencies.) Despite their drastic nature these stabilization programmes initially had widespread support, as the previous monetarist stabilization policies were widely discredited. Also, after years of dictatorship the new civilian governments in Brazil and Argentina, and the popular government of García, were riding on a wave of goodwill and were given the benefit of the doubt. There was also a realization that rampant three digit inflation (which in Argentina reached over 1,000 per cent!) had to be brought under control. While achieving some initial success these stabilization plans were later abandoned, as no consensus could be reached on how to share the heavy burden of adjustment.

Structural heterogeneity, marginality, and the informal sector

The analysis of structural heterogeneity retains significance, especially as differences in productivity between and within sectors have become even more acute in the last decade. Such disparities in productivity lead to increased intra- and inter-sectoral imbalances, widen income differentials, limit the spread of technological progress, and reflect the continuing, if not growing, marginalization. Most new investments and modern technologies go to the most productive enterprises within each sector and much, if not most, of these new investment resources go to the industrial sector.

The discussion on marginality has largely been taken over during the 1970s by informal-sector analysis and by Marxist debates on modes of production. The concepts of marginality and marginal pole of the economy have influenced the Marxist discussion on articulation of modes of production in particular. Whatever the rubric under which authors prefer to discuss the problem of marginality and the marginal pole of the economy, there is little doubt that the issue continues to be relevant, topical, and unresolved.

Marginality is still a problem as labour continues to be marginalized both from and by a modern technology which is largely imported from the advanced countries. This foreign technological progress is biased in favour of upper income products in the context of the Third World. Consumption patterns in underdeveloped countries are increasingly being 'denationalized' or internationalized as growing sectors of the population imitate those of the developed countries. The creation of such dependent consumption habits extends as far as agro-industrial food products (Lajo, 1983). Many enterprises are unable to adapt or adopt the new technology, and as their products become obsolete they have to close down or become part of the petty-commodity sector of the economy. The neo-conservatives' lack of concern with development and their stabilization programmes have increased the mass of the structurally unemployed. These unemployed have to fall back on their ingenuity to devise survival strategies varying from petty activities to casual and low-paid labour in the petty commodity, domestic, or informal sectors of the economy.

Given the capital-intensive nature of advanced technology, the industrial sector has been unable to absorb much labour even in those countries with high rates of industrial growth. The problem is compounded by the rapid rate of population growth and the high rate of rural-urban migration. The problem of absorbing this new contingent into the labour force is even more acute in those countries which experienced a process of 'premature de-industrialization' over the last decade or so as a consequence of neo-conservative policies. Thus, in countries like Chile, Peru, and Argentina the percentage of the total labour force employed by the industrial sector has significantly declined (Wells, 1987: 109). This lack of labour–absorptive capacity of the industrial sector means that most of the new labour force either ends up in the service sector performing a great variety of casual low–productivity activities or remains unemployed. According to some observers this swelling of an heterogeneous service sector reflects a process of 'premature tertiarization' of the economy. In most Latin American economies well over 40 per cent of the labour force was employed in the service sector in 1980 (ibid.: 99).

Marginality analysis could be extended to encompass the recent phenomenon of de–industrialization in some mature developed countries. This creates a new type of unemployed worker who does not even act as a labour reserve, being permanently unemployed. The transition from an old industrial economy, like that of the UK, to a service economy marginalizes those workers who are linked to the decaying traditional industries. When these workers are declared redundant they are unable to find new employment as their skills do not match those of the new industries or the service sector. Furthermore, the neo–conservative development model no longer creates sufficient employment opportunities even for the new generation of young workers. However, the social origins of these marginals, as well as the process of marginalization, differs from that taking place in the Third World. In the developed countries marginal workers are largely former industrial workers and the process of marginalization is not due to dependent industrialization as is the case in the Third World but to de–industrialization and the transition to a service economy.

New industrialization strategies

In the late 1940s and early 1950s when the structuralists or *cepalistas* first advocated import–substituting industrialization, they had to battle against orthodox economists who argued that less–developed countries should continue to specialize in primary–commodity production on the grounds of international comparative advantage. At that time the dispute was over whether Third World countries should industrialize or not; today it is about whether they should follow an import–substituting or an export–oriented industrialization strategy. At present there is a general awareness of, or even a consensus on, the shortcomings of import–substitution policies. Neoclassical economists who advocate an export–oriented industrialization strategy conveniently forget that a couple of decades earlier they were opposed to any kind of industrialization strategy for the Third World – except for one spontaneously and gradually induced by free markets. Their position has changed (though often not publicly admitted) in view of the successful industrialization of the newly industrializing countries in East Asia, i.e. South Korea, Taiwan, Singapore, and Hong Kong (Balassa, 1981). The spectacular breakthrough into manufacturing exports of these four countries in the last couple of decades is hailed as a success of free–market policies and is used as a stick with which to beat the early supporters of import substitution and all those who favour state interventionism in the economy (Ranis and Orrock, 1984).

However, on closer examination a more complex picture emerges from the industrialization experience of the newly industrializing countries (N. Harris, 1987). While some oriented their industrialization to the external market, many entered the export market after having first gone through an import–substitution process. Furthermore, most relied on government intervention, or what Lal (1983) calls *dirigisme*, to get their industrialization under way (Schmitz, 1984: 1–20). Such interventionism took a variety of forms, from protective tariffs to export subsidies. The key difference between the old import–substituting countries and the East Asian newly industrializing countries is that government intervention in the latter was much more selective, flexible, and less enduring, and their ultimate purpose was increasingly to expose the industrial sector to international competition (Colman and Nixson, 1986: 267–325). Meanwhile, in many old import–substituting countries government interventionism degenerated into spiralling protectionism which shielded an increasingly inefficient industrial structure. However, this does not mean that the only or optimal way of remedying the vicissitudes of import substitution is to expose these countries to the full rigours of foreign competition, as is argued by neo–conservatives.

The contrast between the way in which Brazil and Chile have attempted to overcome the problems of import substitution is illustrative. In Brazil the post–1964 state has only gradually and partially exposed the industrial sector to international competition and has strongly supported industrial exports, through subsidies and other measures (Tavares and Coutinho, 1984). Meanwhile, in Chile the post–1973 state thoroughly and mercilessly implemented a rigorous neo–conservative policy which dismantled most of the protectionist barriers within a short time, exposing the industrial sector to fierce foreign competition (Edwards and Cox Edwards, 1987). In Brazil the state industrial sector expanded even further and spearheaded many developments, while in Chile it was almost completely privatized. As a consequence Brazil has become a major industrial power and a large proportion of its exports are industrial commodities, while Chile has suffered a process of premature de–industrialization and most of its exports continue to be primary products, although they have become more diversified and industrialized (Tokman, 1984; Gwynne, 1986). Monetarist policies in Argentina also resulted in industrial decline for a few years (Kosacoff, 1984) but the policies and their outcome were less severe than in the case of Chile.[3]

Those advocating an export–oriented industrialization strategy not only misrepresent the actual experience of the newly industrializing countries but fail to acknowledge that the East Asian model may not be generalizable (Cline, 1982). For a start the 'fallacy of composition' has to be considered, i.e. that if most Third World countries begin to export industrial products this will not only lead to a fall in industrial prices but might also bring forth even more protective barriers by the developed countries against industrial exports from the Third World. It is not necessary to be an export pessimist to recognize that the favourable conditions existing in the world market for industrial exports in the pre–1980s might no longer hold, especially as the expansion of industrial exports has already declined during the recession–prone 1980s. The increasing competition for developed countries' markets, the pressures for greater protectionism in the advanced countries, and new technological developments (such as robotics) which threaten to create new advantages for locating industries in the developed countries will make it more difficult for developing countries to export industrial products.

Thus, it would be foolish to advise Third World countries to opt exclusively for an export–oriented strategy. On the one hand, the chances of replicating the export success of the East Asian countries are slim; on the other hand, the debt crisis, on top of the depressed state of primary–commodity prices and of market opportunities for primary–product exports, should encourage some import substitution, although depriving less–developed countries of capital for undertaking such new investments.

It might therefore be judicious for underdeveloped countries to combine varying degrees of both an inward– and outward–directed development strategy according to changing circumstances. In such a combined strategy exports become a means of achieving further internal development. Such a strategy would seek to break down the barriers between economic sectors by enhancing, for example, the industrialization of agriculture, by stimulating exports of industrial products or primary products, but with as high a degree of industrial processing as possible so as to maximize value added, and by promoting an indigenous technological capacity.

Undoubtedly the state will continue to play an important part in the periphery's development process. In view of the premature de–industrialization of the Southern Cone countries, the task today is to devise an efficient import–resubstitution industrialization strategy as well as promoting industrial exports where it is sensible so to do. The civilian governments which have recently emerged in some Latin American countries have reversed some of the previous neo–conservative and neo–monetarist policies and given greater scope to government intervention and industrialization. Reflecting this new mood, many structuralists would endorse the following comment by a perceptive foreign observer:

> Difficult though it may be, there is a broad commitment in Latin America to harness and use government intervention more productively. That translates into greater selectivity and decentralization of authority; into reliable access to real resources, rather than second–best measures that provoke other disequilibria; into attention to macroeconomic policy as well as to cost pressures that reproduce high rates of inflation; into adequate growth of exports to reduce the constraint on growth emanating from the balance of payments: exports are a means, not an end, important for their regular supply of foreign exchange rather than industrial dynamism; and into acceptance of integration into international financial markets, so long as they compensate for, rather than induce, vulnerability to external and internal shocks.
>
> (Fishlow, 1985: 145)

FINAL REMARKS ON DEVELOPMENT THEORY AND OPTIONS

While in the early 1960s Dudley Seers held out the hope that the new discipline of development economics might overcome the crisis in economics, by the late 1970s he argued that development economics itself was in crisis. On the one hand, he perceived that developed countries were beginning to experience structural problems in the post–industrial era and, on the other hand, that the rapid industrialization of some developing countries, together with the growing interdependence of the world economy, revealed a new situation. He also argued that development economics had not lived up to its promise as it had failed to address the crucial problems of mass poverty and unemployment in the midst of growth in the Third World. In his view,

> To insist on the 'difference in circumstances', i.e. that the industrial countries were a 'special case', seemed revolutionary to some in the 1960s. Indeed, it was then a step forward. It discouraged the naive transfer of neo–classical economics...to continents for which they had not been designed.
>
> (Seers, 1979a: 713)

He then concluded that, 'From a professional point of view, the time has come to emphasize similarities rather than differences in circumstances and to dispose of development economics.' (ibid.: 71.)

Seers argued that the way forward was for economics and development economics to be replaced by development studies because it offered the best hope for an interdisciplinary and world–system approach which was required for understanding and tackling the development problems in both the North and the South. In this context he mentioned that the Latin American school of development provided some useful pointers (ibid.: 714). Paul Streeten echoes similar sentiments by arguing that today it is necessary to stress the 'unity in diversity' and concludes, following Albert Hirschman, that 'the explanation of Southern societies, with different tools of analysis, has often led to new illuminations and discoveries in our own Northern societies, thereby re–establishing the unity of analysis' (Streeten, 1983: 876).

Reform or revolution is still the paramount development dilemma facing Third World countries sixty years after Haya de la Torre and Mariátegui started this important debate. Today, however, this central dichotomy has to be qualified, as development experiences since then have shown that a variety of transitions are possible. Also, the process of transition to a society free from poverty, discrimination, exploitation, and inequality is a far longer and more difficult historical task than originally envisaged. Furthermore, reformists and revolutionaries alike have often neglected or underestimated the possibilities and strengths of a neo–conservative challenge. Neo–conservative theory has provided a powerful ideology and tool of transformation for many counter–revolutionary modernizing elites in recent times in the Third World. Thus, it is the outcome of the class struggle which eventually decides which particular path of transition is followed by society.

There is certainly an urgent need today to develop and assert alternatives to neo–conservative theories and policies in both the South and the North. Given that many issues raised by structuralist and dependency writers are still relevant and that their original analyses retain some validity, it is possible that a new generation of neo–structuralists or neo–*dependentistas* might arise to develop these theories further. However, they would need to address a number of shortcomings and update these schools of thought if they are to make a new contribution to development theory. In this book I have sought to present the strengths as well as the weaknesses of the Latin American theories of development and underdevelopment, and to have shown their potential for further development.

Notes

CHAPTER 1: THE CHALLENGE FROM THE PERIPHERY

1. The list of distinguished contributors reflecting on the state of development economics and studies is indeed very long, and the following is a selection: D. Seers (1979a), J. B. Nugent and P. A. Yotopoulos (1979), J. Toye (1980; 1987), A. O. Hirschman (1981a), I. Livingstone (1981; 1986), D. P. Lal (1983: Chapters 1 and 6), A. K. Sen (1983), P. Streeten (1983; 1985), T. E. Weisskopf (1983), P. T. Bauer (1984: Chapter 10), W. A. Lewis (1984), J. N. Bhagwati (1985: Chapter 1), P. W. Preston (1985; 1987), T. Smith (1985), R. Apthorpe and A. Kráhl (1986), F. Nixson (1986), C. K. Wilber (1986). H. W. Arndt (1987), N. Harris (1987: Chapter 1), B. Hettne (1987), P. F. Leeson (1988), and G. Ranis and T. P. Schultz (1988). For two masterful reflections on the crisis in the sociology of development, see Booth (1985) and Mouzelis (1988). For a discussion of Booth's article, see Vandergeest and Buttel (1988) and Sklair (1988).
2. A common dichotomous categorization within development economics is between classical and neoclassical theories, in which the latter is the mainstream or orthodox position. Sometimes the neo–Marxist position is included in the various classifications of the different streams within the discipline but it is only in recent years that the structuralist position has been acknowledged (Chenery, 1975). Little (1982: 19) even thinks that the essential antithesis is between neoclassical and structuralist theories of economic development. According to Little (ibid.: 20-1), the essential difference between the two positions rests in the fact that the structuralist view the economy in less-developed countries as inflexible and facing major constraints or bottlenecks. They therefore distrust the price mechanism and justify government intervention so as to accelerate the process of economic development. Meanwhile, the neoclassical world is one of flexibility in which prices rule and government intervention or *dirigisme* is spurned (ibid.: 25; Lal, 1983: Chapter 1). However, following Chenery, Little considers as structuralist authors such as Paul Rosenstein–Rodan, Ragnar Nurkse, Gunnar Myrdal, W. Arthur Lewis, and Hans Singer. While such an inclusion might be justified I restrict my analysis in this book to the Latin American structuralist school, namely those authors working in or under the ethos

of the Economic Commission for Latin America (ECLA). The driving force of the structuralist school was Raúl Prebisch who assembled the original team of workers in ECLA (see Chapter 2). Thus, Latin American structuralism should not be confused with other structuralist methodologies, such as that used by social anthropologists and sociologists which is commonly known as structural–functionalism. For an attempt to compare various kinds of structuralism, see Jameson (1986); to explore the links between Latin American structuralism with institutionalist and dependency perspectives, see Street (1967), Street and James (1982), and Dietz and Street (1987); and to trace the origins of structuralism in economics, see Arndt (1985), and of development economics, see Arndt (1972; 1981).

3. It is likely that the writings of the pioneers of development economics such as Paul Rosenstein–Rodan (1943), Kurt Mandelbaum (1947), Hans W. Singer (1950), Paul A. Baran (1952), Ragnar Nurkse (1953), W. Arthur Lewis (1955), Gunnar Myrdal (1957), and later of Dudley Seers, Nicholas Kaldor, and Thomas Balogh, among others, influenced the Latin American structuralist school, but it is difficult to ascertain the extent and exact nature of this influence (Love, 1980; Arndt, 1985). It is interesting to note that, with the exception of Seers, none are Anglo–Saxon. Many are of Central European origin, some from the 'backward' and agrarian Eastern European countries, which probably explains why they favoured industrialization and protectionism as they, in turn, were influenced by the 'infant industry' argument of the German economist Friedrich List (1904) and had observed at close range the rapid industrial development of Germany which was due to protectionist policies and strong state intervention. A most interesting hypothesis is that by Love (1980: 61–2), who thinks that the ideas of the Romanian economist Mihail Manoïlescu (1931) are likely to have influenced those of the structuralists, and Prebisch in particular. For a remarkable study on the influence of populist and neo–populist (largely East European) thinking on modern development theory, see Kitching (1982). However, Kitching surprisingly makes no reference to the seminal essay by Palma (1978), who traces the populist roots of dependency theory.

4. Some other important texts in the theory of modernization are McClelland (1961) and Hagen (1962). For a didactic overview of the modernization sociology of development, see Hoogvelt (1976). For a comprehensive critique of this sociological theory, see Frank (1972a), J. Taylor (1979), and Webster (1984). For critiques of Rostow's theory of stages of economic growth, see Baran and Hobsbawm (1961), Frank (n.d.), Meier (1964: 23–8), and Griffin (1969), who also provides a critique of the theories of dualism. A useful critical overview of modernization, dualism, and Rostow is given by Szentes (1983). For a balanced review and appraisal of the sociology of development and underdevelopment, see Harrison (1988).

5. To my knowledge, the only book which deals with the Latin American contribution to development theory is by Blomström and Hettne (1984), although it tends to focus on the dependency debate. Roxborough (1979) does not set out to assess the Latin American school but his

book is strongly influenced by it and deals with some of its aspects. The book by Kahl (1976) only deals with the contribution by three Latin American sociologists, i.e. Gino Germani, Pablo González Casanova, and Fernando Henrique Cardoso, but puts them within the wider context of the 'new sociology in Latin America'. Guzmán (1976) and O. Rodríguez (1980) give a good and comprehensive overview of the structuralist school, while Chilcote and Edelstein (1974) largely examine the dependency school. For a brief and idiosyncratic view from India of what the author calls 'the Latin American Theory of Underdevelopment', see Vyasulu (1974: 607–12).

6. 'The first approach to the problem of the relationship between imported technology and underdevelopment is to be found in the study prepared by the ECLA team in 1951.' (Furtado, 1980: 212.) Thus, the structuralists can also claim to be one of the forerunners of the debate on 'appropriate technology'. See CEPAL (1952).

7. F. H. Cardoso's and E. Faletto's influential book *Dependency and Development in Latin America*, which was first published in Spanish in 1969, did not appear in English until 1979.

8. On this point I disagree with Hettne (1983: 26) who argues that the dependency school was the first real Third World contribution to the social sciences. In my view the structuralist school should receive this honour, as the *dependentistas* are the heirs of structuralism.

9. Ideas are a social product which, while not respecting national frontiers, are nevertheless grounded in a certain historical reality. Undoubtedly ideas should fertilize each other, especially in the search for a human world free from poverty and oppression.

10. Ernesto 'Ché' Guevara was familiar with Baran's writings and paid tribute to his work on underdevelopment: see the back cover of Baran (1973). Hettne speculates that Baran, who was also an Indian specialist, might have been influenced by Indian writers who were discussing strikingly similar topics to those of the *dependentistas* as far back as the end of the nineteenth century. 'Thus, to formulate a daring hypothesis, the Indian debate on dependency could have had an impact on the Latin American debate through Paul Baran!' (Hettne, 1983: 254).

11. For a flavour of the Latin American debate on modes of production see Bagú (1949), Frank (1967), Vitale (1968), Laclau (1971), Garavaglia (1973), and Bartra (1975). In Chapter 5 I review, albeit briefly, the essence of this debate by focusing on the writings of André G. Frank and Ernesto Laclau.

12. Haya de la Torre formed the Alianza Popular Revolucionaria Americana (Popular Revolutionary American Alliance) or APRA in 1924, which aimed to be a Latin American party with national organizations in each country. The strictly Peruvian party (the Partido Aprista Peruano) was founded in 1928. Likewise in 1928 Mariátegui created the first political organization which a year later became the Peruvian Socialist Party, and a few years later still the Peruvian Communist Party (Angotti, 1986: 37, 54). In 1928 each also published their main book, i.e. Haya de la Torre (1972) and Mariátegui (1971).

13. Simplifying modernization theory argues that the traditional and modern categories (which can be sectors within a country or different countries such as the less–developed and the developed) are separate entities on a continuum. For the traditional to become modern it merely follows a similar process of change to that initially adopted by the modern (Frank, 1972a; D. Johnson, 1973; J. Taylor, 1979: Chapter 1).

CHAPTER 2: THE STRUCTURALIST SCHOOL OF DEVELOPMENT

1. ECLA was, and perhaps still is, the most original and active of the various regional organizations established by the United Nations in the post–war period. In the early 1980s it changed its name to Economic Commission for Latin America and the Caribbean. While the English acronym changed to ECLAC, the Spanish acronym remained the same, i.e. CEPAL. The members and ideas emanating from ECLAC continue to be referred to in Spanish as *cepalistas*. As the main *cepalista* ideas were formulated before the new name I will continue to use the old name and English acronym throughout the text. ECLA regularly publishes two serials: the annual *Economic Survey of Latin America* since 1950, and the quarterly *Economic Bulletin for Latin America*, which was discontinued in 1976 after twenty years of existence and replaced by the twice yearly *CEPAL Review*. For analyses of ECLA's influence, see Lüders (1977) and Bruce (1980).

2. Raúl Prebisch was born in 1901 in Argentina. His father was of German origin and his mother was Argentinian (Popescu, 1986: 11). He received his doctorate from the University of Buenos Aires in 1923. He was Under-Secretary of Finance of Argentina from 1930 to 1932. He collaborated in the foundation of his country's Central Bank, which he directed from 1935 to 1943 (Banco Nacional de Comercio Exterior, 1986: 379). Other posts he has held include: Executive Secretary to the ECLA 1948 to 1962, Director–General of the UN's Latin American Institute for Economic and Social Planning (ILPES), Secretary–General to the UN Conference on Trade and Development (UNCTAD) from 1964 to 1969, and Director of the journal *CEPAL Review* from 1976 to his death (Meier and Seers, 1984: 173). With the return of democracy to Argentina in 1984 he was appointed personal advisor to President Raúl Alfonsín. He remained closely associated with ECLA in Santiago de Chile, where he died at the age of 85. For a concise overview of his ideas see Prebisch (1984), and for some of his many publications see the bibliography at the end of this book. A useful selection of Prebisch's main writings (sometimes published anonymously) while working in ECLA has been made by Gurrieri (1982). There have been many analyses of his writings and thoughts, among them: Alemann (1955), Ramírez Gómez (1966), Baer (1971), Flanders (1972), di Marco (1972), Love (1980; 1986), Gurrieri (1981; 1982a; 1982b), Molero (1981), Parra Peña (1981), Hopenhayn (1982), Bhagwati (1985: Chapters 20 and 21), Clairmonte (1986), Banco Nacional de Comercio Exterior (1987), Flechsig (1987), Hodara (1987b), Torres–Rivas (1987),

and by several authors in issues of *CEPAL Review*.

3. Besides Prebisch, economists associated with ECLA and who made key contributions to the structuralist paradigm include among others the Brazilian Celso Furtado (1965), the Mexican Juan Noyola (1984), and the Chileans Aníbal Pinto (1970; Pinto and Kñakal, 1973) and Osvaldo Sunkel (1966). The main ECLA sociologist at the time was the Spanish exile José Medina Echavarría (1963). Furtado's biographical intellectual essay (1985) provides many fascinating insights into the origins and developments of the ECLA scheme of thought. For Noyola's (and ECLA's) early relationship with the Cuban revolutionary government, see Noyola (1978).

4. For a critical analysis of ECLA's view of the state, see Andrade (1979), and Alvarez (1976).

5. ECLA staff were careful to distinguish between different peripheral countries and therefore did not recommend a uniform inward–directed development strategy. For this purpose they developed a typology for the Latin American continent (including Central America) by using the structuralist method. Relevant criteria for constructing this typology were a country's natural resource endowments, its particular historical insertion into the world economy, the resulting road, rail, port, (etc.) infrastructure, its distribution of income, and the character of the state. These distinctive features were distilled for each country and then grouped together by type. Through this typological device the differential impact which the economic cycles of the centre had and still have on the peripheral countries became easier to assess and more appropriate development strategies for each type of country could be formulated (Furtado, 1970; Sunkel and Paz, 1970: Part Four).

6. The 'developmentalist' perspective is analysed further in Aguilar (1971: 17–34) and in F. Cardoso (1980).

7. Much has been written on the fortunes and misfortunes of the Alliance for Progress – see Levinson and de Onis (1970) – and early issues of *NACLA Report on the Americas*, among others.

Much of the Alliance was military aid stemming from the rightist panic to prevent the spread and eventual success of Cuban–style guerrilla movements throughout Latin America. The most obvious consequence of this military aid was the proliferation of national security doctrines and the advent of a substantial number of military governments with 'a mission to save the nation'. The genuinely civilian aid of the Alliance for Progress seemed conditional on a series of 'social democratic reforms': a modest land reform, compensating the displaced landowners, the modernization of the state apparatus through reforming public administration, etc., and the institutionalization of development planning (in reality 'pseudo-planning', to use Seers' classic expression). The whole thing had a rather watered–down 'New Deal' style, and the reason was not hard to find! It was modelled on a very specific Latin American development experience...that of Puerto Rico after the Second World War, the model called 'Operation Bootstrap'. That model had been conceived under the Governorship of Rexford Tugwell, one of Roosevelt's crucial New Deal advisors in the 1930s, and it had been carried out under the Governorship of Luis Muñoz Marín, who subsequently became an advisor to the Alliance for Progress. The Alliance was headed by Teodoro Moscoso, who had previously headed Puerto Rico's Economic Development Administration known as *Fomento*, which was responsible for implementing 'Operation Bootstrap'.

(Ray Bromley, personal communication, 31 August 1987)

8. A comprehensive and clear exposition of ECLA's main propositions is given by Guzmán (1976). Unfortunately the books by Sunkel and Paz (1970), Guzmán (1976), and O. Rodríguez (1980) are not available in English, but an article by O. Rodríguez (1977) published in English conveys some of his main ideas. Other general analyses of the CEPAL's thought are the articles by Hirschman (1961), Stein and Hunt (1971), Bianchi (1973), FitzGerald (1979: 26–39), Kuri Gaytán (1982), Assael (1984), and Hodara (1987a). For a collection of key essays by CEPAL, see ECLA (1970a); and for a useful collection of essays by major *cepalista* thinkers, see Bianchi (1969). It is only in the last years of his prolific life that Raúl Prebisch set out to develop systematically his ideas on what he termed 'peripheral capitalism' in a series of articles originally published in *CEPAL Review* and later published as a book (see Prebisch, 1981a).

9. These ideas are similar to W. Arthur Lewis's (1954) classic dualist model, but were formulated a few years earlier by Prebisch (ECLA, 1951: Chapter 1). However, Lewis emphasizes the low productivity of the subsistence sector, as this explains the low wages in the capitalist export sector and hence the deterioration of the periphery's terms of trade; while Prebisch stresses other factors, as mentioned further on. For an insightful article which draws upon Lewis's and Prebisch's terms of trade analyses and contrasts them with the orthodox factor price equalization theorem, see Chichilnisky (1981).

10. For early neoclassical critiques of the structuralist thesis on the deterioration of the periphery's terms of trade, see Viner (1953), Ellsworth (1961), Haberler (1961), H. Johnson (1967), and Pincus (1967). Later, other economists, like Powelson (1977) and Streeten (1981a), were also unable to find any evidence for the secular deterioration in the terms of trade of primary products in relation to manufactured products. However, more recent studies show that there has been a long–run deterioration in the periphery's terms of trade, as will be discussed later.

11. There is some dispute as to whether Prebisch interpreted the factor–price equalization theory of international trade correctly (Flanders, 1972).

12. It is possible for an *individual* peripheral country which is a marginal producer of primary products to increase its exports of raw materials substantially without producing a fall in price and thereby achieve a capacity to import which is able to sustain an adequate rate of growth of income for some time. Thus, the primary–commodity export model

might not yet have reached exhaustion in all underdeveloped countries and especially in those which still have unused agricultural land or are rich in minerals.

13. It could be argued that one of the conditions for a fairer distribution of the gains from international trade is that the double factoral terms of trade between the centre and the periphery should remain fairly stable or that they should not deteriorate against the periphery. However, how are we to determine if these terms of trade were fair in the first instance? (The double factoral terms of trade take into account the productivity changes in the production of export commodities by both centre and periphery, as well as price changes. They are calculated by multiplying the commodity terms of trade by the ratio of the productivity index of the periphery's exports to, and the productivity index of its imports from, the centre.) Prebisch suggests that the evolution of the double factoral terms of trade have been even more adverse for the periphery than the commodity terms of trade, as he argues that productivity increased faster in the production of industrial commodities than in primary commodities. As it is very difficult to calculate the productivity changes of the commodities traded in the international market, no clear answer has yet been given as to the long–term evolution of the double factoral terms of trade (Spraos, 1979; 1980)

14. There is some similarity here with Emmanuel's writings on unequal exchange, as both Emmanuel (1972) and Prebisch (1950; 1959) focus on the evolution of productivity and wage differentials between centre and periphery. For explorations of the links between these analyses, see H. D. Evans (1981a) and Edwards (1985: Chapter 4).

15. Another structural feature considered by ECLA in their analysis of the impact of centre technology refers to the structure of Latin American agriculture, which is characterized by the co–existence of large landed estates (latifundia) and small subsistence peasant farms (minifundia). The mechanization of the latifundia would exacerbate the problem of unemployment and underemployment on the minifundia (CEPAL, 1952). Thus, Prebisch (1969) concludes that the introduction of mechanization in the countryside is unlikely to improve rural living standards as the surplus population would remain or even increase.

16. Furthermore, Hirschman points out that

> the theory of structural stagnation...had to be hastily abandoned after a brief lifespan in the mid–sixties because Brazil, that paradigm for the 'exhaustion' of import–substitution early in the decade, suddenly resumed growth *without* prior redistribution of income in the egalitarian direction – in fact with the opposite kind of redistribution.
> (Hirschman, 1981b: 175)

In my view these stagnationist currents surface every so often under different guises and have not been completely abandoned.

17. Campos (1961b: 69; 1967: 106) claims to have coined these labels to categorize these two groups of economists. It is certainly true that the structuralists did not at first use the label 'structuralism' or 'structuralist'

in characterizing their position. Sunkel (1960), for example, sub–titles his seminal article on inflation 'an unorthodox approach', and Olivera (1960) refers at first to the 'non–monetarist' theory of inflation and only later to 'structural' inflation (Olivera, 1964).

18. Seers, writing at the turn of the 1960s on the structuralist analysis of inflation, thinks that there is some confusion as to what is meant by structure by members of the structuralist school since they:

> refer to the 'structures' of income, demand, output, industry, exports, imports, administration, politics, society, etc. Broadly speaking the more leftist structuralists mean by the word *all* these things, because each of them is considered in some way an impediment to economic growth and the achievement of a more egalitarian [*sic*] society. The conclusion may be drawn that social revolution is a necessary condition for an adequate rate of economic growth. On the other hand, the more conservative adherents usually put the main, if not the exclusive, emphasis on the structures of production and trade, since they are naturally less inclined to stress the need for social change.
>
> (Seers, 1962: 192)

Seers also thinks that the structuralist school 'must be the first indigenous school of economics in an underdeveloped area' and that it has 'affinities with Keynesian economics. It is essentially anti–monetarist, and it is on the whole more easily accepted by the Left than the Right' (ibid.: 193).

19. Noyola (1984: 354; orig. 1956) was the first to distinguish between the 'basic inflationary pressures' and the 'propagating mechanisms' of inflation. He in turn was influenced by Kalecki and Aujac, Polish and French economists respectively. Kalecki (1976: 62), in an article first published in Spanish in 1954, spoke of the 'primary inflationary pressure', which he saw as resulting from basic disproportions in productive relations. Kalecki also stressed that supply rigidities in, and monopolization of, economic systems created inflationary pressures. Meanwhile, Aujac (1954), in an article originally published in 1950, argued that inflation was the consequence of the behaviour of social groups. As will be seen later on, these ideas have a strong bearing on the structuralist analysis of inflation. For a clear analysis on the relationship between inflation and import–substituting industrialization, see Furtado (1970: Chapter 12).

20. For useful summaries of the debate see Campos (1960; 1961b), Felix (1961; 1964), Pinto (1961b), Seers (1962; 1964; 1983b), Baer (1967), Malavé Mata (1976), Kirkpatrick and Nixson (1981), Little (1982: Chapter 5), and Cáceres and Jiménez (1983). For empirical analyses of a general kind, see Maynard (1961), Edel (1969), Mikesell (1969), Thorp (1971), Pazos (1972), Wachter (1976), and E. Cardoso (1981). For a selection of country studies, see Grünwald (1961), Harberger (1963), Hirschman (1963), Kaldor (1964; 1983), Sierra (1969), Díaz–Alejandro (1970: Chapter 7), Ffrench–Davis (1973), Kahil (1973), Reichmann (1973), Corbo (1974), and Thorp and Whitehead (1979). For an excellent comprehensive and up–to–date theoretical and empirical

study on inflation and stabilization in less–developed countries, see Colman and Nixson (1986: 402–35).

21. See, for example, ECLA (1955: 38–9), Noyola (1984: 361), Pinto (1964: 60–1), and Prebisch (1971: 381).

22. In the 1970s a group of neo–conservative economists, which Foxley (1983) calls 'structuralist monetarists', emerged in Latin America. In their stabilization programme they consider long–term structural and institutional changes as well as orthodox monetarist policies. Among the structural and institutional changes proposed are the denationalization of state enterprises, the drastic reduction if not elimination of protectionist measures, the introduction of labour legislation which aims at weakening the labour movement, and the partial dismantling of the welfare state by privatizing the social security, health, and higher education systems. This new brand of monetarists thus proposes a very different kind of structural changes to that of the original ECLA–type structuralists. These structuralist monetarists emerged as a reaction to the structural and institutional changes which had occurred since the 1930s in countries like Brazil, Chile, Argentina, and Uruguay, and to the ideas of structuralist and dependency writers: see Chapter 7.

CHAPTER 3: INTERNAL COLONIALISM: ETHNIC AND CLASS RELATIONS

1. This radical view of Latin America's colonial heritage also influenced the structuralist and dependency theories in their search for the roots of the outward–directed and dependent processes of development. An insight into the radical interpretation of Latin American history can be gained by reading Bagú (1949), Prado Jr. (1967), Stein and Stein (1970), Peña (1971: Chapter 5), Galeano (1973), Cueva (1977), and C. Cardoso and Brignoli (1979), among others. For a perceptive analysis of the 'unity and diversity in Latin American history' see Roxborough (1984).

2. I am paraphrasing the title of Galeano's (1971) best seller, where he writes:

Latin America is the region of open veins. Everything from the discovery until our times, has always been transmuted into European – or later United States – capital, and as such has accumulated in distant centers of power. Everything: the soil, its fruits and its mineral–rich depths, the people and their capacity to work and to consume, natural resources and human resources.

(Galeano, 1973: 12)

3. On the rise of *indigenismo* and its original characteristics in Perú, see Alfajeme and Valderrama (n.d.) and T. Davies (1974: Chapter 3). For Mexico, see Warman (1978).

4. For example, Rama (1975: xv, xvi) considers Mariátegui as an *indigenista*. However, Mariátegui (1955: 26–8) was critical of many *indigenistas* of his time, with the exception of Valcárcel. Among the

first leading *indigenistas* in Perú can be mentioned Luis E. Valcárcel (1972), Dora Mayer de Zulen, and Hildebrando Castro Pozo (1924). Of special note in Mexico are: Gonzalo Aguirre Beltrán (1957; 1967), Vicente Lombardo Toledano (1973), and Manuel Gamio. According to Stavenhagen (1965: 55), one of Aguirre Beltrán's (1957) books 'constitutes the most complete theoretical exposition of Mexican nativism'.

5. For an insightful comparison of the ideas held by Mariátegui and Haya de la Torre on the Indian and national questions, see Valderrama (n.d.).

6. Frank became familiar with the writings of the *indigenistas*, as well as those of González Casanova and Stavenhagen, while working during the 1960s in Latin America. See especially his various articles and chapters on internal colonialism in Frank (1967; 1969; 1975).

7. The Sendero Luminoso guerrilla movement, whose actions were initiated in 1980 in the poorest Indian region (Ayacucho), draws inspiration from the writings of Mariátegui. The full name of the organization is Partido Comunista del Perú, *Por el Sendero Luminoso de Mariátegui*, i.e. 'by or following the shining path of Mariátegui'.

8. Mariátegui in his polemic with the *indigenistas* crossed swords particularly with Luis Alberto Sánchez, the leading *Aprista* intellectual in the late 1920s (Castro, 1976).

9. González Casanova is in turn criticized by Frank (1969: 318–20) for holding a dualist position. Frank's critique refers to González Casanova's (1970) first formulations on internal colonialism. Furthermore, Frank emphasizes economic factors in his own analysis of internal colonialism and criticizes González Casanova for neglecting these and stressing instead cultural factors. In my view, González Casanova has to some extent taken these criticisms on board in his subsequent analyses.

10. In the original translation 'owners of the means of production' is wrongly translated as 'owners of raw materials or of production': see the original Spanish article first published in *América Latina*, 6 (3), 1963, and reprinted in González Casanova (1969: 221–50) and in Cardoso and Weffort (1970: 164–83).

11. Although Quijano puts forward this suggestive link between internal colonialism and marginality, he does not develop it further. In González Casanova's view (1968: 480) indigenous communities as well as poor peasants and unskilled workers constitute marginal groups.

12. This issue resurfaces in the polemic of Marini with Fernando H. Cardoso and Lessa which is discussed at length in Chapter 6.

13. For a brief explanation of the Marxist theory of unequal exchange, see note 14 of Chapter 5. For a detailed theoretical analysis, see Edwards (1985: Chapter 4).

14. See Chapter 6 (and especially note 2) for a brief explanation of this aspect of the Marxist labour theory of value.

15. Frank's (1967) thesis that Latin America has been capitalist since its incorporation into the world capitalist system as a consequence of the Iberian conquest was first criticized by Ernesto Laclau (1971), and

started a long debate on modes of production. See especially Romano (1970), Sempat Assadourian (1971), Frank *et al.* (1973), C. Cardoso (1975), Brenner (1977), Dieterich (1978), Foster–Carter (1978), and Wolpe (1980).

16. For a thoughtful examination and critique of various attempts to reformulate internal colonialism within the theory of dependency, see Stoltz Chinchilla (1983).

17. The term 'Chicanos' is mainly used to refer to descendants of the population which lived in Mexican territory annexed by the US in the last century, but it can also be applied to recent immigrants from Mexico.

CHAPTER 4: MARGINALITY: SOCIAL RELATIONS AND CAPITAL ACCUMULATION

1. The literature on squatter settlements in Latin America is vast. Some useful publications are: Hauser (1962), Mangin (1967), Matos Mar (1968), Peattie (1968), Leeds (1969), Cornelius and Trueblood (1974; 1975), Hardoy (1975), Portes and Browning (1976), Portes and Walton (1976), and Cornelius and Kemper (1978).

2. Frank (1966b: 79) prefers to use the term 'unstable floating population' instead of 'marginal population'.

3. DESAL stands for *Centro para el Desarrollo Económico y Social de América Latina* or the Centre for the Economic and Social Development of Latin America. The DESAL marginality approach is located within the modernization paradigm. The writings on urbanization and marginality by ECLA (1963a; 1963b; 1970b) and by Germani (1972; 1980) also belong to this paradigm.

4. See in particular Germani (1966; 1967; 1969–70; 1981), where the author fully develops his modernization paradigm.

5. Franco (1974: 526) goes even further by criticizing the neo–Marxist writers on marginality, who in his view have grossly exaggerated the peculiarities of the Latin American case as, marginality was, and partly still is, common in advanced countries.

6. This analysis by DESAL follows in the tradition of those theories, like Oscar Lewis's (1963; 1966) 'culture of poverty', which blame the victims for their own state of affairs and poverty.

7. In most DESAL studies countless statistical tables are presented with data on social stratification, ethnic and racial composition of the population, distribution of population between rural and urban areas, housing conditions, employment, incomes, social security, education, transport, access to radio, newspapers and television, membership of organizations such as political parties, co–operatives, trade unions, football clubs, mother centres, neighbourhood centres, social clubs and other community organizations, characteristics of the family such as percentage of legally married couples, number of children, illegitimacy, vagrancy, divorce rates, promiscuity and juvenile delinquency, and so on.

8. The shanty towns previously called *poblaciones callampas* (mushroom shanty towns in the sense that like mushrooms they appear overnight) were renamed *poblaciones marginales*, i.e. marginal townships. Their inhabitants were not referred to as marginals, as this could be considered as offensive (previously they were called *callamperos* which is a derogatory term), but as *pobladores*, i.e. settlers or townsmen.

9. Carlos Delgado was a personal adviser of President Velasco Alvarado and together with General Leonidas Rodríguez was the main driving force of SINAMOS (which can also be read as '*sin amos*' or 'without bosses'). During the late 1960s he briefly worked in Chile where he became familiar with, or renewed his acquaintance with, the writings on marginality of ECLA, Germani, DESAL, F. H. Cardoso, Quijano, and Nun, as well as observing at close range the participatory and promotional programmes of the Frei government (Delgado, 1971: 47, 119, 160, 163; Delgado 1975: 19, 75).

10. I am grateful to Ray Bromley for this interpretation of Carlos Delgado's ideas on the social and political integration of lower-class groups.

11. For ECLA's diverse interpretations on marginality, see Rosenblüth (1968), ECLA (1970b), and Faria (1978).

12. It is of interest to note that Quijano produced his first writings on marginality while working for the Social Affairs Division of ECLA while one of Nun's research projects on marginality was undertaken under the auspices of ECLA's Latin American Institute of Economic and Social Planning (ILPES).

13. Only one of Quijano's articles on marginality has been published in English (Quijano, 1974). More recently part of his introduction to his 1977a collection of articles on marginality has been published in English (Quijano, 1983).

14. Nun makes a distinction between relative surplus labour and industrial reserve army which, according to Fernando H. Cardoso (1971: 62), and others, it is doubtful that Marx himself intended to make. As Marx's writings on this point (1976: 781–99, 848–53) are vague, the two interpretations might be possible.

15. It might even be dysfunctional if monopoly capital has to bear some of the cost of welfare and poverty alleviation measures for this marginal mass – if such provisions exist at all. I would add the cost of policing if the marginal mass resorts to thefts, protests, food riots, revolts, and violence in general. In certain Latin American countries 'security' and 'defence' have become major economic activities and absorbers of labour in their own right, such as soldiers, policemen, informers, security guards, night-watchmen, torturers, bodyguards, and so on.

16. In my view, Nun's concept of marginal mass is too broad as it includes all labour which will never be employed by monopoly capital and which does not exert any influence on wage levels paid by monopoly capital. In addition, he makes no attempt to measure the marginal mass. What is of interest to note is that Nun does not equate marginality with unemployment or underemployment *per se*, which is often the case with other writers, among them Córdova (1973).

17. In a joint study Nun, Marín, and Murmis distinguish between three

types of marginality. Type A refers to that part of the population who are not free wage–labourers being inserted into pre–capitalist forms of production or under some degree of extra–economic coercion. This type of marginal population is largely found within the rural sector. It includes those who are tied to the land through debt peonage, various forms of tenancy (labour–service tenants, sharecroppers, etc.), and so on. It also refers to those who are direct producers such as small miners, craftsmen, and smallholders who, through the ownership of some means of production, are able to scrape a living. Type B is mainly composed of that part of the labour force which has been freed from its means of production and/or from extra–economic coercion, and had largely migrated to the urban centres. They are free to sell their labour power but are unable to to find stable and full employment. Type C is that part of the labour force which used to have stable wage employment but is now only able to find employment intermittently and/or in jobs which significantly underutilize its skills (Nun *et al.*, 1969; Murmis, 1969: 417; Nun, 1971: 196–7).

18. This issue is problematic and Quijano should have examined this point by drawing on the 'unequal exchange' discussion.

19. For this quotation of Marx by Quijano (which Quijano quotes in Spanish), I am using the translation of the English edition of *Capital*, i.e. Marx (1976: 798).

20. Although Nun uses a different Spanish edition of *Capital*, the same translation error seems to have been made. Nun also used a French edition which either contained the same mistake, or he failed to notice the discrepancy.

21. The German word *flüssig* is translated in both the Progress Publishers (Lawrence & Wishart) and Penguin editions as 'floating'. *Flüssig* literally means 'fluid' and in this context, to my knowledge, 'readily available'.

22. However, Nun (1979: 7), in a more recent article, abandons the concept of marginal mass, using instead Marx's term of 'floating surplus population' to refer to a case study of the Argentinian car industry. It is difficult to know if he intends to abandon the term marginal mass completely. For a savage critique of Nun's article, see C. Johnson (1979).

23. I am grateful to Ray Bromley for this idea and its formulation.

24. This explains the inverted commas used by Oliveira and Kowarick when refering to the marginals.

25. Much of the following analysis of the contribution of marginal labour to capital accumulation is taken from Oliveira (1985) and Kowarick (1978). Although they examine the Brazilian case, their analysis is of general relevance to other Third World countries.

26. Perlman's (1976: 259) comment that 'the favelados serve in the creation of jobs of diverse sorts of professionals and quasi–professionals, especially social workers, social scientists, and urban planners' is not without irony.

27. The Brazilian case might be exceptional in this regard as it recorded one of the highest, if not the highest, rate of industrial growth in the

post–war period in Latin America. It therefore remains to be seen to what extent data from other Latin American countries confirm this empirical challenge to the marginality hypothesis.

28. Thus, for example, although various of the articles in Bromley and Gerry (eds) (1979) bear on this point, in particular those by Bromley and Gerry (1979), MacEwen Scott (1979), and R. Davies (1979), none examines explicitly the possible relations between marginality and formal–informal sectors. Some of the articles in Bromley (1979) make passing reference to marginality when discussing the relationship between the informal sector and petty commodity production. In a special issue of the *IDS Bulletin* (Institute of Development Studies, University of Sussex, 5 (2–3), 1973) on 'The informal sector and marginal groups', none of the authors refer to the Latin American marginality writers. This omission in the history of ideas is only partially rectified in a succint and recently published article by Peattie (1987). The best, though brief, overview remains that by Tokman (1978b).

29. The benign and exploitative approaches to the linkages between the formal and informal sectors were already identified by Bienefeld and Godfrey (1975: 8). The prolific writings of Portes (1978; 1983; Portes and Walton, 1981) on marginality and the informal sector are probably best classified in between the neo–Marxist and PREALC/structuralist approaches as his analysis combines elements of both. Lomnitz (1978), who has assimilated the marginal sector to the informal sector, views the formal–informal sector linkages as a network of social relationships within an articulated totality.

CHAPTER 5: REFORMIST AND MARXIST APPROACHES TO DEPENDENCY

1. *Dependentistas* who have been forced into exile for some or all of the remainder of their careers include, among others, the Argentinians Oscar Braun, Juan Carlos Marín, Miguel Murmis, José Nun, and Tomás Amadeo Vasconi; the Bolivian René Zavaleta; the Brazilians Vania Bambirra, Fernando Henrique Cardoso, Theotonio Dos Santos, Celso Furtado, Ruy Mauro Marini, and Herbert De Souza; the Chileans Gonzalo Arroyo, Sergio Bitar, Alvaro Briones, Orlando Caputo, Jacques Chonchol, Luis Maira, Roberto Pizarro, Sergio Ramos, and José Valenzuela; the Ecuadorian Agustín Cueva; the Peruvian Aníbal Quijano; and the Uruguayan Eduardo Galeano.

2. By attempting to redress the balance, I hope not to do too much of an injustice to Frank. Those interested in Frank's ideas should find the following of interest, as the origin of some of his ideas can be found in the intellectual climate in Latin America where he lived and worked during the 1960s and early 1970s.

3. When the English edition of Cardoso and Faletto's book was finally published in 1979, it was greeted by some commentators as a 'happening' and 'an event' (Packenham, 1982: 131). Given this late publication in English and 'the English bias of the English speaking world' O'Brien (1984: 5–6) reflects that:

It would be an interesting essay in the sociology of knowledge to trace the connections and links in this process of circulation, for particular interpretations, rather than original versions, seem to have played a key role in the spread of the concept [of dependency].

4. For a fascinating though personalistic and at times speculative ideological history of dependency, which gives further reasons for its widespread influence, see Lehmann (1986).

5. The nationalist theme has a long history in Latin America, as mentioned in Chapter 1. There is, for example, a resemblance between the nationalist discourse of Haya de la Torre and the reformist *dependentistas*.

6. Palma (1978) and Munck (1984) prefer a three–way classification of *dependentistas* as they put Fernando Henrique Cardoso in a category of his own. Although Cardoso tends to occupy the middle ground, on balance his position is closest to the reformists, which seems to be confirmed by his political activities in Brazilian politics over the last decade or so (Lehmann, 1986: 16–20). However,

It is in the marxist tradition that Cardoso finds his preferred theoretical interlocutors, not in Frank and the dependency school. ...He has for long seen 'dependencia' as sharing with official marxism an excessively structured or over–determined view of the world and its history in which there is no place for the subject, for political action, for social movements.

(ibid.: 13–14)

7. For an early and global overview of neo–Marxist approaches to development and underdevelopment, see Foster–Carter (1974) and the subsequent critiques by Bernstein (1979) and J. Taylor (1979).

8. Those who contributed to a Caribbean dependency approach are: Norman Girvan (1971; 1973; Girvan and Jefferson, 1971), George Beckford (1972), Owen Jefferson (1972), Havelock Brewster (1973), Alister McIntyre, Walter Rodney, and Clive Thomas, among others. Some of them spread the dependency vision to Africa by working for some years in Africa and writing books on dependency in Africa (Rodney, 1972; Thomas, 1974).

9. The CESO dependency group included at one time or another the following: Vania Bambirra, Alvaro Briones, Orlando Caputo, André Gunder Frank, Ruy Mauro Marini, Roberto Pizarro, Sergio Ramos, Cristián Sepúlveda, Jaime Torres, José Valenzuela, and Tomás Vasconi, among others. This group dispersed after the military coup of September 1973 but continued to contribute to the dependency debate from exile, although by then the key propositions had already been formulated.

10. There is a dispute, however, over the extent to which Marx later changed his view on this, as indicated in his correspondence with the Russian populists (Dos Santos, 1978: 341) and through his involvement with the Irish question (Munck, 1984: 17). As a consequence of his studies on the Russian peasant commune and its possibilities for a socialist transition, Marx begun to 'perceive the structures unique to

backward capitalism' (Shanin, 1981: 116; Wada, 1981). 'To sum it up bluntly, to Marx the England he knew, "that is more developed industrially", did not and indeed could not any longer "show to the less developed" Russia the "image of its own future".' (Shanin, 1981: 117.)

11. In his analysis of unequal exchange, for example, Marini makes no reference whatsoever to Emmanuel – the main Marxist exponent of the theory of unequal exchange – nor does he examine the debate concerning this issue. His analysis might also have gained precision and greater clarity if he had used Marx's notations and algebraic formulations rather than relying exclusively on words.

12. Marini works within the Marxist labour theory of value and political economy. According to this theory, labour is the only source of value. Workers sell their labour power to capitalists for a wage which capitalists employ for producing commodities. The labour power employed in the production of commodities creates a value which exceeds the exchange value of this labour power (i.e. wage). This difference is the surplus value which is the source of profits and is appropriated by the capitalists (Bottomore *et al.*, 1983: 265–7).

13. In Marxian economics a distinction is made between absolute and relative surplus value. Surplus value as such is the difference between the value produced by a worker and the value of the worker's labour power. The working day can be divided into two parts: 'Necessary labour, in which time the worker is producing an equivalent of what he or she receives as wages, and surplus labour, in which time the worker is producing simply for the capitalist' (Bottomore *et al.*, 1983: 474). The production of absolute surplus value involves 'increasing the total value produced by each worker without changing the amount of necessary labour. This can be done by either an intensive or an extensive extension of the working day' (ibid.). The production of relative surplus value

> requires necessary labour time to be reduced, that is, a fall in the value of labour power, ...which can take place in two ways. Either the quantity of use values the worker consumes, or the socially necessary labour time to produce the same quantity of use values, must be reduced.
>
> (ibid.)

The former method implies a reduction in wages and thus a deterioration of the worker's physical condition. 'The latter method is that by which capitalism has become the most dynamic mode of production to date, continually changing its production methods and introducing technological improvements.' (ibid.)

14. The unequal exchange theory was first put forward by Emmanuel (1972) working within Marxian economics. According to him international trade between developed and underdeveloped countries is unequal because the former exchange goods in which less labour time is embodied for goods in which more labour time is embodied (Edwards, 1985: 63).

In particular, the ratio of advanced country prices to backward country prices is greater than the ratio of the labour time in advanced country commodities to the labour time in backward country commodities, where 'advanced' and 'backward' are defined purely in terms of the wage level in each country. In this way, through exchange, advanced countries appropriate more labour time in exchange than they generate in production. A surplus is transferred from backward countries, reducing the rate of accumulation there for lack of a sufficient investable surplus.

(Bottomore *et al.*, 1983: 500–1)

15. As can be observed there are certain similarities here between Marini's and Furtado's analysis as both see the demand for industrial goods as determining industry's structure of production which is not geared towards the production of mass consumer goods (Marini, 1973: 55–6).

16. A sizeable literature exists on the topic of Latin American authoritarian and corporatist regimes and on Guillermo O'Donnell's thesis of bureaucratic authoritarianism. See particularly O'Donnell (1973; 1977; 1978), F. Cardoso (1975), Malloy (1977), Linz and Stepan (1978), Collier (1979), and Wiarda (1981).

17. For Marini, and indeed most other *dependentistas*, this is the case as well, although Marini does not centre his analysis on technological dependence as most other *dependentistas* do.

18. André Gunder Frank was born in Berlin in 1929 and educated in the United States where in 1957 he received a PhD in economics from the University of Chicago. From 1962 to 1973 he spent most of his time in Latin America as a staff member of universities in Brazil, Mexico, and Chile. Those years were particularly fertile for Latin American social scientists as it was a period of 'paradigm shift' in which the Latin American development theories reached fruition. This shift was, of course, already initiated by earlier intellectuals – most notably José Carlos Mariátegui and Raúl Prebisch, as discussed in Chapters 1 and 2. Thus, Frank in his early creative period was privileged to be able to participate and contribute to this Latin American debate. The other, and pehaps more important, influence on Frank's intellectual formation has been the writings of the US Marxist Paul Baran. Politically the Cuban revolution of 1959 had a major influence on him. His first and probably most influential book, entitled *Capitalism and Underdevelopment in Latin America: Historical Studies of Chile and Brazil*, was published in 1967. In this book he develops his famous theses of 'the development of underdevelopment' and of the capitalist character of the Latin American countries since the colonial period. Although he does not use the term dependence in this book it can be viewed as a contribution to the dependence approach. His next major text, *Lumpenbourgeoisie: Lumpendevelopment*, was published in Spanish in 1970 and then in English in 1972. This book is explicitly placed by Frank within the dependence framework and in it he tries to meet some of the criticisms made of his previous writings, in particular

concerning his insufficient (and some would say inadequate) analysis of class and internal relations of production. His next two major books *World Accumulation 1492–1789* and *Dependent Accumulation and Underdevelopment*, both published in 1978, despite the phrase dependent accumulation in one of them, are already within a world–system perspective, which the author has continued to develop since.

19. It seems that it is only in an essay written in 1969 and published in 1970 that Frank first makes reference to the term dependency (Frank, 1970: 20–1). It is thus paradoxical that he later considers this essay as signalling a swan-song of the dependency writings (Frank, 1977: 356).

20. On world-system theory see particularly Wallerstein (1974; 1980; 1982), Amin (1976), Frank (1980; 1981b), and Amin *et al.* (1982).

21. I am thinking particularly of the book by Cardoso and Faletto (1979), which can be considered as the classical dependency text. It is significant that Frank is never mentioned in this text: neither in the first Spanish version (1969) nor in the expanded English version (1979).

22. For an illustration of this point regarding Eastern Europe's 'second serfdom' and the 'Prussian road' to capitalist agriculture in Latin America, see C. Kay (1974; 1980).

23. See particularly Frank (1967). Frank's 'development of underdevelopment' thesis has been fiercely challenged mainly by historians such as Platt (1980; 1985), Halperin Donghi (1982), and Albert (1983).

24. Although many *dependentistas* have addressed this crucial question the analysis of it is bedevilled with theoretical and empirical difficulties to the extent that no clear answer has yet been found. See the attempts by Caputo and Pizarro (1970), Emmanuel (1972), and Amin (1974; 1977a), among others.

25. In response to criticism from Laclau and other radicals that he cannot properly claim to be a Marxist, Frank (1984: 264) replied in self–defence that he has never claimed to be a Marxist (Lehmann, 1986: 50–1).

26. With regard to theory, for example, when Frank uses Marxist concepts like economic surplus, super–exploitation and sub–imperialism, unequal exchange, and so on, he refers to Baran, Marini, and Emmanuel respectively, as well as to Marx, but without developing them further. The concept of dependence itself had been formulated previously by others, as already mentioned. Furthermore, dependence analysis itself is perhaps best viewed as a paradigm shift rather than a major development in theory – Marxist or otherwise.

CHAPTER 6: DEPENDENCY: DEBATES, CRITIQUES, AND BEYOND

1. F. H. Cardoso (1972c; 1977b) had earlier queried Marini's ideas in two articles on dependency. Marini (1973) briefly replied to Cardoso's 1972c critique in his book on the dialectics of dependence.

2. The value of labour power is the equivalent of the worker's subsistence

wage or the amount of goods and services required for the reproduction of labour. The ratio s/v can also be expressed according to the labour theory of value as the ratio of the hours the worker spends working for a capitalist over the hours the worker spends working for personal consumption (Bottomore *et al.*, 1983: 473–4).

3. In the Marxist theory of labour, constant capital (c) is that portion of capital advanced which is turned into means of production (machinery, equipment, and raw materials), while the variable capital (v) is that portion of capital advanced which is turned into labour power. The sum of constant and variable capital ($c+v$) is the total capital advanced. The labour power which the worker sells for a wage (v) to the capitalist is the only source of surplus value (s) which in turn is appropriated by the capitalist. Thus, the ratio $s/(c+v)$ is the return on capital advanced, i.e. the rate of profit.

4. The underconsumption thesis (i.e. a shortfall of demand for consumption goods) was put forward by Marxist economists as a possible explanation for the realization problem (i.e converting surplus value into profits).

> The demand for wage goods – the output of Department II – could come only from workers (except for a small amount from capitalists), but in their desire to shore up the rate of surplus value and expand the mass of profits capitalists must constantly try to arrest the tendency of real wages to rise. By restricting employment (maintaining a reserve army of labour) as well as real wages, the capitalists put a definite brake on the ability of Department II to sell its goods. The poverty of workers, so necessary in this view to keep up the rate of profit, boomerangs on the system by making it difficult to realize surplus value (convert it into money profits).
>
> (Bottomore *et al.*, 1983: 496)

5. Leys (1977), for example, a well–known critic of the dependency perspective, draws upon a very limited number of dependency writings i.e. an article by Fernando H. Cardoso, an article by Girvan, and a book and article by Frank. In a subsequent article Leys (1978) refers to Frank alone. G. Kay (1975: 103–5), in his critique of the 'theoretical framework' of dependency analysis, likewise makes reference only to Frank. Warren's ferocious and influential attack (1980) rests upon two mimeographed essays by Fernando H. Cardoso, one book by Frank, and an article by Sunkel. Foster–Carter (1979–80) cites only one book by Frank although in a subsequent article he acknowledges that his previous reading of the *dependentistas* was limited. His understanding of dependency was greatly enhanced through reading the book by Cardoso and Faletto (1979) and he reflects that 'a lot of what many people took to constitute dependency theory was in fact the specific extreme and often polemical formulations of Andre Gunder Frank' (Foster–Carter, 1984: 4). For a glimpse of the varied and fertile dependency literature, see Dos Santos (1978) who, for general studies alone, cites over fifty books and articles published in Latin America during the late 1960s and early 1970s (ibid.: 357–8). A profuse collection

of essays on the Latin American dependency debate is contained in Murga F. and Boils (1973) and in Camacho (1979). For a particular thorough and critical survey of the dependency literature, see Hurtienne (1974); and for concise but rich overviews, see Chilcote (1974) and Boeckh (1982). Other critical essays are by Sloan (1977) and Smith (1979). For a comprehensive exploratory review essay on theories of imperialism, dependency, and unequal exchange, see Griffin and Gurley (1985).

6. Some critics have engaged in even worse practices by constructing a dependency straw person which is then easily knocked down. Blomström and Hettne (1984: 69), Munck (1981: 176) and O'Brien (1984: 21–2) have tracked down some of these false critics.

7. But is this commendable advice so very different from F. H. Cardoso's (1972d: 360) suggestion (not referred to by Bernstein but first delivered in a public lecture as early as 1970) that dependency studies should deal with the analysis of concrete situations rather than aspire to become a general theory?

8. For these reasons a Caribbean dependency school emerged in the late 1960s. While influenced by the Latin American dependency school, the Caribbean *dependentistas* realized that the small island economies of the Caribbean displayed peculiarities of their own which the original dependency writings, based largely on Brazil and the Southern Cone countries, were ill–suited to explain. Dependency analysis struck a sympathetic chord as for them the dependence of the Caribbean islands was more obvious given their more recent colonial past. Some of the first English–language translations of dependency writings appeared in *Social and Economic Studies* and other Caribbean journals. For an overview of the Caribbean dependency school see Girvan and Jefferson (1971), Girvan (1973), and Blomström and Hettne (1984: 98–119).

9. For an analysis of the room to manœuvre open to Third World countries in the pursuit of less–dependent development strategies, see: Amin (1977b), Senghaas (1979), Galtung *et al.* (1980), Seers (1981b; 1983a), and Bienefeld and Godfrey (1982). For studies of the difficulties facing countries which attempted or are attempting to overcome dependence by pursuing a socialist development path, see O'Brien (1976), White *et al.* (1983), Chilcote and Edelstein (1986), and Fagen *et al.* (1986).

10. Warren's assault on dependency analysis has generated much controversy. One of the best critiques of Warren, which sets the record straight with regard to dependency, is O'Brien (1984); and other useful critiques are by Ahmad (1983), Weaver (1986), and Slater (1987). The extreme orthodox Marxism of Warren led Seers (1978; 1983a: 31–45), who certainly was no Marxist, to argue (in my view mistakenly) that there is a fundamental congruence between Marxism and neoclassical theories. For a Warrenite critique of African dependency writings, see Sender and Smith (1986).

11. Furthermore, Ray (1973) argues that socialist countries, such as Cuba, are still dependent. For a different view and a more rigorous discussion of various dependency theses concerning Cuba, see Pollitt (1985).

12. For a selection of empirical studies on dependence see: Tyler and

Wogart (1973), Chase–Dunn (1975), Kaufman *et al.* (1975), Jackson *et al.* (1979), Mahler (1980), who give a useful overview, and Delacroix and Ragin (1981).

13. Extensive bibliographies on the dependency literature which contain many references to regional and country studies can be found in the following surveys: Senghaas (1972; 1974), Chilcote and Edelstein (1974), Aguilar *et al.* (1976), Bath and James (1976), Palma (1978), Lindenberg (1982), and Abel and Lewis (1985).

14. See also Blomström and Hettne (1984: 194–200) for an analysis of the paradigmatic, ideological, and political significance of the dependency school.

15. The relationship between dependency theory and Marxism is explored comprehensively in Chilcote (1982).

CHAPTER 7: THE LATIN AMERICAN CONTRIBUTION IN PERSPECTIVE

1. O'Donnell's thesis has its flaws, as shown in the critiques of Serra (1979) and Cammack (1985), but this is not the place to discuss them.

2. For useful texts which begin to explore these issues, see White *et al.* (1983), Fagen *et al.* (1986), and R. Harris (1988).

3. For an insightful analysis which contrasts the 'forced–march industrialization' of Brazil with the de–industrialization of Chile and Argentina, see Hirschman (1987: 19–22).

References

Abel, C. and Lewis, C. M. (eds) (1985) *Latin America, Economic Imperialism and the State: The Political Economy of the External Connection from Independence to the Present*, London, The Athlone Press.

Ady, P. (1967) 'Teaching economic development in the UK: some analytical aspects', in K. Martin and J. Knapp (eds).

Agarwala, A. N. and Singh, S. P. (eds) (1958) *The Economics of Underdevelopment*, New York, Oxford University Press.

Aguilar, A. (1971) 'El capitalismo del subdesarrollo: un capitalismo sin capital y sin perspectivas', *Problemas del Desarrollo*, 2 (8).

Aguilar, A. (1973) 'Imperialismo y subdesarrollo' (primera parte), *Problemas del Desarrollo*, 4 (14).

Aguilar, A. (1974) 'Imperialismo y subdesarrollo' (segunda parte), *Problemas del Desarrollo*, 5 (20).

Aguilar, A. *et al.* (1976) *Capitalismo, Atraso y Dependencia en América Latina*, Mexico, Universidad Nacional Autónoma de México (UNAM).

Aguirre Beltrán, G. (1957) *El Proceso de Aculturación*, Mexico, UNAM.

Aguirre Beltrán, G. (1967) *Regiones de Refugio: El Desarrollo de la Comunidad y el Proceso Dominical en Mestizo América*, Mexico, Instituto Nacional Indigenista.

Aguirre Beltrán, G. (1976) *Obra Polémica*, Mexico, Sepinah.

Ahmad, A. (1983) 'Imperialism and progress', in R. H. Chilcote and D. L. Johnson (eds).

Alavi, H. and Shanin, T. (eds) (1982) *Introduction to the Sociology of "Developing Societies"*, London, Macmillan.

Albert, B. (1983) *South America and the World Economy from Independence to 1930*, London, Macmillan.

Alemann, R. T. (1955) 'Die Theorie der peripherischen Wirtschaft', *Weltwirtschaftliches Archiv*, 74 (1).

Alfajeme, A. and Valderrama, M. (n.d.) 'El surgimiento de la discusión de la cuestión agraria y del llamado problema indígena', in C. I. Degregori.

Alvarez, A. R. (1976) 'El estado en el pensamiento de la CEPAL', *Investigación Económica*, 35 (135).

Amin, S. (1974) *Accumulation on a World Scale: A Critique of the Theory of Underdevelopment*, New York, Monthly Review Press.

Amin, S. (1976) *Unequal Development; An Essay on the Social Formations of Peripheral Capitalism*, Brighton, Harvester Press.

Amin, S. (1977a) *Imperialism and Unequal Development*, Brighton, Harvester Press.

Amin, S. (1977b) 'Self–reliance and the new international economic order', *Monthly Review*, 29 (3).

Amin, S., Arrighi, G., Frank, A. G., and Wallerstein, I. (1982) *Dynamics of Global Crisis*, London, Macmillan.

Andrade, R. de Castro (1979) 'The economics of underdevelopment, the state and politics in ECLA's doctrine (1949–1964)', *Occasional Papers Institute of Latin American Studies, University of Glasgow*, no. 29.

Angotti, T. (1981) 'The political implications of dependency theory', *Latin American Perspectives*, 8 (3–4), issues 30–31.

Angotti, T. (1986) 'The contribution of José Carlos Mariátegui to revolutionary theory', *Latin American Perspectives*, 13 (2), issue 49.

Apthorpe, R. and Kráhl, A. (1986) 'Epilogue: "researching for development"', in R. Apthorpe and A. Kráhl (eds) *Development Studies: Critique and Renewal*, Leiden, E. J. Brill.

Arauco, F. (1974) 'Observaciones en torno a la dialéctica de la dependencia', *Historia y Sociedad*, no. 3.

Arndt, H. W. (1972) 'Development economics before 1945', in J. Bhagwati and R. S. Eckaus (eds) *Development and Planning: Essays in Honour of Paul Rosenstein–Rodan*, London, George Allen & Unwin.

Arndt, H. W. (1981) 'Economic development: a semantic history', *Economic Development and Cultural Change*, 29 (3).

Arndt, H. W. (1985) 'The origins of structuralism', *World Development*, 13 (2).

Arndt, H. W. (1987) *Economic Development: The History of an Idea*, Chicago, University of Chicago Press.

Arroyo, G. and Gross, M. (1969) 'La marginalidad campesina', in DESAL (1969).

Assael, H. (1984) 'El pensamiento de la CEPAL: un intento de evaluar algunas críticas de sus ideas principales', *El Trimestre Económico*, 51 (3), no. 203.

Aujac, H. (1954) 'Inflation as the monetary consequence of behaviour of social groups: a working hypothesis', *International Economic Papers*, no. 4.

Baer, W. (1967) 'The inflation controversy in Latin America: a survey', *Latin American Research Review*, 2 (2).

Baer, W. (1971) 'The economics of Prebisch and the ECLA', in I. Livingstone (ed.); originally published in *Economic Development and Cultural Change*, 10 (2), 1961–2. Also in C. T. Nisbet (ed.).

Baer, W. and Kerstenetzky, I. (eds) (1964) *Inflation and Growth in Latin America*, Homewood (Illinois), Irwin.

Baer, W. and Welch, J. H. (1987) 'Editors' introduction', *World Development*, 15 (8). Also in W. Baer and J. H. Welch (eds) *The Resurgence of Inflation in Latin America*, Oxford, Pergamon Press, 1987.

Bagú, S. (1949) *Economía de la Sociedad Colonial. Ensayo de Historia Comparada de América Latina*, Buenos Aires, El Ateneo.

Bahro, R. (1978) *The Alternative in Eastern Europe*, London, New Left Books.

Baines, J. M. (1972) *Revolution in Peru: Mariátegui and the Myth*, Alabama, University of Alabama Press.

Balassa, B. (1981) *The Newly Industrialising Countries in the World Economy*, Oxford, Pergamon Press.

Bambirra, V. (1972) 'Integración monopólica mundial e industrialización: sus contradicciones', *Sociedad y Desarrollo*, no. 1.

Bambirra, V. (1973) *Capitalismo Dependiente Latinoamericano*, Santiago, Editorial Prensa Latinoamericana (PLA).

Bambirra, V. (1978) *Teoría de la Dependencia: Una Anticrítica*, Mexico, Ediciones Era.

Banco Nacional de Comercio Exterior (1986) 'Raúl Prebisch, 1901–1986', *Comercio Exterior*, 36 (5).

Banco Nacional de Comercio Exterior (ed.) (1987) 'Homenaje a Raúl Prebisch (1901–1986)', *Comercio Exterior*, 37 (5).

Baran, P. A. (1952) 'On the political economy of bachwardness', *The Manchester School*, 20 (1); reprinted in A. N. Agarwala and S. P. Singh (eds), and in C. K. Wilber (ed.) (1973).

Baran, P. A. (1973) *The Political Economy of Growth*, Harmondsworth, Penguin.

Baran, P. A. and Hobsbawm, E. J. (1961) 'The stages of economic growth: a review', *Kyklos*, 14 (2). Also in C. K. Wilber (ed.) (1973).

Barkin, D. (1981) 'Internationalization of capital: an alternative approach', *Latin American Perspectives*, 8 (3–4), issues 30–31.

Barrera, M. (1979) *Race and Class in the Southwest: A Theory of Racial Inequality*, Notre Dame, University of Notre Dame Press.

Bartra, R. (1974) 'El problema indígena y la ideología indigenista', *Revista Mexicana de Sociología*, 36 (3).

Bartra, R. (ed.) (1975) 'Modos de producción en América Latina', special issue of *Historia y Sociedad*, no. 5.

Bath, C. R. and James, D. D. (1976) 'Dependency analysis of Latin America: some criticisms, some suggestions', *Latin American Research Review*, 11 (3).

Bauer, P. T. (1984) *Reality and Rhetoric: Studies in the Economics of Development*, London, Weidenfeld & Nicolson.

Bazdresch, C. (1983) 'El pensamiento de Juan F. Noyola', *El Trimestre Económico*, 50 (2), no. 198.

Beckford, L. G. (1972) *Persistent Poverty: Underdevelopment in Plantation Economies of the Third World*, Oxford, Oxford University Press.

Béjar, H. (n.d.) *La Revolución en la Trampa*, Lima, Ediciones Socialismo y Participación.

Benítez Zenteno, R. (ed.) (1973) *Las Clases Sociales en América Latina*, Mexico, Siglo Veintiuno Editores.

Bernstein, H. (1979) 'Sociology of underdevelopment versus sociology of development?', in D. Lehmann (ed.) *Development Theory: Four Critical Studies*, London, Frank Cass.

Bernstein, H. (1982) 'Industrialization, development and dependence', in H. Alavi and T. Shanin (eds).

Beyer, G. H. (ed.) (1967) *The Urban Explosion in Latin America: A Continent in Process of Modernization*, Ithaca (New York), Cornell University Press.

Bhagwati, J. N. (1965) 'The pure theory of international trade: a survey', in The American Economic Association and The Royal Economic Society, *Surveys of Economic Theory: Growth and Development*, London, Macmillan and New York, St Martin's Press.

Bhagwati, J. N. (1985) *Essays in Development Economics: (Vol. 1) Wealth and Poverty*, edited by G. Grossman, Oxford, Basil Blackwell.

Bianchi, A. (1973) 'Notes on the theory of Latin American development', *Social and Economic Studies*, 22 (1).

Bianchi, A. (ed.) (1969) *América Latina: Ensayos de Interpretación Económica*, Santiago, Editorial Universitaria.

Bienefeld, M. (1980) 'Dependency in the eighties', *IDS Bulletin*, 12 (1).

Bienefeld, M. (1981) 'Dependency and the newly industrialising countries (NICs): towards a reappraisal', in D. Seers (ed.) (1981).

Bienefeld, M. and Godfrey, M. (1975) 'Measuring unemployment and the informal sector: some conceptual and statistical problems', *IDS Bulletin*, 7 (3).

Bienefeld, M. and Godfrey, M. (1978) 'Surplus labour and underdevelopment', *IDS Discussion Paper* (Institute of Development Studies, University of Sussex), no. 138.

Bienefeld, M. and Godfrey, M. (eds) (1982) *The Struggle for Development: National Strategies in an International Context*, Chichester, John Wiley.

Bitar, S. (1988) 'Neo-liberalism versus neo-structuralism in Latin America', *CEPAL Review*, no. 34.

Blomström, M. and Hettne, B. (1984) *Development Theory in Transition The Dependency Debate and Beyond: Third World Responses*, London, Zed Books.

Boeckh, A. (1982) 'Der Beitrag der Dependencia–Ansätze zur Erklärung von Entwicklung und Unterentwicklung in Lateinamerika', in K. Lindenberg (ed.).

Bonfil Batalla, G. (1978) 'Las nuevas organizaciones indígenas', in C. I. Degregori (ed.).

Booth, D. (1975) 'Andre Gunder Frank: an introduction and appreciation', in I. Oxaal, T. Barnett, and D. Booth (eds).

Booth, D. (1985) 'Marxism and development sociology: interpreting the impasse', *World Development*, 13 (7).

Booth, D. and Sorj, B. (eds) (1983) *Military Reformism and Social Classes. The Peruvian Experience, 1968–80*, London, Macmillan.

Bottomore, T. *et al.* (eds) (1983) *A Dictionary of Marxist Thought*, Oxford, Basil Blackwell.

Braun, O. (1973) *Comercio Internacional e Imperialismo*, Buenos Aires, Siglo Veintiuno Argentina Editores.

Braun, O. (with R. Brown and P. Wright) (1984) *International Trade and Imperialism*, The Hague, Institute of Social Studies.

Breman, J. (1985) 'A dualistic labour system? A critique of the "informal sector" concept', in R. Bromley (ed.).

Brenner, R. (1977) 'The origins of capitalist development: a critique of neo–Smithian Marxism', *New Left Review*, no. 104.

Bresser Pereira, L. (1987) 'Inertial inflation and the Cruzado plan', *World Development*, 15 (8).

Brett, E. A. (1985) *The World Economy since the War. The Politics of Uneven Development*, London, Macmillan.

Brewer, A. (1980) *Marxist Theories of Imperialism. A Critical Survey*, London, Routledge & Kegan Paul.

Brewster, H. (1973) 'Economic dependence: a quantitative interpretation, *Social and Economic Studies*, 22 (1).

Bromley, R. (ed.) (1979) *The Urban Informal Sector: Critical Perspectives on Employment and Housing*, Oxford, Pergamon Press; originally published in a special issue of *World Development*, 6 (9–10), 1978.

Bromley, R. (ed.) (1985) *Planning for Small Enterprises in Third World Cities*, Oxford, Pergamon Press.

Bromley, R. and Gerry, C. (1979) 'Who are the casual poor?', in R. Bromley and C. Gerry (eds).

Bromley, R. and Gerry, C. (eds) (1979) *Casual Work and Poverty in the Third World*, Chichester, John Wiley.

Brookfield, H. (1975) *Interdependent Development*, London, Methuen.

Browett, J. (1985) 'The newly industrializing countries and radical theories of development', *World Development*, 13 (7).

Bruce, D. C. (1980) 'The impact of the United Nations Economic Commission for Latin America: technocrats as channels of influence', *Inter–American Economic Affairs*, 33 (4).

Bukharin, N. (1972) *Imperialism and the Accumulation of Capital*, London, Allen Lane.

Bukharin, N. (1973) *Imperialism and World Economy*, New York, Monthly Review Press.

Cáceres, L. R. and Jiménez, F. J. (1983) 'Estructuralismo, monetarismo e inflación en Latinoamérica', *El Trimestre Económico*, 50 (2); no. 198.

Camacho, D. (ed.) (1979) *Debates sobre la Teoría de la Dependencia y la Sociología Latinoamericana*, San José, Editorial Universitaria Centroamericana (EDUCA).

Cammack, P. (1985), 'The political economy of contemporary military regimes in Latin America: from bureaucratic authoritarianism to restructuring', in P. O'Brien and P. Cammack (eds) *Generals in Retreat: The Crisis of Military Rule in Latin America*, Manchester, University of Manchester Press.

Campanario, R. and Richter, E. (1974) 'Superpoblación capitalista en América Latina: un intento de marginalización del concepto de marginalidad', *Estudios Sociales Centroamericanos*, 3 (9).

Campos, R. de O. (1960) 'Inflación y crecimiento equilibrado', *El Trimestre Económico*, 27 (1), no. 105.

Campos, R. de O. (1961a) 'Inflation and balanced growth', in H. S. Ellis and H. C. Wallich (eds).

Campos, R. de O. (1961b) 'Two views on inflation in Latin America', in A. O. Hirschman (ed.).

Campos, R. de O. (1967) 'Economic development and inflation, with special reference to Latin America', in R. de Oliveira Campos, *Reflections on Latin American Development*, Austin, University of Texas Press.

Campos, R. de O. (1970) 'Monetarism and structuralism in Latin America', in G. M. Meier (ed.) *Leading Issues in Economic Development: Studies in International Poverty*, New York, Oxford University Press.

Caputo, O. and Pizarro, R. (1970) *Imperialismo, Dependencia y Relaciones Económicas Internacionales*, Santiago, Centro de Estudios Socio–Económicos, Universidad de Chile (Cuadernos de Estudios Socio–Económicos nos. 12–13, CESO).

Cardoso, C. F. S. (1975) 'On the colonial modes of production of the Americas', *Critique of Anthropology*, nos. 4–5.

Cardoso, C. F. S. and Brignoli, H. P. (1979) *Historia Económica de América Latina*, 2 vols, Barcelona, Editorial Crítica.

Cardoso, E. (1981) 'Food supply and inflation', *Journal of Development Economics*, 8 (3).

Cardoso, F. H. (1968) *Cuestiones de Sociología del Desarrollo en América Latina*, Santiago, Editorial Universitaria.

Cardoso, F. H. (1971) 'Comentario sobre los conceptos de sobrepoblación relativa y marginalidad', *Revista Latinoamericana de Ciencias Sociales*, nos. 1–2.

Cardoso, F. H. (1972a) 'Participación y marginalidad: notas para una discusión teórica', in F. H. Cardoso, *Estado y Sociedad en América Latina*, Buenos Aires, Ediciones Nueva Visión.

Cardoso, F. H. (1972b) 'Dependency and development in Latin America', *New Left Review*, no. 74.

Cardoso, F. H. (1972c) 'Notas sobre el estado actual de los estudios sobre dependencia', *Revista Latinoamericana de Ciencias Sociales*, no. 4.

Cardoso, F. H. (1972d) ¿"Teoría de la dependencia" o análisis concreto de situaciones de dependencia?', *Comercio Exterior*, 22 (4).

Cardoso, F. H. (1973a) 'Imperialism and dependency in Latin America', in F. Bonilla and R. Girling (eds) *Structures of Dependency*, Stanford, California, Institute of Political Studies.

Cardoso, F. H. (1973b) 'Associated–dependent development: theoretical and practical implications', in A. Stepan (ed.) *Authoritarian Brazil: Origins, Policies, and Future*, New Haven, Yale University Press.

Cardoso, F. H. (1975) *Autoritarismo e Democratizacão*, São Paulo, Editora Paz e Terra.

Cardoso, F. H. (1976) 'Foreword', in J. E. Perlman (1976).

Cardoso, F. H. (1977a) 'The consumption of dependency theory in the United States', *Latin American Research Review*, 12 (3).

Cardoso, F. H. (1977b) 'Current theses on Latin American development and dependency: a critique', *Boletín de Estudios Latinoamericanos y del Caribe*, no. 22.

Cardoso, F. H. (1977c) 'The originality of a copy: CEPAL and the idea of development', *CEPAL Review*, no. 4; also published in K. Q. Hill (ed.) (1979), Chapter 2.

Cardoso, F. H. (1980) 'El desarrollo en el banquilllo', *Comercio Exterior*, 30 (8).

Cardoso, F. H. (1982) 'Dependency and development in Latin America', in H. Alavi and T. Shanin (eds).

Cardoso, F. H. and Faletto, E. (1969) *Dependencia y Desarrollo en América Latina: Ensayo de Interpretación Sociológica*, Mexico, Siglo Veintiuno Editores.

Cardoso, F. H. and Faletto, E. (1979) *Dependency and Development in Latin America*, Berkeley and Los Angeles, University of California Press (translation, with new introduction and a post–scriptum, of Cardoso and Faletto, 1969).

Cardoso, F. H. and Weffort, F. (eds) (1970) *América Latina: Ensayos de Interpretación Sociológico–Política*, Santiago, Editorial Universitaria.

Castañeda, J. and Hett, E. (1978) *El Economismo Dependentista*, Mexico, Siglo Veintiuno Editores.

Castells, M. (1974) *La Cuestión Urbana*, Mexico, Siglo Veintiuno Editores.

Castells, M. (ed.) (1973) *Imperialismo y Urbanización en América Latina*, Barcelona, Editorial Gustavo Gili.

Castells, M. (ed.) (1974) *Estructura de Clases y Política Urbana en América Latina*, Buenos Aires, Ediciones SIAP.

Castro, M. A. (1976) (ed.) *La Polémica del Indigenismo*, Lima, Mosca Azul Editores.

Castro Pozo, H. (1924) *Nuestra Comunidad Indígena*, Lima, Ediciones El Lucero.

CEPAL (1952) *Problemas Teóricos y Prácticos del Crecimiento Económico*, Santiago, CEPAL; shortened version published under the name of R. Prebisch in Bianchi (ed.) (1969).

CEPAL (1969) *América Latina: El Pensamiento de la CEPAL*, Santiago, Editorial Universitaria; published in English, ECLA (1970a).

CEPAL (1975) *Integración Económica y Sustitución de Importaciones en América Latina* (Report written by J. Ayza, G. Fichet, and N. González), Mexico, Fondo de Cultura Económica.

Chase–Dunn, C. (1975) 'The effects of international economic dependence on development and inequality: a cross–national study', *American Sociological Review*, 40 (6).

Chavarría, J. (1979) *José Carlos Mariátegui and the Rise of Modern Peru 1890–1930*, Albuquerque, University of New Mexico Press.

Chenery, H. B. (1965) 'Comparative advantage and development policy', in The American Economic Association and The Royal Economic Society, *Surveys of Economic Theory: Growth and Development*, London, Macmillan, and New York, St Martin's Press.

Chenery, H. B. (1975) 'The structuralist approach to development policy', *American Economic Review*, 65 (2).

Chichilnisky, G. (1981) 'Terms of trade and domestic distribution. Export–led growth with abundant labour', *Journal of Development Economics*, 8 (2).

Chilcote, R. H. (1974) 'A critical synthesis of the dependency literature', *Latin American Perspectives*, 1 (1), issue 1.

Chilcote, R. H. (1981) 'Issues of theory in dependency and marxism', *Latin American Perspectives*, 8 (3–4), issues 30–31.

Chilcote, R. H. (1984) *Theories of Development and Underdevelopment*, Boulder, Westview Press.

Chilcote, R. H. (ed.) (1982) *Dependency and Marxism: Towards a Resolution of the Debate*, Boulder (Colorado), Westview Press.

Chilcote, R. H. and Edelstein, J. C. (1986) *Latin America: Capitalist and Socialist Perspectives of Development and Underdevelopment*, Boulder (Colorado), Westview Press.

Chilcote, R. H. and Edelstein, J. C. (eds) (1974) *Latin America: The Struggle with Dependency and Beyond*, Cambridge (Massachusetts), Shenkman Publishing.

Chilcote, R. H. and Johnson, D. L. (eds) (1983) *Theories of Development: Mode of Production or Dependency?*, Beverly Hills, Sage Publications.

Clairmonte, F. C. (1986) 'Prebisch and UNCTAD: the banality of compromise', *Journal of Contemporary Asia*, 16 (4).

Cline, W. R. (1982) 'Can the East Asian model of development be generalised?', *World Development*, 6 (3).

Cockcroft, J. D. (1983) 'Immiseration, not marginalization: the case of Mexico', *Latin American Perspectives*, 10 (2–3), issues 37–8.

Cockcroft, J. D., Frank, A.G. and Johnson, D. L. (1972) *Dependence and Underdevelopment: Latin America's Political Economy*, New York, Doubleday.

Collier, D. (ed.) (1979) *The New Authoritarianism in Latin America*, Princeton, Princeton University Press.

Colman, D. and Nixson, F. (1986) *Economics of Change in the Less Developed Countries*, Oxford, Philip Allan.

Corbo, V. (1974) *Inflation in Developing Countries: An Econometric Study of Chilean Inflation*, New York, North–Holland.

Córdova, A. (1973) 'Empleo, desempleo, marginalidad', in S. Bagú *et al.*, *Problemas del Subdesarrollo Latinoamericano*, Mexico, Editorial Nuestro Tiempo.

Cornelius, W. A. and Kemper, R. V. (eds) (1978) *Metropolitan Latin America: The Challenge and the Response*, Beverly Hills, Sage Publications.

Cornelius, W. A. and Trueblood, F. M. (eds) (1974) *Anthropological Perspectives on Latin American Urbanization*, Beverly Hills, Sage Publications.

Cornelius, W. A. and Trueblood, F. M. (eds) (1975) *Urbanization and Inequality: The Political Economy of Urban and Rural Development in Latin America*, Beverly Hills, Sage Publications.

Cotler, J. (1967–8) 'The mechanics of internal domination and social change in Peru', *Studies in Comparative International Development*, 3 (12); reprinted in I. L. Horowitz (ed.).

Cotler, J. (1968) 'La mecánica de la dominación interna y del cambio social en el Perú', *América Latina*, 11 (1).

Cueva, A. (1974) 'Problemas y perpectivas de la teoría de la dependencia', *Historia y Sociedad*, no. 3; a shortened version published in English as 'A summary of "Problems and perspectives of dependency theory"', *Latin American Perspectives*, 3 (4), issue 11, 1976.

Cueva, A. (1977) *El Desarrollo del Capitalismo en América Latina: Ensayo de Interpretación Histórica*, Mexico, Siglo Veintiuno Editores.

Cueva, A. (1979) 'Problemas y perpectivas de la teoría de la dependencia', in D. Camacho (ed.).

Cumper, G. (1974) 'Dependence, development and the sociology of economic thought', *Social and Economic Studies*, 23 (3).

Davies, R. (1979) 'Informal sector or subordinate mode of production? A model', in R. Bromley and C. Gerry (eds).

Davies, T. M. (1974) *Indian Integration in Peru: A Half Century of Experience, 1900–1948*, Lincoln, University of Nebraska Press.

de Janvry, A. (1982) *The Agrarian Question and Reformism in Latin America*, Baltimore, The Johns Hopkins University Press.

de Janvry, A. and Garramón, C. (1977) ' The dynamics of rural poverty in Latin America', *The Journal of Peasant Studies*, 5 (3).

Deere, C. D. and de Janvry, A. (1979) 'A conceptual framework for the empirical analysis of peasants', *American Journal of Agricultural Economics*, 61 (4).

Degregori, C. I. *et al.* (n.d.) *Indigenismo, Clases Sociales y Problema Nacional*, Lima, Ediciones CELATS.

Degregori, C. I. (ed.) (1978) *Campesinado e Indigenismo en América Latina*, Lima, Ediciones CELATS (Centro Latinoamericano de Trabajo Social).

Delacroix, J and Ragin, C. (1981) 'Structural blockage: a cross–national study of economic dependency, state efficacy, and underdevelopment', *American Journal of Sociology*, 86 (6).

Delgado, C. (1971) *Problemas Sociales en el Perú Contemporáneo*, Lima, Instituto de Estudios Peruanos.

Delgado, C. (1973) *Testimonio de Lucha*, Lima, Ediciones PEISA.

Delgado, C. (1975) *Revolución Peruana: Autonomía y Deslindes*, Lima, Librería Studium.

DESAL (1968) *Tenencia de la Tierra y Campesinado en Chile*, Buenos Aires, Ediciones Troquel.

DESAL (1969) *Marginalidad en América Latina: Un Ensayo de Diagnóstico*, Barcelona, Editorial Herder.

DESAL (1970) *Marginalidad, Promoción Popular e Integración Latinoamericana*, Buenos Aires, Ediciones Troquel.

Díaz–Alejandro, C. F. (1970) *Essays on the Economic History of the Argentine Republic*, New Haven, Yale University Press.

di Marco, L. E. (ed.) (1972) *International Economics and Development: Essays in Honour of Raúl Prebisch*, New York, Academic Press.

Dieterich, H. (1978) *Relaciones de Producción en América Latina*, Mexico, Ediciones de Cultura Popular.

Dietz, J. L. and Street, J. H. (1987) 'Institutionalist and structuralist perspectives on Latin American economic development', in J. L. Dietz and J. H. Street (eds).

Dietz, J. L. and Street, J. H. (eds) (1987) *Latin America's Economic Development: Institutionalist and Structuralist Perspectives*, Boulder (Colorado), Lynne Rienner Publishers.

Dobb, M. (1980) 'Prólogo', in C. Kay *El Sistema Señorial Europeo y La Hacienda Latinoamericana: Estudios sobre el Desarrollo del Capitalismo en la Agricultura*, Mexico, Ediciones Era.

Dore, E. (1983), 'Dependency theory', in T. Bottomore *et al.* (eds).

Dos Santos, T. (1969) *Socialismo o Fascismo: Dilema Latinoamericano*, Santiago, Prensa Latinoamericana (PLA).

Dos Santos, T. (1970) *Dependencia y Cambio Social*, Santiago, Centro de

Estudios Socio–Económicos (CESO), Universidad de Chile.

Dos Santos, T. (1971) 'The structure of dependence', in K. T. Fann and D. C. Hodges (eds) *Readings in U.S. Imperialism*, Boston, Porter Sargent; also published in *American Economic Review*, 60 (2), 1970; in C. K. Wilber (ed.) (1973); in I. Livingstone (ed.) (1981); and in M. P. Todaro (ed.) *The Struggle for Economic Development: Readings in Problema and Policies*, New York, Longman, 1983.

Dos Santos, T. (1972) 'El nuevo carácter de la dependencia', in J. Matos Mar (ed.) *La Crisis del Desarrollismo y la Nueva Dependencia*, Buenos Aires, Amorrortu Editores; originally published as *El Nuevo Carácter de la Dependencia*, Santiago, CESO, 1968.

Dos Santos, T. (1973) 'The crisis of development theory and the problem of dependence in Latin America', in H. Bernstein (ed.) *Underdevelopment and Development: The Third World Today*, Harmondsworth, Penguin Books.

Dos Santos, T. (1978) *Imperialismo y Dependencia*, Mexico, Ediciones Era.

ECLA (1951) *Economic Survey of Latin America 1949*, New York, United Nations Department of Economic Affairs; originally published in Spanish, CEPAL, *Estudio Económico de América Latina 1949*, mimeographed, Santiago, Naciones Unidas, Comisión Económica Para América Latina (CEPAL), 1950. The first part of this survey was reprinted in CEPAL, *Interpretación del Proceso de Desarrollo Latinoamericano en 1949*, Santiago, NU (Naciones Unidas) CEPAL, 1973.

ECLA (1955) 'Inflation and anti–inflationary policy', in ECLA *Economic Survey of Latin America 1954*, New York, UN Department of Economic and Social Affairs, United Nations.

ECLA (1962) 'Inflation and growth: a summary of experience in Latin America', *Economic Bulletin for Latin America* (United Nations), 7 (1).

ECLA (1963a) *Social Development of Latin America in the Post–War Period*, New York, United Nations.

ECLA (1963b) *Urbanization in Latin America*, Santiago, United Nations Economic Commission for Latin America (UN ECLA).

ECLA (1966) *The Process of Industrial Development in Latin America*, New York, United Nations.

ECLA (1970a) *Development Problems in Latin America: An Analysis by the UN ECLA*, Austin, University of Texas Press.

ECLA (1970b) *Social Change and Social Development Policy in Latin America*, New York, United Nations.

Edel, M. (1969) *Food Supply and Inflation in Latin America*, New York, Praeger.

Edelstein, J. (1981) 'Dependency: a special theory within marxist analysis', *Latin American Perspectives*, 8 (3–4), issues 30-31.

Edwards, C. (1985) *The Fragmented World; Competing Perspectives on Trade, Money and Crisis*, London, Methuen.

Edwards, S. and Cox Edwards, A. (1987) *Monetarism and Liberalization: The Chilean Experiment*, Cambridge (Massachusetts), Bollinger Publisher Company.

Ellis, H. S. and Wallich, H. C. (eds) (1961) *Economic Development for Latin America: Proceedings of a Conference Held by the International Economic*

Association, London, Macmillan and New York, St Martin's Press.

Ellsworth, P. T. (1961) 'The terms of trade between primary–producing and industrial countries', *Inter–American Economic Affairs*, 10 (1); reprinted in I. Livingstone (ed.) (1981).

Emmanuel, A. (1972) *Unequal Exchange: A Study of the Imperialism of Trade*, London, New Left Books.

Emmanuel, A. (1982) *Appropriate or Underdeveloped Technology?*, Chichester, John Wiley.

Emmanuel, A., Bettelheim, C., Amin, S., and Palloix, C. (1971) *Imperialismo y Comercio Internacional. El Intercambio Desigual*, Córdoba, Ediciones de Pasado y Presente.

Epstein, E. C. (1987) 'Recent stabilization programs in Argentina, 1973–86', *World Development*, 15 (8).

Esteva, G. (1983) 'Los "tradifas" o el fin de la marginación', *El Trimestre Económico*, 50 (2), no. 198.

Evans, H. D. (1981a) 'Unequal exchange and economic policies: some implications of the neo–Ricardian critique of the theory of comparative advantage', in I. Livingstone (ed.); originally published in *IDS Bulletin*, 6 (4), 1975.

Evans, H. D. (1981b) 'Trade, production and self–reliance', in D. Seers (ed.), Chapter 5.

Evans, H. D. (1981c) 'Monopoly power and imperialism: Oscar Braun's theory of unequal exchange', *Development and Change*, 12 (4).

Evans, H. D. (1987) 'The long–run determinants of North–South terms of trade and some recent empirical evidence', *World Development*, 15 (5).

Evans, P. (1979) *Dependent Development: The Alliance of Multinational, State and Local Capital in Brazil*, Princeton, Princeton University Press.

Evans, P. (1987) 'Class, state, and dependence in East Asia: lessons for Latin Americanists, in F. Deyo (ed.) *The Political Economy of the New Asian Industrialism*, Ithaca (New York), Cornell University Press.

Evers, T. E. and von Wogau, P. (1973) 'Dependencia: Lateinamerikanische Beiträge zur Theorie der Unterentwicklung', *Das Argument*, 15 (4–6), no. 79.

Fagen, R. R., Deere, C. D. and Coraggio, J. L. (eds) (1986) *Transition and Development: Problems of Third World Socialism*, New York, Monthly Review Press.

Faria, V. E. (1976) *Occupational Marginality, Employment and Poverty in Urban Brazil*, Ann Arbor (Michigan), University Microfilms (PhD dissertation, Harvard University).

Faria, V. E. (1978) 'Desarrollo económico y marginalidad urbana: los cambios de perspectiva de la CEPAL', *Revista Mexicana de Sociología*, 40 (1).

Felix, D. (1960) 'Structural imbalances, social conflict and inflation: an appraisal of Chile's recent anti–inflationary effort', *Economic Development and Cultural Change*, 8 (2).

Felix, D. (1961) 'An alternative view of the "monetarist"–"structuralist" controversy', in A. O. Hirschman (ed.).

Felix, D. (1964) 'Monetarists, structuralists, and import–substituting industrialization: a critical appraisal', in W. Baer and I. Kerstenetzky (eds).

Felix, D. (1981) 'Latin American monetarism in crisis', *IDS Bulletin*, 13 (1).

Fernández, R. A. and Ocampo, J. F. (1974) 'The Latin American revolution: a theory of imperialism, not dependence', *Latin American Perspectives*, 1 (1), issue 1.

Ferrer, A. (1975) 'América Latina y los países capitalistas desarrollados: una perspectiva del modelo centro–periferia', *El Trimestre Económico*, 42 (4), no. 168.

Ferrer, A. (1979a) 'Latin America and the world economy', *Journal of Interamerican Studies and World Affairs*, vol. 21.

Ferrer, A. (1979b) 'Notas para una teoría de la independencia', *Comercio Exterior*, 29 (8).

Ffrench–Davis, R. (1973) *Políticas Económicas en Chile 1952–1970*, Santiago, Ediciones Nueva Universidad y CIEPLAN.

Ffrench-Davis, R. (1988) 'An outline of a neo-structuralist approach', *CEPAL Review*, no. 34.

Fishlow, A. (1985) 'The state of Latin American economics', in Inter-American Development Bank (IDB), *Economic and Social Progress in Latin America*, Washington DC, IDB, Chapter 5.

FitzGerald, E. V. K. (1979) *The Political Economy of Peru 1956-78: Economic Development and the Restructuring of Capital*, Cambridge, Cambridge University Press.

FitzGerald, E. V. K. (1981) 'The new international division of labour and the relative autonomy of the state: notes for a reappraisal of classical dependency', paper presented at the Millenium Conference on Political Development in a Changing World Economy.

FitzGerald, E. V. K. and Wuyts, R. (eds) (1988) *The Market Within Planning: Socialist Economic Management in the Third World*, London, Frank Cass.

Flanders, M. J. (1972) 'Prebisch on protectionism: an evaluation', in W. L. Johnson and D. R. Kamerschen (eds) *Readings in Economic Development*, Ohio, South Western Publishing; originally published in *Economic Journal*, 74 (294), 1964. Also published in J. D. Theberge (ed.) and in I. Livingstone (ed.) (1981).

Flechsig, S. (1987) 'Raúl Prebisch – ein bedeutender Ökonom Lateinamerikas und der Entwicklungsländer', *Wirtschaftswissenschaft*, 35 (5).

Flynn, P. (1986) 'Brazil: the politics of the Cruzado plan', *Third World Quarterly*, 8 (4).

Fortín, C. (1984) 'The failure of repressive monetarism: Chile, 1973– 83', *Third World Quarterly*, 6 (2).

Foster–Carter, A. (1974) 'Neo–marxist approaches to development and underdevelopment', in E. de Kadt and G. Williams (eds) *Sociology and Development*, London, Tavistock Publications.

Foster–Carter, A. (1976) 'From Rostow to Gunder Frank: conflicting paradigms in the analysis of underdevelopment', *World Development*, 4 (3).

Foster–Carter, A. (1978) 'The modes of production controversy', *New Left Review*, no. 107.

Foster–Carter, A. (1979–80) 'Marxism versus dependency theory? A polemic', *Journal of International Studies*, 8 (3).

Foster–Carter, A. (1984) 'Theory in development: current trends', *Third Book Review*, 1 (1).

Foweraker, J. (1981) *The Struggle for Land: A Political Economy of the Pioneer Frontier in Brazil from 1930 to the Present Day*, Cambridge, Cambridge University Press.

Foxley, A. (1983) *Latin American Experiments in Neoconservative Economics*, Berkeley, University of California Press.

Franco, R. (1974) 'Sobre los supuestos económicos y sociales de la marginalidad y de la acción política de los grupos marginales en América Latina', *Desarrollo Económico*, 13 (55).

Frank, A. G. (1966a) 'The development of underdevelopment', *Monthly Review*, 18 (4); reprinted in C. K. Wilber (ed.) (1973); and in P. F. Klarén and T. J. Bossert, (eds) (1986).

Frank, A. G. (1966b) 'Urban poverty in Latin America', *Studies in Comparative International Development*, 2 (5).

Frank, A. G. (1967) *Capitalism and Underdevelopment in Latin America: Historical Studies of Chile and Brazil*, New York, Monthly Review Press.

Frank, A. G. (1969) *Latin America: Underdevelopment or Revolution: Essays on the Development of Underdevelopment and the Immediate Enemy*, New York, Monthly Review Press.

Frank, A. G. (1970) *Lumpenburguesía: Lumpendesarrollo, Dependencia, Clase y Política en Latinoamérica*, Santiago, Editorial Prensa Latinoamericana (PLA); published in English as *Lumpenbourgeoisie: Lumpendevelopment, Dependence, Class and Politics*, New York, Monthly Review Press, 1972.

Frank, A. G. (1972a) 'Sociology of development and underdevelopment of sociology', in J. D. Cockcroft, A. G. Frank, and D. L. Johnson; originally published in *Catalyst* (University of Buffalo), no. 3, 1967.

Frank, A. G. (1972b) 'Economic dependence, class structure, and underdevelopment policy', in J. D. Cockcroft, A. G. Frank, and D. L. Johnson.

Frank, A. G. (1974) 'Dependence is dead, long live dependence and the class struggle: an answer to critics', *Latin American Perspectives*, 1 (1), issue 1.

Frank, A. G. (1975) *On Capitalist Underdevelopment*, Bombay, Oxford University Press.

Frank, A. G. (1977) 'Dependence is dead, long live dependence and the class struggle: an answer to critics', *World Development*, 5 (4).

Frank, A. G. (1978a) *Dependent Accumulation and Underdevelopment*, London, Macmillan.

Frank, A. G. (1978b) *World Accumulation 1492–1789*, London, Macmillan.

Frank, A. G. (1980) *Crisis in the World Economy*, London, Heinemann.

Frank, A. G. (1981a) *Crisis in the Third World*, London, Heinemann.

Frank, A. G. (1981b) *Reflections on the World Economic Crisis*, London, Hutchinson.

Frank, A. G. (1984) *Critique and Anti-Critique: Essays on Dependence and Reformism*, London, Macmillan.

Frank, A. G. (n.d.) *Rostow's Stages of Economic Growth Through Escalation to Nuclear Destruction*, mimeographed, Ann Arbor, (Michigan), Radical Education Project.

Frank, A. G., Puiggrós, R., and Laclau, E. (1973) *América Latina: Feudalismo o Capitalismo?*, Medellín, Editorial La Oveja Negra.

Freire, P. (1970) *Pedagogy of the Oppressed*, New York, Herder.

Freire, P. (1972) *Cultural Action for Freedom*, Harmondsworth, Penguin.

Freire, P. (1985) *The Politics of Education: Culture, Power, and Liberation*, South Hadley (Massachusetts), Bergin and Gawey.

Frieden, J. (1985) 'On borrowed time', *NACLA Report on the Americas*, 19 (2).

Friedmann, J. (1973) *Urbanization, Planning, and National Dvelopment*, Beverly Hills, Sage Publications.

Fröbel, F., Heinrichs, J., and Kreye, O. (1980) *The New International Division of Labour*, Cambridge, Cambridge University Press.

Furtado, C. (1964) *Development and Underdevelopment: A Structural View of the Problems of Developed and Underdeveloped Countries*, Berkeley, University of California Press.

Furtado, C. (1965) 'Development and stagnation in Latin America: a structural approach', *Studies in Comparative International Development*, 1 (11).

Furtado, C. (1968) 'La concentración del poder económico en los EEUU y sus proyecciones en América Latina', *Estudios Internacionales*, 1 (3–4).

Furtado, C. (1970) *Economic Development of Latin America: A Survey from Colonial Times to the Cuban Revolution*, Cambridge, Cambridge University Press.

Furtado, C. (1971) 'Dependencia externa y teoría económica', *El Trimestre Económico*, 38 (2), no. 150.

Furtado, C. (1972) 'Externe Abhängigkeit und ökonomische Theorie', in D. Senghaas (ed.) *Imperialismus und Strukturelle Gewalt: Analysen über Ahängige Reproduktion*, Frankfurt am Main, Suhrkamp Verlag.

Furtado, C. (1973) 'The concept of external dependence in the study of underdevelopment', in C. K. Wilber (ed.) (1973).

Furtado, C. (1974a) *Teoría y Política del Desarrollo Económico*, Mexico, Siglo Veintiuno Editores.

Furtado, C. (1974b) 'Underdevelopment and dependence: the fundamental connection', *Working Paper, Centre of Latin American Studies, University of Cambridge*.

Furtado, C. (1980) 'Development: theoretical and conceptual considerations', in J. Pajestka and C. H. Feinstein (eds).

Furtado, C. (1985) *A Fantasia Organizada*, Rio de Janeiro, Paz e Terra.

Galeano, E. (1971) *Las Venas Abiertas de América Latina*, La Habana, Casa de las Américas.

Galeano, E. (1973) *Open Veins of Latin America: Five Centuries of the Pillage of a Continent*, New York, Monthly Review Press.

Galtung, J. (1980) 'Self–reliance: concepts, practice and rationale', in J. Galtung *et al.* (eds).

Galtung, J., *et al.* (eds) (1980) *Self–Reliance: A Strategy for Development*, London, Bogle–L'Ouverture Publications.

Garavaglia, J. C. (ed.) (1973) *Modos de Producción en América Latina*, Córdoba, Ediciones de Pasado y Presente.

García, A. (1972) *Atraso y Dependencia en América Latina; Hacia una Teoría Latinoamericana de Desarrollo*, Buenos Aires, El Ateneo.

Germaná, C. (1977) 'La polémica Haya de la Torre – Mariátegui: reforma o revolución?', *Análisis*, nos. 2–3.

Germani, G. (1966) *Política y Sociedad en una Época de Transición: De la Sociedad Tradicional a la Sociedad de Masas*, Buenos Aires, Editorial Paidos.

Germani, G. (1967) 'The city as an integrating mechanism: the concept of social integration', in G. H. Beyer (ed.) *The Urban Explosion in Latin America: A Continent in Process of Modernization*, Ithaca (New York), Cornell University Press.

Germani, G. (1969-70) 'Stages in modernization in Latin America', *Studies in Comparative International Development*, 5 (8).

Germani, G. (1972) 'Aspectos teóricos de la marginalidad', *Revista Paraguaya de Sociología*, 9 (30).

Germani, G. (1980) *Marginality*, New Brunswick, Transaction Books.

Germani, G. (1981) *The Sociology of Modernization: Studies on its Historical Aspects with Special Regard to the Latin American Case*, New Brunswick, Transaction Books.

Germani, G. (ed.) (1973) *Modernization, Urbanization, and the Urban Crisis*, Boston, Little, Brown and Co.

Ghai, D., Kay, C., and Peek, P. (1988) *Labour and Development in Rural Cuba*, London, Macmillan.

Gilbert, A. and Gugler, J. (1982) *Cities, Poverty, and Development. Urbanization in the Third World.*, Oxford, Oxford University Press.

Girvan, N. (1971) *Foreign Capital and Economic Underdevlopment in Jamaica*, Kingston, Institute of Social and Economic Research, University of the West Indies.

Girvan, N. (1973) 'The development of dependency economics in the Caribbean and Latin America: review and comparison', *Social and Economic Studies*, 22 (1).

Girvan, N. and Jefferson, O. (eds) (1971) *Readings in the Political Economy of the Caribbean*, Kingston, New World.

Godfrey, M. (1977) 'Surplus population and underdevelopment: reserve army or marginal mass?', *Manpower and Unemployment Research*, 10 (1).

Godfrey, M. (1980) 'Editorial: is dependency dead?', *IDS Bulletin*, 12 (1).

Goldrich, D., Pratt, R. B., and Schuller, C. R. (1967–8) 'The political integration of lower–class urban settlements in Chile and Peru', *Studies in Comparative International Development*, 3 (1).

González, G. (1974) 'A critique of the internal colony model', *Latin American Perspectives*, 1 (1), issue 1.

González Casanova, P. (1965) 'Internal colonialism and national development', *Studies in Comparative International Development*, 1 (4); reprinted in I. L. Horowitz, J. de Castro and J. Gerassi (eds) *Latin American Radicalism*, New York, Random House, 1969.

González Casanova, P. (1968) 'Mexico: the dynamics of an agrarian and "semicapitalist" revolution', in J. Petras and M. Zeitlin (eds).

González Casanova, P. (1969) *Sociología de la Explotación*, Mexico, Siglo Veintiuno Editores.

González Casanova, P. (1970) *Democracy in Mexico*, New York, Oxford University Press.

González Casanova, P. (1979) 'Las minorías étnicas en América Latina: del subdesarrollo colonial al socialismo', *Desarrollo Indoamericano*, 14 (47).

Graciarena, J. and Franco, R. (1978) 'Social formations and power structures in Latin America', *Current Sociology*, 26 (1).

Griffin, K. (1969) 'Underdevelopment in theory and history', in K. Griffin, *Underdevelopment in Spanish America: An Interpretation*, London, George Allen and Unwin, Chapter 1; reprinted in C. K. Wilber (ed.) (1973), Chapters 2 and 6.

Griffin, K. and Gurley, J. (1985) 'Radical analyses of imperialism, the Third World, and the transition to socialism: a survey article', *Journal of Economic Literature*, 23 (3).

Griffith–Jones, S. and Sunkel, O. (1986) *Debt and Development Crisis in Latin America: The End of an Illusion*, Oxford, Clarendon Press.

Grilli, E. R. and Yang, M. C. (1988) 'Primary commodities prices, manufactured goods prices, and the terms of trade of developing countries: what the long run shows', *The World Bank Economic Review*, 2 (1).

Ground, R. L. (1984) 'Orthodox adjustment programmes in Latin America: a critical look at the policies of the IMF', *CEPAL Review*, no. 23.

Grünwald, J. (1961) 'The "structuralist" school on price stability and development: the Chilean case', in A. O. Hirschman (ed.).

Gurrieri, A. (1981) 'El progreso técnico y sus frutos. La idea de desarrollo en la obra de Raúl Prebisch', *Comercio Exterior*, 3 (12).

Gurrieri, A. (1982a) 'La economía política de Raúl Prebisch', in A. Gurrieri (ed.) (1982).

Gurrieri, A. (1982b) 'La dimensión sociológica en la obra de Prebisch', *Pensamiento Iberoamericano. Revista de Economía Política*, no. 2.

Gurrieri, A. (ed.) (1982) *La Obra de Prebisch en la CEPAL*, Mexico, Fondo de Cultura Económica.

Gutiérrez, G. (1973) *A Theology of Liberation: History, Politics, and Salvation*, New York, Orbis.

Guzmán, G. (1976) *El Desarrollo Latinoamericano y la CEPAL*, Barcelona, Editorial Planeta.

Gwynne, R. N. (1986) 'The deindustrialization of Chile, 1974–1984', *Bulletin of Latin American Research*, 5 (1).

Haberler, G. (1961) 'Terms of trade and economic development', in H. S. Ellis and H. C. Wallich (eds), Chapter 10; reprinted in J. D. Theberge (ed.) (1968).

Hagen, E. (1962) *On the Theory of Social Change*, Homewood, Dorsey Press.

Halperin Donghi, T. (1982) '"Dependency theory" and Latin American historiography', *Latin American Research Review*, 17 (1).

Harberger, A. (1963) 'The dynamics of inflation in Chile', in C. Christ *et al.*, *Measurement in Economics*, Stanford, Stanford University Press.

Hardoy, J. E. (ed.) (1975) *Urbanization in Latin America: Approaches and Issues*, Garden City (New York), Anchor Books.

Harris, N. (1987) *The End of the Third World: Newly Industrializing Countries and the Decline of an Ideology*, Harmondsworth, Penguin Books.

Harris, R. L. (1987) 'The revolutionary transformation of Nicaragua', *Latin American Perspectives*, 14 (1), issue 52.

Harris, R. L. (1988) 'Marxism and the transition to socialism in Latin

America', *Latin American Perspectives*, 15 (1), issue 56.

Harrison, D. (1988) *The Sociology of Modernization and Development*, London, Unwin Hyman.

Hart, K. (1973) 'Informal income opportunities and urban employment in Ghana', *Journal of Modern African Studies*, 11 (1).

Hauser, P. (ed.) (1962) *L'Urbanisation en Amérique Latine*, Paris, UNESCO; also published in English and Spanish by UNESCO.

Havens, A. E. and Flinn, W. L. (1970) 'Introduction', in A. E. Havens and W. L. Flinn (eds) *Internal Colonialism and Structural Change in Colombia*, New York, Praeger.

Haya de la Torre, V. R. (1972) *El Antimperialismo y el Apra*, Lima.

Hechter, M. (1975) *Internal Colonialism: The Celtic Fringe in British National Development, 1536–1966*, London, Routledge & Kegan Paul.

Helm, D. (1986) 'The economic borders of the state', *Oxford Review of Economic Policy*, 2 (2).

Henfrey, C. (1981) 'Dependency, modes of production, and the class analysis of Latin America', *Latin American Perspectives*, 8 (3–4), issues 30–31.

Hettne, B. (1983) 'The development of development theory', *Acta Sociologica*, 26 (3–4).

Hettne, B. (1987) 'Crises in development theory and in the world', paper presented at the Fifth General Conference of EADI (European Association of Development Institutes), Amsterdam.

Heymann, D. (1986) 'Inflation and stabilization policies', *CEPAL Review*, no. 28.

Hilferding, R. (1981) *Finance Capital: A Study of the Latest Phase of Capitalist Development*, London, Routledge & Kegan Paul.

Hill, K. Q. (ed.) (1979) *Toward a New Strategy for Development: A Rothko Chapel Colloquium*, New York and Oxford, Pergamon Press.

Hilton, R., *et al.* (1976) *The Transition from Feudalism to Capitalism*, London, New Left Review Editions.

Hirsch, F. (1978) 'The ideological underlay of inflation', in F. Hirsch and J. H. Goldthorpe (eds) *The Political Economy of Inflation*, London, Robertson.

Hirschman, A. O. (1961) 'Ideologies of economic development in Latin America', in A. O. Hirschman (ed.).

Hirschman, A. O. (1963) 'Inflation in Chile', in A. O. Hirschman, *Journeys Toward Progress*, New York, Twentieth Century Fund.

Hirschman, A. O. (1971) *A Bias for Hope: Essays on Development and Latin America*, New Haven (Connecticut), Yale University Press.

Hirschman, A. O. (1981a) 'The rise and decline of development economics', in A. O. Hirschman (1981d).

Hirschman, A. O. (1981b) 'On Hegel, imperialism, and structural stagnation', in A. O. Hirschman (1981d).

Hirschman, A. O. (1981c) 'The social and political matrix of inflation: elaborations on the Latin American experience', in A. O. Hirschman (1981d).

Hirschman, A. O. (1981d) *Essays in Trespassing: Economics to Politics and Beyond*, Cambridge, Cambridge University Press.

Hirschman, A. O. (1987) 'The political economy of Latin American development: seven exercises in retrospection', *Latin American Research Review*, 22 (3).

Hirschman, A. O. (ed.) (1961) *Latin American Issues: Essays and Comments*, New York, Twentieth Century Fund.

Hobson, J. A. (1961) *Imperialism: A Study*, London, George Allen & Unwin.

Hodara, J. (1987a) 'Orígenes de la CEPAL', *Comercio Exterior*, 37 (5).

Hodara, J. (1987b) *Prebisch y la CEPAL: Sustancia, Trayectoria y Contexto Institucional*, Mexico, El Colegio de México.

Hoffman, R., *et al.* (1969) 'La marginalidad urbana', in DESAL (1969).

Hoogvelt, A. M. M. (1976) *The Sociology of Developing Societies*, London, Macmillan.

Hoogvelt, A. M. M. (1982) *The Third World in Global Development*, London, Macmillan.

Hopenhayn, B. (1982) 'Algunas notas sobre el "Capitalismo Periférico" de Raúl Prebisch', *Desarrollo Económico*, 22 (86).

Horowitz, I. L. (ed.) (1970) *Masses in Latin America*, New York, Oxford University Press.

Hoselitz, B. F. (1960) *Sociological Aspects of Economic Growth*, Chicago, Free Press.

Howe, G. N. (1981) 'Dependency theory, imperialism, and the production of surplus value on a world scale', *Latin American Perspectives*, 8 (3– 4), issues 30–31.

Hurtienne, T. (1974) 'Zur Ideologiekritik der lateinamerikanischen Theorien der Unterentwicklung und Abhängigkeit', *Probleme des Klassenkampfs*, 4 (3), nos. 14–15.

Ianni, O. (1970) *Imperialismo y Cultura de la Violencia en América Latina*, Mexico, Siglo Veintiuno Editores.

Iglesias, E. (1987) 'Managing the world economy or reshaping world society?', keynote speech delivered at the Fifth General Conference of EADI (European Association of Development Institutes), Amsterdam.

Instituto Nacional Indigenista (1962) *Los Centros Coordinadores Indigenistas*, Mexico, INI.

Inter–American Development Bank (1985) *Economic and Social Progress in Latin America. External Debt: Crisis and Adjustment, 1985 Report*, Washington, DC, Inter–American Development Bank.

International Labour Office (1972) *Employment, Incomes and Equality: A Strategy for Increasing Productive Employment in Kenya*, Geneva, ILO.

Jackson, S., Russett, B., Snidal, D., and Sylvan, D. (1979) 'An assessment of empirical research on *dependencia*', *Latin American Research Review*, 14 (3).

Jaguaribe, H. (1969) 'Dependencia y autonomía', in H. Jaguaribe, A. Ferrer, M. S. Wionczek and T. dos Santos *La Dependencia Político–Económica de América Latina*, Mexico, Siglo Veintiuno Editores.

Jameson, K. P. (1986) 'Latin American structuralism: a methodological perspective', *World Development*, 14 (2).

Jefferson, O. (1972) *The Post–War Economic Development of Jamaica*, Kingston, Institute of Social and Economic Research, University of the West Indies.

Johnson, C. (1979) 'Critical comments on marginality: relative surplus population and capital/labour relations', *Labour: Capital and Society*, 12 (2).

Johnson, C. (1981) 'Dependency theory and processes of capitalism and socialism', *Latin American Perspectives*, 8 (3–4), issues 30–31.

Johnson, C. (1983) 'Ideologies in theories of imperialism and dependency', in R. H. Chilcote and D. L. Johnson (eds) (1983).

Johnson, D. L. (1972) 'On oppressed classes', in J. D. Cockcroft, A. G. Frank, and D. L. Johnson.

Johnson, D. L. (1973) *The Sociology of Change and Reaction in Latin America*, New York, Bobbs–Merrill.

Johnson, D. L. (1981) 'Economism and determinism in dependency theory', *Latin American Perspectives*, 8 (3–4), issues 30–31.

Johnson, D. L. (1983) 'Class analysis and dependency', in R. H. Chilcote and D. L. Johnson (eds).

Johnson, H. G. (1967) 'Analysis of Prebisch's views on the terms of trade', in H. G. Johnson *Economic Policies Towards Less Developed Countries*, London, Allen and Unwin.

Kahil, R. (1973) *Inflation and Economic Development in Brazil, 1946–1963*, Oxford, Clarendon Press.

Kahl, J. A. (1976) *Modernization, Exploitation and Dependency in Latin America: Germani, González Casanova and Cardoso*, New Brunswick, Transaction Books.

Kaldor, N. (1964) 'Economic problems of Chile', in N. Kaldor *Essays in Economic Policy*, vol. 2, London, Duckworth.

Kaldor, N. (1983) 'El papel de las políticas fiscal y monetaria en la inflación latinoamericana', *Investigación Económica*, 42 (165).

Kalecki, M. (1976) 'The problem of financing economic development', in M. Kalecki *Essays on Developing Economies*, Hassocks, Harvester Press.

Kalmanovitz, S. (1975) 'Note critique: "théorie de la dépendance" au théorie de l'impérialisme', *Sociologie du Travail*, 75 (1).

Kalmanovitz, S. (1982) 'Cuestiones de método en la teoría del desarrollo', *Comercio Exterior*, 32 (5).

Kaufman, R. R., Chernotsky, H. I., and Geller, D. S. (1975) 'A preliminary test of the theory of dependency', *Comparative Politics*, 7 (3).

Kay, C. (1974) 'Comparative development of the European manorial system and the Latin American hacienda system', *Journal of Peasant Studies*, 2 (1).

Kay, C. (1980) *El Sistema Señorial Europeo y la Hacienda Latinoamericana: Estudios sobre el Desarrollo del Capitalismo en la Agricultura*, Mexico, Ediciones Era.

Kay, C. (1988) 'Economic reforms and collectivisation in Cuban agriculture', *Third World Quarterly*, 10 (3).

Kay, G. (1975) *Development and Underdevelopment: A Marxist Analysis*, London, Macmillan.

Kirkpatrick, C. H. and Nixson, F. I. (1981) 'The origins of inflation in less developed countries: a selective review', in I. Livingstone (ed.) (1981); originally published in M. Parkin and G. Zis (eds) *Inflation in Open*

Economies, Manchester, Manchester University Press, 1976.

Kitching, G. (1982) *Development and Underdevelopment in Historical Perspective. Populism, Nationalism and Industrialization* London, Methuen.

Klarén, P. F. and Bossert, T. J. (eds) (1986) *Promise of Development: Theories of Change in Latin America*, Boulder (Colorado), Westview Press.

Kosacoff, B. P. (1984) 'Industrialización y monetarismo en Argentina', *Economía de América Latina*, no. 12.

Kowarick, L. (1974) 'Capitalismo, dependência e marginalidade urbana na America Latina: una contribuiçao teórica', *Estudos CEBRAP*, no. 8.

Kowarick, L. (1975) *Capitalismo e Marginalidade Urbana na América Latina*, Rio de Janeiro, Editora Paz e Terra.

Kowarick, L. (1978) 'Desarrollo capitalista y marginalidad: el caso brasileño', *Revista Mexicana de Sociología*, 40 (1).

Kowarick, L. (1979) 'Capitalism and urban marginality in Brazil', in R. Bromley and C. Gerry (eds).

Kuri Gaytán, A. (1982) 'La evolución del pensamiento de la CEPAL', *Investigación Económica*, 41 (162).

Laclau, E. (1971) 'Feudalism and capitalism in Latin America', *New Left Review*, no. 67; reprinted in P. F. Klarén and T. J. Bossert (eds) (1986); and reprinted with an added 'Postscriptum' in E. Laclau *Politics and Ideology in Marxist Theory: Capitalism, Fascism, Populism*, London, Verso, 1982.

Lajo, M. (1983) *Alternativa Agraria y Alimentaria. Diagnóstico y Propuesta para el Perú*, Piura, Centro de Investigación y Promoción del Campesinado (CIPCA).

Lal, D. (1983) *The Poverty of Development Economics*, London, Institute of Economic Affairs.

Lall, S. (1975) 'Is "dependence" a useful concept in analysing underdevelopment?', *World Development*, 3 (11–12); also in S. Lall *Developing Countries in the International Economy*, London, Macmillan, 1981, Chapter 1.

LeBrun, O. and Gerry, C. (1975) 'Petty producers and capitalism', *Review of African Political Economy*, no. 3.

Leeds, A. (1969) 'Significant variables determining the character of squatter settlements', *América Latina*, 12 (3).

Leeson, P. F. (1988) 'Development economics and the study of development', in P. F. Leeson and M. M. Minogue (eds), *Perspectives on Development: Cross-disciplinary Themes in Development Studies*, Manchester, Manchester University Press.

Lehmann, D. (1986) 'Dependencia: an ideological history', *IDS Discussion Paper* (University of Sussex), no. 219.

Lenin, V. I. (1969) *Imperialism, the Highest Stage of Capitalism: A Popular Outline*, Peking, Foreign Languages Press.

Lenin, V. I. (1972) 'A characterization of economic romanticism', in V. I. Lenin, *Collected Works*, vol. 2, Moscow, Progress Publishers.

Lessa, C. (1973) 'Marginalidad y proceso de marginalización', in A. Murga Frasinetti and G. Boils (eds).

Levinson, J. and de Onis, J. (1970) *The Alliance that Lost its Way: A Critical*

Report on the Alliance for Progress, Chicago, Quadrangle Books.

Lewis, O. (1963) *The Children of Sanchez*, New York, Vintage Books.

Lewis, O. (1966) 'The culture of poverty', *Scientific American*, no. 215.

Lewis, W. A. (1954) 'Economic development with unlimited supplies of labour', *The Manchester School*, 22 (2); reprinted in A. N. Agarwala and S. P. Singh (eds).

Lewis, W. A. (1955) *The Theory of economic Growth*, London, Allen & Unwin.

Lewis, W. A. (1984) 'The state of development theory', *American Economic Review*, 74 (1).

Leys, C. (1977) 'Underdevelopment and dependency: critical notes', *Journal of Contemporary Asia*, 7 (1).

Leys, C. (1978) 'Capital accumulation, class formation and dependency – the significance of the Kenyan case', in R. Miliband and J. Saville (eds) *The Socialist Register 1978*, London, Merlin Press.

Lindenberg, K. (ed.) (1982) *Lateinamerika: Herrschaft, Gewalt und internationale Abhängigkeit*, Bonn, Verlag Neue Gesellschaft.

Linz, J. and Stepan, A. (eds) (1978) *The Breakdown of Democratic Regimes: Latin America*, Baltimore, Johns Hopkins University Press.

List, F. (1904) *The National System of Political Economy*, London, Longman (also New York, Augustus M. Kelly, 1885 edition); originally published in German in 1841.

Little, I. M. D. (1982) *Economic Development: Theory, Policy and International Relations*, New York, Basic Books.

Livingstone, I. (1981) 'The development of development economics', *ODI Review*, no. 2; reprinted in I. Livingstone (ed.) *Approaches to Development Studies: Essays in Honour of Athole Mackintosh*, Aldershot, Gower, 1982.

Livingstone, I. (1986) 'The further development of development economics', *Discussion Paper, School of Development Studies, University of East Anglia*, no. 198.

Livingstone, I. (ed.) (1971) *Economic Policy for Development: Selected Readings*, Harmondsworth, Penguin Books.

Livingstone, I. (ed.) (1981) *Development Economics and Policy: Readings*, London, George Allen & Unwin.

Lloyd, P. (1976) 'Marginality: euphemism or concept', *IDS Bulletin* 8 (2).

Lombardo Toledano, V. (1973) *El Problema del Indio*, Mexico, SepSetentas.

Lomnitz, L. (1977) *Networks and Marginality, Life in a Mexican Shantytown*, New York, Academic Press.

Lomnitz, L. (1978) 'Mecanismos de articulación entre el sector informal y el sector formal urbano', *Revista Mexicana de Sociología*, 40 (1).

Love, J. L. (1980) 'Raúl Prebisch and the origins of the doctrine of unequal exchange', *Latin American Research Review*, 15 (3); also in J. L. Dietz and J. H. Street (eds).

Love, J. L. (1986) 'Raúl Prebisch (1901–1986): his life and ideas', paper presented at the XIII International Congress of the Latin American Studies Association (LASA, USA) held at Boston (Massachusetts).

Luxemburg, R. (1963) *The Accumulation of Capital*, London, Routledge & Kegan Paul.

Lüders, R. (1977) 'La Comisión Económica para América Latina: sus políticas y su influencia', *Estudios de Economía*, no. 9.

McClelland, D. (1961) *The Achieving Society*, Princeton, D. van Nostrand.

MacEwen Scott, A. (1979) 'Who are the self–employed?', in R. Bromley and C. Gerry (eds).

Mahler, V. A. (1980) *Dependency Approaches to International Political Economy: A Cross National Study*, New York, Columbia University Press.

Maizels, A. (ed.) (1987) *Primary Commodities in the World Economy: Problems and Policies*, Oxford, Pergamon Press.

Malavé Mata, H. (1976) *Dialéctica de la Inflación: Análisis Estructural de la Inflación y el Subdesarrollo con Especial Referencia al Caso Venezolano*, Caracas, Universidad Central de Venezuela.

Malloy, J. M. (ed.) (1977) *Authoritarianism and Corporatism in Latin America*, Pittsburgh, Pittsburgh University Press.

Mandelbaum, K. (1947) *The Industrialization of Backward Areas*, Oxford, Basil Blackwell.

Mangin, W. (1967) 'Latin American squatter settlements: a problem and a solution', *Latin American Research Review*, 2 (3).

Manoïlescu, M. (1931) *The Theory of Protection and International Trade*, London, P. S. King.

Manzetti, L. and dell'Aquila, M. (1988) 'Economic stabilisation in Argentina: the Austral plan'. *Journal of Latin American Studies*, 20 (1).

Marcel, M. and Palma, G. (1987) *The Debt Crisis: The Third World and British Banks*, London, Fabian Society.

Marcussen, H. S. and Torp, J. E. (1982) *The Internationalization of Capital. The Prospects for the Third World*, London, Zed Press.

Margulis, M. (1968) *Migración y Marginalidad en la Sociedad Argentina*, Buenos Aires, Paidos.

Mariátegui, J. C. (1955) *Siete Ensayos de Interpretación de la Realidad Peruana*, Santiago, Editorial Universitaria.

Mariátegui, J. C. (1971) *Seven Interpretive Essays on Peruvian Reality*, Austin, University of Texas Press.

Marini, R. M. (1965) 'Brazilian interdependence and imperialist integration', *Monthly Review*, 17 (7).

Marini, R. M. (1969) *Subdesarrollo y Revolución*, Mexico, Siglo Veintiuno Editores.

Marini, R. M. (1971) 'El subimperialismo brasileño', *Documento de Trabajo*, Centro de Estudios Socio–Económicos (CESO), Universidad de Chile; published in English as 'Brazilian subimperialism', *Monthly Review*, 23 (9), 1972.

Marini, R. M. (1972) 'Dialéctica de la dependencia: la economía exportadora', *Sociedad y Desarrollo*, no. 1.

Marini, R. M. (1973) *Dialéctica de la Dependencia*, Mexico, Ediciones Era.

Marini, R. M. (1978a) 'World capitalist accumulation and sub–imperialism', *Two Thirds*, no. 1.

Marini, R. M. (1978b) 'Las razones del neodesarrollismo (respuesta a F. H. Cardoso y J. Serra)', *Revista Mexicana de Sociología*, 40 (E).

Marroquín, A. D. (1972) *Balance del Indigenismo*, Mexico, Instituto Indigenista Interamericano.

Martin, K. and Knapp, J. (1967) *The Teaching of Development Economics: Its Position in the Present State of Knowledge. The Proceedings of the Manchester Conference on Teaching Economic Development.* London, Frank Cass.

Martínez, H. and Samaniego, C. (1978) 'Política indigenista en el Perú: 1946–1969', in C. I. Degregori (ed.).

Martner, G. (1970) 'El pensamiento estructuralista y la crisis en las Ciencias Sociales', *Cuadernos de la Realidad Nacional*, no. 4.

Marx, K. (1976) *Capital: A Critique of Political Economy*, Volume One, Harmondsworth, Penguin Books.

Matos Mar, J. (1968) *Urbanización y Barriadas en América del Sur*, Lima, Instituto de Estudios Peruanos.

Mattelart, A. and Garretón, M. A. (1965) *Integración Nacional y Marginalidad: Ensayo de Regionalización Social de Chile*, Santiago, Editorial del Pacífico.

Maynard, G. (1961) 'Inflation and growth: some lessons to be drawn from Latin American experience', *Oxford Economic Papers*, 13 (2).

Medina Echavarría, J. (1963) 'A sociologist's view', in J. Medina Echavarría *et al.* (eds) *Social Aspects of Economic Development in Latin America* (vol. 2), Paris, UNESCO.

Meier, G. M. (ed.) (1964) *Leading Issues in Development Economics: Selected Materials and Commentary*, New York, Oxford University Press.

Meier, G. M. and Seers, D. (eds) (1984) *Pioneers in Development*, New York, Oxford University Press.

Middleton A. (1980) 'The marginalised labour force, the reserve army and the relative surplus population revisited: a comment on Aníbal Quijano', *Occasional Papers, Institute of Latin American Studies, University of Glasgow*, No. 31.

Mikesell, R. F. (1969) 'Inflation in Latin America', in C. T. Nisbet (ed.).

Miller, J. and Gakenheimer, R. A. (eds) (1971) *Latin American Policies and the Social Sciences*, Beverly Hills, Sage Publications.

Mires, F. (1978) 'De la teoría de la dependencia a la teoría de los modos de producción', *Praxisschwerpunkt Entwicklungsplanung und Entwicklungspolitik*, Fakultät für Soziologie, Universität Bielefeld.

Molero, J. (1981) 'Raúl Prebisch y la idea de transformar el subdesarrollo', *Comercio Exterior*, 31 (2).

Morgan, T. and Betz, G. W. (eds) (1970) *Economic Development: Readings in Theory and Practice*, Belmont (California), Wadsworth Publishing.

Moser, C. (1978) 'Informal sector or petty commodity production: dualism or dependence in urban development', *World Development*, 6 (9–10).

Mouzelis, N. P. (1988) 'Sociology of development: reflections on the present crisis', *Sociology*, 22 (1).

Munck, R. (1981) 'Imperialism and dependency: recent debates and old dead-ends', *Latin American Perspectives*, 8 (3–4), issues 30–31.

Munck, R. (1984) *Politics and Dependency in the Third World: The Case of Latin America*, London, Zed Books.

Murga Frasinetti, A. and Boils, G. (eds) (1973) *América Latina: Dependencia y Subdesarrollo*, San José de Costa Rica, Editorial Universitaria Centroamericana (EDUCA).

Murmis, M. (1969) 'Tipos de marginalidad y posición en el proceso productivo', *Revista Latinoamericana de Sociología*, 5 (2).

Myrdal, G. (1957) *Economic Theory and Underdeveloped Regions*, London, Gerald Duckworth; also published under the title *Rich Land and Poor*, New York, Harper & Row.

Nash, M. (1963) 'Approaches to the study of economic growth', *Journal of Social Issues*, 29 (1).

Neira, H. (1975) 'Prólogo', in O. Delgado (1975).

Nisbet, C. T. (ed.) (1969) *Latin America: Problems in Economic Development*, New York, Free Press.

Nixson, F. (1986) '"Economic development": a suitable case for treatment?', in B. Ingham and C. Simmons (eds) *The Historical Dimension of Economic Development*, London, Frank Cass.

Nove, A. (1974) 'On reading André Gunder Frank', *Journal of Development Studies*, 10 (3–4).

Nove, A. (1983) *The Economics of Feasible Socialism*, London, Allen & Unwin.

Noyola, J. F. (1978) *La Economía Cubana en los Primeros Años de la Revolución y Otros Ensayos*, Mexico, Siglo Veintiuno.

Noyola, J. (1984) 'El desarrollo económico y la inflación en México y otros países latinoamericanos', *Investigación Económica*, 43 (169); originally printed in the same journal, 16 (4), 1956.

Nugent, J. B. and Yotopoulos, P. A. (1979) 'What has orthodox economics learned from recent experience?', *World Development*, 7 (6).

Nun, J (1969) 'Superpoblación relativa, ejército industrial de reserva y masa marginal', *Revista Latinoamericana de Sociología*, 5 (2).

Nun, J. (1971) 'Proposte per lo studio della marginalità e della partecipazione in America Latina', *International Review of Community Development*, no. 25–26.

Nun, J. (1972) 'Marginalidad y otras cuestiones', *Revista Latinoamericana de Ciencias Sociales*, no. 4.

Nun, J. (1979) 'Dismissals in the Argentine automobile industry: a case study of the floating surplus population', *Labour: Capital and Society*, 12 (1).

Nun, J., Marín, J. C., and Murmis, M. (1969) 'Marginalidad en América Latina', *Documento de Trabajo, Centro de Investigaciones Sociales, Instituto Torcuato Di Tella* (Buenos Aires), no. 53.

Nurkse, R. (1953) *Problems of Capital Formation in Underdeveloped Countries*, Oxford, Basil Blackwell.

O'Brien, P. J. (1975) 'A critique of Latin American theories of dependency', in I. Oxaal, T. Barnett, and D. Booth (eds).

O'Brien, P. J. (1981) 'The new Leviathan: the Chicago school and the Chilean regime 1973–80', *IDS Bulletin*, 13 (1).

O'Brien, P. J. (1984) 'Dependency revisited', *Occasional Papers, Institute of Latin American Studies, University of Glasgow*, no. 40; also published in C. Abel and C. Lewis (eds).

O'Brien, P. J. (1986) '"The debt cannot be paid": Castro and the Latin American debt', *Bulletin of Latin American Research*, 5 (1).

O'Brien, P. J. (ed.) (1976) *Allende's Chile*, New York, Praeger.

O'Donnell, G. (1973) *Modernization and Bureaucratic–Authoritarianism. Studies in South American Politics*, Berkeley, Institute of International Studies, University of California.

O'Donnell, G. (1977) 'Corporatism and the question of the state', in J. M. Malloy (ed.).

O'Donnell, G. (1978) 'Reflections on the pattern of change in the bureaucratic authoritarian state', *Latin American Research Review*, 13 (1).

Olivera, J. H. G. (1960) 'La teoría no monetaria de la inflación', *El Trimestre Económico*, 27 (4), no. 108.

Olivera, J. H. G. (1964) 'On structural inflation and Latin American "structuralism"', *Oxford Economic Papers*, 16 (3).

Oliveira, F. de (1973) 'La economía brasileña: crítica a la razón dualista', *El Trimestre Económico*, 40 (2), no. 158.

Oliveira, F. de (1985) 'A critique of dualist reason: the Brazilian economy since 1930', in R. Bromley (ed.).

Oteiza, E. (1978) 'Introduction', in Institute of Development Studies Library, 'Bibliography of selected Latin American publications on development', *Occasional Guides, Institute of Development Studies, University of Sussex*, no. 13.

Oxaal, I. (1975) 'The dependency economist as grassroots politician in the Caribbean', in I. Oxaal, T. Barnett, and D. Booth (eds).

Oxaal, I., Barnett, T., and Booth, D. (eds) (1975) *Beyond the Sociology of Development: Economy and Society in Latin America and Africa*, London, Routledge & Kegan Paul.

Packenham, R. A. (1982) 'Plus ça change...: The English edition of Cardoso and Faletto's *Dependencia y Desarrollo en América Latina*', *Latin American Research Review*, 17 (1).

Pajestka, J. and Feinstein, C. H. (eds) (1980) *The Relevance of Economic Theories*, London, Macmillan.

Palma, G. (1978) 'Dependency: a formal theory of underdevelopment or a methodology for the analysis of concrete situations of dependency ?', *World Development*, 6 (7–8). Also published as 'Dependency and development', in D. Seers (ed.) (1981).

Pantin, D. (1980) 'The plantation economy model and the Caribbean', *IDS Bulletin*, 12 (1).

Park, R. E. (1928) 'Human migration and the marginal man', *American Journal of Sociology*, 33 (6).

Parra Peña, I. (1981) 'Leyendo a Raúl Prebisch', *Desarrollo Indoamericano*, no. 66.

Parsons, T. (1948) *The Structure of Social Action*, New York, McGraw-Hill.

Parsons, T. (1951) *The Social System*, London, Routledge & Kegan Paul.

Payer, C. (1985) 'Repudiating the past', *NACLA Report on the Americas*, 19 (2).

Paz, P. (1981) 'El enfoque de la dependencia en el desarrollo del pensamiento económico latinoamericano', *Economía de América Latina*, no. 6.

Paz, P. (1984) 'Juan Noyola Vásquez: precursor de la vertiente progresista del pensamiento estructuralista latinoamericano', *Investigación Económica*, 43 (170).

Pazos, F. (1972) *Chronic Inflation in Latin America*, New York, Praeger.

Peattie, L. R. (1968) *View from the Barrio*, Ann Arbour, University of Michigan Press.

Peattie, L. R. (1987) 'An idea in good currency and how it grew: the informal sector', *World Development*, 15 (7).

Peña, S. de la (1971) *El Antidesarrollo de América Latina*, Mexico, Siglo Veintiuno Editores.

Perlman, J. E. (1976) *The Myth of Marginality: Urban Politics and Poverty in Rio de Janeiro*, Berkeley, University of California Press.

Petras, J. (1981) 'Dependency and world system theory: a critique and new directions', *Latin American Perspectives*, 8 (3–4), issues 30–31.

Petras, J. and Brill, H. (1985) 'The tyranny of globalism', *Journal of Contemporary Asia*, 15 (4).

Petras, J. and Brill, H. (1986) 'The IMF, austerity and the state in Latin America', *Third World Quarterly*, 8 (2).

Petras, J. and Zeitlin, M. (eds) (1968) *Latin America: Reform or Revolution?*, New York, Fawcett.

Phillips, A. (1977) 'The concept of "development"', *Review of African Political Economy*, no. 8.

Pincus, J. (1967) *Trade, Aid and Development*, New York, McGraw–Hill.

Pinto, A. (1956) '¿Es posible detener la inflación?', *Panorama Económico*, Santiago, Editorial Universitaria.

Pinto, A. (1960a) 'Estabilidad y desarrollo: ¿metas incompatibles o complementarias?, *El Trimestre Económico*, 27 (2), no. 106.

Pinto, A. (1960b) *Ni Estabilidad Ni Desarrollo: La Política del Fondo Monetario Internacional*, Santiago, Editorial Universitaria.

Pinto, A. (1961a) 'Los modelos del subdesarrollo: el impacto del capitalismo en América Latina', *Revista de la Universidad de Buenos Aires* (V Época), 6 (1).

Pinto, A. (1961b) 'El análisis de la inflación "estructuralistas" y "monetaristas": un recuento', *Revista de Economía Latinoamericana*, Banco Central de Venezuela, no. 4.

Pinto, A. (1964) *Chile Una Economía Difícil*, Mexico, Fondo de Cultura Económica.

Pinto, A. (1965) 'Concentración del progreso técnico y de sus frutos en el desarrollo latinoamericano', *El Trimestre Económico*, 32 (1), no. 125; reprinted in A. Bianchi (ed.) (1969).

Pinto, A. (1968) 'Raíces estructurales de la inflación en América Latina', *El Trimestre Económico*, 35 (1), no. 137; also in A. Pinto, *Inflación: Raíces Estructurales*, Mexico, Fondo de Cultura Económica, 1973.

Pinto, A. (1970) 'Naturaleza e implicaciones de la "heterogeneidad estructural" de la América Latina', *El Trimestre Económico*, 37 (1), no. 145; also in C. Lara Beautell (ed.) *Dos Polémicas sobre el Desarrollo de América Latina: Textos del Instituto Latinoamericano de Planificación Económica y Social*, Santiago, Editorial Universitaria, 1970.

Pinto, A. (1972) 'Notas sobre el desarrollo, subdesarrollo y dependencia', *El Trimestre Económico*, 39 (2), no. 154.

Pinto, A. (1973) 'Marginalización y dependencia de América Latina', in A. Pinto and J. Kñakal, *América Latina y el Cambio en la Economía Mundial*, Lima, Instituto de Estudios Peruanos.

Pinto, A. (1983) 'Centro–periferia e industrialización. Vigencia y cambios en el pensamiento de la CEPAL', *El Trimestre Económico*, 50 (2), no. 198.

Pinto, A. and Kñakal, J. (1973) 'The centre–periphery system twenty years later', *Social and Economic Studies*, 22 (1); also published in L. E. di Marco (ed.).

Platt, D. C. M. (1980) 'Dependency in nineteenth–century Latin America: an historian objects', *Latin American Research Review*, 15 (1).

Platt, D. C. M. (1985) 'Dependency and the historian: further objections', in C. Abel and C. M. Lewis (eds).

Pollitt, B. (1985) 'Sugar, "dependency" and the Cuban revolution', *Occasional Papers, Institute of Latin American Studies, University of Glasgow*, no. 43.

Popescu, O. (1986) 'Raúl Prebisch in memoriam', *Desarrollo Indoamericano*, no. 84.

Portes, A. (1978) 'The informal sector and the world economy: notes on the structure of subsidized labour', *IDS Bulletin*, 9 (4).

Portes, A. (1983) 'The informal sector: definition, controversy, and relation to national development', *Review*, 7 (1).

Portes, A. and Browning, H. L. (eds) (1976) *Current Perspectives in Latin American Urban Research*, Austin, Institute of Latin American Studies, University of Texas Press.

Portes, A. and Walton, J. (1976) *Urban Latin America*, Austin, University of Texas Press.

Portes, A. and Walton, J. (1981) *Labor, Class, and the International System*, New York, Academic Press.

Powelson, J. P. (1977) 'The strange persistence of the "terms of trade"', *Inter-American Economic Affairs*, 30 (4).

Pradilla, E. C. (1984) *Contribución a la Crítica de la "Teoría Urbana" del "Espacio" a la "Crisis Urbana"*, Mexico, Universidad Autónoma Metropolitana (Xochimilco).

Prado Jr., Caio (1967) *The Colonial Background of Modern Brazil*, Berkeley, University of California Press.

PREALC (1978) *Sector Informal: Funcionamiento y Políticas*, Santiago, Programa Regional del Empleo para América Latina y el Caribe (PREALC), Oficina Internacional del Trabajo (OIT).

PREALC (1987) *Adjustment and Social Debt. A Structural Approach*, Santiago, PREALC/ILO.

Prebisch, R. (1949) *El Desarrollo Económico de la América Latina y Algunos de sus Principales Problemas*, mimeographed, Santiago, Naciones Unidas, Comisión Económica para América Latina (CEPAL); also in *El Trimestre Económico*, 16 (3), no. 63, 1949.

Prebisch, R. (1950) *The Economic Development of Latin America and its Principal Problems*, New York, United Nations (translation of Prebisch, 1949); reprinted in *Economic Bulletin for Latin America*, 7 (1), 1962.

Prebisch, R. (1959) 'Commercial policy in the underdeveloped countries', *American Economic Review. Papers and Proceedings*, 49 (2).

Prebisch, R. (1961) *Economic Development, Planning and International Co-operation*, Santiago, NU/CEPAL.

Prebisch, R. (1963) *Toward a Dynamic Development Policy for Latin America*,

New York, United Nations.

Prebisch, R. (1964) *Towards a New Trade Policy for Development*, (Report by the Secretary General of UNCTAD), New York, United Nations.

Prebisch, R. (1968) 'Development problems of the peripheral countries and the terms of trade', in J. D. Theberge (ed.); originally published in United Nations, *Towards a Dynamic Development Policy for Latin America*, New York, United Nations.

Prebisch, R. (1969) 'Industrialización y desarrollo', in CEPAL (1969, Chapter 2); also in ECLA (1970a), Chapter 2. A longer version was originally published (but not under Prebisch's name) in CEPAL, *Problemas Teóricos y Prácticos del Crecimiento Económico*, Santiago, NU/CEPAL, 1952. A shortened version of the latter can also be found in Bianchi (ed.) (1969).

Prebisch, R. (1971) 'Economic development or monetary stability: the false dilemma', in I. Livingstone (ed.); originally published in *Economic Bulletin for Latin America*, 6 (1), 1961.

Prebisch, R. (1981a) *Capitalismo Periférico. Crisis y Transformación*, Mexico, Fondo de Cultura Económica.

Prebisch, R. (1981b) 'Dialogue on Friedman and Hayek from the standpoint of the periphery', *Cepal Review*, no. 15.

Prebisch, R. (1984) 'Five stages in my thinking on development', in G. M. Meier and D. Seers (eds) *Pioneers of Development*, New York and Oxford, Oxford University Press for World Bank.

Prebisch, R. (1986a) 'Address delivered by Dr Raúl Prebisch at the twenty–first session of ECLAC', *Cepal Review*, no. 29; also published under the title 'Renovar el pensamiento económico latinoamericano, un imperativo', *Comercio Exterior*, 36 (6), 1986.

Prebisch, R. (1986b) 'Notes on trade from the standpoint of the periphery', *CEPAL Review*, no. 28.

Preobrazhensky, E. A. (1965) *The New Economics*, Oxford, Oxford University Press.

Preston, P. W. (1985) *New Trends in Development Theory. Essays in Development and Social Theory*, London, Routledge & Kegan Paul.

Preston, P. W. (1987) *Rethinking Development*, London, Routledge & Kegan Paul.

Quartim de Moraes, J. (1972) 'Le statut théorique de la rélation de dépendence', *IV Seminaire Latino–Américain*, CETIM, Geneva. Also in E. Anda *et al.* (eds), *Dépendence et Structure de Classes en Amérique Latine*, Paris, Centre Europe – Tiers Monde, 1972.

Quijano, A. (1966) 'Notas sobre el concepto de "marginalidad social"', Santiago, CEPAL, mimeographed; published in Quijano (1977a).

Quijano, A. (1971) *Nationalism and Capitalism in Peru: A Study in Neo–Imperialism*, New York, Monthly Review Press.

Quijano, A. (1973) 'El marco estructural condicionante de los problemas de participación social en América Latina', in A. Murga Frasinetti and G. Boils (eds).

Quijano, A. (1974) 'The marginal pole of the economy and the marginalised labour force', *Economy and Society*, 3 (4); reprinted in H. Wolpe (ed.) (1980).

Quijano, A. (1977a) *Imperialismo y "Marginalidad" en América Latina*, Lima,

Mosca Azul Editores.

Quijano, A. (1977b) *Dependencia, Urbanización y Cambio Social en Latinoamerica*, Lima, Mosca Azul Editores.

Quijano, A. (1983) 'Imperialism and marginality in Latin America', *Latin American Perspectives*, 10 (2–3), issues 37–38.

Rabinowitz, F. F. and Trueblood, F. M. (eds) (1971) *Latin American Urban Research*, Beverly Hills, Sage Publications.

Raffer, K. (1987) *Unequal Exchange and the Evolution of the World System Reconsidering the Impact of Trade on North–South Relations*, London, Macmillan.

Rama, A. (1975) 'Introducción', in J. M. Arguedas *Formación de una Cultura Indoamericana*, Mexico, Siglo Veintiuno Editores.

Ramírez Gómez, R. (1966) 'ECLA, Prebisch, and the problem of Latin American Development', *Studies in Comparative International Development*, 2 (8).

Ramos, J. R. (1987) *Neoconservative Economics in the Southern Cone of Latin America, 1973–1983*, Baltimore, Johns Hopkins University Press.

Randall, V. and Theobald, R. (1985) *Political Change and Underdevelopment: A Critical Introduction to Third World Politics*, London, Macmillan.

Ranis, G. and Orrock L. (1984) 'Latin American and East Asian NICs: development strategies compared', in E. Durán (ed.) *Latin America and the World Recession*, Cambridge, Cambridge University Press.

Ranis, G. and Schultz, T. P. (1988) *The State of Development Economics: Progress and Perspectives*, Oxford, Blackwell.

Ray, D. (1973) 'The dependency model of Latin American underdevelopment: three basic fallacies', *Journal of Interamerican Studies*, 15 (1).

Reichmann, T. (1973) *Persistent Inflation and Macroeconomic Equilibrium: The Case of Chile*, Ann Arbor (Michigan), University Microfilms, PhD disssertation, University of Harvard.

Roberts, B. (1978) *Cities of Peasants. The Political Economy of Urbanization in the Third World*, London, Edward Arnold.

Rodney, W. (1972) *How Europe Underdeveloped Africa*, London, Bogle–L'Ouverture Publications.

Rodríguez, A. (1983) 'Los científicos sociales latinoamericanos como nuevo grupo de intelectuales', *El Trimestre Económico*, 50 (2), no. 198.

Rodríguez, O. (1977) 'On the conception of the centre–periphery system', *CEPAL Review*, no. 3.

Rodríguez, O. (1980) *La Teoría del Subdesarrollo de la CEPAL*, Mexico, Siglo Veintiuno Editores.

Romano, R. (1970) 'A propósito de "Capitalismo y Subdesarrollo en América Latina" de André Gunder Frank', *Desarrollo Económico*, 10 (38).

Rosales, O. (1988) 'An assessment of the structuralist paradigm for Latin American development and the prospects for its renovation', *CEPAL Review*, no. 34.

Rosenblüth, G. (1968) 'Problemas socio–económicos de la marginalidad y la integración urbana', *Revista Paraguaya de Sociología*, 5 (11); also published under the same title in the same year by CEPAL, Santiago.

Rosenstein–Rodan, P. N. (1943) 'Problems of industrialisation in Eastern and

South–Eastern Europe', *Economic Journal*, 53 (2–3); also in A. N. Agarwala and S. P. Singh (eds).

Rostow, W. W. (1960) *The Stages of Economic Growth: A Non–Communist Manifesto*, Cambridge, Cambridge University Press.

Rowthorn, R. (1980) *Capitalism, Conflict and Inflation: Essays in Political Economy*, London, Verso.

Roxborough, I. (1979) *Theories of Underdevelopment*, London, Macmillan.

Roxborough, I. (1984) 'Unity and diversity in Latin American history', *Journal of Latin American Studies*, 16 (1).

Samuelson, P. A. (1948) 'International trade and the equalisation of factor prices', *Economic Journal*, 58 (230).

Samuelson, P. A. (1949) 'International factor–price equalisation once again', *Economic Journal*, 59 (234).

Sarkar, P. (1986) 'The Singer-Prebisch hypothesis: a statistical evaluation', *Cambridge Journal of Economics*, 10 (4).

Schmitz, H. (1984) 'Industrialisation strategies in less developed countries: some lessons of historical experience', *Journal of Development Studies*, 21 (1).

Schteingart, M. (ed.) (1973) *Urbanización y Dependencia en América Latina*, Buenos Aires, Ediciones SIAP.

Seddon, D. (ed.) (1978) *Relations of Production*, London, Frank Cass.

Seers, D. (1962) 'A theory of inflation and growth in under–developed economies based on the experience of Latin America', *Oxford Economic Papers*, 14 (2).

Seers, D. (1964) 'Inflation and growth: the heart of the controversy', in W. Baer and I. Kerstenetzky (eds) (1964).

Seers, D. (1967) 'The limitations of the special case', in K. Martin and J. Knapp (eds); originally published in *Bulletin of Oxford Institute of Economics and Statistics*, 25 (2), 1963.

Seers, D. (1978) 'The congruence of marxism and other neo–classical doctrines', *IDS Discussion Paper* (Institute of Development Studies, University of Sussex), no. 136; also published in K. Q. Hill (ed.) (1979), Introduction.

Seers, D. (1979a) 'The birth, life and death of development economics (Revisiting a Manchester Conference)', *Development and Change*, 10 (4).

Seers, D. (1979b) 'Patterns of dependence', in J. J. Villamil (ed.).

Seers, D. (1980) 'The cultural lag in economics', in J. Pajestka and C. H. Feinstein (eds).

Seers, D. (1981a) 'Inflation: the Latin American experience', *IDS Discussion Paper* (University of Sussex), no. 168.

Seers, D. (1981b) 'Development options: the strengths and weaknesses of dependency theories in explaining a government's room to manoeuvre', *IDS Discussion Paper* (University of Sussex), no. 165; also in D. Seers (ed.) (1981), Chapter 6.

Seers, D. (1983a) *The Political Economy of Nationalism*, Oxford, Oxford University Press.

Seers, D. (1983b) 'Structuralism *vs* monetarism in Latin America: a reappraisal of a great debate, with lessons for Europe in the 1980s', in K. Jansen (ed.)

Monetarism, Economic Crisis and the Third World, London, Frank Cass.

Seers, D. (ed.) (1981) *Dependency Theory: A Critical Reassessment*, London, Frances Pinter.

Semo, E. (1975) *La Crisis Actual del Capitalismo*, Mexico, Ediciones de Cultura Popular.

Sempat Assadourian, C. (1971) 'Modos de producción, capitalismo y subdesarrollo en América Latina', *Cuadernos de la Realidad Nacional*, no. 7; reprinted in J. C. Garavaglia (ed.).

Sen, A. K. (1983) 'Development: which way now ?', *Economic Journal*, 93 (372).

Sender, J. and Smith, S. (1986) *The Development of Capitalism in Africa*, London, Methuen.

Senghaas, D. (1972) *Imperialismus und strukturelle Gewalt. Analysen über abhängige Reproduktion*, Frankfurt am Main, Suhrkamp Verlag.

Senghaas, D. (1974) *Peripherer Kapitalismus. Analysen über Abhängigkeit und Unterentwicklung*, Frankfurt am Main, Suhrkamp Verlag.

Senghaas, D. (1977) *Weltwirtschaftsordnung und Entwicklungspolitik. Plädoyer für Dissoziation*, Frankfurt am Main, Suhrkamp Verlag.

Senghaas, D. (1979) 'Dissoziation und autozentrierte Entwicklung. Eine entwicklungspolitische Alternative für die Dritte Welt', in D. Senghaas (ed.) (1979) *Kapitalistische Weltökonomie. Kontroversen über ihren Ursprung und ihre Entwicklungsdynamik*, Frankfurt am Main, Suhrkamp Verlag; published in English as 'Dissociation and autocentric development', in R. L. Merritt and B. M. Russett (eds) (1981) *From National Development to Global Community*, London, Allen & Unwin.

Senghaas, D. (1985) *The European Experience. A Historical Critique of Development Theory*, Leamington Spa, Berg Publishers.

Senghaas, D. (1988) 'European development and the Third World: an assessment', *Review*, 11 (1).

Serra, J. (1979) 'Three mistaken theses regarding the connection between industrialization and authoritarian regimes', in D. Collier (ed.).

Serra, J. and Cardoso, F. H. (1978) 'Las desventuras de la dialéctica de la dependencia', *Revista Mexicana de Sociología*, 40 (E).

Sethuraman, S. V. (ed.) (1981) *The Urban Informal Sector in Developing Countries: Employment, Poverty, and Environment*, Geneva, International Labour Office.

Shanin, T. (1981) 'Marx and the peasant commune', *History Workshop Journal*, no. 12; also published in T. Shanin (ed.) (1983) *Late Marx and the Russian Road: Marx and 'The Peripheries of Capitalism': A Case Presented*, London, Routledge & Kegan Paul.

Sheahan, J. (1987) *Patterns of Development in Latin America: Poverty, Repression and Economic Strategy*, Boston, Allen and Unwin.

Sierra, E. (1969) *Tres Ensayos de Estabilización en Chile: Las Políticas Aplicadas en el Decenio 1956–66*, Santiago, Editorial Universitaria.

Singer, H. W. (1950) 'The distribution of gains between investing and borrowing countries', *American Economic Review: Papers and Proceedings*, 40 (2); also in J. D. Theberge (ed.), in T. Morgan and G. W. Betz (eds), and in H. W. Singer (1978).

Singer, H. W. (1975) 'The distribution of gains from trade and investment revisited', *Journal of Development Studies*, 11 (4); reprinted in H. W. Singer (1978).

Singer, H. W. (1978) *The Strategy of International Development: Essays in the Economics of Backwardness* (edited by A. Cairncross and M. Puri), London, Macmillan.

Singer, H. W. (1982) 'The Terms of Trade Controversy and the Evolution of Soft Financing. Early Years in the UN: 1947–51', mimeographed, Washington, DC, International Bank for Reconstruction and Development/The World Bank; published as *IDS Discussion Paper* (University of Sussex), no. 181, 1982. Also in G. M. Meier and D. Seers (eds).

Singer, P. (1973) 'Urbanización, dependencia y marginalidad en América Latina', in M. Castells (ed.); also published in M. Schteingart (ed.).

Sklair, L. (1988) 'Transcending the impasse: metatheory, theory, and empirical research in the sociology of development and underdevelopment', *World Development*, 16 (6).

Slater, D. (1987) 'On development theory and the Warren thesis: arguments against the predominance of economism', *Society and Space (Environment Planning D)*, 5 (3).

Slater, D. (ed.) (1985) *New Social Movements and the State in Latin America*, Dordrecht, FORIS Publications.

Sloan, J. W. (1977) 'Dependency theory and Latin American development: another key fails to open the door', *Inter-American Economic Affairs*, 31 (3).

Smith, T. (1979) 'The underdevelopment of development literature: the case of dependency theory', *World Politics*, 31 (2).

Smith, T. (1985) 'Requiem or new agenda for Third World studies?', *World Politics*, 37 (4).

Spalding, R. J. (ed.) (1987) *The Political Economy of Revolutionary Nicaragua*, London, Allen & Unwin.

Spraos, J. (1979) 'The theory of deteriorating terms of trade revisited', *Greek Economic Review*, no. 1.

Spraos, J. (1980) 'The statistical debate on the net barter terms of trade between primary commodities and manufactures', *Economic Journal*, 90 (1).

Spraos, J. (1983) *Inequalising Trade? A Study of Traditional North/South Specialisation in the Context of Terms of Trade Concepts*, Oxford, Clarendon Press.

Staniland, M. (1985) *What is Political Economy? A Study of Social Theory and Underdevelopment*, New Haven, Yale University Press.

Stavenhagen, R. (1965) 'Classes, colonialism, and acculturation. Essay on a system of inter–ethnic relations in Mesoamerica', *Studies in Comparative International Development*, 1 (6); reprinted in J. A. Kahl (ed.) *Comparative Perspectives on Stratification: Mexico, Great Britain and Japan*, Boston, Little Brown, 1968, and in I. L. Horowitz (ed.).

Stavenhagen, R. (1968) 'Seven fallacies about Latin America', in J. Petras and M. Zeitlin (eds).

Stavenhagen, R. (1970) 'Marginality, participation and agrarian structure in Latin America', *International Institute for Labour Studies Bulletin*, 7.

Stavenhagen, R. (1971a) *Sociología y Subdesarrollo*, Mexico, Editorial Nuestro Tiempo.

Stavenhagen, R. (1971b) 'Cómo descolonizar las ciencias sociales?', in R. Stavenhagen (1971a).

Stavenhagen, R. (1973) 'Comentario', in R. Benítez Zenteno (ed.).

Stavenhagen, R. (1974) 'The future of Latin America: between underdevelopment and revolution', *Latin American Perspectives*, 1 (1), issue 1.

Stavenhagen, R. (1986) 'Ethnodevelopment: a neglected dimension in development thinking', in R. Apthorpe and A. Kráhl (eds).

Stein, S. J. and Hunt, S. J. (1971) 'Principal currents in the economic historiography of Latin America', *Journal of Economic History*, 31 (1).

Stein, S. J. and Stein, B. H. (1970) *The Colonial Heritage of Latin America: Essays on Economic Dependence in Perspective*, New York, Oxford University Press.

Stoltz Chinchilla, N. (1983) 'Interpreting social change in Guatemala: modernization, dependency, and articulation of modes of production', in R. H. Chilcote and D. L. Johnson (eds.).

Stonequist, E. (1937) *The Marginal Man: A Study in Personality and Culture*, New York, Charles Scribner's Sons.

Street, J. H. (1967) 'The Latin American "structuralists" and the institutionalists: convergence in development theory', *Journal of Economic Issues*, 1 (1–2); also in J. L. Dietz and J. H. Street (eds) (1987).

Street, J. H. and James, D. D. (1982) 'Institutionalism, structuralism, and dependency in Latin America', *Journal of Economic Issues*, 16 (3).

Streeten, P. (1979) 'Development ideas in historical perspective', in K. Q. Hill (ed.), Chapter 1; also in P. Streeten (1981b), Paper 5.

Streeten, P. (1981a) 'World trade in agricultural commodities and the terms of trade with industrial goods', in P. Streeten (1981b), Paper 11.

Streeten, P. (1981b) *Development Perspectives*, London, Macmillan.

Streeten, P. (1983) 'Development dichotomies', *World Development*, 11 (10).

Streeten, P. (1985) 'A problem to every solution', *Finance and Development*, 22 (2).

Sunkel, O. (1960) 'Inflation in Chile: an unorthodox approach', *International Economic Papers*, no. 10.

Sunkel, O. (1963) 'El fracaso de las políticas de estabilización en el contexto del proceso de desarrollo latinoamericano', *El Trimestre Económico*, 30 (4), no. 120.

Sunkel, O. (1966) 'The structural background of development problems in Latin America', *Weltwirtschaftliches Archiv*, 97 (1); also in C. T. Nisbet (ed.).

Sunkel, O. (1967a) 'La inflación chilena: un enfoque heterodoxo', in T. Halperin Donghi (ed.) *Inflación y Estructura Económica*, Buenos Aires, Editorial Paidos.

Sunkel, O. (1967b) 'Política nacional de desarrollo y dependencia externa', *Estudios Internacionales*, 1 (1).

Sunkel, O. (1969) 'National development policy and external dependence in Latin America', *Journal of Development Studies*, 6 (1).

Sunkel, O. (1972a) *Capitalismo Transnacional y Desintegración Nacional en América Latina*, Buenos Aires, Ediciones Nueva Visión; also published in English as 'Transnational capitalism and national disintegration in Latin

America', *Social and Economic Studies* (University of the West Indies), 22 (1), 1973.

Sunkel, O. (1972b) 'Big business and "dependencia": a Latin American view', *Foreign Affairs*, 50 (3).

Sunkel, O. (1973) 'The pattern of Latin American dependence', in V. L. Urquidi and R. Thorp (eds) *Latin America and the International Economy*, London, Macmillan.

Sunkel, O. (1977) 'The development of development thinking', *IDS Bulletin* (University of Sussex), 8 (3); reprinted in J. J. Villamil (ed.) (1979), Chapter 1.

Sunkel, O. (1979) 'Un esquema general para el análisis de la inflación', *Desarrollo Indoamericano*, 14 (49); originally published in *Economía* (Revista de la Facultad de Ciencias Económicas de la Universidad de Chile), no. 62, 1959.

Sunkel, O. and Fuenzalida, E. F. (1979) 'Transnationalization and its consequences', in J. J. Villamil (ed.) (1979), Chapter 3.

Sunkel, O. and Paz, P. (1970) *El Subdesarrollo Latinoamericano y la Teoría del Desarrollo*, Mexico, Siglo Veintiuno Editores.

Sutcliffe, R. B. (1973) 'Introduction', in P. A. Baran, *The Political Economy of Growth*, Harmondsworth, Penguin Books.

Szentes, T. (1983) *The Political Economy of Underdevelopment*, Budapest, Akadémiai Kiadó.

Tavares, M. da C. (1964) 'The growth and decline of import substitution in Brazil', *Economic Bulletin for Latin America*, 9 (1). A slightly revised version was published under the title 'El proceso de sustitución de importaciones como modelo de desarrollo reciente en América Latina', in A. Bianchi (ed.) (1969).

Tavares, M. da C. (1974) *Acumulaçao de capital e industrializaçao no Brasil*, Tesis de libre docencia, Universidad Federal de Rio de Janeiro.

Tavares, M. da C. and Coutinho, L. G. (1984) 'La industrialización brasileña reciente: impasse y perspectivas', *Economía de América Latina*, no. 12.

Tavares, M. da C. and Serra, J. (1973) 'Beyond stagnation: a discussion on the nature of recent developments in Brazil', in J. Petras (ed.) *Latin America: From Dependence to Revolution*, New York, John Wiley.

Taylor, J. G. (1974) 'Neo–marxism and underdevelopment: a sociological phantasy', *Journal of Contemporary Asia*, 4 (1).

Taylor, J. G. (1979) *From Modernization to Modes of Production: A Critique of the Sociology of Development and Underdevelopment*, London, Macmillan.

Taylor, L. (1983) *Structural Macroeconomics: Models for the Third World*, New York, Basic Books.

Theberge, J. D. (ed.) (1968) *Economics of Trade and Development*, New York, John Wiley.

Thirlwall, A. P. and Bergevin, J. (1985) 'Trends, cycles and asymmetries in the terms of trade of primary commodities from developed and less developed countries', *World Development*, 13 (7).

Thomas, C. Y. (1974) *Dependence and Transformation: The Economics of the Transition to Socialism*, New York, Monthly Review Press.

Thorp, R. (1971) 'Inflation and the financing of economic development', in

K. Griffin (ed.) *Financing Development in Latin America*, London, Macmillan.

Thorp, R. and Whitehead, L. (eds) (1979) *Inflation and Stabilization in Latin America*, London, Macmillan.

Thorp, R. and Whitehead, L. (eds) (1987) *Latin American Debt and the Adjustment Crisis*, Pittsburg (PA), University of Pittsburg Press.

Tokman, V. (1978a) 'Informal–formal sector relationships: an exploration into their nature', *CEPAL Review*, no. 5.

Tokman, V. (1978b) 'An exploration into the nature of informal–formal sector relationships', *World Development*, 6 (9–10).

Tokman, V. (1984) 'Global monetarism and the destruction of industry', *CEPAL Review*, no. 23.

Toranzo, C. (1977) 'Notas sobre la teoría de la marginalidad', *Historia y Sociedad*, no. 13.

Torres–Rivas, E. (1969) *Procesos y Estructuras de una Sociedad Dependiente: Centroamerica*, Santiago, Editorial Prensa Latinoamericana (PLA)

Torres–Rivas, E. (1970) 'Desarrollo, integración y dependencia en Centroamérica', *Estudios Internacionales*, no. 12.

Torres–Rivas, E. (1971) 'Reflexiones en torno a una interpretación histórico–social de Guatemala', *Alero* (Suplemento), 3 February, 48–58.

Torres–Rivas, E. (1987) 'Estado y sociedad en Prebisch', *Comercio Exterior*, 37 (6).

Touraine, A. (1977) 'La marginalité urbaine', *Boletín de Estudios Latinoamericanos y del Caribe*, no. 22; Spanish translation published as 'La marginalidad urbana', *Revista Mexicana de Sociología*, 39 (4), 1977.

Touraine, A. (1987) *Actores Sociales y Sistemas Políticos en América Latina*, Santiago, PREALC/OIT.

Toye, J. (1980) 'Does development studies have a core ?', *IDS Bulletin* (Institute of Development Studies, University of Sussex), 11 (3).

Toye, J. (1987) *Dilemmas of Development: Reflections on the Counter–Revolution in Development Theory and Policy*, Oxford, Basil Blackwell.

Tyler, W. G. and Wogart, J. P. (1973) 'Economic dependence and marginalization: some empirical evidence', *Journal of Interamerican Studies and World Affairs*, 15 (1).

Valcárcel, L. E. (1972) *Tempestad en los Andes*, Lima, Editorial Universo.

Valderrama, M. (n.d.) 'Los planteamientos de Haya de la Torre y de José Carlos Mariátegui sobre el problema indígena y el problema nacional', in Degregori, C. I. *et al.*

Valenzuela, J. S. and Valenzuela, A. (1979) 'Modernization and dependence: alternative perspectives in the study of Latin American underdevelopment', in J. J. Villamil (ed.).

Vanden, H. E. (1986) *National Marxism in Latin America: José Carlos Mariátegui's Thought and Politics*, Boulder (Colorado), Lynne Rienner Publishers.

Vandergeest, P. and Buttel, F. H. (1988) 'Marx, Weber, and Development Sociology: Beyond the impasse', *World Developmen*, 16 (6).

Vasconi, T. A. (1971) 'Dependencia y superestructura', in T. A. Vasconi and I. Reca *Modernización y Crisis en la Universidad Latinoamericana*,

Santiago, Centro de Estudios Socio–Económicos (CESO), Universidad de Chile.

Vasconi, T. A. (1972) 'Cultura, ideología, dependencia y alienación', in J. Matos Mar (ed.) *La Crisis del Desarrollismo y la Nueva Dependencia*, Buenos Aires, Amorrortu Editores.

Vasconi. T. A. and García, M. A. (1972) 'Las ideologías dominantes en América Latina', *Sociedad y Desarrollo*, no. 1.

Vekemans, R. (1970) *Marginalidad, Promoción e Integración Latinoamericana*, Buenos Aires, Ediciones Troquel.

Vekemans, R. and Silva Fuenzalida, I. (1969) 'El concepto de marginalidad', in DESAL (1969).

Veltmeyer, H. (1983) 'Surplus labor and class formation on the Latin American periphery', in R. H. Chilcote and D. L. Johnson (eds) (1983).

Vilas, C. M. (1987) 'Troubles everywhere: an economic perspective on the Sandinista revolution', in R. J. Spalding (ed.).

Villamil, J. J. (ed.) (1979) *Transnational Capitalism and National Development: New Perspectives on Dependence*, Brighton, Harvester Press.

Viner, J. (1953) *International Trade and Economic Development*, Oxford, Clarendon Press; also published in New York, Free Press, 1952.

Vitale, L. (1968) 'Latin America: feudal or capitalist?', in J. Petras and M. Zeitlin (eds).

Vyasulu, V. (1974) 'On the Latin American view of underdevelopment', *Economic and Political Weekly*, 13 April.

Wachter, S. M. (1976) *Latin American Inflation: The Structuralist– Monetarist Debate*, Lexington (MA), Lexington Books.

Wada, H. (1981) 'Marx and revolutionary Russia', *History Workshop Journal*, no. 12.

Wallerstein, I. (1974) *The Modern World–System I: Capitalist Agriculture and the Origins of the European World–Economy in the Sixteenth Century*, New York, Academic Press.

Wallerstein, I. (1980) *The Modern World–System II: Mercantilism and the Consolidation of the European World–Economy 1600–1750*, New York, Academic Press.

Wallerstein, I. (1982) 'The rise and future demise of the world capitalist system: Concepts for comparative analysis', in H. Alavi and T. Shanin (eds).

Walton, J. (1975) 'Internal colonialism: problems of definition and measurement', in W. A. Cornelius and F. Trueblood (eds).

Warman, A. (1978) 'El pensamiento indigenista', in C. I. Degregori (ed.).

Warren, B. (1973) 'Imperialism and capitalist industrialization', *New Left Review*, no. 81.

Warren, B. (1980) *Imperialism: Pioneer of Capitalism*, London, New Left Books (Verso).

Weaver, F. S. (1986) 'The limits of inerrant marxism', *Latin American Perspectives*, 13 (4), issue 51.

Webster, A. (1984) *Introduction to the Sociology of Development*, London, Macmillan.

Weeks, J. (1981) 'The difference between materialist theory and dependency theory and why they matter', *Latin American Perspectives*, 8 (3–4), issues 30–31.

Weeks, J. and Dore, E. (1979) 'International exchange and the causes of backwardness', *Latin American Perspectives*, 6 (2), issue 21.

Weisskopf, T. E. (1976) 'Dependence as an explanation of underdevelopment: critique', mimeo, Center for Research on Economic Development, Ann Arbor, University of Michigan.

Weisskopf, T. E. (1983) 'Economic development and the development of economics: some observations from the left', *World Development*, 11 (10).

Wells, J. (1987) *Empleo en América Latina: Una Búsqueda de Opciones*, Santiago, PREALC/OIT.

White, G. *et al.* (eds) (1983) *Revolutionary Socialist Development in the Third World*, Brighton, Wheatsheaf Books.

Wiarda, H. J. (1981) *Corporatism and National Development in Latin America*, Boulder (Colorado), Westview Press.

Wilber, C. K. (ed.) (1973) *The Political Economy of Development and Underdevelopment*, New York, Random House.

Wilber, C. K. (ed.) (1986) *The Methodological Foundations of Development Economics*, Oxford, Pergamon Press.

Winn, P. (1986) *Weavers of Revolution. The Yarur Workers and Chile's Road to Socialism*, New York, Oxford University Press.

Wolpe, H. (1975) 'The theory of internal colonialism: the South African case', in I. Oxaal, T. Barnett, and D. Booth (eds).

Wolpe, H. (ed.) (1980) *The Articulation of Modes of Production*, London, Routledge & Kegan Paul.

Wyn Williams, S. (1983) 'The theory of internal colonialism: an examination', in D. Drakakis–Smith and S. Wyn Williams (eds) *Internal Colonialism: Essays Around a Theme*, Monograph no. 3, Developing Areas Research Group, Institute of British Geographers; Edinburgh, Department of Geography University of Edinburgh.

Zammit, J. A. and Palma, G. (eds) (1973) *The Chilean Road to Socialism. Proceedings of an ODEPLAN–IDS Round Table*, Brighton, Institute of Development Studies, University of Sussex.

Author Index

Aguilar, A. 128, 232
Aguirre Beltrán, G. 64-5, 73, 237
Amin, S. 26, 156, 184, 245-7
Angotti, T. 17, 174
Arauco, F. 171
Arndt, H. W. 228-9
Assael, H. 232
Aujac, H. 235

Baer, W. 231, 235
Bagú, S. 230, 236
Bambirra, V. 128, 139, 148-54, 167, 173, 177-8, 192, 194, 211, 241-2
Baran, P. 12-13, 144, 229-30, 244-5
Barerrera, M. 86
Bartra, R. 71, 79, 157, 230
Bernstein, H. 176, 179, 182-3, 189-92, 242, 246
Bhagwati, J. N. 31, 228, 231
Bianchi, A. 233
Bienefeld, M. 121, 163, 174-5, 185, 241, 247
Blomström, M. and Hettne, B. 128, 179, 190-2, 229, 246-8
Bonfil Batalla, G. 71
Booth, D. 155, 174, 191-2, 194, 228
Braun, O. 127, 216, 241
Brenner, R. 157, 176, 180-2, 205-6, 238
Brewer, A. 140-3, 183
Bromley, R. 88, 96, 185, 233n, 239n-41
Bukharin, N. 139-42, 173

Campanario, R. and Richter, E. 108, 115
Campos, R. de O. 54-5, 234-5
Caputo, O. and Pizarro, R. 140, 143, 242, 245
Cardoso, F. H. 88, 91, 106-10, 114, 118, 130, 134-9, 160, 165-6, 177-8, 190, 198, 229n, 232, 237-42, 244-6
Cardoso, F. H. and Faletto, E. 125-7,

134, 159, 170-1, 187-8, 212, 230, 241, 245
Castañeda, J. 178-80, 182, 188-90, 192
Castells, M. 90, 118
CEPAL (*Comisión Económica para América Latina*) 39, 40, 45-6, 230-2, 233-4; *see also* ECLA
Chenery, H. B. 31, 228
Chilcote, R. H. 192-3, 230, 247-8
Cockcroft, J. 108, 116, 124, 162
Colman, D. and Nixson, F. 236
Córdova, A. 118, 239
Cotler, J. 66, 72-3
Cueva, A. 172, 176, 190-4, 241

de Janvry, A. and Garramón, C. 116
Deere, C. D. and de Janvry, A. 115
Delgado, C. 98, 239
DESAL (*Centro para el Desarrollo Económico y Social de América Latina*) 90, 93-7
Díaz-Alejandro, C. F. 235
Dobb, M. 157, 182
Dore, E. 173, 176, 182, 205
Dos Santos, T. 127-9, 135, 139-40, 143, 149-57, 162-3, 167, 177, 181-2, 211, 241-2, 246

ECLA (Economic Commission for Latin America) 26, 29-30, 32-4, 36, 39, 45-8, 230-2, 233, 238-9; *see also* CEPAL
Echevarría, J. M. 232
Edelstein, J. 192, 230, 247–8
Emmanuel, A. 26, 179, 216, 234, 243, 245
Esteva, G. 120
Evans, H. D. 216, 234

Fagen, R. R. 247-8
Felix, D. 47, 201, 235

Subject Index